The Happy Youth of a Desperate Country

JAPAN LIBRARY

The Happy Youth of a Desperate Country

The Disconnect between Japan's Malaise and Its Millennials

Noritoshi Furuichi

Translated by
Raj Mahtani

Japan Publishing Industry Foundation for Culture

The Happy Youth of a Desperate Country: The Disconnect between Japan's Malaise and Its Millennials
by Noritoshi Furuichi. Translated by Raj Mahtani.

Published by
Japan Publishing Industry Foundation for Culture (JPIC)
3-12-3 Kanda-Jinbocho, Chiyoda-ku, Tokyo 101-0051, Japan

First edition: March 2017

This book is a translation of the paperback edition of *Zetsubō no kuni no kōfuku na wakamono-tachi,* first published in 2011 and then released in paperback form in 2015, both published by Kodansha Ltd.

English publishing rights arranged with Kodansha Ltd., Tokyo.

Jacket and cover design by Hisanori Niizuma
Jacket and cover photograph by Akihito Sumiyoshi

As this book is published primarily to be donated to overseas universities, research institutions, public librar-ies and other organizations, commercial publication rights are available. For all enquiries regarding those rights, please contact the publisher of the English edition at the following address: japanlibrary@jpic.or.jp

Printed in Japan
ISBN 978-4-916055-83-5
http://www.jpic.or.jp/japanlibrary

Table of Contents

Translator's Note

All Japanese names appearing in the text are written in the Western order, i.e. with first name followed by family name, while the names of Japanese historical figures appear in the Japanese order, i.e. with family name followed by first name. In addition, all Japanese words are romanized, and wherever deemed appropriate, macrons have been applied to indicate long vowel sounds, except in place names, such as towns or prefectures, and in the official romanized names of organizations, groups, and associations showing no macrons.

This English edition is based on a reissue of the work that contains approximately two hundred additional footnotes, offering a probing reexamination—by the author himself, then aged thirty—of the portrait of "young people" that he had created when he was twenty-six. As such, the book, an exemplary sociological treatment, not only appeals to academics, but, as the subtitle suggests, to "millennials" or "young people" as well. To that end, the author's voice, at times, shifts from an objective tone to a more subjective and casual, yet entertaining, witty, and ultimately personal one, mixing—in effect—a blogger's flair with astute scholarly observations. I have attempted to retain this exhilarating voice in this translation as much as possible to not only reflect how exuberant the author is, as an individual, but to also convey the sense of how truly groundbreaking the nature of his perspective and line of argument advanced in this book has been in Japan, where the animated public discourse on youth has been seeing young people—as Tuukka Toivonen, an Oxford-based sociologist of youth and social innovation sharply points out in the August 26, 2012 issue of *The Asia-Pacific Journal*—as either "lazy moral degenerates with no work ethic" or as victims burdened with disproportionate costs suffered during "Japan's two so-called Lost Decades" of economic decline.

Preface to the English Edition

The first edition of this book, "The Happy Youth of a Desperate Country," was published in September of 2011. At that time in Japan the memory of the Great East Japan Earthquake, which had occurred on March 11 of the same year, was still lingering vividly in everyone's mind. The whole country was enveloped in such an atmosphere of despair that it was, indeed, appropriate to call Japan a "desperate country."

However, 3/11 didn't suddenly push Japan into this state. After the collapse of the bubble economy in 1991, economic stagnation had continued for a span of more than twenty years. In addition, due to the rapidly dwindling birthrate and aging population, the increase in social-security costs and inequalities between generations had become permanent problems.

In particular, young people appeared to find themselves in miserable straits; there emerged "black companies," which exploited the younger generation as an expedient disposable workforce; *freeters*, or job-hopping part-timers, would continue to land unstable employment amid circumstances that made it difficult to acquire good jobs; "parasite singles," unable to become independent, remained in their parents' homes. In Japan, neologisms that were emblematic of the "unhappiness" of young people appeared one after another.

There is no shortage of topics expressing the fact that Japan is a "desperate country." But why, then, are young people, who are supposed to be at the greatest disadvantage in this "desperate country," happy? The provocative title of this book ended up sparking off a huge war of words upon its release in Japan.

Various opinions began to mount, including criticisms from scholars. "There's no way young people are happy," they said, unwilling to alter their convictions. Young people, expressing their personal denunciation, told me they weren't happy. And then there were cool, detached analyses stating that this book was a "consolation device"—a coping mechanism—to comfort the Japanese who had lost their self-confidence after the earthquake disaster.

However, there was one more major reason why this book went beyond my expectations and became topical. And that was the fact that at the time it was released, in 2011, I was a "youth" myself at twenty-six. The idea of a youth theory written by a youth still in his twenties must have been a novel one. Inspired by this book, many special features related to "young people" were put together for TV, newspapers, and magazines.

Given that this book addressed the limits of "youth theory," in a sense it was ironic that I myself, at the time of its publication, was solicited by various media for my views as a "youth." Still, because I was in my twenties when I wrote it, perhaps this book has managed to present a vivid account of the "young people" of the 2010s. Being a "young person" back then, I was able to casually ask for stories from other youngsters I ran into in the streets, while freely venturing into all sorts of places to collect data. I feel that kind of casual spirit pervades this work.

In other words, in two distinctive ways, this book turned out to be one that I could only have written in 2011. Firstly, it captures the mood peculiar to the circumstances that ensued in the immediate aftermath of the Great East Japan Earthquake. Secondly, it is a youth theory written by a youth who was still in his twenties.

Thus, when the book was re-released in a paperback edition in 2015, the text and footnotes of the hardcover edition were, for the most part, kept intact. This English edition is a translation of the paperback edition. However, since most people nowadays are unlikely to be interested in information from 2011, instead of correcting and revising the text, I have supplemented it with new footnotes containing the latest data. These are indicated with a star symbol (★) along with a reference number. In addition, I have added postscripts to selected chapters discussing how my views have changed with reference to certain sections.

Since this book was originally written with a Japanese audience in mind, I am uncertain to what extent you, dear reader, will be able to relate to its context. But I probably won't have to worry; if you've picked up this book, you're likely to be a commendable individual with an interest in Japanese youth.

In fact, many experiences of Japan depicted in this book, although unique, should prove useful for people living in other countries as well. Generally speaking, the level of interest in "young people" has been on the rise in developed nations. For example, in the U.K., a work titled *Jilted Generation*, published in 2010 by two reporters for the *Guardian* newspaper, attracted much attention. While the U.K. is said to have a class-based society, this book inveighs against the "unhappiness" commonly faced by that nation's youth. According to the authors, even though the average income continues to decline, taxes and housing expenses keep rising. Apparently, buying a house independently has never been more difficult than it has become today, and many young people have no choice but to live together with their parents.

In addition, in Western countries like the United States and Italy, young people are living with their parents longer. Problems such as the expansion of temporary or contract employment for the young due to deregulation, as well as spiking rents and tuition costs, are common to many developed countries, albeit in varying degrees. Just as the term "parasite single" has emerged in Japan, analogous words like *twixter* in the United States, *nesthocker* in Germany, and *mammoni* in Italy have appeared in various countries.

The number of nations that can be described by the phrase "desperate country," which appears in the title of this book, is escalating rapidly. Finding a "hopeful country" is more challenging by far, even if you search the whole world—including the United States, which has seen the election of a president drawing a remarkable level of attention the world over; the U.K., which has decided to withdraw from the European Union; and the various countries of Europe thrown into confusion by movements to clamp down on immigration.

In a time when desperation and despair prevail in the world, how should people live? This book describes how Japanese youth are adapting to the climate of desperation and despair, so I hope it will be able to contribute, as much as possible, to the happiness of the reader, or to that of the society the reader lives in.

Introduction

Is it true that Japanese youth are unhappy?
I received a question sometime around the end of 2010, before the Fukushima earth-quake occurred, from Mr. Martin Fackler, a forty-four-year-old Iowan who was the Tokyo bureau chief of the *New York Times*. "Why aren't Japanese youth rising up, given the unfortunate and dire circumstances they find themselves in?" Mr. Fackler was writing a piece on the generation gap in Japan at the time; he said he still couldn't get a handle on the feelings of Japan's youth.[1/★1]

Many in the youth age bracket inevitably lead precarious lives marked by irregular employment. With the rate of job offers to university graduates remaining low, there are even students who go on to graduate without securing jobs. In Japan, where the aging of society is forecast to keep gaining momentum, the burden on the working generation promises to only get heavier and heavier.

With that in mind, Mr. Fackler's concern was basically this: Why weren't young

---

1. The interview I gave at that time became the basis for the *New York Times* article, "In Japan, Young Face Generational Roadblocks" (January 28, 2011). Putting together additional interviews with Yuki Honda and Takafumi Horie, the piece expertly sums up the challenges youth in Japan face due to intergenerational inequities.

★1. What surprised many people at first, soon after the publication of this book, was the usage style I adopted for footnotes. While their inclusion in a scholarly work isn't unusual, there still weren't that many books out there that lined up footnotes in fine print below the text in this way. However, I have come to adopt this style because I am convinced that notes are far easier to reference when they appear at the bottom of running text than when they appear at the end of a book. What's more, it now appears that, since the publication of this book, there are more books with footnotes presented in this way, so I'm convinced that this is an unsung achievement of this work. While it sounds really cool and laudable, as you'll see in the course of reading the book, there are many footnotes that are nothing more than mere mutterings and gripes of mine. The footnotes that were added in the 2015 paperback edition are denoted with the ★ symbol next to consecutive numbers. These can be read as updates to the text that was written in 2011.

people in Japan, despite finding themselves in such a dire situation, willing to rise to the challenges facing them in society? The answer I (a Tokyo native, then twenty-six) gave him was simple: "Because the youth of Japan are happy."

Certainly, when you look at it from a macro perspective, it may be true that the social structure of Japan, including aspects of generational disparities, is stacked against the younger generation. However, when you consider the actual ways young people lead their everyday lives, it becomes questionable to say that they—or rather we—are actually unhappy or miserable.

Perhaps it's too much to expect to see further economic growth in Japan anymore. At the same time, though, in this country, there are plenty of amenities available that make daily life colorful and pleasurable. Even if we happen to be short of money, depending on our creativity, we can spend our days quite decently.

For example, we young people find basic clothing items at UNIQLO and Zara, turn to H&M for stylish outfits, enjoy lunch and coffee breaks at McDonald's, and hang out with friends for a few hours; at home, where we're surrounded by furniture acquired from the mega-chain Nitori and IKEA, we watch YouTube videos while Skyping with friends. Come nighttime, we gather at a friend's home and share a hot-pot meal together.

So in this way, even without spending too much money, it is quite feasible to spend our days fairly pleasantly.★²

In reality, it has become clear from a variety of surveys that the levels of satisfaction with life and happiness among modern youth have been the highest on record for these past forty years. For example, according to the Cabinet Office's *Public Opinion Survey on the Life of the People*, as of the year 2010, 70.5 percent of youth in their twenties responded that they were currently satisfied with life. That's right; despite all those claims of disparities and intergenerational inequities in Japanese society, 70 percent of Japanese youth are satisfied with life today.★³

What's more, the level of satisfaction among youth is higher than that recorded for other generations—it drops to 65.2 percent among those in their thirties, 58.3 percent among those in their forties, and down to 55.3 percent among those in their fifties. The life-satisfaction levels of older generations, who are likely to be concerned about

---

★2.   The greatest difference between the time I wrote this book and the year 2015 could be the advent and penetration of the free calling and messaging app LINE. This service launched in June, 2011, so the phenomenon that is LINE wasn't reflected in the original book at all. For this reason, the paperback edition reflects, in hindsight, how much LINE has changed the lives of the young. In a nutshell, I believe that our lives haven't changed that much.

★3.   Since then, the level of life satisfaction has risen further; in a 2015 survey, 79.3 percent of twenty-somethings responded that they were "satisfied" with their current lives.

the well-being of young people, are lower by far.

Furthermore, the life-satisfaction level among today's youth is higher than that reported by people in their twenties in the past. The life-satisfaction level recorded in the late 1960s, when Japan was still experiencing a period of rapid economic growth, was around 60 percent. In the 1970s, the nation even saw a year when the level fell as low as around 50 percent. But since the latter half of the 1990s, the satisfaction level has begun to register at about 70 percent.

The flip side of economic growth

Even compared to the young people of the past, those living in 2011, I feel, are happier. To make the comparison with the present age, let's go back thirty years to 1980 or thereabouts and take a peek at the lives of the young back then. The 1980s, prior to the burst of the bubble economy, is at times depicted as a wonderful, dreamlike society. Certainly the economy was growing steadily, and even after suffering the first oil shock in 1973 and the second one in 1979, Japan was sustaining, until the burst of the bubble, an average economic growth of 3.8 percent (from 1974 through 1990).

However, a soaring economy isn't necessarily tied to people leading happy, fulfilling lives; they are altogether two separate issues. As a matter of fact, the flipside of economic growth is the emergence of distress and distortions, the byproducts of a growth society.

First of all, working fathers had a terribly tough time. The number of employees working for an extended period of more than sixty hours per week, including unpaid overtime, began rising rapidly in 1975. By 1980, approximately 4.5 million people, or a little under 20 percent of all employees, were already working such long hours, and this number only continued to rise through the 1980s.[2] This is because in Japan, where firing an employee is problematic and discouraged, when the company's overall workload increases, employers respond by boosting the workload per individual employee already working for them, instead of increasing the number of new hires.

Even the children lived through a terribly tough time. After all, the 1980s was also the time when the exam wars—that is, excessive competition in entrance examinations—began to intensify. In 1979 the Preliminary Standard Entrance Examination for Public Universities began. This test, which is equivalent to today's National Center Test for University Admissions, in effect paved the way to the practice of ranking uni-

---

2.   Kōji Morioka, *Kigyōchūshin shakai no jikan kōzō* (The structure of time in a business-centric society), Aoki Shoten, 1995. At that time the legal weekly workload was forty-eight hours, and the five-day workweek system had yet to gain currency.

versities. Furthermore, the proportion of students who went on to attend general (as opposed to vocational) senior high schools rose, paving the way to the practice of ranking high schools as well.

In those days, everyone believed that if you went to a good school, you could get into a good company, and if you got into a good company, you could lead a good life. But inextricably associated with this idea was also the intimation of a relentless rat race.

In 1980, the "metal-bat murder incident" made waves. This case concerned a twenty-year-old second-year student at a cram school in Tokyo who killed his parents with a metal bat while they were asleep in bed. The young man was a member of an elite family: he lived with his father, who had graduated from The University of Tokyo, and his older brother, who had graduated from Waseda University, a renowned private university. At the trial, it was recognized on circumstantial grounds that the crime was indirectly motivated by mounting psychological pressure to perform well on the entrance exams.[3]

The situation in some junior high schools and high schools went beyond the pale due to control-oriented, regimented educational practices put into place to deal with the problem of school violence. While in 1973 the number of reported cases of violence perpetrated against teachers was seventy-one, in 1982 that number skyrocketed to 843. Stories of student violence perpetrated against teachers often received widespread coverage in the media, while the number of incidents involving police intervention also rose.

Meanwhile, draconian educational practices were carried out openly with impunity. At the former Kiyō Senior High School in Gifu prefecture, the teachers in charge of routine dress-code and baggage checks carried bamboo swords as they waited for the students to arrive at the school gates every morning, enforcing a bizarre school tradition that favored physical punishment. In 1985, there was even a case in which a teacher at a school-trip destination beat a student to death. The student's crime: bringing a hair dryer on the trip.[4]

Many schools were carrying out a form of militaristic education which, while not always so drastic as to result in death, was nonetheless draconian. Countless schools at

---

3.   "Kinzoku batto satsujin: Nobuya Ichiryū ni chōeki 13-nen" (Nobuya Ichiryū, the metal-bat murderer: Sentenced to thirteen years in prison), *Asahi Shimbun*, April 26, 1984, morning edition. The backdoor-admissions scandal was symbolic of another aspect of the competitive exam wars. That affair revealed that famous private universities, including Waseda University, had leaked entrance-exam questions.

4.   "Kagaku bampaku kengaku no kōkōsei, taibatsu de shokkushi" (High school student dies from shock after being subjected to physical punishment while on field trip to the International Exposition, Tsukuba, Japan, 1985), *Asahi Shimbun*, May 10, 1985, morning edition.

that time believed physical punishment to be natural, and a good number of them enforced preposterous regulations, such as mandating that students not only had to seek permission to travel outside the school district, but were also forced to wear their school uniform whenever they did so.[5]

Would you want to be young in the eighties?

Let's take a look at the *Consumer Confidence Survey*, a survey of single workers released by the Economic Planning Agency back in 1980. Of the people under age thirty who had left their parents' home for work, only 9.9 percent owned an air conditioner, 57.3 percent owned a washing machine, and just 47.9 percent even owned a vacuum cleaner. Can you imagine your life without an air conditioner?

Even in the case of TV, the ownership rate for a black-and-white television set was 21.5 percent, 67.3 percent for a color television set; incredibly, the ownership rate of telerecording devices was a mere 1.1 percent. Thirty years ago, when the television set was still an expensive item, many young people still watched TV on black-and-white sets. Among those living in their family homes who had a TV set for their personal use, the ownership rate, even when taking into account both black and white and color television sets, still only amounted to 50 percent.[6]

Compared to the present, overall prices were naturally lower. The starting salary for a university graduate was about 120,000 yen (in contrast to 200,000 yen today). However, when you look at the goods being sold at the time, many of them were actually more expensive than they are now. For example, shampoo and toothbrushes cost more in 1980 and a liter of gasoline cost 155 yen. Electrical appliances such as TVs, stereos, and cameras were more expensive as well. The fax machine released in 1979 by Matsushita Graphic Communication Systems (known today as Panasonic) cost

---

5. While I can't be certain how much impact the draconian practices of control-oriented educational policies have had, Aichi prefecture, which is in the vanguard for such practices, had the highest number of abuse-related deaths in Japan in the late 1990s; in 2000, it had the highest number of cases recognized as bullying incidents. This timing coincides with the start of the school attendance of children born to parents who, around 1980, were in junior high and in the thick of the control-oriented education movement. (Toshihiro Kawamoto, *Na bakari daigakusei* [College student in name only], Kobunsha, 2009.)

6. What's more, it's doubtful that they were experiencing happiness due to freedom from the trappings of materialism. According to the same survey, compared to one year ago, the percentage of young people who responded "My life has improved" was 9.1 percent, the percentage responding "My life hasn't changed" was 57.3 percent, and the percentage responding "My life has become worse" was 33.6 percent. It's also doubtful that they were hopeful about the future. Only 7.2 percent agreed that "My life will improve in the coming year," while 49.2 percent said, "My life will remain unchanged in the coming year," and as high as 43.6 percent believed that "My life will get worse." (All respondents were youth under thirty who had left their family homes and were living in either boarding houses or apartments.)

480,000 yen. The color television set released by Hitachi in 1980, featuring a twenty-six-inch screen, cost 265,000 yen. This price amounted to two months' starting salary, making the television set slightly out of reach. The decline in the prices of these electric appliances would, in fact, have to await the rise of the newly industrializing economies (the NIEs nations).

But in 1980 many things had yet to make their appearances in the world. Needless to say, there was no Wii, no PlayStation, nor even the Nintendo Entertainment System. When it came to games, fans were pleased by the mere technological achievement of making it possible to play Space Invaders at home. That's how low the bar was at the time.

Obviously, the Internet and the cell phone were nonexistent.[7] Telephone service hadn't even been privatized yet, and the telephone itself was not something you bought, but something you rented from the Nippon Telegraph & Telephone Public Corporation (now NTT). Push-button telephones had become widespread only in offices, and in many households a black rotary dial model was permanently set somewhere near the entrance, as though enshrined.[8]

International call rates were also incredibly high. In 1979 a three-minute call to the United States would have set you back a pricey 3,200 yen.[9] Today, it isn't unusual to find a telephone-service provider charging less than thirty yen for a three-minute call. But if you use Skype or Google Chat, you can talk face-to-face with people all around the world virtually for free.

In 1980 Japan, Disneyland was still nonexistent,[10] not to mention the fact that the manga comics *One Piece*, *Dragon Ball*, *Fist of the North Star*, and *City Hunter* had yet

---

7.   Today, there is already a generation born after the Internet and cell phones have become commonplace and ordinary. Just the other day, a high school student asked me how people had contacted their friends before cell phones and email existed. I was certainly surprised to realize that such a clueless generation had emerged at last, but, truth be told, I was stumped myself, unable to recollect just how I used to contact my friends myself during that inconvenient period of my life. Just how did people in the past manage, anyway?

8.   While push-button telephones were released in 1969, the usage fee was high compared to the fee for dial phones, so they failed to catch on for household use. When this fee finally came down in 1982, more than four million subscriptions for push-button terminals resulted. A newspaper article at the time alluded to "young people" in headlines like "Schoolgirls are attracted to stylish mini push-button telephones," and "Black telephones are *dasai* [nerdy]." ("Naze ninki pusshu fon" [Why are push-button phones popular?], *Yomiuri Shimbun*, February 3, 1983, morning edition.)

9.   One newspaper of the time carried a story about a person who had run up a stratospheric phone bill amounting to millions of yen after making phone calls to his ex every day for a time in an attempt to get back together (*Asahi Shimbun*, January 20, 1979, morning edition).

10. Disneyland opened in 1983 amid tremendous enthusiasm. But at the time of its launch, attractions such as the Electrical Parade or Big Thunder Mountain were nonexistent.

to begin their serialization.[11] Nor were anime films like *Nausicaä of the Valley of the Wind* and *Castle in the Sky* released in theaters.

Convenience stores had made their appearance, but compared to the present, they were far fewer in number. Many of them back then were, in reality, just dimly lit general stores calling themselves convenience stores after some remodeling; at that time, 7-Eleven had only approximately 1,000 outlets (compared to some 13,000 as of 2011) and Lawson had only 500 outlets (which had about 9,700 stores as of 2011).[★4] Naturally, these stores didn't yet act as agencies for collecting utilities fees, nor did they have bank ATMs installed.

Residential environments weren't all that favorable, either. Japanese at the time had accepted, with a slightly self-mocking air, the criticism from Europe that "Japan was a nation of workaholics living in rabbit hutches."[12] Studio apartments were uncommon, too. Such accommodations began to gain in popularity only after the mid-1980s. The ones that were enjoying popularity were fifteen- to twenty-square-meter apartments that came with a six-tatami-mat-sized Western-style room, along with a bath, a toilet, and a kitchen. It was a time when the "Western-style room" was so novel that it had to be specially mentioned in flyers.[13] Reportedly, the inhabitants of one-room apartments didn't associate with their neighbors, and often got entangled in disputes with local residents who complained that many of them ignored rules for the proper disposal of garbage.[14]

So what do you think? That was the 1980s—a time when people now in their fifties were the young ones. As I see it, they seem to be the misfortunate, unhappy lot, not the young people today. While "misfortunate" is a subjective label, at the very least I feel lucky not to have been born in those days. Because I don't really want to sweat that much to study for exams, and because I can't imagine my life without the Internet or cell phones.

---

11.   *Dr. Slump* began its serialization in 1980, however; and *Cat's Eye* was serialized starting in 1981.
★4.   There were approximately 17,900 7-Eleven outlets in 2015, and approximately 12,300 Lawson outlets. Now, how about that? Convenience stores are still on the rise.
12.   The first recorded instance of the expression "rabbit hutches" appeared in a 1979 European Commission report. It came about in the process of translating, and it wasn't the manifestation of any intent to express contempt for Japan. An examination of the public opinion polls of the time, however, reveals that approximately 60 percent believed this expression had gotten it right when describing Japan's existing conditions (*Asahi Shimbun*, June 26, 1979, morning edition).
13.   At that time, tatami mats were mainstream, as evidenced in a newspaper story boldly asserting, "The current custom of welcoming the new year with a new tatami mat remains unchanged from the past" (*Asahi Shimbun*, October 27, 1981, morning edition).
14.   "Fueru wanrūmu manshon funsō" (The rising number of one-room-apartment disputes), *Asahi Shimbun*, September 28, 1983, morning edition.

Young people who lead lives with a new kind of "happiness"

When he was twenty-one, the renowned actor Takeru Satō (originally from Saitama), who played the role of the samurai Okada Izō in the historical 2010 TV saga *Ryomaden/The Legend of Ryoma Sakamoto*, said that if he could be reborn he would, without a doubt, prefer to be born again in the present age than in the Edo period (1603–1868). This was, he said, because—unlike the Edo period when you were required to slay people—the present age lets you savor the "happiness of taking an overnight trip to the sprawling suburbs of Chiba with your friends to enjoy a barbecue party."[15]

He doesn't wish to particularly create a furor and instigate a revolution like Sakamoto Ryōma did, nor does he want to be worshipped as a hero like Ryōma, who gave up his life for the country. To Satō, what's important isn't such heroism, but the modicum of happiness he can find in traveling to Chiba with his friends and staying there overnight to have a barbecue party.

As epitomized by Satō's words, what's spreading among young people, more and more, are the values of treasuring slivers of happiness in our days—those smaller pleasures of life, such as intimate relations with those close to us. Young people don't believe that tomorrow will be better than today. Young people don't wish for anything drastic as the renewal of the Japanese economy, nor do they hope for a revolution. This way of life goes hand in hand, you might say, with the well-rounded, mature society of our modern day and age.

But of course, the situation isn't so simple that we can declare, with absolute certainty, that young people are therefore happy. Certainly, in terms of the infrastructure and living environment, it's safe to say that young people today are living under the most affluent conditions on record in human history.

However, just as Mr. Fackler of the *New York Times* anxiously points out, from now on the disparities between generations will only get worse, and the burdens of the working generation, mainly comprised of the younger age group, will only keep increasing.

The trend seen in Japan of the dwindling birth rate and an aging population shows no sign of stopping; the birth rate has yet to recover from the low rate of 1.3. As for social security, until now one elderly person was being supported by three members of the working generation, but within the next fifteen years, this figure is predicted to change to one elderly person per two people.[*5]

An enormous budget deficit is also in the process of being left behind for future generations. The national debt will, in effect, have to be paid by them. Some insist that

---

15.   *AERA*, November 1, 2010 issue.

this is tantamount to a con being pulled off by, say, an aged grandfather using his grandchild's credit card without permission.[16]

Furthermore, the preceding generation has also left behind the legacy of a nuclear power plant with an uncontainable radioactive leak. It will likely take at least dozens of years to completely decommission the nuclear reactor at Fukushima Daiichi Nuclear Power Station, where the notorious accident occurred, and to make the site available for redevelopment and reuse.[17/★6] That's just about how long it will take for today's youth to mature into senior citizens.

No matter how convinced you might be that the modern youth of Japan are "happy," the foundation of life itself—the basis of their "happiness"—is starting to gradually decay. And yet amid this social structure, which is in a way warped, a strange sense of stability, of equilibrium, is emerging among these very youths—one that indeed arises from their perceiving themselves as being happy.

Amid this perceived stability, what are young people thinking and feeling? Where do they come from? Where are they going?

As you will recall, when Mr. Fackler of the *New York Times* asked me, "Why don't the youth of Japan rise up?" I told him it was because Japanese youth are happy. Buried in this answer are a number of other hidden ramifications, and I intend to reveal them in this book.

The structure of this book

This book is designed to help you gain, through reading just this single volume, a rough grasp of modern Japanese youth. Regrettably, it's just that—a rough grasp, and not a comprehensive, all-encompassing one. To begin with, since I'm dealing with the subject of the living beings called young people, it's impossible to describe everything about them.

Thus this book isn't *The Complete Manual to Understanding Young People (the ulti-*

★5. The average number of births per woman in Japan rose to 1.43 in 2013, but fell again in 2014. Within the past fifteen years, in which the second-generation baby boomers reached the age of marriage and childbearing, it wouldn't have been surprising to see the occurrence of a "third baby boom."

16. Manabu Shimasawa and Tsutomu Yamashita, *Mago wa sofu yori ichi-oku en son o suru* (The grandchild will be 100 million yen worse off than his grandfather), Asahi Shimbun Publications, 2009.

17. While provisional estimates of how long it would take to realize a full decommissioning vary greatly, many show that even a planned and systematic decommissioning would take as long as around thirty years (Shin'ya Nagasaki and Shin'ichi Nakayama, eds., *Hōshasei haikibutsu no kōgaku* [The engineering science behind radioactive waste], Ohmsha, 2010).

★6. According to the information made available in Tokyo Electric Power's timetable, completion of decommissioning from the year 2015 will take thirty to forty years to complete, which would mean that decommissioning would finish anywhere between 2045 and 2055. What a terrible future!

mate collector's edition). Nonetheless, I believe it can prove to be a complementary re-source—an analytical filter or lens, if you will—for helping you understand the youth of modern Japan. For instance, it can at least comprise a valid part of, say, some 2011 compendium of references on youth.★7

For this reason, I'd be happy if you would consider this book as a starting point or a launchpad for a discussion on contemplating young people. You may think that it's rather brazen of me to be selling something that's just a starting point, but I ask your forgiveness. I have included in this book topics and findings of field reports that have been sorely lacking in arguments and theories concerning young people to date.

In certain places, you might find me putting on a scholarly air and presenting various seemingly tortuous arguments, but it is my hope that you will read these sec-tions in particular with a healthy dose of skepticism. After all, scholars—myself in-cluded—tend to write in an ambiguous and abstruse style when our confidence eludes us.★8

In chapter 1, I will begin by asking what this entity called "young people" is in the first place. What I came to understand after surveying the landscape of youth talks and discourses, including those circulating in prewar times, is that the *wakamono* (young person) is a certain kind of illusion.

In the second chapter, I will mine data and investigate how accurate various per-ceptions, discussed the world over, are when it comes to young people. Just how true are the generalizations you often hear these days—e.g., that young people don't buy things, that they don't travel abroad, that they're indifferent to politics, that they're introverted herbivores (a reference to men who shun sex and prefer quieter lives, a.k.a. grass eaters).

In chapters 3 and 4, drawing on multiple fieldwork findings, I will try to shed a multifaceted light on young people. Through an examination of youth who got excited over the World Cup, and youths who participated in a protest demonstration concern-ing the Senkaku Islands dispute, I will ponder "Japan" and "young people."

In chapter 5, I will deal with the Great East Japan Earthquake, which occurred as I was writing this book. In the aftermath of the tragedy, I heard many people saying that 3/11 triggered a complete transformation of Japanese society. However, a look at the reactions of young people so far reveals nothing unexpected★9—unlike the

---

★7.   I've made updates for the paperback edition, so I believe it's now at least worthy of being included in the collection of references on youths (early 2010s edition). My wish to have this book serve as a starting point to explore the subject of "young people" still remains.

★8.   Although it's not for me to comment on the "me" of four years ago, if I may say so myself, I like it that I'm being quite honest here.

tsunami.

In the sixth and final chapter, I will contemplate the thematic premise of this book—that the young people of Japan are happy—through the lens of generational disparities and the labor problem. Consequently, I question the sustainability of this thematic premise: what will the future really hold for Japan twenty years from now, thirty years from now? Will young people still be happy then?

I have also included, as a supplement, a record of my conversation with the actor Takeru Satō. Given Satō-san's name value, it's no exaggeration to say that this section is the heart of this book.★10

Though the chapters are interrelated, each one can be read independently, so feel free to dive in and start reading at any point. But apparently my prose is too long-winded for the whole book to be digested in a single sitting, so as an author I recommend a reading pace of a chapter a day.

Incidentally, I refer to various interviews and publications in this book, and whenever necessary, I also include the age and birthplace of the people I quote.[18] This is because when someone talks about "young people," I feel that their age and where they are originally from sheds valuable light on their standpoint.

On a separate note, some names mentioned are pseudonyms.

★9. Back then, the tsunami that destroyed the Fukushima Daiichi Nuclear Power Station was often described as being "beyond expectations."

★10. After this, Takeru Satō went on to coolly score a series of hits, appearing in the movies *Rurōni Kenshin*, a romance about a Meiji era swordsman, and *Kanojo wa uso o aishisugiteru* (She loves lies too much), as well as in the TV drama *Tennō no ryōriban* (The emperor's cook). Thereafter, from the summer of 2014, he suddenly began to get hooked on "Jinroh" (Werewolf, a party game involving deception) and Real Escape Game's physical adventure games in which players attempt to escape from a locked room within a set time limit, using their wits.

18. The ages I mention were calculated based on how old the person who made the remark was at the time of the publication of the source literature or at the time when they made the remark. In cases where quotes from magazines are given unrevised, I have written down the assumed age of the person at the time the text first appeared. Whenever an exact date of birth was uncertain, I have taken the liberty of assuming the date of birth to be the date of publication of the work in which the remark appears, and calculating the age accordingly. Basically, all ages given are those of "that time," but I explicitly say so only where this was difficult to tell. So please take note that these ages aren't strictly accurate; they're presented to give you a rough idea.

Chapter 1
The Rise and Fall of "Young People"

We love to talk about our young people. From championing hopeful views on how they can transform Japan to despairing their detachment from consumerism, there's always someone rambling on about "young people." However, the phrase "young people"—that is to say, the concept behind the term as we mean it today—hasn't been around that long. In this chapter, by examining the historical characterization of "young people" as a group, as well as discussions about them, I will attempt to redefine the term itself, which tends to be tossed around ambiguously. Furthermore, I will clarify the reasons why discussions and narratives about "young people" keep recurring again and again throughout the ages.

1. Who Are "Young People"?

Are today's youth so outrageous?

There's an anecdote many people are fond of bringing up when talking about the younger generation. It concerns an inscription found on an artifact unearthed from remains dating back several thousands of years. The words read, "Young people today are outrageous!" While the setting may vary—Mesopotamia in some versions and Egypt in others—I expect many of you have heard this story at least once. Although the inscription is actually an urban legend,[19] the notion that even people back in ancient times were grumbling about "today's outrageous youngsters" isn't all that surprising.

However, what we have to keep in mind here is that the implications of the expression "young people" on such an artifact would have been considerably different from what we, in the modern age, mean when we say the term. First, there's the issue of age classification to consider. For example, in ancient Rome, there was a time when adolescence (*adulescentia*) referred to the age bracket ranging from fifteen to thirty, while youth (*juventus*) referred to the age bracket ranging from thirty to forty-five.[20]

In modern Japan, too, the definition of "young people" is inconsistent. In its employment policy, the Ministry of Health, Labour and Welfare defines the "youth demographic" as those aged fifteen through thirty-four years old. However, in the government's National Youth Development Policy, the age bracket for the term "youth" is between eighteen and thirty. The age eligibility for volunteers recruited by the Japan International Cooperation Agency (JICA) for the Overseas Cooperation Volunteers group, though, is twenty to thirty-nine.[★11] It's all quite confusing, really.

But what's even more puzzling than the age issue is the matter of when the term "young people" first emerged.

You might be thinking, "Wait, surely young people have been around from the old days, haven't they?" Of course, teenagers and twenty-somethings have existed from time immemorial. Even the usage instances of words that refer to young people can be traced back to a considerably distant past. In the case of *wakamono* (young people), the term appears as a rallying cry in a passage from the *The Tale of Heiji* written around 1220. *"Akugenta wa nido made teki o oidasu zokashi. Susume ya, wakamono!"* (Mark my words, Akugenta [Minamoto no Yoshihira] repelled his enemies twice. Onward, young men!)

Instances of the more refined term *wakōdo* (young man or youth) appear in *The Gossamer Years* written around 974, and in the *As I Crossed a Bridge of Dreams* written

---

19.   One early source is the first edition of Kunio Yanagita's *Momen izen no koto* (Stories from pre-cotton times) published in 1939 by Iwanami Shoten. In this work, Yanagita says, "I heard from an elderly British professor, Professor Archibald Sayce, that in the handwritten diary of a scribe belonging to a medieval dynasty, which was discovered at an excavation site of certain Egyptian historic ruins, there was a note that read, 'The young these days take full advantage of their intellect and delight in their flippant ways. It's deplorable.'" But that is hearsay. In the English-speaking world, an oft-quoted remark is "When I was young, we were taught to be discreet and respectful of elders, but the present youth are exceedingly disrespectful and impatient of restraint." This comment is attributed to the ancient Greek philosopher Hesiod, who was active in the eighth century BC. Multiple dissertations refer to Eugene Pumpian-Mindlin's "Omnipotentiality, Youth, and Commitment" in the *Journal of the American Academy of Child Psychiatry*, 4–1 (1965), but that paper contains no information on the original source.

20.   Augusto Freschetti, "Roman Youth" in *A History of Young People* edited by Giovanni Levi and Jean-Claude Schmitt, Belknap Press, 1997.

★11.   In recent years, there have even been youth-support measures that target people up to forty-four years old. This is because of the aging of the first generation of so-called *freeters* (job-hopping part-timers) who were created by the "employment ice age," a period that spanned from the early nineties to the mid-2000s. If the definition of "youth" keeps expanding in this way, the notion that "Japan will one day turn into an entire nation of young people" (see chapter 6) will cease to be a joke.

around 1059.[21]

But the problem isn't so simple. In present-day Japan the term *wakamono*, in most cases, is used to refer not just to an individual, but collectively to the entire twenty-something generation. For example, in a sentence like "The *wakamono* these days don't buy cars," the term tacitly refers to a group of Japanese men and women in the age range from twenty to around thirty.

In other words, understanding of the term is based on the idea that "Japanese people in their twenties and thereabouts comprise a group of people who share traits in common with each other." This concept would have been unthinkable in the past, at least until the Edo period (1603–1868). It wouldn't have possibly occurred to anyone back then to talk about, say, a "twenty-year-old peasant" and a "twenty-year-old samurai" in the same breath, as if they were of the same rank, as if they were equals.

Furthermore, though I'm unsure about samurai, I doubt that peasants ever imagined Japan as a nation. Even if an Edo-period villager had said, "Young people today are useless," his implication, at most, would have been that, compared with his own generation when they were young, the youngsters in his village were even more worthless good-for-nothings.

Thus, a number of conditions had to be met before the subject of "young people" could be discussed in the way we do today. Naturally, this book, which deals with the theme of "young people," must consider how to go about defining this expression. But that's a problem; the issue is much too complex, and I'm still at a loss. So let me just say for now that this matter of definition will be mulled over. In the meantime, I'll ask you to turn your gaze with me to the history of discourses and narratives on young people in Japan. For now, understand that when I talk about "discourses regarding young people" or "narratives about young people," I am referring collectively to interpretations that talk about young people as a particular group, rather than limiting my discussions to "discourses on youth" put forward by researchers.

21.　The *Kagerō nikki* contains the line, "*Ware ima wa oi ni taritote, wakōdo motomete, ware o kandō shi tamaeru naran*" (Maybe now that I am getting old, you are throwing me over for some young boy). (English translation from *The Gossamer Years*, Tuttle Publishing, 1973.) The *Sarashina nikki* contains the line, "*Ware wa ito wakōdo ni aru beki ni mo arazu, mata otona ni seraru beki oboe mo naku*" ("…but even though I could not be regarded as a novice, neither could I be treated as an old hand)." (English translation from *As I Crossed a Bridge of Dreams*, Penguin, 1989.)

2. The Eve of the "Discourse on Young People"

When the young were called "youth"

Up to this point, I have been using the term *wakamono* (young people) over and over
again (and will continue to do so henceforth); but in fact, the widespread use of this
expression in Japan occurred in the not-too-distant past, having started to generally
prevail from the late 1960s through the 1970s. Until then, the word *seinen* (youth), a
more refined way of referring to the young, enjoyed wider currency. Even today, a de-
rivative of this term, *seishonen*, still appears in governmental white papers.[22]

In the history of the Japanese language, the expression *wakamono* dates further
back than the more elegant *seinen*. So why did the term *seinen* have wider currency
until the 1960s? The story goes all the way back to the Meiji era (1603–1868).[23]

In the mid-1880s, with the enactment of the Great Japanese Imperial Constitution
and the establishment of the Imperial Diet just around the corner, the movement for
democratic rights began to stagnate. At that time, the terms *Shin Nihon* (New Japan)
and *seinen* began to gain currency, and the intellectuals of the day seemed to sense that
they were witnessing the end of one era and the beginning of a new one. Consequently, a bright spotlight was trained on the term *seinen* as if it were a revelation—a newly
discovered expression for referring to souls entrusted with championing this New
Japan.[24]

The word *seinen* didn't, therefore, merely refer to someone's age. At the heart of the
"*seinen* boom" were the young controversialists of the magazines *Kokumin no tomo*
(The nation's friend) and *Nihonjin* (The Japanese), who had willingly adopted the term
seinen with the intent of ridiculing the "elderly of the Tempō era"—those folk failing
to keep up with *bunmei kaika*, the Westernization movement sweeping across Japan
during the Meiji era. In effect, these young iconoclasts were asserting that they them-

---

22.   In the narrative parts of this book I use the term *wakamono* (young people), and not *seinen* (youth).
23.   I prefer not to go back in history—but I do, since existing studies that look back on "youth discourses"
       are, for the most part, indifferent to the developments before the 1960s. In this sense, though the scope
       may be limited, I feel it is nonetheless meaningful for this chapter to look back in retrospect on discourses
       on youth that took place during prewar times. However, I would like to address, as future subjects, the
       vagueness of the boundaries defining "youth discourse" and the problem of the exhaustiveness, or the lack
       thereof, of the source materials, especially in light of the fact that accounts of the Meiji and Taishō eras are
       evidently insufficient.
24.   Naoe Kimura, *Seinen no tanjō* (The birth of youth), Shin-yo-sha, 1998. But the word is said to have come
       into vogue after Hiromichi Kozaki, in 1880, translated "Young Men's Association" as "Seinen Kai" (youth
       group). (Teruhiro Tani, *Seinen no seiki* [The century of youth], Douseisha, 2003.)

selves—that is, the youth, not the old-fashioned bunch who were born in the Tempō era (1830–44)—were the ones worthy of assuming the mantle of leadership in ushering in "The New Japan."[25] Apparently, this "*seinen* boom" lasted until the early 1890s.

Rather than originating with adults who were discussing young people, the use of the word *seinen* emerged exclusively from discussions of young people by the young themselves (i.e., self-referential discourse). What's more, even though the phenomenon was widespread to some extent, it was in vogue only among some privileged intellectuals who were able to contribute their opinions to magazines.

The changing meaning of *seinen*

The period spanning the final years of the Meiji era and the early Taishō era (1912–26) saw the earliest instance of the youngster-bashing phenomenon in Japan. It was all about bemoaning young people and sex—the same old story that continues to make adults frown to this day.

Books that flourished back then were those that discussed how disturbed and depraved young people were in their sexual pursuits. Such publications included the 1907 *Seinen shijo daraku no riyū* (The reasons behind the descent of young men and children into decadence) by Yutaka Hibino, a forty-one-year-old resident of the Owari domain who was famous in some parts for having introduced the sport of marathon running into educational circles; and the 1917 *Seinen to seiyoku* (Youth and sexual appetite) by forty-seven-year-old Owari resident Akira Fujinami, a pathologist known for his research into the *Schistosomiasis japonica* parasite.[26]

Adults became alarmed by the "free love" fad and the rampancy of sexually transmitted diseases, and began to view the nurturing of wholesome young people as the major factor—a top priority—that could sustain the advancement of the Japanese empire. To this end, the gist of the "young people and sex" school of criticism, which targeted students who traveled to Tokyo to study, dealt with how onanism was harmful.[27]

---

25.   What's interesting about this group is that they took pride in staying away from any particular political movement. They would pen novels, publish their opinions in magazines, and even create hobby groups, but they referred to young people who were committed to political movements as "ruffians," looking down on them as anachronistic fools who were deeply and eternally attached to the Japan of a bygone time. This was because the formation of a centralized government, which the Meiji government had initiated, was already nearing completion; in their view, it was futile to challenge such a formidable authority. Talk about an "apathy generation," yeah?

26.   Hiroshi Komatsu, *Nihon no rekishi 14: "Inochi" to teikoku Nippon* (The history of Japan 14: "Life" and the Empire of Japan), Shogakukan, 2009.

27.   Manabu Akagawa, *Sekushuaritei no rekishi shakaigaku* (Historical sociology of sexuality), Keiso Shobo, 1999.

The *Gendai seinen-ron* (Modern discourse on youth), a work by thirty-six-year-old Gingetsu Itō of Akita prefecture, can also be said to be an early example of the genre.[28] Instead of being focused on the subject of youth per se, however, this book uses the metaphor of youth to advance the discussion of "the future of Japan."

If you asked me to pick a Taishō-era bestseller that could be characterized as a book about young people as seen from our modern-day perspective, I would offer the work *Taishō no seinen to teikoku no zento* (The youth of the Taishō era and the future of the empire) by the journalist Soho Tokutomi, who, when he completed the work, was fifty-three years old and a resident of the Higo province.[29]

In this work, while recounting the odyssey of youth since the Meiji era, Tokutomi laments the lack of patriotism in the young people of the Taishō era; he says they have become disinclined to harbor grand ambitions. According to Tokutomi, these Taishō-era youth felt as entitled as "third-generation scions of wealthy men—in other words, young masters." With the foundations of the "empire" called Japan having already been established, the young, he reasons, were slacking off and leading carefree lives of apathy.

As there seem to have been various types of these "young masters," Tokutomi attempts to identify five categories of personality that describe the young: the "model *seinen*," a stability-oriented youth who is loyal to his seniors and is also adept at reading a situation or sensing the prevailing mood; the "success-oriented *seinen*," a youth who is self-centered and obsessed with becoming rich; the "anguished *seinen*," a youth who is beset with angst over the laissez-faire mores of the present age (that is, the Taishō era) and stays indoors, feeling powerless; the "hedonistic *seinen*," a youth who is a slave to carnal desires, leading a life of decadence; and the "colorless *seinen*," a youth who, without having a distinct individuality of his own, drifts through life, following others blindly. While they are nothing like those found in *Yoki rironteki jinkaku shisutemu ruikei-ron* (Expectancy theory concerning a system of personality types),[30] a work by thirty-four-year-old Shinji Miyadai of Miyagi prefecture, which employs complex statistical analyses, these five personality types seem valid even to this day.[31]

---

28.   Gingetsu Itō, *Gendai seinen-ron* (Modern discourse on youth), Kyōkadō Shoten, 1907.

29.   Soho Tokutomi, *Taishō no seinen to teikoku no zento* (The youth of the Taishō era and the future of the empire), Minyūsha, 1916. Comprising 160 chapters, with 646 pages in the main volume alone, this work is a masterpiece that concurrently discusses the subjects of youth and the nation.

30.   Shinji Miyadai, Hideki Ishihara, and Akiko Ōtsuka, *Zōho: Sabukaruchā shinwa kaitai* (Supplement: Deconstructing the subculture myth), Chikumashobo, 2007.

31.   Incidentally, Yasuo Nagayama points out that the personality types conceived by Tokutomi resemble the descriptions applied to modern-day youth: *antei shikō* (the stability-oriented types), *kachi gumi* (the winners), *hikikomori* (the shut-ins), *otaku* (the geeks), and *freeters* (the job-hopping part-timers). (*Taitei botsugo* [After the demise of the great emperor], Shinchosha, 2007.)

Tokutomi's views on young people were immediately challenged by the thirty-nine-year-old thinker Sakuzō Yoshino of Miyagi prefecture.[32] Yoshino claimed that Tokutomi's work was merely incurring young people's ill will, since all he was doing was, in effect, randomly tossing around abstract platitudes like "Love your nation" when, to begin with, there was neither any infrastructure nor any social security system in place. He went on to mock Tokutomi, saying that the only people who would fall for his sloppy arguments were the elderly and country folk; the nation's most influential youth, who were graced with some good judgment, would not be swayed. (Even though this essay by Yoshino is nearly a hundred years old now, I'd love to distribute copies of it to self-proclaimed nationalists who put tradition on a pedestal.)

But Tokutomi's *seinen-ron*—that is, his discourse on youth—wasn't as bad as Yoshino made out. After all, it didn't just offer a one-sided conclusion like "Young people these days are outrageous!" His discussion was meticulous, taking into account the changing social landscape of the time. In addition, he didn't fail to criticize the nation itself for having brought about the rise of these five types of *seinen*.

The discourse on youth prompted by the war

In Japan, talking about the *seinen* as a generation began to come into style in the late 1930s. The frequency with which the word *seinen* appeared in newspaper stories also saw a rapid rise at this time (see figure 1.1).

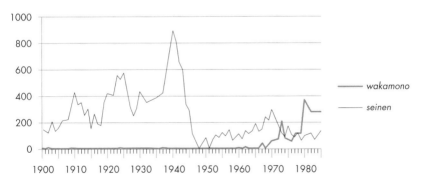

Figure 1.1 Variations in the usage frequency of the words *wakamono* (young people) and *seinen* (youth)

This is a graph showing the number of instances of these words appearing in the electronic edition of the *Asahi Shimbun*, as determined through a "headline and keyword analysis." The graph excludes advertisements and synonyms.

---

32.   Sakuzō Yoshino, "Sohō sensei no 'Taishō no seinen to teikoku no zento' o yomu" (Reading master Sohō's "The youth of the Taishō era and the future of the empire"), *Chūōkōron*, January 1917.

Fifty-one-year-old Tokyo native Ikutarō Shimizu recollects that, in those days, the public debate on young people had become a major theme in the journalism of the time.[33] But why did the discourse take off in the 1930s? As everyone probably knows— except "those youngsters these days, ignorant of history"—in 1937 the Japan-China War was fully underway, and in 1938 the National Mobilization Act was established by the first Konoe cabinet. In effect, it was a time when the whole of Japan became embroiled in war.

War is a phenomenon that has a leveling effect: it engenders a certain kind of equality among people.[34] Whether you're rich or poor, or whether your father is a politician or a criminal, in principle, you, like everyone else, must fight for your country. The ones who actually proceed to the front lines, however, and even face the possibility of having to sacrifice their lives, are those around twenty years of age. Of course, these "youths" are, for the most part, male.

Thus, the public debate on youth carried out during this time was entirely about those who were qualified to become Imperial Army soldiers; that is, the debate was limited to just males. A discourse on young people fails to be valid unless the people talking about it assume that members of the young generation share common characteristics. When war looms, whether you're a young man leading a glamorous life in the city or a young man leading a drab existence in a destitute out-of-the-way village, you, as a citizen like everyone else, are subject to military conscription. In other words, it became possible, when discussing young people, to talk about all of them on an equal footing, as "soldiers" for the "citizens of the country."[35] In other words, it was a sort of fantasy of equality brought about by the war that laid the foundations of the youth discourse that took place under wartime conditions.

For example, in his 1937 book, *Sensō to seinen* (War and youth), the critic Kōshin Murobuse (forty-five years old, Kanagawa) defines *seinen* (in this case, young man) as "one who is incomplete," and attempts to aggressively evaluate such a person.[36]

---

33.   Ikutarō Shimizu, ed., *Seinen* (Youth), Yuhikaku Publishing, 1959.

34.   The notion that war and the military draft bring about equality is, strictly speaking, the product of rhetoric espoused by the government and the establishment. In reality, the question of just what kind of "equality" was realized has been up for debate, and has been the subject of various ongoing studies and discussions. (Rieko Takada, *Gakureki, kaikyū, guntai* [Academic background, social class, and the military], Chuokoron-Shinsha, 2008.)

35.   Starting in 1939, compulsory education for boys was extended, requiring all boys up to age nineteen to attend school. Before that point, students had only been required to attend up to primary school, so there were boys who were still in their early teens, or even as young as ten or twelve, dropping out to enter the job market. On the other hand, the elite who were admitted into one of the imperial universities would remain students until their twenties. Given this situation, I believe you can see why it's difficult to make blanket statements about all "young people."

36.   Kōshin Murobuse, *Sensō to seinen* (War and youth), Nippon Hyoron Sha, 1937.

This is because he felt the urgent need to help the transition of a "senescent Japan," on its deathbed as it faced the crisis of living under wartime conditions, to the era of *Seinen Nihon*, a "youthful Japan." Consequently, he appeals the merits of a war for the liberation of Asia, declaring, "Young men, fight, fight with this noble awareness in mind." Toward the end, though—perhaps because he himself had become overwhelmed with emotion—Murobuse lapses into sentimental babble: "Embrace Japan with the arms of love, and ignite the spirit of a youthful Japan with the flames of passion."

Dai Nihon seinen (The youth of Great Japan)

Incidentally, when it became clear that Japan's defeat was imminent, Murobuse promptly turned into a recluse before going on to postwar activity as an author of works theorizing on TV and mass culture. So as it turns out, all he ever did was stir up youth from his privileged position, never having to risk his life, before ultimately fleeing. Now, how convenient was that? This aspect of convenience, it should be noted, relates to other discourses on youth as well.

Seinen magazines that glorified youth

Now let's take a look at a magazine for young men published in 1938, titled *Dai Nihon seinen* (The youth of Great Japan). With its book review section covering the second-oldest book of classical Japanese history, *The Nihongi: Chronicles of Japan from the Earliest Times to A.D. 697*, and with the *manzai* (comic dialogue or commentary) on current affairs running in its entertainment pages, which featured the theme of "physical examinations for conscription,"[37] this magazine was quite hip for its time, a periodical in sync with its wartime milieu. Since the company behind it went on to become today's *Mainichi Shimbun*, the magazine was likely a major publication

---

37. The "situational *manzai*" (comic dialogue) is made up of the following interchange between Nihon Tarō and Aikyō Hanako:
     Hanako: With those glasses of yours, I doubt you'll pass the physical exam.
     Tarō: Oh, I'm not bothered about these glasses. In fact, I'm confident that I'm going to pass with flying colors, grade A!
     Hanako: Are your glasses *kōkekkō* [really awesome]?
     Tarō: Yes, they're *bekkō* [tortoiseshell-rimmed].
     (*Dainihon seinen*, January 1, 1939, king-size issue).
     (Translator's note: Part of the humor of this joke is found in the rhyming wordplay between *kōkekkō* and *bekkō*, which both include the character 甲 [*kō*, shell], but the humor mainly hinges on the double meaning of this character, which, in this context, means "Grade A" or "top-notch" in the first instance, and refers to "tortoiseshell" in the other.)

back then.

In each issue of this magazine, a big-name politician appears to convey words of gratitude to the *seinen shokun* (young gentlemen). For example, the minister of the navy at the time, Mitsumasa Yonai (fifty-eight years old, Iwate), offered this shout-out to young people: "In these critical times we live under today, the expectations we harbor for you—you young gentlemen who are the backbone of the people of this nation—are immensely vast." He also says, "What we must expect from you young gentlemen, no matter what kind of poverty you may encounter, is to continue to persevere and believe in yourself, to continue to brim with ample self-confidence, while leveraging your intelligence to push on toward meeting your expectations."[38] Similarly, the then minister of justice, Suehiko Shiono (fifty-eight years old, Nagano), said, "To fulfill this crusade for founding the continent is our honorable duty, and our responsibility," adding, "You young gentlemen will find it an honor on your part to be shouldering, along with us, the burden of the great deed that must be brought to fruition for the future." He then incites them to action: "Rise up, young gentlemen!"[39]

Even the secretary of state for the Home Department, Nobumasa Suetsugu (fifty-eight years old, Yamaguchi), as expected, flatters the youth contingent, saying, "The young men of a nation are always burdened with the baggage called 'the coming era.'" He then goes on to encourage youngsters to "commit to the idea of the national polity of traditional Japan, and put this into practice."[40] However, he doesn't specify in his writing just what this "idea of national polity" might be.

What's interesting about adults like Suetsugu is that rather than flatly stating that they don't understand young people today, they express high expectations for young people on the grounds that the future of Japan depends on its youth. In a sense, you could describe them as "understanding adults."

To wit, the way General Takashi Hishikari (sixty-seven years old, Kagoshima) spoke was precisely the way an "understanding adult" would speak:

> There are those who say things like the youth in the old days, compared to the youth of today, used to be one way or another, or that they were far greater and more honorable, but I'm against such talk. I can't help feeling sorry for the young ones today when people torment them by bringing up examples of their counter-

---

38.   *Dainihon seinen*, May 15, 1938.
39.   *Dainihon seinen*, October 1, 1938.
40.   *Dainihon seinen*, September 1, 1938.

parts in the past. Those bygone days and the present are totally different ages.[41]

Well, it may have been only natural to pretend to be understanding. The young men for whom they had such high hopes were, after all, precious resources who would go to the lengths of sacrificing their own lives for the cause of the great Japanese empire.

The hunted youth

Of course, there were some young people who had noticed the sinister attitude of their elders. To illustrate, let me now invite you to take a look at the writings of a student who was twenty years old when he wrote the work below—an excerpt from *Kike wadatsumi no koe* (Listen to the voice of the sea god), the famous posthumous collection of last wills and testaments of student soldiers killed in battle in the final years of World War II. Although this student had entered Kyoto Imperial University in 1942, he went on to join the army in 1943; in 1945, he was killed in action in Myanmar. He was twenty-two years old.

> Though journalists and the public make a great fuss about us, we have rather passed the point of merely being annoyed, and are now experiencing indignation in our hearts. When I think about how those who advocated mobilizing students for the war had several years ago approved of student-hunts, I can clearly see now, at this late hour, that society was never concerned about the things that each and every one of us had seriously contemplated and ruminated in our heart of hearts, that all they saw was us guys getting drafted and plucked out of our reveries midway through; that is to say, that all they really saw was the change in our social station, our occupation. I have come to the keen realization that while there certainly are some students being manipulated by journalists, when all is said and done, they fail to see, even just a little, that we students being rounded up back in those days and we students today are one and the same human beings.[42]

The student-hunts he refers to are the crackdowns on cafés, movie theaters, and dance halls carried out in 1938 by the Metropolitan Police Department. They arrested students they deemed to be truants and, after having them write an oath of repentance,

---

41.   *Dainihon seinen*, January 1, 1939, king-size issue. But Hishikari, in the latter half of the work, suddenly begins to say, "What's lacking in today's youth is training." So, in the end, he may just have been a savvy smooth-talker, and nothing more.

42.   Compiled by the Nihon Senbotsu Gakusei Kinenkai (memorial foundation for the student war dead), *Kike wadatsumi no koe* (Listen to the voice of the sea god), Iwanami Shoten, new edition, 1995.

made them salute in the direction of the Imperial Palace. It is said that during the February student-hunt, they managed to arrest a total of 3,486 people within the course of just three days. The justification behind the roundup was that it was outrageous that, at a time when an all-out mobilization program was in place, students who were exempt from military service were playing truant in cafés.

Back then, the so-called student-hunts had developed into a full-blown social controversy, embroiling people in contentious disputes over the rights and wrongs of the practice. For instance, students at Waseda University, while protesting against the practice of student-hunting, set up a council appealing students to use self-restraint and self-discipline to resist the urge to visit places of entertainment. The government responded, too, in a way that was hardly characteristic of a monolithic, inflexible organization: the Ministry of Education at the time protested against the police regulating not only crime prevention measures, but public morals as well.[43]

Anti-real-life happiness in wartime Japan

Well, ultimately, the various discussions pertaining to student-hunts were, more often than not, settled with the words, "a serious situation."[44] A look at the newspapers of the time shows letters to the editor carrying complaints as along the lines of, "Given the situation we find ourselves in today, the behaviors engaged in by students are disgraceful and inexcusable: they dress up in American-style overcoats (the kind that low-wage earners can't afford); they amuse themselves at cafés, mahjong parlors, and dance halls; and even hold hands with girls and strut about together in a public show of affection!"[45]

In present-day lingo, this can be described as *riajū hihan* (criticism against being content with real life, or "offline life"). Originating on the Internet, the expression *riajū* is online jargon which came into widespread use from around 2007; it refers to a person satisfied (*jūjitsu*) with his or her real life (*ria*), as opposed to an online virtual life. It could also refer to the state of such satisfaction. Typically, persons involved in a romantic relationship or those who keep themselves busy in their work are often called *riajū*.

In this day and age, if someone criticizes a person for being a *riajū*, or for leading

---

43.   "Ikisugita gakusei gari: Mombushō ga kōgi" (The student hunts that went too far: The Ministry of Education protests), *Asahi Shimbun*, June 18, 1938, Tokyo evening edition.

44.   "Yō wa gakusei no tame ni" (Bottom line: It's all for the students), *Asahi Shimbun*, June 22, 1938, morning edition.

45.   "Dokusha gan: Furyō gakusei gari" (Reader's view: Delinquent-student hunts), *Yomiuri Shimbun*, February 19, 1938, morning edition.

a fulfilling life in the real, offline world, it would just come off as jealousy. But in war-time Japan, by merely adding the words "serious situation," any message was instantly rendered into a fantastic glorification of war.

Thus, even though a major public debate about young people was taking place during wartime, not all of the views articulated in the debate praised youth. In particular, criticism against university students was loud.

The philosopher Kiyoshi Miki (forty years old, Hyogo) published the famous essay "Gakusei no chinō teika ni tsuite" (On the decline of intelligence among students) in the May 1937 issue of the literary magazine *Bungeishunjū*. In this essay, he claims that there was a decline in the level of intelligence among "students after the incident" (students who entered high school after the occurrence of the Manchurian Incident). He says that "high school students in the past used to have a youthful curiosity, healthy skepticism, and passionate idealism, and for this reason, devoured all kinds of books." He was probably talking about himself.

He goes on to assert, of contemporary students attending school, that "they believe that all they should do is graduate, without ever developing any substantial interest in social issues or in society itself." Enter the rise of the "*King* students"—those who only read the popular entertainment magazine *King*, which used to be published by Kodansha. Judged by today's standards, this magazine is so text-heavy that if any friend of mine were to be reading such a thing, I'd end up respecting him; but naturally, Miki had no respect for *King*—he was just mocking it. Headlines such as "Students of The University of Tokyo Can't Do Fractions" and "The Decline in the Academic Ability of University Students" have appeared in the news recently, and the prototype of the argument underlying these kinds of criticisms can be found in Miki's essay.[46]

The lament of nostalgic granddads

Sōichi Ōya (thirty-six years old, Osaka), a pundit who was as critical of students as Miki was, also writes as follows:[47] "Students these days lack any kind of knowledge or thoughts and ideas found outside of technical expertise, and are also poor at self-reflection." In effect, he says, there's a surfeit of utilitarian "pseudo-intellectual" students around. A newspaper reporter appearing in the forum of a magazine called *Nihon hyōron* (Japan review) offers the following comment. "Back in 1931, 1932, when so-called social movements were flourishing, this thing called the university used to be

---

46.   But to be fair to Miki, what he's engaged in is criticizing educational authorities, rather than in simple student bashing. He's accusing the recent educational administration of neglecting to train students in critical thinking and cultivating them to only be bureaucratic and adept at attaining high scores on tests.

47.   Sōichi Ōya, "Ruiji interi no hanran" (The flooding of like-minded intellectuals), *Chūōkōron*, March 1937.

severely criticized, but I feel the students of that time, as human beings, were more well-rounded than the bunch you see these days. The present young ones all seem to fit into the same mold, each of them looking like sons of civil servants, you know."[48]

In fact, arguments such as this one were all fueled by nostalgia for the leftist movement that came to life in the early years of the Shōwa era (1926–89).[49] Under the influence of ideologies like Taishō democracy, the elite students of the Taishō era (1912–26) had become receptive to Marxism and socialism. Furthermore, in the early Shōwa era, the rise in the number of students leaning toward left-wing politics became a social issue of concern. The movement had apparently seen a moderate upsurge, with the students carrying out demonstrations on college campuses and distributing flyers. However, later studies clearly show that many students participated in such activities because they "feared being left out."

In other words, the general argument put forth by Miki et al. represents a kind of nostalgia for the days of the speakers' own youth, when the leftist movement and student commotions still made waves, when the students of that time, hence, were "more well-rounded as human beings," in contrast to the kids these days, whose "level of intelligence is on the decline." That reminds me, I think I heard an earful of a sermon like this recently from an elderly man of the *Zenkyōtō sedai* (the "all-campus joint struggle generation," who were in college from 1965 to 1972; in short, the angry young men).

To add to this discussion, other noteworthy events happening in the late 1930s included the popularization of universities and the culture boom. It was a time when the number of university students was growing, albeit gradually, and students at the imperial university and those at private universities were beginning to differentiate themselves. This differentiation saw the imperial side claiming that private schools were at fault since they admitted students without requiring them to study, just lumping them together and treating them indiscriminately as worthless.[50]

In addition, from 1936 through 1941, the twelve-volume series known as *Gakusei sōsho* (Student library) was published and became a bestseller by the standards of the day. Individual titles in this series performed remarkably well, too: *Gakusei to kyōyō* (Students and culture) went into its twenty-fourth edition three years after its publica-

48.   "Zadankai: Wakaki interi wa kataru" (Roundtable forum: Young intellectuals discuss), *Nippon hyōron*, September 1938.

49.   Yō Takeuchi, "Sakei gakusei no gunzō" (Left-wing students) in *Furyō, hīrō, sakei* (The juvenile delinquent, the hero, and the leftists) edited by Yō Takeuchi and Kyōko Inagaki, Jimbun Shoin, 2002.

50.   Rieko Takada, *Gakureki, kaikyū, guntai* (Academic background, social class, and the military), Chuokoron-Shinsha, 2008.

tion; *Gakusei to seikatsu* (Students and daily living) went into its thirty-third edition three and a half years after its launch; and *Gakusei to dokusho* (Students and reading) sold 29,000 copies in a single year.[51]

The *Gakusei sōsho* series comprised a kind of how-to manual for becoming cultured. Through this series, one could not only know, with ease and clarity, what books were recommended for students, but could learn how to write prose correctly, too.

Thanks to this "cultural enrichment boom," many who had never been interested in becoming cultured or literate suddenly became men of culture—overnight sophisticates—to the dismay of self-proclaimed "true" intellectuals. You would have witnessed a similar scene at The University of Tokyo in the year 2010, when Michael J. Sandel's works were catching on.

Did the vices of liberalism ruin young people?

Positioned halfway between youth bashing and the argument advocating that "young people are our hope" is the argument proposed by Kazunobu Kanokogi (fifty-three years old, Tokyo), who was a professor and doctor of literature at the former Kyushu Imperial University.

While counting on young people to "lead Greater Asia," he felt uneasy about the influences of democratic trends and liberalism. Due to the impact of the "vile global climate" that prevailed in the aftermath of World War I, he says, "Young people jumped on the democracy bandwagon, and in turn, lapsed into adopting liberal manners and attitudes." He goes on to say that they consequently began in numerous ways, to display a lack of the training, cultivation, and education befitting the *Nihon seinen* (youth of Japan).[52] He exhorts to the young men of the time to "Strive to be obedient, to learn to submit!"

Though this discourse dates back as far as seventy years, for some reason I experienced déjà vu when I realized that it was reminiscent of the "postwar democracy" critique. Even more familiar, though, is the argument put forward by the dramatist Kunio Kishida (forty-nine years old, Tokyo), who decried the sorry sight of young people on the train hesitating to give up their seats to the elderly.[53]

According to Kishida, "…ever since the Taishō era, Japan has been losing sight of the goal it should have been advancing toward, on account of being preoccupied with welcoming and adopting all sorts of trends." The Japanese people confused "European"

51.　Yō Takeuchi, *Kyōyō shugi no botsuraku* (The fall of intellectualism), Chuokoron-Shinsha, 2003.
52.　*Dainihon seinen*, May 15, 1938.
53.　Kunio Kishida, "Fūzoku no hidōtokusei" (The amorality of manners and customs), *Bungeishunjū*, June 1940.

with "modern"; and as for "Western thought" and the "ancient customs of our country," it became admissible to just adopt them superficially. The group that exemplifies this tendency, he says, is young people. This notion perfectly applies to the present as well, if you replace "Taishō era" with "postwar Japan."

To confirm how their "youth talk," or narrative on young people, is no different from the kind of youth talk we hear today, let's have a look at one that was published in 2007. It was written by an elderly man: a seventy-one-year-old educationalist from Chiba prefecture named Yoshihiro Noguchi.

According to Grandpa Noguchi, one of the causes contributing to the "confusion among young people and to their downfall" is postwar democracy.[54] He expresses regret at the fact that "Our postwar educational institutions, unmoored by the currents of postwar democracy, neglected to carry out the kind of in-depth scrutiny necessary for realizing how fraught with danger are flowery and flattering words such as freedom, equality, individuality, and leisure." Now, if you replace the expression "postwar democracy" mentioned here by Noguchi with "post–World War I liberalism," you'll get a classic discourse on youth that can apply just as aptly to the 1930s. I'd certainly like to seal up this classic work of youth literature and store it for safekeeping deep in the archives of a library.

"The alien other" vs. "the expedient ally"

I think by now you can see a basic theme emerging—one of youngster bashing that has, regrettably, been going on to this day without abating at all since the 1930s. Basically, the bashing comes in two patterns. The first compares today's young people to the young people of old and saying that the present young ones are no good. This is seen in the criticism aimed at the *wakadanna* (young masters; i.e., heirs to property or businesses) and at left-wing students. The second pattern expresses disapproval of young people out of envy. This applies to the likes of the *riajū* student criticism that rails against being content with real, "offline" life.

What both these patterns have in common is the adults' conviction that "young people" are different from them—that youth are "alien others." Adults can therefore criticize without limit, and in doing so, they can boost their sense of self-worth, their superiority.

At this juncture, I'd say it becomes clear why politicians posed as "understanding

---

54.   "Kaitō ranma: Nihon kyōiku gijutsu gakkai meiyokaichō, Yoshihiro Noguchi—Gakkō ga katei o yowaku shita" ("Gordian Knot" column by the honorary chairman of the Japan Society for Educational Skill, Yoshihiro Noguchi— School has weakened the home), *Sankei Shimbun*, February 19, 2007, Tokyo morning edition).

adults" and declared that young people were their hope. These "understanding adults" weren't talking about young people as they existed, but about pie-in-the sky, ideal versions of them. Since they were dealing with an idealistic image of youth, they didn't need to compare young people to themselves, nor did they need to feel jealous of them. If anything, since they even expected them to give up their lives for the cause of the great Japanese empire to which they belonged, rather than considering them to be "alien others," they saw young people as convenient, expedient allies to be exploited.

"Expedient allies"—in name, they're individuals who belong on "this side" as opposed to "the other side." That's why if they die they can be honored at Yasukuni Shrine in the name of the entire country, and even potentially be enshrined as heroes (that is, to be given the status of a great honorable spirit of the war dead). But, in substance, they're not "on this side"—they're not "us." The politicians who declare that young people are our hope won't be going to the front, nor will they be granting young people—those very people who are supposed to represent hope—any rights, not even the right to vote, which was only given to men age twenty-five years and above.

An emblematic book is the *Kokubō kokka to seinen no shinro* (National defense and the path of youth), authored in 1941 by Kurazō Suzuki (forty-seven years old, Ibaraki), who was an undercover intelligence officer responsible for censorship. In this book he passionately preaches the necessity of establishing the Greater East Asia Co-Prosperity Sphere, and just how critical young people were to this end.[55]

According to Suzuki, the stain of the ideology called *jiga kōri* (self-centered utilitarianism)—a legacy of the Edo period—getting entangled with ideologies such as individualism, liberalism, and democracy imported from Europe and America starting in the Meiji period, the Great Japanese Empire was being afflicted with the spread of "infectious ideological diseases." Suzuki maintains that youth are the ones who remain, comparatively speaking, lightly afflicted, thanks to the fact that they're still young; they comprise the "nation's hope," making them indispensable to the creation of Greater East Asia.

---

55. Kurazō Suzuki, *Kokubō kokka to seinen no shinro* (The trajectories of the national defense state and youth), Dai-Nippon Yūbenkai Kodansha, 1941. This book is memorable for its front cover showing a macho, half-naked man pointing far away into the distance with a self-absorbed look in his eyes. Such an image is certainly in keeping with the persona of the publishing company Kodansha, which, in tandem with the Great Japanese Empire, stirred up excitement in the war. Incidentally, the image of Kurazō Suzuki as an "evil overlord of censorship" only became entrenched after the war. In reality he was someone who was enthusiastic about education, spending his days, after the end of the war, as the director of the public hall of Kumamoto (Takumi Satō, *Genrontōsei* [Censorship], Chuokoron-Shinsha, 2004).

It's interesting to see that Suzuki's rejection doesn't stop at "Western" ideologies such as democracy and liberalism; it extends even up to the Edo period. At any rate, it's clear that the young people Suzuki talks about, and even praises, are nonentities; they simply don't exist yet.

The persistence of the "expedient ally" rhetoric

You might be wondering, given the terror of war, how people could seduce the young by calling them the nation's hope and send them off to the front lines. No way! But this rhetoric wasn't just limited to wartime. You often see it in the present age too.

For example, the wartime assertion that young people were the hope of the nation was remarkably echoed in the pro-entrepreneur policies of the 1990s. After the economic bubble burst Japan proposed various schemes to increase the number of companies. A look at the messages transmitted by the government and the business world back then reveal that entrepreneurs were supposed to be the saviors of the Japanese economy: they would shoulder the burden of job creation while valuing the principles of working for the greater public good and embracing an ethical viewpoint. If they failed, however, entrepreneurs would, by definition, assume responsibility.[56/★12] Indeed, the entrepreneur was, in effect, an "expedient ally."

And this sentiment isn't limited just to entrepreneurs today. Many adults, including politicians and management executives and even *bunkajin* (intellectuals), assert their wish to see young people try hard. That, in and of itself, should be a welcome thing. I myself have been the beneficiary of various perks simply on account of being young. In fact, the likely reason why I'm able to come out with a book like this is exactly because I'm a young person, a *wakamono*.[★13]

However, the argument that young people are our hope tacitly regards young people, at times, as "expedient allies." To just exhort young people to try hard without giving them any privileges or rights or concrete benefits and opportunities is the height of irresponsibility. But hey, unlike the young people who went on to become soldiers of the imperial army, at least you don't end up dying when you become an entrepreneur and launch a company in modern-day Japan—barring extraordinary circum-

---

56.   Noritoshi Furuichi, "Posuto 1991" (Post-1991) in *G2* no. 6, 2010.
★12.   An elaborate compilation of the stories mentioned here can be found in Noritoshi Furuichi's "Tsukurareta 'kigyōka'" (The made "entrepreneur") in *Shakaigaku hyōron* (Japanese Sociological Review), 63–3, 2012.
★13.   After the publication of this book, society's willingness to cheer young people on grew, giving rise to the creation of various opportunities to do just that. In 2012, NHK began airing the talk show *Nippon no jiremma* (Japan's dilemma), which focused on polemicists born after 1970. In addition, conventions and roundtable conferences held by the government also helped to increase opportunities to study young people.

stances, of course.

3. The Postwar Discourse on Young People

The après-guerre crimes adults can't quite understand

The long war finally ended, bringing to a close the age when the slogan for the young was "Life lasts just twenty years." One phrase that came into vogue immediately after the war was "après-guerre." Though this expression is French for "postwar," in Japan it was appropriated to refer to young people living in the immediate aftermath of war. The term is loaded with the nuances of nihilism and decadence.[57]

What catapulted this expression into an overnight sensation was the Hikari Club incident. Akitsugu Yamazaki, a twenty-four-year old student from Chiba who was at The University of Tokyo at the time, started a money-lending business that made waves as a company helmed by a student from this prestigious institution. But when it came to light that he had allegedly violated the Price Control Law, his cash flow came to a standstill, and, after defaulting on his debts, at the age of twenty-seven, he committed suicide. His unusual suicide note, titled "Cyanide Suicide To Settle All Loans," also made it into the news.

The Hikari Club incident went on to be dubbed an *apure hanzai* (postwar crime). After this incident, other *après-guerre* crimes (that is, incidents named as such) ensued one after another. In effect, talk of "*après-guerre* crimes" became trendy. Rokurō Sahara, in his newspaper editorial titled "Apure gēru no shakaigaku" (The sociology of après-guerre), points out that the confusion occurring in the aftermath of the war had led to an increase in the number of robbers and the rise in black markets, among other criminal phenomena.[58] In 1951, Shisō no Kagaku Kenkyū Kai (Association for the Study of the Science of Thought) published a piece titled *Sengoha no kenkyū: Apure gēru no jittai kiroku* (Study of the postwar generation: A record of the reality of *après-guerre* times).

In 1953, the *Yomiuri Shimbun* put together a special feature called "Apure hanzai

---

57.　"*Après*" wasn't just a term for "youngster bashing." A young man who was eighteen at the time declared, "We may be *après*, but I think we're the ones who will be shouldering the world moving forward." He goes on to add, "I want to study more, to grasp the real image—the true shape and form—of *après*." (*Asahi Shimbun*, January 8, 1955, Tokyo evening edition.) Apparently, ever since the old days, young people—whose level of education and self-awareness were so high that they'd end up sending letters to newspapers—have been engaged in the act of soul-searching.

58.　"Apure gēru no shakaigaku" (The sociology of *après-guerre*), *Yomiuri Shimbun*, December 10, 1949.

hakusho" (White paper on après-guerre crimes),[59] The article states, "A series of what are called *après-guerre* crimes has been occurring. These are quite beyond the comprehension of adults, being characterized by the fact that the motives behind them, and their modus operandi, are tainted with such a level of absurdity as to boggle the mind." The piece then adds that it's apparently the "great burden entrusted to adults to clarify and expose the secret of this young generation." The writing style of the reporter of this piece is surprisingly light and pleasant for someone who's supposedly an "adult."

According to this same article, the hallmarks of an *après-guerre* crime are that "the motivation behind the crime is vague or nonexistent, and that the act is extremely impulsive." Attached to this piece is also a grateful comment from a teacher, Sōichi Ōya (fifty-two years old, Osaka). According to Mr. Ōya, the reason behind the rise in *après-guerre* crimes was that the "grammar of everyday living" had been thrown into disorder. "In the old days in society there used to be this thing called discipline. It was a systematic form of social training. This has disappeared." And apparently, for this reason, young people "commit murder with the same kind of frivolous feeling one would have when saying, 'Let's play mahjong!'"

I don't know exactly what time period Mr. Ōya, who was born in the year 1900, is referring to when he talks about the "old days," but the past—the prewar days as well as during the war—is riddled with cryptic and brutal crimes, including an eighteen-year-old boy murdering nine people one after another (1942); a fourteen-year-old, after killing two little girls, engaging in necrophilia (1939); a twenty-year-old murdering five members of his family just to test how many people he could kill (1934); a fourteen-year-old, inside a classroom, murdering his classmate by stabbing him repeatedly in the chest and arms with a knife (1932); a twenty-year-old, after squandering his money in a spree of womanizing, going on to rob and murder a business tycoon (1928); and a seventeen-year-old monk raping and murdering a girl in his neighborhood (1927).[60]

---

59. "Apure hanzai hakusho" (White paper on après crimes), *Yomiuri Shimbun*, August 31, 1953, morning edition.

60. Erurō Kanga, *Senzen no shōnen hanzai* (Prewar juvenile crimes), Tsukiji Shokan, 2007. However, it is a fact that, compared to the present age, the postwar period saw a higher rate of violent crimes. In 1954, there were 4,367 arrests for brutal crimes committed by boys age nineteen or younger—404 of them for murder alone. The peak of such crimes occurred in the 1960s, after which the rate of violent crimes committed by juveniles continued to decline dramatically (Takayoshi Doi, *Hikōshōnen no shōmetsu* [The demise of juvenile delinquents], Shinzansha, 2003). In 2010, only forty-six juveniles age nineteen or under were arrested for murder. This is around half of the number arrested in the year 2000. (National Police Agency, *Heisei 22-nen no hanzai jōsei* [The state of crime in 2010].)

Sociology enters the fray

In 1953, the first full-scale study on young people by a sociologist, *Seinen shakaigaku* (The Sociology of the young), was published.[61] Since this is a collection of papers written by multiple authors, the level of quality varies by the paper, but judging from the standards of modern sociology, the overall content of this work is in no way inferior. In essence, the tome refers to the available research on youth carried out in Europe and America and applies it to concrete cases observed in Japan, just as comparative research is done today.

However, what's interesting is that the *seinen* described in this work are truly diverse. The editor's intention appears to have been to delineate commonly shared attributes that differentiated young people as a generation, but the actual content of the book ends up being an analysis based on a predefined, detailed categorization of the different types of youth: urban *seinen*, rural *seinen*, and misbehaving *seinen* (juvenile delinquents).

The sociologists of the time had too much good sense to discuss *seinen* as a generation. This was because young people, even if they are the same with respect to their age, are, in reality, diverse.

As of 1950, the urban population of Japan didn't even comprise 40 percent of the overall nation. Most Japanese were living in rural communities. The lifestyles of young people living there and the lifestyles of their counterparts in cities were poles apart. But even when talking about the young people living in cities, you couldn't easily lump them together in a group; most were factory workers, but some were engaged in the metal-machine industry and others engaged in the cotton-spinning industry; these two groups were not only totally different in terms of their lifestyles, but in terms of their male-to-female ratio as well.

At a time when urban Tokyo was abuzz with news of the so-called "pink group"—a gang of runaway high school students who hotel-hopped, haunted dance halls, and turned to theft when they had trouble coming up with the money to cover their entertainment expenses—a lot of young people in rural areas would immediately pursue professions in the agriculture and forestry industry after graduating from junior high. So, as you can see, there was no way anyone, at such a time, could have easily asserted, in the breezy way we do today, that "all young people are [insert your favorite adjective here]."

---

61. Prior to this, among works by sociologists on the subject of young people, there is Ryōzō Takeda's "'Shūhenjin' no shakaigaku" (The sociology of the "marginal man"; *Risō*, 176, 1947). Takeda characterized young people as *shūhenjin* (marginal people) and attempted to analyze them as such. However, these works are basically essays.

Meanwhile, in the field of psychology, the active study of young people had been ongoing since prewar days. This is believed to be because psychologists were focused on youths as a "biological generation"; unlike sociologists, who attach great weight to social relevancy, psychologists didn't feel the need to consider the social disparities among youth. And indeed there's no denying that, biologically speaking, young people of urban environments and young people of rural environments are one and the same.[62]

The emergence of the young as consumers

After a slight delay in the "après" (postwar) period, it was teenagers—specifically, the *jūdai* generation, or those aged between ten and nineteen—who jazzed up the world. This group is distinguished from the "après" generation in terms of being younger, as well as never having experienced defeat in war.[63] These are the people who would be around seventy years old today (as of 2011).

In describing these teenagers, a newspaper of the time said they watched the movie *Jūdai no seiten* (Sex manual for teenagers), had sweethearts, hummed jazz tunes to themselves—even while eating—formed jazz bands that did concert tours, lost themselves in sports, and satisfied their vanities a little by collecting autographs from popular actresses. Although I personally can't imagine teens like this, their lives genuinely appeared this way to the eyes of adults.[64]

What's noteworthy here, though, is that the behaviors viewed as being characteristic of teenagers were, for the most part, tied to consumption. To enjoy these pastimes, whether movies or jazz music, money was necessary.

To put it differently, it can safely be said that in the mid-1950s the market and media had discovered teenagers as customers; it was the birth of the argument that "young people are consumers."

Of course, for companies, it was a clever ploy to make customers out of the most populous generation. In terms of the percentage of the overall population, the society of the 1950s was far younger than ours is today. As of 1955, 20.3 percent of the total

---

62. For example, when I read Yoshitomo Ushijima's *Seinen no shinri* (Youth psychology; Ganshodo, 1940), which I found in the Keio University library, I observed that the author, while referring to theories by foreign psychologists, dispassionately discusses subjects such as "the development of self-consciousness" and "rebellious age" through the lens of biology. Although the author touched on Japanese cases, his only sources were female students at Tsuda College, where he worked. It's a very biased study on "the psychology of youths." Incidentally, the last time this book was checked out was January 23, 1945. At that rate, the next time will probably be around 2075.

63. Kōji Namba, *Zoku no keifugaku* (The genealogy of tribes), Seikyusha, 2007.

64. "Mokushiroku tīnējā" (Teenagers of the apocalypse), *Yomiuri Shimbun*, October 5, 1953, morning edition.

population comprised youngsters between ten and nineteen years old.[65/★14]

In fashion shows for teenagers held by the apparel industry, the items exhibited included loungewear that resembled mantles, "exuding a youthful loveliness expressed through their stand-up collar and closed cuffs"; skirts with "a loose and relaxed-fit with pleats or flares"; and hats that weren't "pretentious."[66]

For marketers, teenagers were good customers; at the same time, they were the object of adults' high hopes and envy. Yoshizō Kawamori (fifty-six years old, Osaka), who was a professor at the Tokyo University of Education, points out that the teenagers in their late teens, unlike the "après" generation, had still been in their infancy at the time of war, and were therefore not subjected to the confusion that had unfolded in its immediate aftermath. They were spared from the "various restraints" of the time, such as the imperial system and the norms of patriarchy, "in a very natural way, without suffering any considerable hardships."[67] While he expresses high hopes for "these youngsters who have a freedom beyond compare to what we had in our times," his tone is envious and spiteful.

The postwar period can also be said to have been, in a certain way, the most difficult time to engage in youngster bashing. Before the war, it was possible to apply the logic that suggested that young people were "good until a certain point in time, but not anymore"; for instance, it was possible to say things like, "Students prior to the Manchurian Incident were wonderful!" or "Young people were spoiled by the currents of liberalism introduced after World War I."

However, after losing the war, Japan was compelled to abandon its former values. In other words, even though many people willingly discarded them,[68] without those values, people began to find themselves at a loss as to how to criticize youth; there were no grounds anymore for youngster bashing. In the "après" period, the adults managed to pull off youngster bashing by positioning criminal youth as poster boys and girls for their entire generation.

But the "teens" were consumers. On top of that, they weren't even tainted with the

---

65.   Cabinet Office Statistics Bureau, *1955 Population Census*.

★14.   As of August 2015, the number of young people in their teens had dropped so low that they accounted for only 9.1 percent of the total population.

66.   "Tīnējā no tame no fuku" (Clothes for teenagers), *Yomiuri Shimbun*, November 24, 1955, morning edition. If you look at this article, you can understand that teens, rather than being the kind of consummate consumers on a par with adults, occupy a place somewhere between the "adult" and the "child."

67.   "Wakai Nihon: Kenjitsu ni natta hai-tīn" (Young Japan: Young people in their late teens have become trustworthy), *Yomiuri Shimbun*, March 30, 1959, evening edition.

68.   John Dower, author; Yōichi Miura et. al, translators, *Zōhoban: Haiboku o dakishimete* (Original title: *Embracing Defeat: Japan in the Wake of World War II*), enlarged edition, Iwanami Shoten, 2004.

prewar values the Japanese at the time should have been rejecting. Thus, to criticize the "teens," some other logic or rhetoric needed to be conceived. It was quite a challenge.[69] Given such a situation, you can see that, comparatively speaking, the present age is a good time for bashing. After all, you could boldly reason, "Postwar democracy has ruined the Japanese" because postwar democracy has been ongoing for nearly seventy years.

When Shintarō Ishihara was young

At long last, a story appeared that would serve as a model justification for youngster bashing. This was the story of the Taiyō-zoku (Sun Tribe). In 1955, the novel *Taiyō no kisetsu* (Season of the sun), by Shintarō Ishihara, a twenty-three-year-old Hyogo native who went on to serve as the governor of Tokyo from 1999 to 2010, won the prestigious Akutagawa Prize. It was immediately adapted for film and went on to became a social phenomenon. Apparently, society was shocked by the attitudes and dry sensibilities of a group of youngsters who never got caught up in the conventions of the day—the members of the Sun Tribe depicted in Ishihara's book. Incidentally, believe it or not, in the same year the author won the Akutagawa Prize, his other movie, *Nisshoku no natsu* (Summer of the eclipse)—for which he was tapped to come up with an original screenplay while also appearing in the film—was also released.

Today, the seventy-eight-year-old Ishihara says, "Young people should be required to work for a year in occupations that demand they abuse their bodies for the good of others, like jobs in the Self-Defense Forces, the police force, firefighting, and the Japan Overseas Cooperation Volunteers. This way, by challenging their mind and body while serving the public, they can train their brainstem, the part that controls emotions."[70] What an excellent thing to say! But I wonder if he's forgetting how a young man called Ishihara was once blessed with opportunities by society back in his youth. I think he obviously is.[71]

---

69. Even on the educational front and in households, confusion ensued, with many adults apparently flinching upon hearing things like, "You're old-fashioned, Mother!" In the work titled *Danjo kyōgaku to sono michibiki kata* (Coeducation and its methodologies; Iwasaki Publishing, 1950) released by Keio Chutobu Junior High School, you can even find instructions for parents on how to respond if their child accuses them of being old-fashioned in their thinking.

70. "Kinkyū chokugen: Oya no shi o kakushi, tomurau koto o shinaku natta dōbutsu ika no Nihonjin ni shohō suru 'gekiyaku.'" (Frank and urgent talk: "Dramatic entertainment" prescribed for Japanese people who have become less than animals as they hide the deaths of their parents and no longer even mourn), *SAPIO*, October 13–20, 2010.

71. Incidentally, Shintarō Ishihara has apparently been arrogant since his early days. A newspaper of the time sourly describes his "impudent actions," explaining that he was in the habit of calling the shots for location hunts as well as fitting sessions. Furthermore, when asked about his motivation in life, he declared, with haughty indifference, that it was the breaks he took to rest up for his next full-length novel (*Yomiuri Shimbun*, July 12, 1956, evening edition).

The "Sun Tribe" phenomenon swept the country through the cinema, as this was the largest mass-media outlet before television became widespread in Japan.[72] Apparently, it was all the rage back then to go around in sunglasses and a Hawaiian shirt, wearing a hairstyle known as the "Shintarō cut"—a look that is only spotted nowadays on passé beach resorts.

What was found to be controversial about *Taiyō no kisetsu* and the initial series of the "Sun Gang" movies, though, was their depiction of violence and sex, which was considered too radical for the time. In the end, legal action against the film was abandoned, but the Ministry of Education was intent on considering how they could, in one way or another, restrict minors from viewing the movie. One newspaper of the time prominently featured a news story about a boy who, influenced by the "Sun movie" and motivated by a love scene therein, had assaulted a five-year old girl.[73] Many other reports of Sun Gang–related crimes followed in quick succession, and the paper eventually ended up running tips from a police detective—advice like, "You should watch out for telltale signs like the type of clothes worn, or the vibes you get from certain bodily postures" and "Let's judge a person by his or her appearance."[74]

"Straighten that crowd out"

Around 1964, the Miyuki-zoku (Miyuki Tribe) whipped up a media frenzy. This was a group of young men and women who would don the trappings of Ivy League fashion, including long skirts, while loitering around Miyuki Street in the upscale Ginza district, carrying large rice bags.[★15]

Wait, what? Rice bags?! Why on earth? Apparently because "It's cool, and it's original. There's no rice store in Paris, right?"[75]

What's interesting is that the Miyuki Tribe was the target of a wholesale police

---

72. A newspaper reporter who went through adolescence in the age of the Taiyō-zoku (Sun Tribe) recollects, "The Taiyō-zoku, I felt, were nothing other than cool and novel in the way they broke down old-fashioned social mores and took a stand against the grownups." ("Mame teppō" [Peashooter], *Yomiuri Shimbun*, August 12, 1973, morning edition.)

73. "Eigakan de yōjo osou" (Little girl assaulted in movie theater), *Yomiuri Shimbun*, August 25, 1956, morning edition.

74. "Jūdai Taiyō-zoku" (Teenagers of the Sun Tribe), *Asahi Shimbun*, July 27, 1956, Tokyo evening edition.

★15. The name "Miyuki-zoku" is evocative of the woman's name "Miyuki," but the group included men as well.

75. "Sazaesan o sagashite" (In search of Sazae-san), *Asahi Shimbun*, February 6, 2010, morning edition. Apparently, in an episode of the animated television series *Sazaesan* airing at the time that touched on the subject of the Miyuki-zoku, the line "feminization of men" came up in the dialogue. This shows that the men of the Miyuki Tribe were the forerunners of today's "herbivorous men." In addition, though they were known collectively as a tribe, their fashion was diverse, and not all of them carried rice bags. (Kōji Namba, *Zoku no keifugaku* [The genealogy of tribes], Seikyusha, 2007.)

crackdown in September of 1964. Since these youngsters were just walking around on a street in Ginza, naturally they couldn't be charged on the grounds of violating any traffic laws or even any minor offense. So the police rounded them all up at once on a Saturday afternoon, when the group would normally gather after school, to admonish them and offer guidance. Apparently, after briskly apprehending and reprimanding the juveniles loitering in the street, the police would send them off in "special" micro-buses, one after another, to the police station, where they were forced to write oaths that they would "never again wander around busy streets." Supposedly, even though they protested, "We're not into bad stuff, you know," the members of the Miyuki Tribe complied, letting the police apprehend them anyway.[76] A police detective in the Juve-nile Division at that time explains the reasoning behind the wholesale roundup: "It was to straighten out a spineless bunch [of kids] who didn't even study or work." Un-like those apprehended in the student hunts of the 1940s, members of the Miyuki Tribe weren't required to face in the direction of the Imperial Palace and salute, but the scene was nonetheless similar. —Funny, considering that postwar democracy was sup-posed to have been firmly rooted in Japanese society by the 1960s.[77]

Of course, the reason behind the Miyuki Tribe clampdown is clear—the Tokyo Olympics were slated to be held in October, 1964. It would spoil the atmosphere to have young people with rice bags hanging around in Tokyo where a national event drawing worldwide attention was to be held—and in particular, to have them standing around in Ginza, an upscale district for adults. Thus it was that the first street fashion ever to appear in my country vanished in the span of a single summer.[78]

The emergence of "young people" is imminent

The possibility of living a lifestyle like that enjoyed by the "teenagers," the Sun Tribe, and the Miyuki Tribe, was limited to young people living in urban areas. When the words "teens" and "Sun Tribe" were popular, the standard of living in Japan was below that of prewar times. Only when in 1956, when the annual economic white paper declared that the postwar period had ended, did various economic indicators begin to

---

76. *Asahi Shimbun*, September 13, 1964, morning edition; and September 20, 1964, morning edition.
77. To be precise, the role of the "nation" in Japan became significant again from the 1960s through the 1970s. The Tokyo Olympics were held in 1964, and the Osaka World Exposition was held in 1970; these two events, referred to as "national projects," have often been described as parts of a continuum lasting from prewar days. In addition, it was around this time that topics such as "the cultivation of patriotism" and "the courage to protect the country" came to be actively discussed. In 1963, the magazine serialization of *Dai tōa sensō kōtei-ron* (A positive view of the Greater East Asia War) by Fusao Hayashi began. Apparently the memory of war disappears in twenty years.
78. Kazuo Jō and Naoki Watanabe, *Nihon no fasshon* (Japan's fashion), Seigensha Art Publishing, 2007.

surpass the prewar ones.

Many of the younger generation were living in poverty. In 1955, the starting salary for men who had graduated junior high was 4,090 yen; for women who had graduated junior high it was 3,890 yen. These amounts were below the poverty threshold. Nonetheless, the reason behind the movie *Taiyō no kisetsu* becoming a hit, and the reason cities had begun to teem with youth who idolized the so-called "Sun Tribe," was most likely the emerging desire among young people to emulate the lives of the upper middle class.[79]

As a matter of fact, at the time plenty of how-to books on how to be "successful" were published and became popular among salaried workers. For example, the bestsellers of that time included a book titled *Seikō suru aidea no tsukamikata* (How to get ideas for achieving success), which suggested everyday habits that could help one get promoted to upper management in one's company, and another one titled *Sararīman sanjū-roku no kagi* (Thirty-six keys for the salaryman), which urged salaried workers to be constantly conscious of elevating their status and accumulating wealth.[80]

Then, in the 1960s, the period of rapid economic growth began at last, with a growth rate registering a tremendous average of 10.4 percent per year. The structure of industry changed drastically as well, and many young people came out from rural communities to pursue both high wages and urban culture. To the eyes of those who had led monotonous lives eating seasonal vegetables every day in villages where refrigerators were not yet widespread, the city would have certainly looked shiny and glittery.[81]

The eating habits of the Japanese changed, too. It was around this time that processed meats like ham and sausage became available, and the consumption of animal protein, fatty foods, and vitamins was on the rise. Even clothes changed—the appearance of synthetic fibers gave rise to a remarkable variety in fashion.

Subsequently, what proved to be vital for the emergence of "young people" as a bloc was the expansion of the media environment. Only 15.9 percent of households owned a black-and-white television set in 1958, but five years later, in 1963, this rate jumped all the way up to 88.7 percent. The period also saw the launching of a succes-

---

79. Kenji Hashimoto, *"Kakusa" no sengoshi* (The postwar history of "social polarization"), Kawade Shobo Shinsha, 2009.

80. "Ureru seikatsu shinansho" (Guidebooks on living are selling well), *Yomiuri Shimbun*, February 12, 1958, evening edition. Like discourses on youth, business books, too, seem to have failed to evolve in the past fifty years.

81. For example, the penetration level of the electric refrigerator in rural areas in 1967 was 58 percent. But TV ownership in rural areas was as high as 95 percent, which was practically the same as the national average of 96 percent (Cabinet Office, *Sanson chiiki no jūmin no ishiki chōsa* [Survey on the attitudes of the residents of mountain villages], 1967). This was the time when information broadcast on TV was the same everywhere, even when the standard of living diverged markedly from the standard in urban areas; it was a time of such striking regional differences.

sion of youth-oriented magazines, with *Heibon Panchi* (Ordinary punch) and *Shūkan Pureibōi* (Weekly playboy) publishing their inaugural issues in 1964 and 1966 respectively.

In other words, the early 1960s were significant in two ways: this was the time when the stage was set for the emergence of both a culture commonly shared by a generation and experiences commonly shared by a generation. First of all, people tended to flock to urban areas as a function of population dynamics. Secondly, experiences, conveyed through the media, became easier to share than ever. The "common culture," or consensus culture, as envisaged by the Sun Tribe and the Miyuki Tribe, was fueling the drive to objectify middle- to upper-class life and take part in it. From this juncture, the emergence of "young people" as a bloc was just a step away.

4. The Myth of the 100 Million Middle Class and the Emergence of "Young People"

The arrival of the youth discourse boom

From the late 1960s through the 1970s, we see an uptick in the number of discourses on the young taking place. A look at just a few of the typical works published during this period shows a multitude of titles including the 1968 work *Gendai no seinen zō* (A contemporary portrait of youth) by Munesuke Mita, a thirty-one-year-old from Tokyo; the 1973 *Shinigai no sōshitsu* (The loss of death's raison d'être), by Shun Inoue, a thirty-four-year-old from Miyagi; 1975's *Kopī taiken no bunka* (Culture of replicated experiences) cowritten by Hideaki Hirano, a forty-three-year-old from Taipei, and Osamu Nakano, a forty-one-year-old from Nagano; and the 1978 *Moratoriamu ningen no jidai* (The age of the moratorium being) (1978) by Keigo Okonogi, a forty-eight-year-old from Tokyo.

In 1971, the highly celebrated magazine *Shakaigaku hyōron* (Social sciences review),[82] which is still being published today, put together a special feature titled *Seinen mondai* (The problems of youth). Even the government, in 1978, released a work titled *Wagakuni no wakamono jinkaku-ron* (A discussion on the personalities of our country's young people). It was an amazing flood of commentary on youth.

A cursory glance at ongoing public discussions of the time reveals various individuals readily asserting that, compared to the youth of Europe and America, Japan's

---

82.   Well-known only among sociologists, that is.

young people lacked public spirit, or a sense of civic responsibility, and harbored a strong resentment against society; that they lacked a spirit of independence, and that their attitude toward their work was devoid of any sense of purpose.[83] Another argument suggested that there was a rise in the number of young people who couldn't grow into adulthood, with the loss of an intermediary step necessary for becoming an adult; specifically, the stage in the process of growing up called the identity moratorium.[84]

What I'd like to call your attention to here, beyond the details of those arguments, is the fact that the adults of that time were attempting to somehow grasp "young people" as a generation. They were quite intentionally trying to depict young people in a simple fashion as being of a certain type, as evidenced in descriptions of modern youth as *kapuseru ningen* (capsule beings) or *moratoriamu ningen* (moratorium beings).

Of course, those making such arguments were themselves aware of the limits of talking about "young people" as a generation. Inoue points out that generationalism "tends to overlook the individualistic and hierarchical diversity inherent in a 'generation,' so 'generation-centric' ideas are dangerous things." Nonetheless, he says, we should still talk about "young people" as a generation, because there exists a consensus about the situation they, as a generation, find themselves in, and about the experiences they share in common.[85]

In those days, alongside studies made by Inoue and Okonogi, many other empirical studies on young people were being carried out by sociologists and psychologists. Even by today's standards, these scholarly works are sound and worthy of respect. But many of them have been lost in the mists of time. What still comes up today, instead, are the "capsule beings" from the "Culture of Copycat Experiences" and Keigo Okonogi's "moratorium beings." The reason is simple: bona fide research results are dull.

Anyone reading "The age of the moratorium being"—even an old man in his dotage—could become an authority on the topic and say important-sounding things like, "Young people these days are called 'moratorium beings,' you know." The reader can come to feel as though he or she has gained an understanding of young people as "alien others." On the other hand, though, studies backed by reams of data conclude that "young people" are not so easy to categorize. Even if you force yourself to read these data-rich studies, unless you're a researcher yourself, the only impression you'll likely take away will be some-

---

83. *Wagakuni no wakamono jinkaku-ron* (Our country's theories on youth personalities), Juvenile problems section in the Prime Minister's Office, 1978.

84. Keigo Okonogi, *Moratoriamu ningen no jidai* (The age of the moratorium being), Chuokoron-sha, 1978.

85. Shun Inoue, "Seinen no bunka to seikatsu ishiki" (Youth culture and attitudes toward life), *Shakaigaku hyōron* (Japanese Sociological Review) 22–1, 1971. For an earlier critique of generationalism, see Yasujirō Hayasaka, ed., *Sedai-ron* (Generationalism), Nihon YMCA Dōmei Shuppanbu (the publishing division of the Japan YMCA alliance), 1967.

thing along the lines of, "Oh, so young people come in a variety of flavors."

Consequently, as Satoshi Kotani (thirty-six years old, Tottori) offered candidly,[86] the types of arguments on young people that went on to increase were those that ignored the diversity found among young people, only to cherry-pick and exaggerate the lifestyles and psychological traits considered to be distinct to them.

The myth of the "hundred-million-member middle class" and the emergence of "young people"

In this period, one more significant change occurred. In the youth narrative, the expression *seinen* (youth), which had been in common use until then, came to be replaced by *wakamono* (young people), by choice (figure 1.2). Nakano, a sixty-two-year-old sociologist from Nagano who dominated the youth discourse of his time, looks back and says, "There was a certain, how should I say, mood about the sixties that made people hesitate to use the expression *seinen*."[87]… there was a transformation in the state of civilization and society, and in the positional relation between the people of this age group and society; everyone was feeling this."[★16]

It was a period of high economic growth. In addition, the members of the baby boom generation (born between 1947 and 1949) had just reached the age of around twenty at that time. The phenomenon of baby boomers, a sizeable generation with no experience of war, creating an original culture of their own is common to developed countries. Given the emergence of this generation, it was unsurprising that the issue of "young people" became topical.

But it wasn't just that the number of young people actually increased. Another shift occurred in Japanese society from the late 1960s through the 1970s: the penetration of the "middle-class consciousness."

Economic disparities hadn't disappeared, but toward the 1970s in Japan, many came to think of themselves as being middle-class. This was a manifestation of the famous *ichi-oku sō-chūryū* (hundred-million-member middle class) myth, which was the belief in a universal middle class—that is to say, the entire population of Japan. According to the *Public Opinion Survey Concerning People's Lifestyles*, the percentage of

---

86.   Satoshi Kotani, ed., *Wakamono-ron o yomu* (The youth-theory reader), Sekaishisosha, 1993.

87.   Osamu Nakano, "Wakamonozō no hensen" (Changes in the image of young people) in *Raifukōsu no shakaigaku* (The sociology of life courses) edited by Shun Inoue et al., Iwanami Shoten, 1996.

★16.   For a book featuring a careful discussion on the shift from "*seinen*" (youth) to "*wakamono*" (young people), see Masashi Miura's *Seishun no shūen* (The end of youth), Kodansha, 2012 (first edition 2001). According to this book, the expression "*seinen*," disappeared, along with the distinctively Japanese idea of "youth." Apparently, when the normative nuance contained in the expression "*seinen*" became undesirable, the expression "*wakamono*" came into use instead.

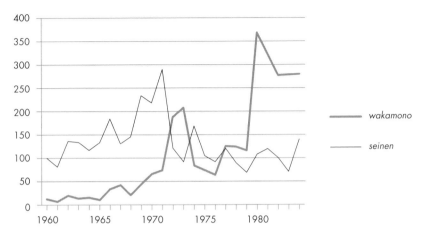

Figure 1.2   Fluctuations in the usage frequency of the words *wakamono* (young people) and *seinen* (youth)

This graph shows the number of hits determined through a "headline and keyword analysis" of instances appearing in the electronic edition of the *Asahi Shimbun*. The graph excludes advertisements and synonyms. (Magnification of the right side of figure 1.1.)

individuals identifying themselves as "middle class," rose from 72.4 percent in 1958 to 87 percent in 1964, and to 90.2 percent in 1973.[88]

Generationalism becomes popular when class theory suffers a disconnect with reality. But generationalism, to begin with, is a considerably forced rationale: it sweeps all other identifiers such as race, gender, and community under the rug; it lumps together the well-off with the destitute, the boys with the girls, and the Japanese with the Koreans and other foreigners residing in Japan—pigeonholing them all as "young people" as long as their ages are close together.

After the mid-1960s, the usage of the expression "generation" in newspapers also rose (figure 1.3). What happened, in effect, was the spread of a way of thinking that facilitated the discussion of society and people through the lens of "generation" rather than on the basis of class and community.

And these days the implication of the adjective *kokuminteki* (national) has likely

---

88.   It's natural that the "middle" is large, since among the five multiple-choice answers for the question asking the respondent's circumstances— "top," "upper middle," "center middle," "lower middle," and "bottom"—the word "middle" appears three times. Nonetheless, it is a fact that the number of people answering "middle" rose in 1970, and this is a trend that can even be confirmed in other surveys. It must, however, be added that the people of that time also struggled with the finding that showed 90 percent of respondents were middle-class, causing the submissions of various critiques from early on. ("Kokumin seikatsu hakusho ni miru seikatsuishiki" [Attitudes on life seen in the white paper on the national life], *Asahi Shimbun*, July 2, 1967, Tokyo morning edition.)

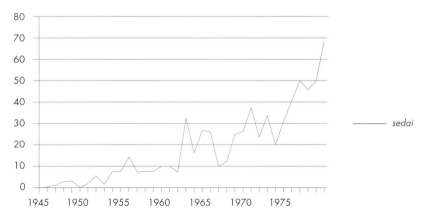

Figure 1.3 Fluctuations in the usage frequency of the word *sedai* (generation)
This graph shows the results of a full-text search of the electronic edition of the *Yomiuri Shimbun*.

changed. Today a "national idol" refers to a person who is liked across generational lines; until the early 1960s, however, a "national idol" was one who was liked across class lines.

For instance, the actress Sayuri Yoshinaga, in the 1962 film *Kyūpora no aru machi* (A town with a cupola), plays the role of a poor girl who juggles school and work; in the 1963 film *Dorodarake no junjō* (A mud-stained pure heart), she plays a diplomat's daughter. Thus Yoshinaga played the roles of girls from every social stratum, from the upper class to the lower class and everything else in between. She was a presence who cut across class lines, which is precisely why she had won popularity among young people of every social rank.[89]

The fantasy that the class system had been abolished, and that, as a result, society had been transformed into a place where everyone was middle class is the *ichi-oku sō-chūryū* myth. The popularity of "youth discourse," in fact, paralleled the progress of this myth.

In this shift from *seinen* (youth) to *wakamono* (young people) more may be found than just a change in terminology. Just as people began to call themselves "middle class" or mainstream, recognizing Japan as an *ichi-oku sō-chūryū* society—that is, one made up of nothing but the middle class—people in general, when discussing "young people," began to gloss over the differences among youths; outside of their age, the other attributes of young people were no longer an issue, despite the fact that dispari-

---

89.   Kenji Hashimoto, *"Kakusa" no sengoshi* (The postwar history of "social polarization"), Kawade Shobo Shinsha, 2009.

ties still remained.

To stretch the point, the concept of the *wakamono* emerged somewhere between the late 1960s and the 1970s as a homogenous group, whose attributes, other than age, didn't matter; in effect, its diversity had been brushed under the carpet.

The sewn-up "youth argument"

By the 1970s, in fact, the archetypes of the "youth arguments" that have lasted to this day had, for the most part, already come into shape. Let me sum up the different youth arguments that have appeared so far. First, there are the prewar arguments of the "alien other" and the "expedient ally." Then, in the 1950s, we see the appearance of the "youth as consumer" argument, such as the "teens" theory, which frames young people as the main constituents of mass consumption. In addition, arguments praising or bashing youths—by focusing to an excessive degree on an aspect of some peculiar, atypical group of youths—spread in the wake of arguments concerning the Sun Tribe.

Only a few more missing pieces to fill.

An argument discussing young people in the context of their relationship with the new media came up in the 1970s. In the 1975 work *Kopī taiken no bunka* (Culture of replicated experiences), the authors Hirano, a forty-three-year-old from Taipei, and Nakano, a forty-one-year-old from Nagano, coined the term "capsule beings".

According to these authors, the advent of the information society accelerated the diversification of values, leading to the dissolution of ideologies. In this "society of extreme fluidity," the scheme of bureaucratic control over the masses through mass-media manipulation, as hypothesized by mass sociology, is no longer viable.

Enter the "capsule beings," a reference to hypothetical young persons who, surrounded by information-processing appliances such as the radio and record player, attempt to achieve emotional balance within the space of their private rooms.

The expression "capsule beings" might lead you to imagine alienated youths living in isolation, shut inside each of their respective capsules, but what Hirano and Nakano were trying to show was a new type of kinship among young people.

These youngsters took an interest in late-night radio, when radio stations, from the latter half of the 1960s, began to launch programs targeting youths that became an integral part of youth culture.[90] Listening to the same late-night radio programs, each of these young people would share the same information in the comfort of their own

---

90.   Among the sources looking back on those days, there are such works as "Yamini nagareru koe" (Voices drifting in the dark) in the manga series *Kochira Katsushika-ku Kameari kōen-mae hashutsujo 172 kan* (This is the police station in front of Kameari park in Katsushika ward, vol. 172; Shueisha, 2010) by Osamu Akimoto (fifty-seven years old, Tokyo).

chambers, behind closed doors.

There, "resonances" occurred among multiple fellow capsules. While on the one hand, you could say that these young people who stayed inside their rooms while listening to the radio or music or making phone calls were, in a sense, shut-ins. But on the other hand, they weren't necessarily ignorant of events taking place in the outside world, since they were connected to the outside via information devices such as the radio.

That's right—this argument could equally apply to our times as well, if you replace "radio" with "the Internet," "cell phone," or "Twitter." What's interesting about "Culture of Copycat Experiences" is that it anticipated other arguments you might find today in the modern discourse on young people.

For example, in the same book, you find passages like, "These days a gathering of young people doesn't necessarily lead to a sustained gabfest, apparently. Gathered in the same room, they read magazines or comics, or play the guitar." Just like nowadays, right?

The final point I'd like to draw from the book is the idea that late-night radio is also a modern incarnation of the "festival." The authors state, "Modernity, whose progress has been an uphill battle, erases from society all that is 'extraordinary and special,' even stripping the 'festival' of its substance to render it a mere shell of its former glory."

But people still sought out public spaces upheld as sacrosanct. In times devoid of such festivals, the authors say, what came to be artificially stage-managed as "festivals" were the late-night radio programs, the rock concert events, and car-free "pedestrian paradises."[91]

This is likely because, in addition to the fact that the groundwork was already fully laid for talking about "young people" without regard to their individual differences—as previously pointed out—a living environment similar to the one in which we find ourselves in the present age had been building up since the 1970s.

Subsequent youth discourses

From this point forward, the public conversation on young people gets animated, but the patterns of most "young people" narratives have already all taken shape and

---

91.   Among sources that describe the "festivals" of the 2010s with a similar logic, there is Noritoshi Furuichi's "TGC (TOKYO GIRLS COLLECTION) no shōtai" (The Truth about the TOKYO GIRLS COLLECTION [T.G.C.]) in *G2* no. 7, 2011. In the field of sociology, despite the passage of thirty-five years, can it really be that only the writing style has changed? [★17]

★17.   The essay is included in Noritoshi Furuichi's *Hatarakikata wa "jibun" de kimeru* (Decide for yourself how you would like to work; Kodansha, 2014). Look for the cat-ear cover, which I commissioned Inio Asano (thirty-four years old, Ibaraki) to draw. This design is evocative of the *riajū* (real-life) mindset.

emerged full-blown by this time. Let me just roughly confirm them here.[92] The 1980s discourse on young people is said to have started with the *shinjinrui-ron* (new species argument) and ended with the *otaku-ron* (geek argument).[93]

The hallmark of the *shinjinrui-ron* is its anticipation that young people would possess a high media literacy and a high propensity to consume.[94] Since the 1980s saw a new media environment rapidly beginning to take shape, with the advent of personal computers and VCRs, young people were praised to the skies as the "constructive beneficiaries" of this new media environment. This is "capsule being" 2.0.[95]

Furthermore, according to Ken'ichirō Horii, a forty-eight-year-old from Kyoto, ever since the year 1983, Christmas had become commercialized for young people.[96/★18] So apparently it was around this time that society had begun to circulate information via the mass media on how young people should behave, in order to have them spend money. This is the popular version of the "young people are consumers" argument, but this idea, which sees the marketplace being galvanized by the targeting of "young people," reaches its peak in the late 1980s during the bubble period. The excitement surrounding the concept of young people as consumers surged enormously, with the marketplace, marketing companies, and scholars conspiring together.

On the other hand, however, *otaku*-bashing began in the latter half of the 1980s. Until only quite recently young people were idolized as information-gadget whizzes, but then they were suddenly treated like criminals. In effect, as soon as the kids stop being "expedient allies" called "consumers," the adults immediately begin to treat them as "alien others."

---

92. To survey youth discourses that surfaced from the 1970s through the 1980s, I recommend *Wakamono-ron o yomu* (The youth-theory reader) edited by Satoshi Kotani (Sekaishisosha, 1993); for youth discourses that surfaced in the 1990s and the 2000s, I recommend *Wakamono to aidentiti* (Young people and identity) edited by Tomohiko Asano (Nihon Tosho Center, 2009). In addition, if you'd like to examine an individual treatment of the postwar youth culture, you'll find a detailed account in Kōji Namba's *Zoku no keifugaku* (The genealogy of tribes; Seikyusha, 2007). Without these three books, the present volume would not have been written.

93. Shinji Miyadai, *Seifuku shōjo-tachi no sentaku* (The choices of girls in uniform), Kodansha, 1994.

94. Satoshi Kotani, ed., *Wakamono-ron o yomu* (The youth-theory reader), Sekaishisosha, 1993.

95. Along with media theories, the *kodomo no shōmetsu-ron* (disappearance of children theory) was also making waves at the time. This theory says that the spread of TV has dissolved the line separating children from adults, which had been drawn by the print media. In this sense, "children" at this time had been subsumed under "young people."

96. Ken'ichirō Horii, *Wakamono goroshi no jidai* (The age of youth homicides), Kodansha, 2006.

★18. In reality, in 1954 the men's fashion magazine *Danshi senka* (Men's specialized subjects) ran a special feature titled "Kimi no heyade koibito to mukaeru☆futaridake no kurisumasu" (Welcoming your lover in your room☆A Christmas for just the two of you). However, with its instructions on how to make a Christmas tree using a potted plant found in one's garden, and on how to make decorations out of plywood, this feature makes it clear that in Japan "Christmas" wasn't a common event at all yet. It was unrelated to the bubbly, consumerist society of the 1980s.

The end of the youth discourse?

From the early 1990s, pundits begin to proclaim the end of the "youth discourse." When he still had black hair, Kotani, a thirty-six-year-old from Tottori, said that young people wouldn't be starting trends anymore.[97] This was because, as indicated by an average of 1.5 births per woman, Japan, at that time, was already heading toward social stagnation and aging. Consequently, one after another, critics began to point out that young people could no longer be regarded as a single, monolithic group.[98] To this end, the use of labels ending in the suffix *-zoku* (tribe) began to wane, and from the 1990s onwards, the labels ending in the suffix *-kei* (lineage) became mainstream instead.[99] Furthermore, the young people themselves, it is said, came to attach greater importance to communicating with friends—that is, to developing and sustaining a world of intimacy—rather than holding on to an awareness of themselves as a group united by a common culture distinct to a generation.[100]

Thus, "young people" talk or narratives came to analyze more niche topics, such as high school girls going on dates with older men in exchange for money/and or luxury gifts (the so-called *enjo-kōsai joshi kōsei*); motorcycle messengers; cell phone novels; net-café refugees, aka the "cyber-homeless"; and Peace Boat.

Amid such a zeitgeist, if you tried to talk about "young people" in a vague sense, it would end up being the kind of discussion this author dreads; even if you can articulate your argument well, with this type of talk all you end up saying is, "There are young people like this or that. All in all, there are all sorts of young people."[101] Since such discussions are steeped in the 1980s framework of "youth talk," they could be even called "zombified youth discussions."

On the other hand, ever since the year 2000, in works that were popular even though they were mainly about young people, the narrative pattern of illustrating relations between society and "young people" increased. The titles of this ilk that still remain fresh in my memory are *Kibō kakusa shakai* (The social polarization of hope) by Masahiro Yamada (forty-seven years old, Tokyo), *Kānibaruka suru shakai* (The carnivalization of society) by Kensuke Suzuki (twenty-nine years old, Fukuoka), *Karyū*

---

97.   Satoshi Kotani, ed., *Wakamono-ron o yomu* (The youth-theory reader), Sekaishisosha, 1993.
98.   Shinji Miyadai, Hideki Ishihara, and Akiko Ōtsuka, *Zōho: Sabukaruchā shinwa kaitai* (Supplement: Deconstructing the subculture myth), Chikumashobo, 2007 (first edition 1993).
99.   Kōji Namba, *Zoku no keifugaku* (The genealogy of tribes), Seikyusha, 2007. The term *kei* (descent) indicates looser connections than *zoku* (family or tribe).
100. Mamoru Yamada, "Wakamono bunka no sekishutsu to yūkai" (Separation and fusion of youth culture) in *Kōza shakaigaku 7: Bunka* (Sociology lecture 7: Culture) by Takashi Miyajima, University of Tokyo Press, 2000.
101. A good example is Yōhei Harada's *Chikagoro no wakamono wa naze dame nano ka* (Why are today's young people useless?; Kobunsha, 2010).

shakai (Downstream society) by Atsushi Miura (forty-six years old, Niigata), and *Haipā meritokurashīka suru shakai* (The transformation of society into a hyper-meritocracy) by Yuki Honda (forty years old, Tokushima).

Borrowing the words of Akihiro Kitada (thirty-eight years old, Kanagawa), to deliberately put it in a more complex fashion, "Modern society is structured in such a way that its big-picture macro viewpoint, or all-encompassing frame of reference, itself inevitably shrinks to a more micro, localized viewpoint."[102] For this reason, in terms of the history of philosophical thought, a withdrawal toward the local, as well as the renewed ambition to regard the totality of society, is pointed out. Indeed, the discourse on youth today is in the process of bifurcating into studies carried out in the more local domain of the enthusiast on the one hand; and on the other, broader, sweeping social discourses that tend to develop into major discussions.

In fact, if we were to fully embrace such a dichotomy, it would become possible to sustain a macro viewpoint that beholds the totality without compromising the ability to observe fragmented parts at the same time. This is because, though universality may not be assumed a priori, the stance of inquiring into and investigating universality is part of the bedrock of modern science.[103]

Even from this point, the bashing of youngsters as "alien others" will likely go on, as will the empirical studies carried out by academicians. But I'm not so sure about the "youth as consumers" argument, which took shape around 1970 along with the establishment of the *ichi-oku sō-chūryū* myth and youth-culture discourses pursued by academics. When people started doubting the *ichi-oku sō-chūryū* society—that is to say, when people stopped believing that "young people" shared the same traits in common just because they were similar in age—these two lines of thought should have started looking flimsy and dubious. With this in mind, it will be interesting to see just how the discourse on young people will turn out going forward.

102.　Toshiki Satō (with expository comments provided by Akihiro Kitada), *Shakai wa jōhōka no yume o miru* (Society dreams of informatization), Kawade Shobo Shinsha, 2010.

103.　Although many are apt to see sociology as a complex subject, the only thing a social scientist can ultimately do is accumulate bits and pieces of knowledge and make an effort to place them in a larger context. While there's nothing wrong with thinking deeply about the subject, sociologists need to produce a steady stream of output, even if they haven't reached any conclusions yet. If they don't, the gap between their academic circle and the real world outside will only keep getting wider.

5. And the Youth Discourse Goes On

Youth discourse is terribly strained

Along with the emergence of an overwhelmingly populous group called the baby-boom generation and the fantasy of a classless society where all social hierarchies are abolished (as evidenced by the embrace of the *ichi-oku sō-chūryū* myth), the idea of "young people," and by extension, "youth discourse," became established. However, even after the members of the baby-boom generation ceased to be young themselves, theories on young people describing them as a group with a unique culture of their own nonetheless continued to be mass produced.

In other words, youth discourse only somehow manages to stay valid as an argument, because its validity—that is, its truth—is terribly stretched. For example, in 2011 there were approximately 20,130,000 young people (defined as Japanese nationals aged fifteen to twenty-nine).[104/★19] These young people include the *sawayaka-kei danshi kōkōsei* (vibrant high-school-boy type)[105] who attends Aoyama Gakuin High School wearing a Hermès watch; the twenty-three year old illustrator[106] who doesn't own a TV or access the Internet, but gets his information fix from the radio; and the nineteen-year old boy sentenced to death as the defendant in the trial of the Ishinomaki serial murder case.

You can see now, can't you, how difficult it is to find common traits shared among twenty million individuals? There are gender differences and regional differences to consider, and on top of those, there's the wealth gap to account for. Of course, while being aware of such disparities, discourses on youth nonetheless tried to talk about "young people" as a generation.

However, it became quite a challenge to keep doing just that with the popularization of the middle-class disintegration and social polarization theories that began in the latter half of the 1990s. In effect, the *ichi-oku sō-chūryū* mentality became passé.[107]

---

104. Press release from the Statistics Bureau, *Population Estimates* (approximate figure as of April, 2011).

★19. Approximately 18,720,000 people in August, 2015. This means that the number of "youths" has decreased by approximately 1,410,000 within a span of four years.

105. "Oheya o minna ni misechauyo" (I'm going to show the room to everyone) in *HR* no. 4, 2010.

106. "Hitorigurashi gyararī" (Single life gallery), *Tokyo Graffiti*, October 2010.

107. In reality, economic disparities have been existing since the so-called age of *ichi-oku sō-chūryū* (hundred-million-member middle class), and these disparities began to widen starting in the 1980s (Kenji Hashimoto, *"Kakusa" no sengoshi* [The postwar history of "social polarization"], Kawade Shobo Shinsha, 2009).

Since this argument was based on the notion that there were no differences among the members of a generation, as a discourse on "young people," it was in deep trouble.

Furthermore, the "youth are consumers" argument that started with the "teens" theory was also teetering on the brink of a crisis. After all, young people, who were supposed to have been discovered as the main constituents of economic consumption, were refusing to buy things.

The argument that young people don't buy things is popular today. But this is possible only because the premise that young people *do* buy things continues to be a consensus view. For this reason, just how long this stereotype will last is suspect. Which brings me to the question: Will youth discourse just go on to disappear as it is?

In short, talking about young people won't end for some time to come. After all, there's an argument that's still alive and well even though it's sketchier than youth discourse. It's the famous Nihonjin-ron (theories and discussions about the Japanese). Nihonjin-ron attempts to talk to 120 million Japanese nationals about their alleged common traits. Occasionally, a Nihonjin-ron argument—such as the one championed by *Tatsuru Uchida* (fifty-nine years old, Tokyo) in *Nihon henkyō-ron* (Japan: A nation of outliers), with an air of unconcern for the social polarization argument—becomes a huge hit.[108] Now, that's enviable.

Another thing ensuring the longevity of debates about young people, though, is that there's a charm about youth discourse that's absent from Nihonjin-ron discussions.

The youth discourse is a means for adults to search their souls

Another reason why debates on youth are unending is, as sociology has it, due to the confusion between the "aging effect" and the "generation effect." In other words, what people perceive as a generational shift or a change in times is, in reality, simply the phenomenon of them getting old and falling behind the times. This illuminates not only youth discourse, but most of the arguments claiming that the Japanese have degenerated. Furthermore, youth discourse is a means of self-affirmation.

When a person candidly submits, "Young people today are outrageous," he or she is saying so from a standpoint of not being young anymore. At the same time, this person is likely confirming that he or she lives in another place far removed from the place occupied by the "outrageous" different youth—the alien others—in other words, he or she, unlike those deplorable "others," is a denizen of "decent" society.

In other words, the kind of talk that considers young people to be outrageous and

---

108. *Tatsuru Uchida, Nihon henkyō-ron* (Japan: A nation of outliers), Shinchosha, 2009.

"alien others" is, to those who are no longer young but middle-aged or elderly, at once a self-affirmation and a means of doing some soul-searching.

If you meekly recognized that you felt different, then you would end up occupying an alien presence in society—that is, you'd be a misfit in society's eyes. Conversely, by characterizing what appears different to you as "different," you yourself can avoid being "different" or a misfit.

The "young people are our hope" argument is the exact opposite of this. By regarding young people as expedient allies, this argument is confirming the ties between yourself and society. "Today's young people," the reasoning goes, "are on the same side as mine, so a society in which I'm also included is all right."

Well, in that case, instead of engaging in youngster bashing, why not make personal attacks? That may be the right way to go, but it's scarier to criticize individuals—and you wouldn't want to take responsibility when the attack is personal, would you? Criticizing an entire generation, rather than an individual, is a milder act, the path of least resistance. And framing the criticism as a discourse on young people is somewhat more plausible too. However, how effective this plausibility will continue to be in the future remains to be seen.

Young people as a negative reflection of society

"Young people," to adults, are also ideal scapegoats. For instance, when cars don't sell, people blame "young people's disenchantment with cars." But the implication behind the expression "disenchantment with cars" here is that young people in the past used to ride in cars, but not the young ones these days. So it's rather odd, don't you think, to describe young people today as having become disenchanted with cars? According to the implication, they never had a connection with automobiles in the first place.

The number of new-automobile sales in Japan had begun to fall in 2001 from its peak in 2000. As Kōsuke Motani (forty-six years old, Yamaguchi) pointed out, in most regions of Japan, except in the large cities, a car isn't a luxury, but a necessity. It's something you can't afford to *not* buy just because you get tired of it. So why did the sales of cars take a nosedive? The answer is simple: Japan's demographics experienced a structural change, with the number of elderly people rising and the number of the young falling.[109]

If the reason for the slump in car sales is a change in demographics, then the problem is hopeless. But if the reason is a shift in the psychology of young people, there is

---

109.   Kōsuke Motani, *Defure no shōtai* (The truth about deflation), KADOKAWA, 2010. Apparently, however, car sales are declining at a faster pace than the population is. I will discuss this in more detail in chapter 2.

still hope. This is why it's a clever decision to protect the assumption that the phenomenon of declining automobile sales is caused by "young people's disenchantment with cars." This way, car companies can feel secure for the time being, and advertising agencies and self-styled youth marketers can rack up new business, and the media can get grist for their news stories.

This attitude, though, of believing it's acceptable to blame "young people" for just about anything and everything is reminiscent of the treatment Jews were subjected to in Nazi Germany. During wartime Germany, much was made of strict rules that demanded discipline, such as hard work and abstinence. However, not everybody was able to observe those rules. Subsequently, people projected what they themselves failed to do on the Jews who were considered different from themselves—who were, in effect, the "alien others."[110]

However, unlike the Jewish people in this scenario, Japan's young people aren't entirely what you can call "alien others." Generally speaking, there surely is no one—at least not in Japan—who, having been young himself once, regards young people living in the same country to be one hundred percent "alien others." And that's why, says forty-four-year-old Tokyo native Asao Naitō, unlike criticisms aimed at Jewish people, which cease with their exclusion, the criticisms against young people will never stop.[111]

But I don't believe the situation is as grave as Naitō fears. Youth discourse is, after all, just that—discourse; this could be a problem if some of the baseless arguments found in it were to have an impact on policymaking. But I wonder just how many people take seriously characterizations of Japanese youths as "turning into monkeys,"[112] or having a "game brain."[113] These kinds of statements should be left to regrettable middle-aged adults and the elderly who, for crying out loud, can't search their own souls without talking about young people.

The ambiguity of "young people" is a good thing

From the old days, "young people" have been associated with various images. In the

---

110. Theodor W. Adorno et al. (authors); Yoshihisa Tanaka, et al. (translators), *Ken'ishugiteki pāsonariti* (original title: *The Authoritarian Personality*), Aoki Shoten, 1980. However, since "race" and "religion" are key variables in the genocide that occurred in Germany, it must be asked to what extent this case is valid in any argument concerning Japanese youths.

111. Asao Naitō, "'Kōzō' shakai zōo no mekanizumu" (The Structural mechanism of hatred in society) in *Nīto tte iu na!* (Don't say NEET!) by Yuki Honda et al., Kobunsha, 2006.

112. Nobuo Masataka, *Keitai o motta saru* (Monkeys with cell phones), Chuokoron-Shinsha, 2003. Come to think of it, Nobuo Masataka's "scholarliness" began its collapse around this time.

113. Akio Mori, *Gēmu nō no kyōfu* (Horror of the gaming brain), NHK Publishing, 2002. The folks of the generation that once went crazy over Space Invaders are now in their fifties. We're now on the brink of seeing a wave of the "gaming brain" sweeping the whole country of Japan.

famous painting by Eugène Delacroix, *Liberty Leading the People*, the young people of Paris are depicted as a symbol of the progressive spirit. In Nazi Germany, youths were expected to possess a "wisdom that can cultivate creativity." In the world of sports, many matches favor the physical prowess of those around age twenty, so these individuals are naturally admired and spoken highly of.

In this chapter, too, we have seen many discourses and theories regarding young people. In the youth discourse of the postwar years, the novelty of young people was particularly emphasized, as seen in the statement, "Young people today are unprecedented in such-and-such a way." This is resonant of a marketing strategy for cars. After all, the car industry developed by selling old models as new after just changing their exterior and name, even though the construction remained largely unchanged.[114]

Lately, the term "digital natives" has been popularly used to refer to a generation that has been familiar with the trappings of information technology since birth. However, by and large, during the time of "capsule beings" and the time of the *shinjinrui*, the young were said to be a generation that had known TV ever since they could remember.[115]

Thus, discourse on youth, in a sense, was possibly a discourse on society carried out under the borrowed guise of youth. "Young people" are an indeterminate entity, appearing substantial one moment and not so the next. Consequently, the designation proves to be so open to interpretation that it becomes easy to associate youth with all kinds of images of your choosing. Furthermore, young people are continuously supplanted.

For this reason, nobody complains when one youth argument or theory is superseded by another. To the contrary, such an outcome is welcomed, eliciting surprised reactions, such as, "Oh, wow—so these are the new youngsters now!"

Moreover, no one wants to listen to a convoluted discussion, but anyone can talk about young people. Compared to discussing the changes in the Japanese economy, a rather demanding topic, talking about young people is easy. All you have to do, after all, is look back on your own young days, make commonsense judgments, and mention topics you've picked up a passing knowledge of somewhere, such as, "It seems young people these days don't watch TV, huh?"

---

114.   This section deals with the argument concerning Toshiki Satō's (forty-seven years old, Hiroshima) *jōhōka shakai* (information-oriented society) (*Shakai wa jōhōka no yume o miru* [Society dreams of informatization], Kawade Shobo Shinsha, 2010). Satō's talk is so complex that half of it is beyond my grasp. For this reason, I have used it as food for thought rather than referring to it directly.

115.   Hideaki Hirano and Osamu Nakano, *Kopī taiken no bunka* (Culture of replicated experiences), Jiji Press, 1975.

The significance and limits of talking about young people

Up to this point, I have been relentlessly pointing out the limits of youth discourse. However, I don't believe that talking about young people is devoid of any significance. If I were to declare that to be the case, the significance of this book, along with its raison d'être, would disappear.

How, then, should I go about discussing "young people"? As a matter of fact, this question has already been answered in the 1970s.

As Taijirō Hayasaka, a forty-four-year-old from Miyagi, pointed out, "The matter of observing that a certain phenomenon exists, and the matter of employing this phenomenon as a tool in the service of creating meaning or an evaluation" are two separate affairs.[116] In this chapter I may have painted the arguments with too broad a brush, but each of those discussions about young people, in their own way, reveal important discoveries and make key points relevant to their respective times.

In effect, what I have been driving at in this chapter is the fact that there are patterns to be observed in discussions and narratives on youth; I wasn't trying to make the point that young people themselves haven't changed. The only problem, though, is tying a "phenomenon" to an evaluation or value judgment in a reckless, slipshod fashion. Change and decay aren't the same thing.

If anything, the need to study phenomena in detail is greater than ever. We are now aware—unlike in the 1980s—that we can no longer talk about "young people" as a monolithic presence.

What's important is to steer clear from thinking about a particular phenomenon as being an issue of an individual young person, or peculiar to young people. Instead, we should view a particular phenomenon as an issue that should be considered alongside the realities of the existing social structure. We'll be on the right track if we keep taking this kind of natural and genuine approach.[117]

But I'm not saying that the magic bullet here is to just make use of statistical data, either. As Inoue (thirty-three years old, Miyagi) said with restraint, "As expected, there's a problem in easily summing up the big picture or coming up with an archetype just because of a statistical 'average picture' or some numbers showing the existence of

---

116. Taijirō Hayasaka, ed., *Sedai-ron* (Generationalism), Nihon YMCA Dōmei Shuppanbu (the publishing division of the Japan YMCA alliance), 1967.

117. "Young people" don't necessarily have to be the main subject. For example, it has been a long time since there was an outcry about the decline in birthrate, but if we think about the childbearing age, you can see that it's also a "youth" problem. If, instead of asking, "Why have young people stopped having children?" we ask, "Why has Japan's birth rate declined?" we can consider not only changes in youth psychology, but also problems related to social structure, including changes in social security and income differences. In reality, many studies on birth rates are conducted in this fashion. [*20]

modal trends."[118]

The subjects of youth studies—those high school girls who engage in "compensated dating," and motorcycle messengers, for example—are certainly in the minority in terms of numbers. But obviously, in the field of statistics, the people who account for the majority are, in many cases, surprisingly levelheaded and ordinary.

Nonetheless, we should also keep in mind that the characteristics and peculiarities exhibited by the minority aren't necessarily isolated phenomena. After all, you cannot ignore the possibility that the minority express, with relative clarity, things that exist vaguely, or are latent, in the majority. The accumulation of revelations, no matter how small-scale they may be, is by no means pointless.

Of course, at the same time, though, we must not forget to keep a close eye on the social context. The aim of this book is to structurally portray as social issues the issues of "young people," which are prone to being appropriated—that is to say, co-opted—for personal identity purposes and cultural matters.

What I believe to be a key element of this constructive portrayal—this framework—is the transformation of Japanese society that took place after the bubble economy collapsed in 1991. With the burst of this bubble, what had been assumed, since the 1970s, to be mainstay models of Japanese meritocracy—"the good school, the good company, the good life"—all collapsed. Furthermore, major companies were no longer able to offer the traditional guarantees of the Japanese business model to young people, such as the *nenkō joretsu* (Japanese seniority-wage system) and lifetime employment. This is the milieu young people find themselves in today; one shaped by the aftermath of the collapse of the middle-class dream.

The genealogy of youth theories

I'll conclude this chapter with a summary of the arguments regarding young people we have been referring to up to this point (see figure 1.4).

In this chapter I have classified the youth arguments into the following four broad categories: The "alien other," the "expedient ally," the cultural argument, and empirical

★20.   While what has been pointed out in this footnote is also fact, in Japan, it is often the case that even the issue of the declining birthrate is discussed as a problem of youth consciousness; the kind of talk that claims that the rise of bachelors is due to the rise of *sōshoku-kei danshi* (herbivorous men). But since the number of children people can have in a lifetime is limited, there is no direct correlation between libido and the rise in the number of bachelors. For details, refer to Noritoshi Furuichi's book with the eye-catching cover showing someone who seems to be a nice person, *Hoikuen gimukyōikuka* (Making nursery schools compulsory; Shogakukan, 2015).

118.   Shun Inoue, "Seinen no bunka to seikatsu ishiki" (Youth culture and attitudes toward life) in *Shakaigaku hyōron* (Japanese Sociological Review) 22–2, 1971.

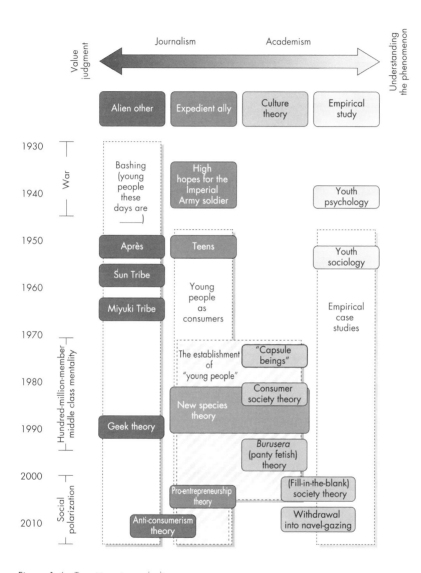

Figure 1.4   Transitions in youth discourse

studies.

Note that the kind of youngster bashing that regards young people as "alien others" has been going on for more than a hundred years, but in the wartime period, we
saw the rise of the argument that viewed young people as "expedient allies."

To make a long story short, the level of public debate on young people conducted by grownups has shown no sign of progress at all for over an entire century. However, "youth discourse" in the modern sense is believed to have emerged concurrently with the *ichi-oku sō-chūryū* mindset. This is because any argument that entirely denies local differences, economic disparities between rich and poor, and gender to talk about youth as if they were all cut from the same cloth, just because they happen to belong to the same age bracket, won't be perceived as realistic unless there's a consensus among people that social divisions in the nation have disappeared.

Which is why, in the present age, when the term "social polarization" is in the air, the very survival of discourse on youth is threatened. At the least, people can no longer talk about "young people" in the same vein as they used to prior to the burst of the bubble—nor should they be doing so. And that's where it's meaningful to talk about "young people."[119]

Thus, in the end, this book will mainly shine a spotlight on the twenty-somethings who lived in the immediate aftermath of the burst of the economic bubble. When I use the expression "young people" in this book, it's no different from the way many use it in everyday parlance.

Now, how do young people actually live in modern society, what are their lives really like? Compared to the past, in what ways can you say their lives have changed? Let's explore some answers in the next section onward.

Postscript: Discourse on Youth Still Goes On

On the jacket of the hardback edition of *The Happy Youth of a Desperate Country* were blurbs written by Chizuko Ueno (sixty-three years old, Toyama) and Eiji Oguma (forty-nine years old, Tokyo). Ueno's blurb said, "This book, authored by a lighthearted yet cynical youth, sentences youth discourse to death and will undoubtedly trigger off the launch of a new youth theory."[★21]

As pointed out by Ueno, in this first chapter, I had intended to boldly put forward the idea that "discussions on young people" were no longer necessary. The "youth dis-

---

119.   However, as a marketing tool, theories on youth will become less and less significant. In the first place, the population is small, and the idea that young people are in the vanguard, creating new fads is a sort of fantasy derived from the "youth as customer" theory.

★21.   From Eiji Oguma I received the sarcastic remark, "If you don't neglect your training from now on, you will be promising."

course" with which we have become familiar appeared in tandem with the *ichi-oku sō-chūryū* mindset. So, naturally, I was convinced that "youth discourse" itself would disappear, now that more people were beginning to share the view that they were, in reality, living in a socially polarized society.

However, the situation turned out to be quite to the contrary. And as Ueno also predicted,★22 this book went on to trigger the launch of a new youth theory. In the meantime, the same old "youth discourses" continued to be mass produced; soon after the publication of this book, we saw the releases of hackneyed works such as *Satori sedai* (The enlightenment generation) by Yōhei Harada (thirty-seven years old, Tokyo), and *Tsukushi sedai* (The devoted generation) by Kōhei Fujimoto (thirty-five years old, Kanagawa).★23

In addition, we're continuing to see all sorts of problems being reduced to the "youth mentality" and interpreted through that lens—problems such as the falling birthrate and the rise in the number of people staying single, which are clearly related to social institutions and the working environment, rather than the "youth mentality." I myself can't tell you how many times elderly politicians and economic experts have told me something along the lines of, "The birthrate's declining because of the rise in the number of herbivorous men, right?" If you look into factors that discourage young people from making the decision to marry and have babies, you'll find such factors as the employment climate and other economic circumstances, but the entire matter, in the eyes of these elders, is settled by reducing and attributing the problem to young people's "herbivore" mindset.

So I can't help asking the question, just how the hell much longer will we have to continue to put up with the mass production of such "youth discourses"?

According to the fifty-year-old literary critic from Niigata, Minako Saitō, literary works that became explosive bestsellers in the postwar period shared the following common characteristics: The writer was young; the work marked the writer's debut, or was released around the time of debut; the writer had personal charm; and works that appeared to depict contemporary youth occasionally became sensational bestsellers.★24

Specifically, these characteristics apply to *Taiyō no kisetsu* by Shintarō Ishihara

---

★22. Damn!

★23. It's not that these books are meaningless. When you create a product plan, or when you persuade clients, "plausibility" is extremely important. In this sense, a "youth theory" that provides a "plausible" picture of youth is also necessary. On the other hand, among the books that appeared after the publication of this one, the most highly recommended source of reference is Kazuo Katase's *Wakamono no sengo shi* (The postwar history of young people; Minerva Shobo, 2015).

★24. Minako Saitō, "Kaisetsu: Kerukoto no imi" (Commentary: The meaning of kicking) in *Keritai senaka* (*I Want to Kick You in the Back*) by Risa Wataya, Kawade Shobo Shinsha, 2007.

(twenty-four years old, Hyogo), *Almost Transparent Blue* by Ryū Murakami (twenty-four years old, Nagasaki), and more recently, *I Want to Kick You in the Back* by Risa Wataya (nineteen years old, Kyoto) and *Kirishima, bukatsu yamerutte yo* (The Kirishima thing) by Ryō Asai (twenty-one years old, Gifu).

While this can be understood as just a manifestation of the love affair Japanese have with youth novels, Saitō says, it can also safely be paraphrased as a love affair the Japanese have with discourses on youth.[25]

If the Japanese are fond of youth novels, the maniacal attraction to the youth "mindset" is understandable. Discourse on young people in Japan has, perhaps, been consumed in the same fashion as "youth novels,"[26] which as a matter of course require the reader to be focused on the "mindset" of the characters.

In addition, the presence of mass media such as television is still powerful, even though its impact has waned.[27] Thus, as long as the mass media continue to have an interest in young people, discourses on youth will likely continue to be recycled.

However, going forward, I can't imagine these "youth discourses" will endlessly continue to be spotlighted as much as they have been. Today, in Japan, young people are rapidly dwindling in number. A small population means that, firstly, young people, as consumers, are unattractive. In addition, it's also coming to light that youth culture isn't always at the vanguard of popular trends.

If I may add another touch of cynicism here,[28] we may have no choice but to wait for the changing of the guard between generations before we are liberated from the shackles of generationalism. At present, many people, led by the middle-aged and elderly, still remain interested in "young people" for better or for worse. However, when these people disappear, and are superseded by a majority that does not view young people to be so influential, "youth discourse" will likely come to an end.

---

[25]. In other countries, you generally don't see so many books on "youth theories" routinely lining the bookshelves of general bookstores. In countries where issues of race, class, and evident economic inequalities exist, people don't readily judge others based on generation alone.

[26]. When you think in this way, you can explain why "youth theories" still hold sway in the present age when poverty has become a serious social concern, and when protests against the threat of the "disappearance of the countryside" are being made with a sense of impending crisis. Because these are "youth novels," what's attracting attention is, perhaps, not our relationship to society, but the consciousness of young characters. Among studies that deal with the subject from a different point of view, asserting that generationalism is a youth theory while arranging the genealogy of youth theories, there is Yasuo Nagayama's *"Sedai" no shōtai* (The truth about "generations"; Kawade Shobo Shinsha, 2014).

[27]. The reason why this book sold well is largely attributable to the coverage it received from the *Asahi Shimbun*, a national newspaper, and to the coverage from the TV show *Asamade nama terebi!*, "*Kurōzu appu gendai*" (Live TV until morning! "Close-up on the present age").

[28]. A touch of cynicism? Yeah, sure, how very rich of me to say so in this book, which is already overflowing with so much irony and sarcasm that I still find surprising after four years.

Chapter 2
The Restless Young

Apparently, young people are getting more and more introverted. In this chapter, for the most part, we will examine the available data and consider whether young people are truly becoming inward looking, and if they are, in what ways they are becoming so, and why they're turning out to be this way. The key word to keep in mind here is "*muramura*" (restlessness), or to put it more euphemistically, "consummatory."

1. Inward-Looking Youth

The editorial image of young people in 2011
Newspaper editorials running on the Seijin no Hi (Coming-of-Age Day) holiday are fun to read. This is because each and every newspaper takes the liberty of making various assumptions about young people, and goes on to lecture "young people" as they please, based on those preconceptions. We saw in the preceding chapter just how freewheeling, self-indulgent, and arbitrary the "youth discourses" engaged in by adults have been; however, since I also belong in the adult camp, I make it a point to read the editorials every year in an unenthusiastic, detached frame of mind instead of becoming upset.

The common thread running in every newspaper in 2011 was that editors lamented the introverted orientation of young people while still having sympathy for their predicament of having been born in times of such despair and hopelessness, and encouraged them to hold on and persevere.[120]

The *Asahi Shimbun* apparently feels that "When we see you guys in the train, absorbed in your games and cell phones, we get seriously worried, wondering whether you're okay." The *Yomiuri Shimbun*, pointing to the decline in the number of students studying abroad and the low usage of Facebook, bemoans that young people are "inward looking."[121] The *Mainichi Shimbun*, citing low voter turnout, blasts, "You people should be thinking about seeking to lower the voting age even more," and the *Sankei Shimbun* concludes that it's not becoming for young people to "spill their frustrations online" and be pessimistic and resigned, saying things like "Society is never going to get better anyway."[122]

Undoubtedly, you often hear these days that young people have become inward-looking. While I believe the terms "inward looking" and "introverted" have various meanings, if the images of young people as depicted by those newspapers are to be believed, the portrait of today's youths will show that young people have utterly resigned themselves to the despairing ethos of the times, choosing to pursue security and certainty in their lives above all else. Furthermore, though they have the potential to connect with the world via the Internet, they're not actually interacting as much as they'd like due to their lack of proficiency in English. The number of students studying abroad has dwindled, as has the number participating in the Japan Overseas Cooperation Volunteers program. Young people also don't pursue success so aggressively that they need to push others out of their way; they'd rather cherish close friends. Young people don't engage in activism, either, to attempt to change society, nor do they vote in elections.

Yes, that's correct. Each of these descriptions feels right, making you nod your head in agreement and say, "Indeed." But if making you just say, "Indeed," settles the matter, then I feel you will never forgive me as the author of this book, which includes "young people" in its title. So let me dig deeper now, and seriously examine, together with the relevant data, whether the generalization that young people are "inward looking" is true.

---

120. In addition, Sakamoto Ryōma received coverage from the *Asahi*, *Yomiuri*, and *Sankei* newspapers. This must be the influence of the NHK TV saga *Ryomaden/The Legend of Ryoma Sakamoto*. If I could arbitrarily create a Sakamoto Ryōma Prize, I'd award it to *Asahi Shimbun*, which said, "The clouds aren't found 'above the hill' [a reference to the historical novel on the Meiji era by Ryōtarō Shiba]; they're found on the Internet."

121. According to the *Yomiuri Shimbun*, more than 500 million people from all parts of the world have joined Facebook and are exchanging information via the medium of English. However, the number of Japanese people using the service is small. Incidentally, Facebook's current level of multilingual support has advanced to a considerable degree, and the fact that exchanges are being carried out in various languages is evident to anyone after using Facebook for just a brief period.

122. What I found interesting about the *Sankei Shimbun* editorial was that, after opening with the promise to "deliver a message from the heart" and consequently saying all sorts of things arbitrarily, the author of the editorial reflected that his ramblings were the self-centered opinions of an adult. I would have liked to have seen more confidence than that from someone speaking on behalf of a conservative newspaper.

2. Young People Want to Contribute to Society

Surprisingly social

First, let's take a look at the attitudes and mindset of young people. While there are vast numbers of surveys out there on the attitudes of the young, many are no more than quick time-killers or marketing data; many do indeed show specific findings, but they fail to make comparisons, and by extension, to prove the findings truly specific and unique.[123]

For example, if, compared to another generation, only young people show a particular numerical value, this data will certainly be worthy of consideration. In addition, if some kind of shift or change is recognized in comparison to the youth of a previous generation, then that data, too, will be worthy of analysis.

To that end, the *Public Opinion Survey on Social Awareness* carried out by the cabinet office is an excellent resource. Since it has contained some of the same questions that have been asked for more than thirty years, this survey comes in handy when you want to roughly follow the shifting attitudes of Japanese people.[124] The question in this survey asking respondents whether they view themselves as "society-centric" or "individual-centric" is one of the classics that has endured for over thirty years. Respondents are asked to choose which of the following two ways of thinking approximates their own: "We should pay more attention to the affairs of the nation and society" or "We should attach great importance to enhancing our personal lives."

Now, if the claim that young people tend to be "inward looking" is true, the number of young people considering themselves to be "individual-centric" should also be high. An examination, though, of the latest data from 2011 data reveals that 55 percent of young people in their twenties said they were "society-centric," while 36.2 percent said they were "individual-centric"; the rest either said "I can't say necessarily" or "I don't know."[125]

Wait, what? Surprisingly, it seems that today's young people are inclined to think

---

123. Another technique often employed by researchers is to clarify the correlations of every question through statistics software, based on data collected through detailed questionnaires.

124. Recent ones are released on the Internet these days, so anyone seeking to get their tax money's worth, no matter how little, should try taking advantage of them. However, the fact that they contain the same questions that have been asked for dozens of years now means that the level of questions is that of several decades ago, so there's naturally a limit.

125. Incidentally, the 2011 survey was carried out in January, so the results of the survey don't reflect the impact of the earthquake disaster. Researchers should be looking forward to the results of the 2012 survey.[*29]

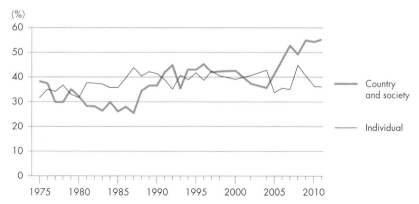

Figure 2.1   Are you society-centric or individual-centric? (Respondents in their twenties)
(*Public Opinion Survey on Social Awareness*)

about the nation and society. Furthermore, albeit by a narrow margin, the percentage of "society-centric" responses was higher among the young than among the elderly. Of those seventy and over, 54.1 percent responded "society-centric," and 30.6 percent responded "individual-centric."

What's more, compared to the past, the number of "society-centric" youths has increased considerably. Figure 2.1 indicates the change in the percentages of "society-centric" and "individual-centric" twenty-somethings, which shows that the percentage of "society-centric" youths was a little under 30 percent in the 1980s, gradually rose above 40 percent by the 1990s, and exceeded 50 percent within the last five years. The youth of these recent years are the most "society-centric" to date since the survey was initiated.

In the same survey concerning social awareness, there is a question about the respondent's attitude toward contributing to society: "Usually, as a member of society, do you feel like being of some help to society?" According to the 2011 survey, 59.4 percent of twenty-somethings indeed wished to contribute to society.★[30] In the 1983 survey, this number was only 32 percent. This means that, just within a span of less

---

★29.   In the survey carried out in January 2012, "society-oriented" twenty-somethings declined to 50.2 percent, while "individual-oriented" twenty-somethings went up to 40.2 percent. According to the survey of that year, the percentage of "society-oriented" twenty-somethings was the lowest among all generations. So did the earthquake end up making young people "individual-oriented"? Just as I was pondering this, it came to my attention that the same survey showed that "awareness of contributing to society" had risen to 70.1 percent. A plausible hypothesis is that, while the earthquake disaster did lead more young people to begin to think that they would like to do something for society, they also came to find significance in valuing their individual lives. And that's why, when they were asked to choose between "society" and the "individual" in an either-or format, the number of "society-oriented" youths appears to have decreased.

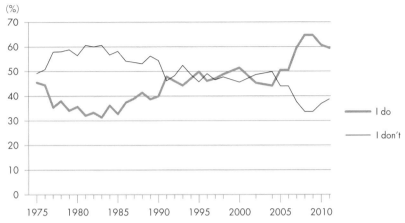

Figure 2.2 Do you think about being of help to society? (Respondents in their twenties) (*Public Opinion Survey on Social Awareness*)

than thirty years, the number of youths wishing to be resourceful to society actually doubled (figure 2.2). So young people these days are not only "society-centric," but are also yearning to actually contribute to society.

Philanthropy boom

Indeed, young people these days seem to be surprisingly concerned about society. Several examples come to mind. For example, in 2005, Kōta Hada (twenty-one years old, Hyogo) and Hiroaki Ishimatsu (twenty-one years old, Oita), who were both medical students at the time, happened to find out that the sum of 1.5 million yen would be enough to build a school in Cambodia. They gathered some friends together, held a charity event, and eventually managed to reach their goal of opening an elementary school.[126] In the autumn of 2011, the story of their great efforts was told in a movie starring Osamu Mukai (twenty-nine years old, Kanagawa).

But Hada and Ishimatsu weren't the only ones doing such good. A student organization called SWITCH, which was established in 2009, holds events and donates the proceeds to the street children of Bangladesh. In addition, the group also joined forces

---

★30.   In the 2015 survey, the percentage of twenty-somethings who said they wished to be helpful to society rose to a height of 67.2 percent. Meanwhile, the percentage of "society-oriented" people saw a slight decrease to 49.3 percent.

126.   Kōta Hada, *Boku-tachi wa sekai o kaeru koto ga dekinai* (We can't change the world), Shogakukan, 2010. You can enjoy reading about the activities of Hiroaki Ishimatsu, who took over the reins of the group from Hada, in *Maji de gachi na borantia* (Seriously earnest volunteers; Kodansha, 2009).

with the travel agency H.I.S. to organize a study tour called the "Bangladesh International Exchange Trip."[127]/[★31]

Many young people who aim to contribute to society also take part in the round-the-world sea voyage known as Peace Boat. Travelers can join optional tours at various destinations, such as a tour investigating the Cambodian mine issue (for a price of 98,000 yen), allowing travelers to contribute to society in their own way and take pleasure in it, too.

The media are also covering more stories on young social entrepreneurs. Eriko Yamaguchi (twenty-five years old, Saitama), launched a company called Mother House, leveraging the experience she gained as an intern in Bangladesh while attending Keio University. The company locally produces high-quality bags made from hemp fiber and imports them to Japan for sale. This is the kind of business model that's attracting attention: one that helps promote a developing country's self-reliance, instead of supporting it with arbitrary donations and sponsorships.

Young people aren't just paying attention to foreign countries, though. The "Green Bird" project, a volunteer operation for picking up garbage that began in Harajuku, has spread across Japan. The total number of participants picking up garbage in 2009 is said to have reached 24,000, many of them being youths.[★32]

As I will cover in detail in chapter 5, the responses to the 2011 Great East Japan Earthquake and tsunami remain fresh in public memory. Young people volunteered in many ways, from raising funds in every city in Japan to actually visiting the disaster-stricken areas, appealing online for power-saving measures, and so on. So strong was their zeal to help that it was as if they had been just waiting to come across such an opportunity.

Thus, a phenomenon that might be called a "philanthropy boom" is taking place among young people. Their actions appear to be overturning the pessimism of adults and inspiring the view that young people are not in the least bit "inward looking." Furthermore, they even have their sights set on countries overseas.

But unfortunately, that's not where the story ends.

---

127.   Official blog of the student group SWITCH: http://ameblo.jp/switch012/
★31.   The student group SWITCH continues to be active to this day. However, they now declare that their main goal is to enrich their student life rather than to carry out philanthropic work overseas. Apparently, their main activity these days is running the "Charity Sports Festival" project, a sports day for undergraduates.
★32.   While the number of Green Bird participants peaked at 28,000 in 2010, 24,000 participants still remain today.

The number of young volunteers hasn't grown much

Let's verify the available data properly. Referring to the *Basic Survey of Social Living Practices* conducted by the Ministry of Internal Affairs and Communications, let's take a look at the percentage of people who carried out volunteer work year before the survey was carried out.

Regrettably, this survey takes place only once every five years, and the most recent data available is for 2006. Nonetheless, the data shows that the number of twenty-somethings participating in volunteer work has been fairly flat since the 1970s. Moreover, their rate of participation in volunteer work was lower than that of any other age bracket (figure 2.3).

In other words, though the number of "society-centric" youths increased, along with the number of young people wanting to "contribute to society," it's clear that there has been no increase in the number of youths actually participating in activities that can help them contribute to society.

In the world of volunteerism and welfare, 1995 is considered to be ground zero—the inaugural year for volunteering. When the Great Hanshin-Awaji Earthquake struck on January 17 of that year, a total of 1.3 million people from all across the country rushed over to offer assistance in the stricken areas, many of whom were volunteering for the first time.

According to research carried out at the time, 66.6 percent of earthquake disaster volunteers were novices, and over 30 percent were between the ages of twenty and twenty-four; the average age was a young 26.3. The timing also happened to coincide with the period of spring vacation for college students (among whom include 18- to

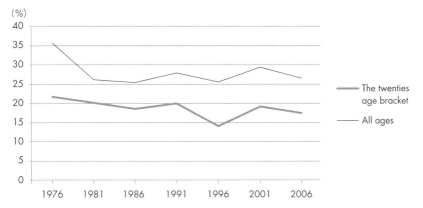

Figure 2.3   Participation rates for volunteer activities
(*Basic Survey of Social Living Practices*)

19-year-olds), so 60 percent of the volunteers were, in fact, university students.[128]

In addition, in 1998 the non-profit organization (NPO) law took effect, making it possible for groups without a large amount of operating capital to become corporate entities. While today you can establish an NPO or a general incorporated foundation by simply registering, prior to the establishment of this law, if you intended to form a grassroots volunteer organization you were left with no choice but to operate as a voluntary association, which had no rights as a juridical person or corporate entity.

However, the evidence shows that the concept of an "inaugural year for volunteering" and the formation of the NPO law failed to catalyze any particular uptick in the volunteer population. But bear in mind that if the study had been carried out in 1995, the graph might have turned out quite differently, since the 1996 survey had inquired about the volunteer experiences gained during the past year—that is, looking back one year from October 1996—which would have effectively excluded those who only volunteered at the time of the earthquake disaster.

At any rate, you can see that, despite the salience of an "inaugural volunteer year," the idea of volunteering didn't take root in Japan that much. I look forward to the 2011 survey, though, which should reflect the number of volunteers present at an earthquake disaster.[129/★33]

Do young people really feel disconnected from politics?

Young people who see themselves as "society-centric" and are eager to contribute to society should certainly be going to the elections to vote. While you might have second thoughts about volunteering, all you have to do to vote is visit the local polling center.

---

128. "Borantia nanawari ga hajimete: Hanshindaishinsai hassei kara sankagetsu" (First-time volunteers comprise 70 percent: Three months after the Great Hanshin Earthquake struck), *Asahi Shimbun*, April 17, 1995, morning edition. This is an attitude survey conducted via interviews by the *Asahi Shimbun* in affected areas, including Kobe, from the middle to the end of March, 1995. There were 709 respondents.

129. However, an examination of the *World Youth Survey*, which targeted people aged eighteen to twenty-four, reveals that the percentage of young people in Japan answering that they were "currently active as volunteers," had risen from 3.3 percent in 2002 to 5.6 percent in 2007. In addition, while 31.7 percent of young people in 2002 answered that they had previously volunteered, by 2007, this figure had risen to as high as 43.9 percent. Since having participated in any volunteer activity just one time qualifies respondents to answer, "I have volunteered before," we can't put much stock in these responses, but it is nevertheless estimated that the number of youths undertaking volunteer activities has steadily increased.

★33. According to the *Shakai seikatsu kihon chōsa* (Basic survey of social living practices) carried out in October, 2011, the percentage of twenty-somethings taking part in volunteer activities was 18.9 percent. While this percentage has slightly risen from 17.2 percent recorded in 2006, it is still less than the 26.3 percent value recorded for all generations. In addition, in the *Shinsai-go no kifu: Borantia-tō ni kansuru ishiki chōsa* (Attitude survey concerning donations and volunteering after the earthquake disaster) carried out by the Japan NPO Research Association (JANPORA), the percentage of those who did not take part in any relief efforts was highest among the twenty-something generation. It looks like the earthquake disaster didn't contribute to any increase in the number of volunteers in Japan.

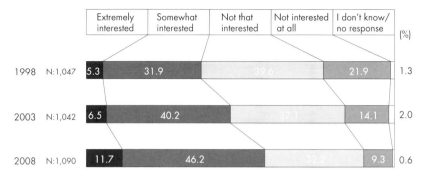

Figure 2.4 Level of interest in politics
(*World Youth Survey*)

Besides, these days even shopping districts offer incentives, as seen in puzzling ads like, "If you vote, we'll give you a free cup of coffee!"

A look at attitude surveys also shows an increase in the level of interest in politics. For instance, the *World Youth Survey* shows that the percentage of young people between the ages of eighteen and twenty-four who answered that they were "interested in politics" had shot up from 37.2 percent at the time of the sixth survey conducted in 1998 to 46.7 percent in 2003, before soaring as high as 57.9 percent in 2008 (figure 2.4). This reveals that a significant number of youths became interested in politics just within the span of ten years.[*34]

However, if you take a look at voter turnout by age at the elections for electing members of the House of Representatives, you will see that the turnout of youths in their twenties ever since 1967—which is as far back as the data on record can confirm—has been in a constant decline (figure 2.5). In the 1970s, approximately 60 percent went to the polls, but by the 1980s this number had dropped to 50 percent, and in 1993 it finally dropped below 50 percent, only to fall as low as 36.4 percent in 1996, at the forty-first Lower House election.

However, the turnout saw a rebound starting in 2005; at the Lower House election in 2009, which was marked by the excitement of seeing the transition of power to the Democratic Party take place, 49.5 percent of twenty-somethings showed up to vote.

★34. According to the *Wagakuni to shogaikoku no wakamono no ishiki ni kansuru chōsa* (Survey on attitudes of the young people of our country and various other countries; for some reason, the title has changed from *Sekai seinen ishiki chōsa*, or *World Youth Survey*), the percentage of youths interested in politics has fallen as low as 50.1 percent. However, it should be noted that there is a change: those surveyed in the *Sekai seinen ishiki chōsa* were between eighteen and twenty-four, whereas in the *Wagakuni to shogaikoku no wakamono no ishiki ni kansuru chōsa* (man, that title is long) they were between thirteen and twenty-nine.

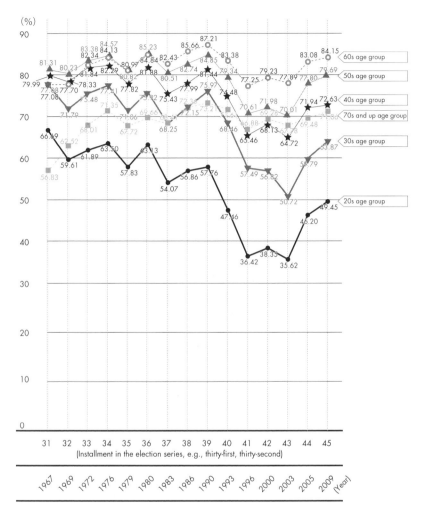

Figure 2.5 Changes in age-specific voter turnouts for Lower House elections
(The Association for Promoting Fair Elections)

Hey, if you try, the sky's the limit, right?

Apparently, a decent number of young people had become convinced that a course correction was necessary after all, finally awakening to the possibilities of politics and beginning to feel that it was up to them to make a difference in this nation.

Just to make sure, though, let's check the turnout recorded for the latest election, the twenty-second Upper House election held in 2010. The overall turnout was 57.9 percent, and the turnout for the youths in their twenties was—wait, what? It was 36.2

percent? That's hardly changed from the 36 percent turnout of twenty-somethings seen in 2007 for the twenty-first Upper House election.

What's more, even at the 2005 and 2009 Lower House elections, in which there was a rise in overall young-voter turnout, the turnouts for those in their thirties and above were, in fact, considerably higher than the turnouts for twenty-somethings. The year 2005, called the year of the "Postal Privatization Election," saw enthusiasm for Jun'ichirō Koizumi and the Liberal Democratic Party sweep across Japan, bringing about an overall turnout of 67.5 percent. In the year 2009, at the election that was pivotal for the transition of power from the Liberal Democratic Party to the Democratic Party, the overall turnout was 69.3 percent, a record high ever since the combined single-seat constituency and proportional representation system were introduced in 1996.

As an editorial in the *Mainichi Shimbun* fretted, the claim that young people don't go to the polls is apparently true. However, since the lowest turnout on record happened around 1995, those grownups in their thirties and forties today who were in their twenties back then have no justification for complaining that young people these days don't go to the polls. Still, there's no denying that the turnout has gone down compared to that in the generations before theirs.★35

3. Isolated, Galápagosized Youth

Are young people truly averse to traveling abroad?

Next, let's take a look at the disconnect with the world outside Japan that youths allegedly feel—the very same disconnect cited as evidence of their inward-looking disposition.

An examination of the overall statistics for Japan reveals that the number departing for overseas destinations exceeded ten million for the first time in 1990, and reached a record high of 17,810,000 in 2000. In subsequent years, due to the impact of the 9/11 terrorist attacks and the outbreak of the SARS epidemic in Asia, the number of people departing for overseas destinations fell to 13,270,000, but these past several years have seen the number growing from some 16 million to around 17 million.★36

★35. The turnout among twenty-somethings for the 2012 Lower House elections was 37.9 percent, whereas in 2014 it was 32.6 percent. This is the lowest generation-specific turnout on record since 1967. However, the 2014 election also saw the worst postwar turnout on record for all generations, at 52 percent. So the loss of interest in politics is not at all limited to young people.

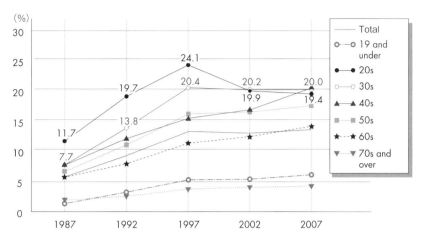

Figure 2.6 Changes in the rate of overseas departures

(Yuichi Hirooka, *Wakamono no kaigai ryokō banare* [A discussion concerning young people's disconnect with overseas travel], 2008)

Meanwhile, the number of twenty-somethings departing for overseas destinations peaked in 1996 before pursuing a long-term downward trend after 1997. The number of people departing for overseas destinations in 1996 was 4,630,000, but ten years later, in 2006, this number had dropped to as low as 2,980,000.

Let's examine this on a departure-rates basis. Despite the fact that in 1997 twenty-somethings accounted for 24.1 percent of overseas departures, which is tantamount to one in four people, by 2002 this number had fallen to 19.9 percent; in 2007, too, the number was a mere 19.4 percent (figure 2.6). While there once was a time when twenty-somethings (especially twenty-something girls) were traveling overseas more frequently than any other generation, after the 2000s, other generations got ahead. In 2010 the percentage of twenty-somethings among overseas travelers was 19.7 percent.[★37]

Young people these days don't even travel abroad; does that sound outrageous? But as many as 20 percent of twenty-somethings still do travel abroad. Besides, 20 percent is merely a return to the level seen around 1992. Girls, in particular, are traveling at a rate of one in four. As it turns out, the young people of the 1990s were traveling

---

★36.   The overall number of Japanese people traveling to overseas destinations reached a record high of 18,490,000 in 2012. Subsequently, under the influence of the weak yen, this number dropped as low as 16,900,000.

★37.   By 2014, the number of twenty-somethings traveling to overseas destinations had fallen to 2,700,000. However, seen on a departure-rate basis, this is 20.8 percent, indicating an upward trend.

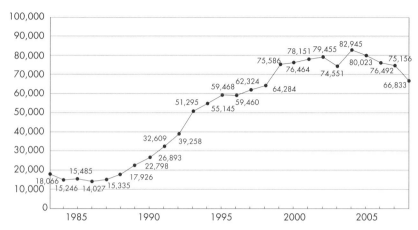

Figure 2.7 Changes in the number of students traveling to study abroad
(Ministry of Education, Culture, Sports, Science and Technology[130])

abroad excessively.[★38]

Let's now also take a look at the change in the number of students studying abroad. To be sure, the number of Japanese students studying abroad has continued to decline every year from its peak of 83,000 in 2004, dropping as low as 67,000 in 2008.[★39]

Figure 2.7 shows the shifts in the number of students studying abroad, but can you spot something strange about this picture? The number of students studying abroad peaked not in the bubble period, but in the more recent mid-2000s. The figure of 67,000 people studying abroad in 2008 certainly marks an 11 percent drop from the previous year, but in effect it also indicates a return to the 1998 level.

Moreover, in the meantime, the population of young people in Japan has de-

---

★38. The highest rate of overseas departures of young people occurred in the late 1990s; in 1996 in particular, 34.2 percent of women between twenty-five and twenty-nine had traveled abroad. Compared to that time, the overseas departure rate in the late 2000s was declining, but it began rising once again after 2010. For further details, refer to Tetsu Nakamura, Sachiko Nishimura, and Noriko Takai, *Wakamono no kaigairyokō banare o yomi toku* (Decoding young people's disengagement from overseas travel), Horitsu Bunka Sha, 2014.

★39. According to the Ministry of Education, Culture, Sports, Science and Technology, the number of students studying abroad in 2011 had declined to 57,501, but by 2012, the figure had bounced back to 60,138, showing a slight recovery. The Ministry of Education, Culture, Sports, Science and Technology launched the "Tobitate! Ryūgaku JAPAN" (Fly Away! Study Abroad Japan) campaign in an attempt to double these figures and bring the number of undergraduates studying abroad as high as 120,000.

130. In terms of the rate of students studying abroad, the late 1980s—supposedly the height of the bubble period—saw approximately 0.1 percent; in the mid-1990s, this figure grew to approximately 0.3 percent; but by about 2005, it finally exceeded 0.5 percent. However, despite the fact that the percentage of young people studying abroad was at a record-high level, it still only amounted to just one out of 200 students studying abroad. To consider this a "youth" problem is a considerable stretch.

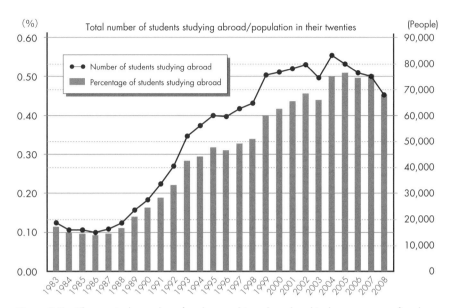

Figure 2.8 Changes in the number of students studying abroad and in the percentage of students studying abroad[131]

creased. The number of young people in their twenties—a cohort assumed to comprise the most number of students studying abroad—fell nearly 30 percent during the period spanning from 1996 to 2010. Thus, when considering "the rate of students studying abroad" in terms of the population of those who are of suitable age to study abroad, the number of students studying abroad is still at a record-high level (figure 2.8). This percentage is more than double the number registered in the bubble period.

In other words, compared to the bubble era, more young people have been studying abroad in this present day and age—a time decried as one of economic slump and social polarization. Yet grownups continue to have the impression that the number of students studying abroad has gone down. This is probably because they're missing the point that the destination of choice for students studying abroad has diversified; up until now many students were strongly inclined toward studying in countries found in the Anglosphere, such as the United States, but students these days have begun to turn

---

131.   For this graph, I referred to the blog *Bokura no jiyū wa koko ni aru* (Our freedom is right here). This blog offers a far more meticulous investigation into young people's lack of engagement with overseas travel and their disinclination to study abroad, so if you're interested, I urge you to check it out. http://wirfere.wordpress.com/

their attention to countries like China as well.[132]

The number of young people working abroad is also rising. To illustrate this, let me point you to the working holiday arrangement, which was initially introduced when a treaty was signed with Australia in 1980.[133] As of January 2011, Japan had signed visa-related treaties with eleven countries, including New Zealand and Canada.[★40]

In 1981, the number of participants in this program was 884, and by 1990, it had soared to 8,974. In 2008, a total of 20,868 Japanese people were taking advantage of the working holiday visa. After the 2000s, though, the figure remained fairly flat, but even so, more than twice as many young people were working abroad than had been the case in the bubble period.[★41]

Is it true that young people are going local?

Stories of young people becoming inclined to live in local communities instead of longing to live in major urban centers are often raised as yet another manifestation of their inward-looking disposition. For example, the TV show, *Kume Hirosi keizai supesharu: Shin Nipponjin arawaru* (Hiroshi Kume's economy special: The arrival of a new species of Japanese!) featured a class of young people labeled "the one-mile tribe." This group of "new Japanese," as defined by this television program, referred to "twenty-something youths who don't spend money." The program added that the number such young people, who never ventured beyond a radius of less than 1.6 km from their homes in their daily lives, was on the rise.[134]

---

132. Source: A press release from the Ministry of Education, Culture, Sports, Science and Technology titled "Nihonjin no kaigai ryūgakusha sū ni tsuite" (On the number of Japanese students studying abroad), December 22, 2010.

133. The mission of this scheme is to "cultivate young people with a broad international perspective, and in turn promote mutual understanding and amicable relations between the two countries, while approving the employment in the other country of young people between the ages of eighteen and twenty-five" (or up to thirty in some nations). Lately, intermediaries such as "Last Resort" have emerged, offering a comprehensive lineup of services for handling everything from visa acquisition to providing local pickup services and securing helplines.

★40. In 2013, Norway, too, became a working-holiday destination. Speaking as someone who actually experienced studying abroad there, I found the place to be a very pastoral and boring country. Though most people speak English there, the official language is, naturally, Norwegian. If you're thinking, "Great, what a bargain, I can learn two languages now," think again; you'll just end up failing to gain a command of either language.

★41. While many adults are angry about the fact that young people are introverted, according to a survey conducted by NHK, 28 percent of high school students actually wish to study abroad (NHK Broadcasting Culture Research Institute, *NHK chūgakusei, kōkōsei no seikatsu to ishiki chōsa 2012* [The 2012 survey on the way of life and attitudes of junior and senior high school students], NHK Publishing, 2013). That the rate of Japanese students studying abroad is nevertheless sluggish likely indicates that economic circumstances are having a large impact. In fact, the same survey clearly shows that the students who are positive about studying abroad are those whose standard of living is high.

134. Aired on June 1, 2008 via the TV Tokyo Network.

Since 2003, the sightseeing guidebook *Rurubu* has been publishing "micro-guide editions," which provide information on a municipality-specific basis, such as information on Machida city and Shinagawa ward. The motivation behind the founding of this periodical is "to offer a magazine that can help residents rediscover their own town." Some of its issues are so popular that they are repeatedly reprinted. The idea that even one's own hometown can become a "sightseeing destination" must sound incredible to people who immediately think of Hawaii when they think about traveling.[135]

A "delivery entrance examination service" carried out in Ikebukuro by Kokushikan University, whose campus is located in Setagaya, Tokyo, was apparently received well.[136] The admissions department of this university explains that they intend to "help students take their exams in a relaxed state of mind" by providing the opportunity to take their exams near where they live. It takes thirty minutes to commute to Setagaya from Ikebukuro by train, so this service, too, might be another instance of the trend toward localization or catering to local needs.

What surprised me the most, though, was the image of youths portrayed by thirty-three-year-old Tokyo native Yōhei Harada (thirty-three years old, Tokyo) of the ad agency Hakuhodo.[137] Apparently, he had met a pair of twenty-one-year-old girls who, he says, couldn't write the kanji characters for "Shinjuku," a major downtown area in Tokyo. According to Harada, this was because they had been spending their days only in Matsudo, in Chiba prefecture, which is adjacent to the Tokyo metropolitan area. Even if they did go to Tokyo on rare occasions, they only went as far as Nippori or Ueno—stops on the Jōban Line they could reach without changing trains. Consequently, the Shinjuku area remained a foreign territory to them.

But wait, there's more. The girls said they were intent on visiting "Odaiba," a redeveloped waterfront area in Tokyo, because "after a year, Odaiba's going to disappear." Apparently this was some kind of misunderstanding, but to these girls who lived in Matsudo, "Odaiba" didn't seem all that real.

Surprised that Matsudo had become such an alarming place, I took a trip down to Matsudo one Sunday in the early afternoon to listen to the stories of the young people there.[138] The first people I interviewed were a couple at a video arcade in the station plaza. Daisuke, a twenty-four-year-old man living in Urayasu, Chiba, and Hikari, a

---

135.   "Nihon no 'tabi' dai-kaimei" (The great revelation about trips taken by the Japanese), *Weekly Toyo Keizai*, March 28, 2009.

136.   "Gakuryoku tte nandarō" (What is academic ability?), *Asahi Shimbun*, February 19, 2010, morning metropolitan edition.

137.   Yōhei Harada, *Chikagoro no wakamono wa naze dame nano ka* (Why are today's young people useless?), Kobunsha, 2010.

twenty-five-year-old woman living in Matsudo, were classmates at a junior high school. They said they had begun dating a little over a year before. When I asked where they frequently went together, they answered, "Matsudo and Urayasu. That's where we go to have fun." So the trend of going local was making headway in Matsudo, after all. When I asked whether they also went to Tokyo, just to make sure, the answer was, "Yes—quite often, in fact. It's nearby, after all." Huh?

"We drop by places like Shibuya, Shinjuku, and Ueno. We often shop at the department stores—Isetan, Marui, Takashimaya—because in Matsudo the shops really don't cater to young people. Matsudo is all right for watching movies or for just everyday shopping, but that's not enough, you know…" Apparently not. But to begin with, Daisuke's workplace was in Shinagawa, and so, as it turned out, he commuted to Tokyo nearly every day.

Feeling that I should be talking to people who appeared to be more local,[139] I approached a seventeen-year old male high school student, Hiroaki, and a nineteen-year-old male undergraduate, Takashi, at a park in front of a Daiē supermarket.

They were fellow Yu-Gi-Oh! card-gamers who had become acquainted about half a year ago at a local gaming shop. They were there at Daiē, they said, for a card tournament. Both of them were living in their parents' homes, and neither had any intention of moving out. Hiroaki, who was planning on finding employment next year, said, "I want to live where many of my friends are around"; Takashi said, "I'm satisfied living in my hometown." However, they apparently visited Tokyo often, too—Takashi, in particular, went to Akihabara often.

Hmmm . . . let me see, now. You can't call that going local, can you?

In Matsudo I interviewed thirteen men and women whose ages ranged from seventeen to thirty-two. While nearly all of them lived near Matsudo, they said they also frequently went to Tokyo. An eighteen-year old female undergraduate whose visits to Tokyo were the most infrequent among the group responded, "I don't know much (about Tokyo) yet, so I don't go there that much. I only go about once or twice a month." Unfortunately, I didn't come across any youngsters like the ones Harada had interviewed.

---

138. July 18, 2010. On that day, after interviewing in Matsudo, I conducted fieldwork at IKEA in Minamifunabashi and at La La Port. If you take a look at just the trajectory of my movements, you'll notice that is, indeed, the trajectory of a normal way of spending a holiday. Well, frankly, it was all just something like a leisure activity anyway.

139. A bias has appeared at this juncture, so, as social research, it's unsatisfactory. In the first place, when I interviewed "young people" in Matsudo on a Sunday afternoon, the sample was already considerably slanted, since youths who had not become "localized" were probably nonexistent in Matsudo. Considering all that, the fact that I didn't run into any young people who had become "localized" is truly unfortunate.

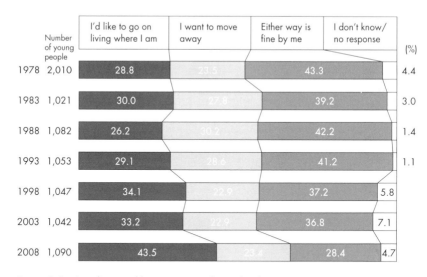

Figure 2.9   Attitude toward living permanently in a local community (*World Youth Survey*)

Well, it appears that taking a proper look at the data, once again, would be a good idea.

Apparently, in the long term, young people are getting local

In the *World Youth Survey*, which covers youngsters between eighteen and twenty-four, there is a question asking, "Do you wish to always go on living in the area (city, town, or village) you're living in right now?" As you can see in figure 2.9, the number of young people who say they want to continue living where they are shows an upward trend.

In particular, in the eighth findings of the survey carried out in 2007 (which was announced in 2008), the number of respondents who wished to go on living where they were went up by about 10 percent, from 33.2 percent in 2003. Certainly, in an attitudinal sense, it appears that young people are inclined becoming toward local-centrism.[140/★42]

---

140.   Nevertheless, compared to other age groups, more young people seem to be attracted to cities. According to the *Daitoshi ni kansuru yoron chōsa* (Public opinion poll regarding large metropolitan areas) conducted by the Cabinet Office in 2012, 76.8 percent of people in their twenties indicated that they were attracted to large metropolitan areas. This is considerably higher than the average recorded for all generations, which was 59.4 percent. Of course, feeling an attraction for a place and actually living there are two different things.

So what, then, is the actual state of population migration? According to the *School Basic Survey*, the percentage of people enrolling into universities in the same cities and districts as their high schools is trending upward. This figure, which was 35.5 percent in 1990, and 38.8 percent in 2000, rose up to 42 percent in 2010. The number of people entering local universities is, without a doubt, seeing an increase.[141/★43]

Furthermore, among those who found employment soon after graduating from high school, 80.4 percent were working within their local prefecture in 2010.[142]

If we examine the last ten years, we see that the highest rate of in-prefecture employment (indicative of a local-centric bias) was 82.5 percent in 2004, and the lowest rate of in-prefecture employment (indicative of less local-centrism) was 78.1 percent in 2009.[★44] While it can't really be said that the level of local-centrism has risen in the past several years, since the rate of in-prefecture employment forty years ago in 1970 was 68.7 percent. In the long run, then, the number of high school graduates working outside the prefecture has, without a doubt, decreased.[143]

The population inflow into the three major metropolitan areas (Tokyo, Osaka, and Nagoya), in terms of all age groups, is also seeing a long-term downward trend. While the 1960s saw an influx that surpassed 600,000 people, after the burst of the economic bubble in the early 1990s, the trend shifted to an outflow. And if we look at recent figures, we see that the influx of people into the three major metropolitan areas, which comprised 930,000 people in 2001, dropped all the way down to 790,000 in

---

★42.   In the survey carried out in 2013, the number of young people answering that they wished to continue living in their hometown decreased to 30.3 percent. But this may have been influenced by the changed target age of the survey. While in 2014 Yōhei Harada (thirty-seven years old, Tokyo), of the advertising agency Hakuhodo, defined those youths who became localized—that is to say, those who became inclined to live in their hometown—as "mild Yankees" (translator's note: In Japanese, the term "Yankee" usually refers to juvenile delinquents), in reality, it seems difficult to say that the inclination of young people to become localized has become stronger.

141.   The percentage of people whose high school is in the same metropolis or district as the university they entered (Ministry of Education, Culture, Sports, Science and Technology, *Gakkō kihon chōsa* [School data survey]). However, the proportion in 1980 was 38.1 percent, which was the same level recorded in 2000. Thereafter, the lowest percentage of students who went on to college in their prefectures was seen in 1992, at 34.9 percent.

★43.   According to the *Gakkō kihon chōsa* (School data survey), the percentage of people entering universities located in the same metropolis or district as their high school was 42.1 percent. While this figure was 42.3 percent in 2013, in the end, it still can't be said that the inclination of young people to become "localized"—that is to say, to live in their hometown—has become stronger.

142.   Here, I have applied in reverse the rate of employment outside the prefecture among those who seek employment after graduating from full-time high schools (Ministry of Education, Culture, Sports, Science and Technology, *Gakkō kihon chōsa* [School data survey]).

★44.   The rate of in-prefecture employment in 2014 was 81.6 percent. As expected, even in the early 2010s, it apparently cannot be said that the inclination toward living in one's hometown had grown stronger.

143.   The rate of in-prefecture employment among high school students was 75.7 percent in 1980, while in 1990 it was 76.2 percent, showing, in the long run, an upward trend.

2010.[144/★45]

Thus, the inclination toward becoming "local-centric" appears to be true in the long term. But strictly speaking, this argument holds up only when a comparison is made to the "Japanese Economic Miracle," the record period of economic growth that took place from the post–World War II era to the end of the Cold War. In those days, the farming population was huge, and second- or third-born sons who couldn't find employment in their hometown had no choice but to move out to cities. These were the so-called *kin no tamago* (golden eggs; promising young people).

Farming households would send off their unemployed second- and third-born sons to the city, where companies sought young people from rural districts as sources of cheap labor.[145] So it was this sharing of mutual goals between two communities that triggered the migratory movement; in other words, it was not an emotional matter like local-centrism is.[146] In fact, the data shows that farming households hoped to see more employment opportunities inside their hometown, suggesting that not everyone moved out to cities willingly.

Nowadays, with the development of local cities, the real countryside—a place without universities or workplaces—has become scarce, while modest cities have seen a rise. This is likely one of the factors keeping young people from moving out of their local cities and districts.

Meanwhile, the proportion of new students enrolling in The University of Tokyo from central places of origin (that is, the Kanto area) and provincial places of origin has remained, for the most part, unchanged from the 1970s to the present.[147/★46] Thus, the "inclination toward becoming local" may be a sign of a bipolar split between young people heading for Tokyo nonetheless and young people foregoing urban centers to live modest lives instead.

---

144. Ministry of Internal Affairs and Communications, *Jūmin kihon daichō jinkō-idō hōkoku: Heisei 22-nen kihon shūkei kekka* (Basic tabulation of the 2010 report on internal migration in Japan derived from basic resident registers). However, in 2010, people in their twenties comprised the largest group migrating between metropolises and districts. For example, among the 390,000 people who moved to the city of Tokyo, 42.4 percent were people in their twenties. Unfortunately, since the statistics for incoming and outgoing migrations by age were only released starting in the year 2010, there is no way to make comparisons with prior years.

★45. Among the 400,000 people who moved into the city of Tokyo in 2014, the ratio of twenty-somethings was 43.8 percent. As expected, statistical surveys are just tedious unless they're seen in the context of a long-term time span. I'm feeling depressed right now, working on the footnotes to the paperback edition in chapter 2, which, for the most part, involves nothing but this kind of tedious work.

145. Kazutoshi Kase, *Shūdan shūshoku no jidai* (The age of searching for jobs en masse), Aoki Shoten, 1997.

146. *Jimotoka* (becoming local) brings to mind young people loitering in front of a convenience store, but this country, to this day, still has many places that can be called "genuine countrysides," which are devoid of convenience stores. Young people living in such provinces can't even *jimotoka*, which is to say, become local.

4. Young People Who Don't Buy Things: A Case of Anemic Consumption

Is "reluctant consumption" for real?

Lately, you often hear the elderly complaining, "Youngsters don't buy things anymore! At this rate, the Japanese economy is in for some dark times ahead." But there are various kinds of "things." So, on what grounds can they complain that "young people don't buy things"? How can they make the argument that young people feel disconnected from consumerism?

To find some answers, let's try taking a look at the latest bestseller covering this disconnect. It's titled *Ken shōhi: Sedai no kenkyū* (Reluctant shopping: A generational study) by Hisakazu Matsuda, a fifty-three-year-old marketer from Hyogo. In this book, he labels young people who shy away from shopping for consumer items as *ken shōhi sedai* (a generation of reluctant shoppers). The eye-catching back-cover blurb features a line uttered by a hip young woman—the type who tends to have a blasé outlook on life. She says, "Buying a car is dumb, isn't it?"

It seems that this line—"Buying a car is dumb, isn't it?"—is something a young person actually said to the author. The beginning of the book is littered with such snippets of dialogue, which apparently made the author cringe and doubt his ears; statements like, "I don't want a large-screen TV! My cell phone's 1-seg TV is good enough," and "How can I have fun traveling overseas where no one understands Japanese?"

A book like this might normally end with the line, "And that's why young people these days are no good." But, as might be expected from a professional marketer, Matsuda draws on meticulously collected statistical data, including an online survey of 2,000 respondents, which he attempted at the company where he serves as the representative director.[148] Furthermore, for some reason, he refers to scholars of the past,

---

147.   The *Tokyo daigaku gakusei seikatsu jittai chōsa* (The University of Tokyo student life fact-finding survey) asks The University of Tokyo students for the addresses of their family households. This shows that the percentage of Tokyo city residents has remained constant, at the 30 percent level, for the past forty years. In the 1970s people from the wider Kanto region comprised 50 percent of the student population, but from the late 1980s the figure began to rise, and according to the survey in 2009, it was at 59.5 percent. At any rate, it can be said that it has remained at the same level for the last ten years.

★46.   In the 2013 survey, the percentage of students whose place of origin was Kanto was 60.4 percent, with no detectable changes these several years. I'm sorry for yet another trivial footnote, but, hey, it's a drag for me, too, okay?

including Wilhelm Dilthey and Karl Mannheim, while discussing the utility and limitations of generationalism. The whole work ultimately comes off as an essay written by a college student eager to impress with an excessive use of abstruse words.[149/★47]

At first, Matsuda refers to the *Annual Report on the Family Income and Expenditure Survey* conducted by the Ministry of Internal Affairs and Communications, to check the changes in the average number of purchases of cars and television sets made by households with more than two inhabitants. The figures clearly show that the average number of purchases of cars and television sets made by twenty-somethings is seeing a downward trend.

After this, using data from his online survey—his pride and joy—Matsuda reveals that the inclination toward "reluctant consumption" is strong among the young generation, particularly among the post-bubble generation born between 1979 and 1983. "Reluctant consumption" refers to the behavior exhibited by people who, despite seeing increases in their personal income, nonetheless wish to reduce their expenditures.[150]

The theme running through this book, from beginning to end, is "Oh, my God! Young people no longer want cars or consumer electronics! They don't even want to travel overseas!"

This is because, if we are to believe the author's data, the members of the post-bubble generation—supposedly the most strongly inclined to "shop reluctantly"—are spending more than any other generation on fashion, furniture, interior decoration, and games. In short, he says that the problem lies in the fact that consumption trends are veering toward not overseas travel or large-screen TV sets, but toward more everyday items closer to personal lives, such as clothing, food, and home decor.

When I first heard the expression "reluctant consumption," I thought it was pointing to a more alarming trend away from consumption, or even consumerism. But, as it turns out, all the expression is really referring to is simply an unremarkable disenchantment with cars, household electrical appliances, and overseas travel.[151]

---

148.   To consult a dissertation that sums up the problems of Internet research and matters that require attention when examining the findings, refer to Takahiro Nagasaki's "Intānetto chōsa no rekishi to sono katsuyō" (The history and usage of Internet research) in *Jōhō no kagaku to gijutsu*, 58–6, 2008. One of the points to keep in mind is the fact that the responses are biased, since the surveys seek answers from only those who use the Internet, and on top of that, mainly from those who are registered as monitors with the research company.

149.   It's too bad his treatment of the difficult classic he had taken the trouble to read doesn't come alive in his discussion.

★47.   I really didn't have to use such stinging words of criticism.

150.   At the time of the survey, people born between 1979 and 1983 were between the ages of twenty-five and twenty-nine. While I doubt that the large number of people thinking about saving as much as possible for the future to prepare for marriage and childrearing is a recent phenomenon, I can't tell for sure, since the survey doesn't contain any comparisons with past records.

In that case, I'm basically on the same page. Without a doubt, a sense of disenchantment with cars is spreading among young people. An examination of the *National Survey on Consumption* reveals that automobile purchases incurred by people under thirty dropped from 6,475 in 1989 to 4,414 in 1999, and to as low as 3,351 in 2009.[152]

In addition, even the Forecast for Vehicle Demand[153] shows that the percentage of primary drivers under age thirty fell from 18 percent in 1997 all the way down to 8 percent in 2009.[★48] This drop is more rapid than the pace of decline seen in the population of young people between eighteen (the age when you're eligible for a driver's license) and twenty-nine years of age.

And the claim that young people aren't buying as many durable consumer goods is also true. According to the *National Survey on Consumption*, the amount of money young people under twenty-nine spend on durable products like household appliances, and the rate of ownership of those products within this group, is certainly less compared to people aged above thirty. However, their expenditure on game consoles and PCs, which are bona fide household appliances in their own right, is considerably more than any other generation. Thus, the assertion that young people don't buy household appliances is a slight exaggeration.

Thanks to "you," sales have been ruined

If you look at other studies, you can confirm similar trends. According to a survey carried out by the *Nikkei Ryūtsū Shimbun* newspaper (presently known as the *Nikkei Marketing Journal*), in 2011, males in their twenties, compared to those in their thirties (the second-generation baby boomers) and those in their forties (the bubble gen-

---

151. In Taku Yamaoka's *Hoshigaranai wakamono-tachi* (Desireless youth; Nikkei Publishing, 2009), what's mainly covered are things like automobiles and alcohol. Why do old men like cars? If I ever have the opportunity to write a theory on the middle-aged, I'd definitely like to consider this as a theme.

152. For this part, I made use of a survey of "total households" which combined single households and households with more than two people. Since, strictly speaking, this is a survey based on the breakdown by the age of the head of the household, I can't confirm the patterns of young people living in their parents' home. Nevertheless, I feel it's better than the *Family Income and Expenditure Survey* that Matsuda used; the survey is limited to households with more than two people living in them. In addition, with a sample size of approximately 60,000 households, the *National Survey of Family Income and Expenditure* is more accurate (the *Family Income and Expenditure Survey* has a sample size of approximately 8,000 households.) The values show average costs.

153. Japan Automobile Dealers Association, *2009-nendo jōyōsha shijō dōkō chōsa* (2009 passenger-car market trends in Japan).

★48. This was 7 percent in the 2013 survey. On the other hand, in 1997, 15 percent of main drivers were sixty years or older, but by 2013, this number had shot up to 34 percent. However, the percentage of twenty-somethings with a driver's license in 2014 was 83.7 percent, tending to still remain at a high level (*The White Paper on Police 2015*). Incidentally, the percentage of twenty-somethings with a driver's license in 1991 was also high, at 84.8 percent.

eration) spent more on fashion, books, cosmetics, and games. Females in their twenties spent more money on wining and dining with friends and colleagues, and on communication costs.[154]

In addition, the desire among young people in their twenties to purchase branded goods from sources like United Arrows and Chanel was higher than among those in their thirties and forties. This generation also has more disposable income per month than second-generation baby boomers and members of the bubble generation. The average amount of monthly spending money, in the case of twenty-somethings, was 50,277 yen (US$434.20, as of January 10, 2017), but 13.2 percent reported having more than 100,000 yen (US$863.63, as of January 10, 2017).

Well, what do you know? Those twenty-year olds are all big spenders. But if you think about it, it's not surprising at all, because surely people in their twenties, many of whom are single, have more money they can spend freely than those in their thirties and forties, a cohort with more people getting married and undertaking parental care.★[49]

So it's absolutely not the case that young people have stopped buying things. It's just that the things they buy and the scale of the things they buy have changed. They don't buy cars as much as they used to. They don't drink alcohol either; nor do they travel overseas. But they do buy clothing-, food-, and home-related items, and they do incur expenses for sustaining their human relations, such as communication costs.

They are, as the advertising magazine published by Hakuhodo puts it, "Young people who engage in sustainable consumption, abstaining from excessive consumption or aggrandizement."[155] For this reason, it's certainly safe to say that the nature of this consumption trend is "inward-looking."

However, since the decrease in the youth population has been so rapid, a few factors, such as the fact that "young people have stopped buying cars" and that "young people no longer travel overseas," have likely had an unwarranted, excessive impact. The population of twenty-somethings has dropped by 26 percent since 1996, fifteen

---

154. *Nikkei Marketing Journal*, January 5, 2011. An online survey intended for men and women between the ages of twenty-five and twenty-nine, thirty-five and thirty-nine, and forty-five and forty-nine. Apparently, the sample size for each age group was approximately 1,000, and responses were collected from an aggregate of 3,242 people.

★49. To delve deeper into the relationship between young people and money, you should first of all read Naoko Kuga's *Wakamono wa hontō ni okane ga nai no ka?* (Is it true that young people really don't have money?; Kobunsha, 2014). The level of disposable income and savings of young people is higher than it was in the bubble period; furthermore, these amounts have also been revealed to be more than what the current middle-aged and elderly have. It looks as though young people today, despite being told that they don't have any money, are, in fact, not only richer than young people of the past, but also wealthier than the middle-aged and elderly people of the present time.

155. *KŌKOKU*, October 2010.

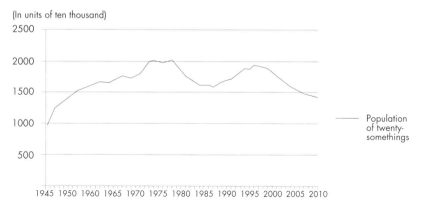

Figure 2.10   Changes in the population of twenty-somethings
(Based on the *Historical Statistics of Japan* provided by the Statistics Bureau[157])

years ago; and by 21 percent since 2001, ten years ago. So naturally, if the denominator for young people drops by as much as 20 percent, consumption will appear to fall (figure 2.10).[156/★50]

If you're going to complain about young people not buying things from you, before you levy that complaint against youngsters, I want you to lash out at the policy-makers responsible for having lowered the Japanese birth rate to such an abysmal level in the first place, and the citizens who supported their policies at the time. In other words, I want most of you—the majority of the population—to blame your past selves.[158]

In addition, as we confirmed in chapter 1, the idea that young people are trendsetters who launch fads is a myth created in the 1980s. The population of "young people" was quite sizable at the time, and they also likely prided themselves in being instigators

156.   In the postwar years, the period that saw the most number of people in their twenties was when the baby-boom generation reached adulthood; the population of twenty-somethings in 1976 was twenty million. The next peak occurred when the so-called "second-generation baby boomers" became adults; the population of twenty-somethings in 1996 was similar, comprising 19,130,000 people.

★50.   The population of twenty-somethings continued to decline steadily after that, and by August 1, 2015 it was 12,750,000. It was 13,170,000 at the time of the book's publication in 2011, which indicates that "young people" have been steadily decreasing in number every year. This "youth shrinkage" may have been the most significant change that occurred between the time of the original publication of the book and the publication of the paperback edition. I have the feeling that a book titled *Youth Extinction* might come out soon.

157.   With regard to 2010 and 2011, I referred to *Population Estimates*.

158.   By the way, twenty years hence, the population of people in their twenties will decline a further 20 percent, to approximately 10,970,000, so you better be prepared. Well, I suppose when I say "you," I mean the folks of my generation. We're the ones who need to be prepared the most.

of fads, or arbiters of fashion.[159]

That means the truth behind the "young people don't buy things" argument is the irony that the marketers and advertising agencies, who should have been making the consumers dance to their tune, were being made to dance, before they knew it, to the tune of the myth they themselves had once created.

The "nuanced picture" of young people

We have been using the available data to examine whether young Japanese have become "inward-looking." But, in the end, my analyses have yielded nothing but vague conclusions. Although it can't be said that young people are "inward-looking" to the extent the world suggests, neither can it be said with finality that they are "outward-looking."

Though young people's desire to contribute to society is on the rise, in reality, they aren't really taking part in efforts to do so. In addition, the number of young people going to the polls to vote is continuing to decline without a doubt. Large-scale protest demonstrations don't take place either. So all that fretting in the newspaper editorials is understandable.[160/★51]

Even though it can be said that, compared to the bubble period, the number of students studying abroad has increased, these past several years have seen a precipitous decline in the figure, and I feel the downward trend is likely to continue. Even the number of youngsters taking part in the working holiday scheme is remaining stagnant. In gross terms, the number of twenty-somethings departing for overseas destinations has undeniably decreased.

But even if you stick to the argument that the number of young people traveling overseas hasn't actually decreased from the past, you will still have no grounds for claiming that young people are, therefore, not "inward-looking." Even if you combined the number of students studying abroad and the number of young people traveling abroad on a working-holiday visa, the total wouldn't even reach 100,000. Roughly speaking, this adds up to a ratio of 1 in 200.

---

159. In terms of population volume, the number of twenty-somethings in the early 1980s wasn't that large. So, to be precise, it is believed that the influence of the "youth festival," which has been going on since the late 1970s, has been significant.

160. Incidentally, the *Mainichi Shimbun*, in its editorial, had expressed concern over young people's lack of engagement with politics, and had even put together a special feature titled "Demo shinai wakamono-tachi" (Young people stay away from demonstrations; March 1, 2011, evening edition), but when a 10,000-person-strong anti-nuclear demonstration took place in Koenji, the paper didn't report the event at all.

★51. As I point out in chapter 4, protest demonstrations became a routine spectacle after 2011. Even the media these days will gladly cover demonstrations led by young people, including those carried out by SEALDs.

The number of youths demonstrating an attachment to their place of birth is also on the rise, and the population migrating to large metropolitan areas is dwindling. However, young people attending upper-ranking schools continue to aim for admission to well-known universities located in urban areas. Thus, you cannot make the sweeping generalization that young people are, as a rule, "inclined toward living in their hometowns."

Even with regard to consumption, though there's no denying that the number of young people buying cars is dwindling, young people don't skimp on the goods and products they desire. In fact, compared to other generations, their appetite for consumption is even greater in certain respects. However, it is also true that the nature of the consumption trend has shifted from an "outward-looking" one to an "inward-looking" one.

How should I put it? It's really a fine line. Depending on your interpretation of the data, you can conclude that young people are "inward-looking" or "not inward-looking." Surely, this nuanced picture is one of the reasons we find the image of young people so confusing.

But for the time being, I'll be evasive and just say that, while young people can be said to be inward-looking, they aren't as inward-looking as they're said to be, and it's not that they have suddenly become inward-looking within the past several years. In the next section, I'll draw an additional auxiliary line of analysis called "consummatorization" to improve a little on this argument.

5. The "Happy" Youth of Japan

Ever-growing level of satisfaction with life

Starting around 2005, various media outlets began to feature close-up accounts of "unhappy youth" or "pitiful youth"; such stories would cover the incessantly rising level of irregular employment; how the working poor were working for low wages; how the job-hunting front was getting harsher and harsher; and the emergence of "net-café refugees," the modern incarnation of the homeless.

But to those who are convinced of this image of "unhappy youth," I have some surprising data for you—data which I myself found in a certain book.[161] Since everyone was jumping at the chance to take a look at it, I've passed it around to all sorts of people myself. Yuki Honda (forty-five years old at the time, Tokushima) was also surprised.

For some reason, youngsters today apparently feel they're happy. According to multiple public opinion polls, many modern youth feel satisfied with their present life. What's more, their level of satisfaction is higher than that seen in any other time: higher than in the 1970s, when young people were apparently energetic; higher than in the 1980s, when the *shinjinrui* (new species) were making strides; higher than in the 1990s, when society was still in a festive mood, despite suffering from the burst of the economic bubble.

According to the Cabinet Office's the *Public Opinion Survey on the Life of the People*, as of 2010, 65.9 percent of males in their twenties and 75.2 percent of females in their twenties reported being "satisfied" with their current lives.[162] Despite being told so much that we live in a socially polarized society, and that young people are an unhappy lot, approximately 70 percent of today's twenty-somethings are satisfied with life. The level of satisfaction among males in particular has risen by nearly 15 percent in the past forty years (figure 2.11).[★52]

In the late 1960s, when the period of high economic growth was supposedly still underway, the life satisfaction level of young people in their twenties was around 60 percent. In the 1970s, there was even a year in which this level fell as low as around 50 percent. But by the late 1990s, surveys indicated it had bounced back to 70 percent. So modern-day youth apparently feel "happier" than the young people of the past.

A similar trend can be confirmed in the survey on Japanese value orientations conducted by the NHK Broadcasting Culture Research Institute. In response to the question, "At present, how happy are you?" the number of individuals answering "I am satisfied" doubled over the period between 1973 to 2008. Even in the *World Youth Survey* and the *Chūgakusei kōkōsei no seikatsu to ishiki chōsa* (Survey on the way of life and attitudes of junior and senior high school students), the level of well-being rises the closer we approach the 2000s.[★53]

In addition, if we examine the life satisfaction level by well-being and generation, we see that the numerical values are lower for middle-aged individuals—specifically for

---

161.   Shūji Toyoizumi, *Wakamono no tame no shakaigaku* (Sociology for young people), Seiunsha, 2010. I have referred to this book for descriptions of happiness found in this chapter. It was written by someone who has been originally studying apparently esoteric thinkers such as Habermas and Arendt, so there are a few places I'm not quite able to follow, but of the books on young people that have appeared in recent times, this is among the better ones.

162.   An aggregation of "I am satisfied" and "I am somewhat satisfied." With regard to surveys on "Japanese attitudes" also, the study shows throughout its text the aggregate values of "I am satisfied" and "I am somewhat satisfied." But even if we limit our examination of changes strictly to "I am satisfied," we can confirm a similar upward trend.

★52.   In the *2015 Public Opinion Survey on the Life of the People*, 79.3 percent of twenty-somethings (74.7 percent male, 83.6 percent female) responded, "I am satisfied." This means that within the span of these five years, the level of satisfaction had risen by nearly 10 percent.

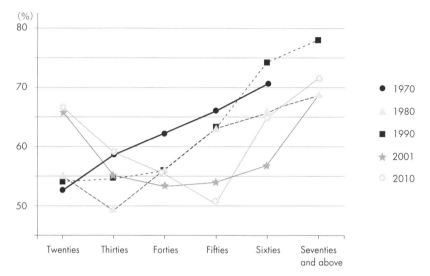

Figure 2.11   Changes in life satisfaction levels by age (men)[163]

those in their forties and fifties. So, as it turns out, those who were worried, saying that young people were unhappy, were themselves greatly unhappy.

I'm not dissatisfied, but I'm worried

But the story doesn't end with the epiphany, "Oh I see, so the youngsters are happy. Great! Let's move on." Some available data does call into question whether young people are actually happy.

In the previously mentioned the *Public Opinion Survey Concerning People's Life-styles*, another question asked with respect to the life satisfaction level was, "In the course of your daily living, do you ever feel worried or anxious?" According to the

---

★53.   According to the survey conducted by the NHK Broadcasting Culture Research Institute in 2012, a whopping 94percent of junior high students and 97 percent of high school students responded that they were "happy." Before long, the percentage of students answering "I am very happy" increased too; by 2012, the percentage of junior high students and high school students answering "I am very happy" had risen to 55 percent and 42 percent respectively from 1982, when the percentage of junior high students answering "I am very happy" was 36 percent, and the percentage of high school students answering the same was 24 percent. Compared to those in their twenties, these young people are likely apt to feel more happy, having fewer points of contact with society (NHK Broadcasting Culture Research Institute, *NHK chūgakusei, kōkōsei no seikatsu to ishiki chōsa, 2012* [The 2012 survey on the way of life and attitudes of junior and senior high school students], NHK Publishing, 2013).

163.   In the surveys carried out in 1970, there was no category for "Seventy years old or above"; it was just "sixty years old or above," so the values in the diagram referring to people in their sixties actually refers to all respondents above sixty. The *Public Opinion Survey on the Life of the People* was not carried out in 2000 for some reason, so 2001 values are shown.

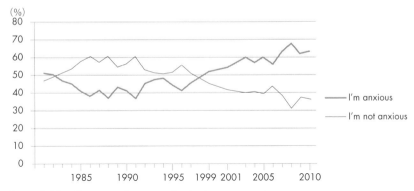

Figure 2.12   Changes in the anxiety levels of twenty-somethings

survey carried out in 2010, 63.1 percent of twenty-somethings said they did feel worried or anxious.★54

When examining the shifts in the levels of anxiety after the 1980s, as can be confirmed by the responses to the same question, the percentage of twenty-somethings who answered "I am worried" was under 40 percent in the late 1980s, but began to rise from the early 1990s after the end of the bubble period, reaching 67.3 percent in 2008. Meanwhile, the percentage of twenty-somethings responding "I have no worries" has been seeing a constant downward trend after the collapse of the bubble economy (figure 2.12).

So more than half of all young people say they feel happy while simultaneously feeling anxious. What on earth does this mean?

In addition, when young people are asked weighty questions, their anxieties become clear. According to the *kokusai hikaku chōsa* (cross-national comparative research) carried out by the Japan Youth Research Institute, in response to the statement, "The twenty-first century will bring about societies filled with hope for all humankind," 62.1 percent of Japanese youths said, "I don't think so." Relative to other countries, this numerical value expresses an extraordinary level of despair.

Furthermore, the level of satisfaction registered in response to the weighty question, "Are you satisfied with your country's society?" was much lower than the reported level of life satisfaction, which is a less weighty metric, relatively speaking.

According to the *World Youth Survey*, as of 2008, the overall level of satisfaction

---

★54.   According to the 2015 survey, 60 percent of twenty-somethings reported feeling "anxious." Although the level of life satisfaction rose, the percentage of people feeling "anxious" apparently did not increase. In fact, "anxious" leveled off among all generations.

with the society of one's own country was 43.9 percent. The level of dissatisfaction for the same, on the other hand, amounted to 54.1 percent. With the satisfaction level in the United States registering at 67.6 percent, and the satisfaction level in the U.K. registering at 61.2 percent, Japan turns out to be the second-worst country in terms of satisfaction levels among the five countries targeted for comparison.★[55]

The level of satisfaction with society peaked at 51.3 percent in 1988, around the eve of the bubble era. As if synchronized with the period of high economic growth in Japan, the level of satisfaction with society had risen to this point from 25.9 percent registered in 1972, when the survey was launched. But from the time of the 1993 survey, the satisfaction level begins to decline.

It all starts to look like a jigsaw puzzle at this point, so let me try to clarify by putting the findings in order here. The figures expressing young people's satisfaction with life and their level of happiness have been, for the most part, optimal values to date over the past forty years. Despite being told that we live in a time of social and inter-generational polarization and rising irregular employment, young people feel themselves, at present, to be "happy."

On the other hand, the percentage of young people feeling anxious about life is just as high. And for the number of young people who have hopes for the future and are satisfied with society is low.

Now, how should we interpret these findings?

The true character of "happy" young people

Former Kyoto University professor Masachi Ōsawa (fifty-two years old, Nagano) has drawn the following inferences about the mindset of the survey respondents.[164] At what kind of time does a person answer, "I'm unhappy now," "I'm not satisfied with my life now"? According to Ōsawa, it's when a person can think that they are unhappy right now, but expect to become happier in the future.

This is because, for those people who still see possibilities remaining in their lives for the future, or those who are hopeful about what may be in store in their lives ahead,

---

★55. In the *Wagakuni to shogaikoku no wakamono no ishiki ni kansuru chōsa* (Survey on attitudes of the young people of our country and various other countries), which was carried out in 2013, the level of satisfaction with Japanese society among Japanese youths had tanked to 31.5 percent. Except for France, this value is the lowest among the seven countries targeted by the survey. Incidentally, the best figure was the one for Germany's youth, at 72.1 percent. In addition, at 28.8 percent, Japan had the smallest percentage of young people who answered, "I believe my country's future is bright."

164. Masachi Ōsawa, "Kanō naru kakumei dai-ikkai 'Kōfuku da' to kotaeru wakamono-tachi no jidai" (The first possible revolution: The era of youths who answer that they are "happy") in *at+* no. 7, 2011. Professor Ōsawa's astonishment at "happy youths" is overblown.

saying "I'm unhappy now" doesn't mean that they're completely rejecting themselves.

Conversely, when a person is unable to believe that they will ever be any happier than they feel at present, they cannot but answer, "I'm happy with my life now." In other words, Ōsawa says, when a person no longer has hope for their future, they answer, "I am happy now," "I am satisfied with my life now."

In reality, in many surveys, it is common to find high happiness and life satisfaction levels among the elderly. On the surface, it seems odd that an elderly person whose physical fitness has waned is more satisfied with his or her present life than a person who is still young. However, the elderly can no longer conceive of a future in which they can be much happier than they are today. And that's why they have no other option but to respond, "I am satisfied with my life right now."

Corroborating Ōsawa's opinion is the fact that oftentimes it is generally during dark times, such as during a recession, when life satisfaction levels of twenty-somethings rise (figure 2.13). For example, the peak of life satisfaction in the 1980s occurred before the bubble, in 1985. The peak in the 1990s occurred in 1996, when the bubble economy had already ended—the year after the Aum Shinrikyō incident and the Great Hanshin-Awaji Earthquake occurred. The peak of the 2000s occurred in 2006, when the discourse on social polarization became galvanized.

When people begin to think that tomorrow won't get any better than today, that's when they answer "I am happy at the present time." With this understanding, you can see why the life satisfaction levels of young people were low during the period of high economic growth and the bubble period. They were able to believe that tomorrow would be better than today. They were even hopeful that their lives would get steadily better. And that's why, even though they felt unhappy at present, they were still able to

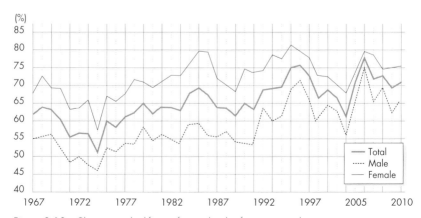

Figure 2.13   Changes in the life satisfaction levels of twenty-somethings

have hopes for their future, believing that someday they would find happiness.

For example, a certain twenty-year-old man who had come up to Tokyo from Akita (a prefecture in the Tohoku region) sometime in the 1950s on a group-employment program was working approximately ten hours every day at a car-maintenance factory. Being bad-mouthed, bullied, and harassed by his senior colleagues was a daily occurrence. Developing an inferiority complex because of his Akita accent, he rarely went out on his days off, and never made any friends. While his life was hellish, his only comfort was his faith in the idea that after all this hardship, he would surely begin to see a bright future.[165]

However, today's youth can no longer naively believe that tomorrow will get better. What lies before them is nothing more than the "eternal everyday"—which is the very reason they can say "I'm happy at the present time." In other words, when people lose hope for the future, they can become "happy."[★56]

The emergence of consummatory young people

The real nature, or true character, of happy youths can be explained by the term "consummatory." Just think of it as a word meaning self-sufficient or self-contained, rooted in a sensibility that values an intimate kind of happiness found in the here and now.

It can also be paraphrased as a way of life that prioritizes relaxing in and enjoying the company of friends, as opposed to pushing yourself for achieving some kind of goal.[166] What I'm basically driving at here is that it can be said—couldn't it?—that the true nature of "happy young people," or what's behind their emergence, is the increase in the number of young people who are able to feel they are really very happy at the present moment, instead of living for a future in which they assume happier things are in store for them.[167]

With this understanding, you can see why young people's satisfaction levels fall when you ask them about weighty big-picture subjects like "society," compared to lighter small-scale subjects like "satisfaction with everyday living." Though they are

---

165. Susumu Sasaki, *Shūdan shūshoku sedai ga Nihon o sukutta!* (The generation of en-masse employment has saved Japan!), Tokyo Tosho Shuppan Kai, 2010. A self-published work, this book's prose lacks finesse to a surprising degree, but on the flip side, its artlessness strikes a chord.

★56. To this day, I remain attracted to this view, but at the same time, research findings opposing this hypothesis have also been released. For details, refer to this chapter's postscript.

166. Originally a concept put forth by Talcott Parsons, a sociologist of old, it is used here to connote a meaning close to "self-satisfaction" (Ryōzō Takeda, translation supervisor, *Shakai kōzō to pāsonariti [shinpan]* [Social structure and personality (new edition)], Shinsensha, 2001). For a reference on "young people becoming consummatory," you will find no better source than Shūji Toyoizumi's *Wakamono no tame no shakaigaku* (Sociology for young people; Seiunsha, 2010). Among other works of its kind, this one is the most skillfully organized.

dissatisfied with "society," which is a large-scale world of its own, they are satisfied with their own smaller self-contained world.

In reality, this phenomenon of becoming self-contained, or consummatory, didn't begin suddenly in recent years. Researchers of several decades ago have also pointed out a similar trend.

In 1970s Japan, industrialization advanced, satisfying materialistic desires for commodities such as food, clothing, and shelter in the process. It was the economist Yasusuke Murakami (forty-four years old, Tokyo) who pointed out that people in such a situation, don't go on to work hard and become thrifty in order to pursue economic affluence, but instead adopt behaviors reflecting consummatory values.[168]

The youth researchers of that time also made similar remarks. The sociologist Akira Hamashima (forty-seven years old, Tokyo) pointed out that affluent societies give birth to youths who immerse themselves in the familiar "here and now" instead of investing their time in some far-off future.[169] He said that in times when people lose their common goals and sense of purpose in life, young people begin to harbor feelings of helplessness and indifference toward politics, and recluses—those individuals who withdraw into their private lives—emerge. A know-it-all pundit of our times might say something similar.

The same applies to the 1980s, just prior to the advent of the bubble economy. Tetsuya Chikushi (forty-nine years old, Oita), in referring to young people of that time, pointed out that a particular kind of youth was beginning to prevail—the kind who was oriented toward his or her immediate surroundings; whose field of vision never went beyond a radius of two meters.[170] This isn't strange, given that the pattern

---

167.   For example, even in the 2010 *Nihonjin no jōhō kōdō chōsa* (2010 survey on the information behavior of the Japanese), the percentage of those who answered, "I'm more interested in events that take place in my small, personal circle of people than in events that take place in '*seken*' [society at large]" was higher the younger the age group was, registering at 79.4 percent among tweens and teenagers, and at 74.3 percent among twenty-somethings. The ratio was 57.5 percent among people in their fifties, and 50.6 percent among people in their sixties (Yoshiaki Hashimoto, *Media to Nihonjin* [Media and the Japanese], Iwanami Shoten, 2011). However, you need to be wary of the wording when reading such statistics. According to the *Public Opinion Survey on Social Awareness*, there has been a rise in the number of society-oriented youths, as mentioned above. However, even in this survey, if you rephrase the multiple-choice response to "more interested in personal matters than in *sekai* and *shakai* [world and society]" the results may change drastically. In sum, the word "*seken*" (society), compared to "*sekai*" (world) and "*shakai*" (another word for society), is lackluster.

168.   Yasusuke Murakami, *Sangyō shakai no byōri* (The pathology of industrial society), Chuokoron-Shinsha, 2010. The first edition came out in 1975.

169.   Akira Hamashima, "Gendai shakai to seinensō" (Modern society and the rising generation) in *Gendai seinen-ron* (Contemporary youth theory) edited by Akira Hamashima, Yuhikaku Publishing, 1973. This book reveals how the field of "youth theory" has failed to achieve any considerable progress for the past forty years.

of the youth narrative, which had been ongoing since around 1970, was nearing completion, as I stated in chapter 1.

Either way, there is no mistaking that Japan had arrived at a turning point around 1973, when the period of high economic growth—a time when economic development was critical—had come to a close, and the negative aspects of the economic growth, such as environmental pollution, had surfaced, and when the oil shock was shifting the growth in a negative direction. In this sense, it can be said that Japanese society began to gradually develop into a self-contained, or consummatory, society from the 1970s.

However, this does not mean that the 1970s seamlessly transitioned into the 2010s. The 1970s and the 1980s, it can be said, were an age of meritocracy[171] and systemization, an age that saw the whole of Japan fall under the spell of the middle-class dream of "the good school, good company, and good life," as symbolized by the exam wars that peaked in the 1980s. It was a time when even young people with a consummatory sense of values would graduate from their youth by working as a wage slave in a company.

However, after the 1990s, when the middle-class dream collapsed and the number of young people who didn't become card-carrying members of companies increased, the number of youth who could indefinitely remain consummatory is believed to have also increased.

What's more, during the period after the 1990s, which is considered to be the "lost twenty years," life satisfaction sees a sudden rise for some reason.

Now let me draw another line of analysis to shed more light on the reason why modern youths are happy. That line is "friends."

6. Tribal Youth

Invincible in the company of friends

What turned out to be remarkable after the 1990s was the fact that the role of peers

---

170.   Tetsuya Chikushi et al., *Wakamono-tachi no kamigami 1* (The gods of young people 1), Shinchosha, 1987. First edition, 1984.
171.   "Meritocracy" refers to a structure that empowers people to govern society not through leveraging social status or lineage, but through leveraging "individual ability." In Japanese this term is often translated as *gyōseki shugi* (achievement-based principle). Its nuance approaches "education-driven society" or "examination rat-race society."

and friends, to young people, increased in importance. In the *Kokumin seikatsu senkō-do chōsa* (National survey of lifestyle preferences) carried out by the cabinet office, respondents were asked to rate their level of happiness on a scale of one to ten, and to indicate items that mattered when judging their level of happiness.[172] The results showed that, in response to the latter, surprisingly, 60.4 percent of young people between fifteen and twenty-nine had answered, "relationships with friends," a figure that proved to be significantly higher compared with other generations.[173]

In response to the question, "At what times do you feel a sense of fulfillment or sense of purpose in life?" the number of youths answering "When I'm with my peers or friends" is also on the upswing.[174] In 1970, the percentage of people reporting a sense of fulfillment when together with peers or friends was 38.8 percent, but in 1980 this figure rose all the way up to 58.8 percent, increasing to 64.1 percent in 1990 and stabilizing at around 74 percent after 1998. This value, even when seen from a global perspective, is high.[175/★57]

Speaking of young people valuing their peers and friends, the man who coined the buzzword of 2010 comes to mind. Yūki Saitō (twenty-two years old, Gumma), who was the captain of Waseda University's baseball club, voiced the following signature remark when his team scored a decisive victory in the last season of the Tokyo Big Six Baseball League. "I have been told over and over again that I have something special. Today I affirmed just exactly what that something is . . . it's friends."

This line is too long for a buzzword, and I have no idea where it began to catch on, but as words symbolic of modern youth, none are more deserving of being enshrined in popular culture.[176/★58] What's interesting, too, is that with slight alterations to the text, this line would sound like something said in the manga series *One Piece.* The theme run-

---

172.   Cabinet Office, *Kokumin seikatsu senkōdo chōsa 2010-nen* (National survey of lifestyle preferences, Fiscal Year 2010).

173.   Among citizens as a whole, the top priority was "health situation," registering at 69.7 percent; people responding "relationships with friends" ranked sixth in importance, accounting for 38.5 percent. While the question categories are different, in the survey on attitudes conducted by sociologists in 1968, more than 60 percent of people between fifteen and twenty-nine answered that "health" was "the most important thing"; compared with other responses, such as "love" and "freedom," the percentage is noticeably higher (Munesuke Mita, *Gendai no seinen-zō* [A contemporary portrait of youth], Kodansha, 1968).

174.   Mamoru Yamada, "Wakamono bunka no sekishutsu to yūkai" (Separation and fusion of youth culture) in *Kōza shakaigaku 7: Bunka* (Sociology lecture 7: Culture) edited by Takashi Miyajima, University of Tokyo Press, 2000.

175.   Cabinet Office, the *Eighth World Youth Survey, 2009.*

★57.   In the *Wagakuni to shogaikoku no wakamono no ishiki ni kansuru chōsa* (Survey on attitudes of the young people of our country and various other countries), 80.3 percent of young people reported feeling a sense of fulfillment "when I'm together with friends and peers." However, among those with partners, 89.8 percent answered, "when I'm together with my lover."

ning throughout that modern-day scripture, whose total circulation exceeds 200 million copies, can be summed up as "Living for friends."[177]/[★59] In *One Piece* the pursuit of self-interest is disdained in favor of devotion to friends. In a world where villains aren't black and white, where absolute evil is nonexistent, Luffy (nineteen years old, Foosha Village) and his mates continue to persevere in their endless quest of searching for friends.

This situation applies to real-life youth. In a time when "youth culture" is said to no longer exist, the quick and easy way to affirm that one is not alone is to be physically together with friends. The sociologist Mamoru Yamada (thirty-eight years old), points out that youths of the present age have come to seek the basis of their identity in "the very act of taking part in various relationships and groups," such as in close human relations.[178]

This stance of valuing such close friendships may appear, from the outside, to be inward-looking. In fact, Yamada fears that these relationships between youths may "spiral backward into a closed, exclusionary colony," adding that, in reality, youth who value friends in the community to which they belong are reminiscent of the inhabitants of a tribal village society.

But no one is describing Saitō or the straw-hatted pirate crew in *One Piece* as "inward-looking." That's because, everyone is aware of the great achievements of these individuals. As the sociologist Shinji Miyadai (thirty-five years old, Miyagi) once pointed out, one peer group—an insular "island universe"—is hard to see from other insular "island universes."[179]

---

176. On the Internet, someone ridiculed the line, remarking, "What he has is a handkerchief, right?" He went on to acquire the nickname "Handkerchief Prince" on account of the fact that he used one to wipe away his sweat as he stood on the pitcher's mound.

★58. I wonder if his friends are still supportive of him today, as his performance failed to meet the high expectations people had set for him when he joined the professional league.

177. Tatsuru Uchida, "Machiba no *One Piece*-ron 1: 'Ryūdō suru mono' e no hitamukina shinrai" (Streetside *One Piece* theory 1: Single-minded faith in "all things that flow") in *ONE PIECE STRONG WORDS* by Eiichirō Oda, Shueisha, 2011.

★59. With the aggregate worldwide circulation of *One Piece* in 2013 exceeding 300 million copies, the achievement was entered into the Guinness Book of World Records as the greatest circulation of a work by a single author. The reason behind the caveat of the "single author" descriptor is probably because the number-one worldwide bestseller is the (genuine) Holy Bible. However, the circulation of *One Piece* keeps growing, and the more it does, the closer it gets to the Bible.

178. Mamoru Yamada, "Wakamono bunka no sekishutsu to yūkai" (Separation and fusion of youth culture) in *Kōza shakaigaku 7: Bunka* (Sociology lecture 7: Culture) edited by Takashi Miyajima, University of Tokyo Press, 2000. However, it's debatable whether young people today are actually unaware of themselves as a generation. For instance, I believe that the "*yutori sedai*" (the generation that received a form of relaxed education) is a point of reference for the identity of many of these young people. That being said, perhaps what makes it different today, relative to the time when there was said to be a youth culture, is the fact that this point of reference serves as just one of the many anchors of identity.

179. Shinji Miyadai, *Seifuku shōjo-tachi no sentaku* (The choices of girls in uniform), Asahi Shimbun Publications, 2006. The first edition came out in 1994. Recently, the term "cluster" is often used as a close substitute to the concept of "island universe."

In this sense, concluding one-sidedly that young people are inward-looking is, it can be said, something akin to a lament arising from an ignorance of the "island universe" called young people. Because, in my eyes, the so-called fathers—those who have worked in just one company after graduating from university, and who do nothing but take part, day in and day out, in the rat race, and who have no awareness of hobbies outside of golf and mahjong—are considerably more inward-looking.

As long as we get together, we're happy

Young people: they're like tribal villagers, spending their days in a small world of friends. This is the very essence of the reason behind the happiness of young people living in the present age.

In sociology this is called relative deprivation, calling attention to the fact that often-times people measure their happiness in the context of the standard set by the group to which they belong. For example, if someone working part-time at a convenience store for an hourly wage of 900 yen noticed that a co-worker whose job was identical to hers was nonetheless receiving 980 yen per hour, she would lose her cool and probably say to herself something like, "What a jerk! He's doing the same work as I am, so why does he earn an extra eighty yen an hour? Is he the store manager's favorite or something?"

But when this same person looks at a glamorous celebrity earning an annual income of several billions of yen, though she might feel a crush on them, she wouldn't ever seriously compare herself to the star, because to her—a convenience-store clerk—the celebrity is a person of another world.

For the same reason, the level of life satisfaction tends to rise during a recession. When the economy of the entire country is gloomy, everyone is troubled, so an individual doesn't feel deprived. But when the economy improves, prosperous individuals appear around you, and since expectations for the future are heightened, even if your income goes up slightly, you will nevertheless feel deprived.★[60]

That's why, as long as young people go on living in the small world of the here and now, no matter how poor the world becomes, no matter how serious the generation gap proves to be, their happiness will remain intact.

If the measure of their happiness is based on having friends who belong to the same small world they belong to, the world outside of this circle of friends is irrelevant, no matter what the situation.

★60. It is known that in many countries around the world, economic growth contributes to a decrease in the level of people's well-being. This is called the "unhappy growth paradox" (Atsushi Ishida, *Sōtaiteki hakudatsu no shakaigaku* [Sociology of relative deprivation], University of Tokyo Press, 2015).

Thus, what took place in the 1990s was not so much the emergence of "island universes," but rather, more appropriately, the collapse of society—a relapse, as it were, to a time before the mass media prevailed, when people had no choice but to live in "island universes" called small villages.

If there is a distinguishing characteristic of the "island universes" appearing after the 1990s, it's that this thing called society—a nationwide consensus fueled by TV and magazine outlets whose significance peaked in the 1970s and the 1980s—had begun to gradually collapse.

In a time when society no longer serves as a reference group, the small world called the "island universe" becomes everything. Young people, without thinking that tomorrow will be better than today, live in the here and now with their friends. In other words, they're happy because they're gathered together.

From tribal comfort to restlessness

Young people, while treasuring their peers and friends, live in village-like communities. But this state of congregating and coming together, of milling about and mixing around, doesn't last for long.

This is because, first of all, groups of peers and friends are far more fragile than collectives that are mediated by the rule of law, such as families and companies.

And when the days spent with a group of the same old friends lasts for too long, young people, at times, begin to feel a sense of entrapment. This is because, unlike Saitō, who has the goal of becoming number one in Japan, and the straw-hatted pirates for whom every day is an adventure, to many people, living with friends is a boring, everyday affair in which nothing happens. What expresses this youth scene well is the song titled "SEASONS" by Ayumi Hamasaki (twenty-one years old, Fukuoka).[180]

> *I had given up, feeling something a little amiss in the days that kept repeating themselves; I had told myself, before I even tried, that it's the fault of the strange, unnatural times we live in.*

---

180.   Ayumi Hamasaki, "SEASONS" (2000). The trajectory of her songs overlaps with the trends of the times (as they have been depicted by the media). At the time of her debut, she sang about things like lacking a sense of belonging, and a quotidian feeling of hopelessness, but in 2004 she loudly extolled the virtues of neoliberalism ("INSPIRE"). She then started talking about an entrepreneurial sort of "creative disruption" (2007's "talkin' 2 myself"). Nonetheless, recently she has appeared to finally settle on the subject of "love" (2010's "Virgin Road").[★61]

★61.   Subsequent releases include "You & Me" (2012), which tells of summer memories; "Last Minute" (2014), about parting with a loved one; and "Story" (2015), about a sworn meeting in "the next life." The "love" theme remains unchanged throughout.

When I talk to young people around age twenty, I often hear the lines, "I want to do something," and "It's wrong to keep on going like this."

Hiroaki Ishimatsu (twenty-one years old, Oita), who launched the volunteer group GRAPHIS in 2005 to support relief efforts in Cambodia, was feeling that something was missing in his college life of picking up girls and attending mixers day in and day out.[181] While he said he had fun leading the playboy life, the feeling that something was lacking only kept growing inside him. So, it seems that even *riajū* (people leading fulfilling real lives, as opposed to online ones) experience ennui.

It was in these circumstances that Ishimatsu was invited, through a friend, to take a look at a proposed plan to build an elementary school in Cambodia, to which he immediately responded, "I'll do it, I'll do it!" adding, "I've finally found something I can truly devote myself to."

This action taken by Ishimatsu holds the key to understanding the patterns of youth behavior. For example, why is it that, even though statistically the number of young people who long to make contributions to society has continued to rise, the number of them actually taking part in activities that could help them do just that hasn't increased as much? Why is the youth voter turnout continuing to fall?

The answer lies in the fact that there are no readily available, attractive, and easy-to-find avenues that can help youths break away from their cooped-up sense of entrapment.[182]

They will say, "I want to do something; it's wrong to keep on going like this, but I don't know what to do." So if they can find answers—that is, avenues, or clear-cut reasons to become restless and take action—they will wholeheartedly swing open the doors.

As I discuss in detail in chapter 5, the earthquake-disaster volunteers are emblematic of this. If something appears that is so extraordinary as to change the dull, everyday lives of youths, and if a channel linking the "extraordinary" to their ordinary daily existence is secured, then even they, who are supposedly inward-looking, will be galvanized into action.★[62]

So in this sense, young people can be considered to be *muramura*—seized with a

---

181.   Hiroaki Ishimatsu, *Maji de gachi na borantia*, (Seriously earnest volunteers), Kodansha, 2009.

182.   According to the 2010 *Nihonjin no jōhō kōdō chōsa* (2010 survey on the information behavior of the Japanese), people who responded "politics are too difficult for me to understand" accounted for 71.4 percent of teenagers and 65.3 percent of people in their twenties (Yoshiaki Hashimoto, *Media to Nihonjin* [Media and the Japanese], Iwanami Shoten, 2011). Yeah, politics are definitely too difficult. Even when there are things in the world we can't agree with, like TEPCO or nuclear power, we still remain clueless as to what, specifically, should be done about such problems.

restless desire to take action.[183] In effect, while holding on to the restlessness of wanting to make a difference, young people just go on getting together with like-minded individuals and keep having the same kinds of exchanges, over and over again. And if something extraordinary comes their way—something so extraordinary that it motivates them to break away from their tribal comfort zone—they'll get restless and take the plunge into the world of this extraordinary something.

But this state of restlessness, this state of being seized by the desire to take action, fails to endure. That's because no matter how extraordinary it may be, before long the extraordinary will go on to become the ordinary, and will sink into the fabric of everyday life.

So the extraordinary is, to the young people who cluster together, something like a tribal festival. In the next chapter, we'll consider the relationship between youth and Japan as a nation, turning to the World Cup for clues, a once-in-four-year tribal festival for youth.

Postscript: Hope and Despair in 2015

The most frequently referenced part of the hardcover edition of *The Happy Youth of a Desperate Country* is the argument that appears in this chapter. In particular, the claim that young people are happy seems to have shocked many adults.

Until this claim was made, in Japan, the argument that young people are unhappy was popular. As evidenced in buzzwords like *hikikomori* (people withdrawing from society), NEET (those Not in Education, Employment or Training), *freeter* (job-hopping part-timer), and working poor, "young people" had become a byword for the weak or the underdogs. Amid the firm entrenchment of such conventional wisdom,

---

★62. The sense of danger arising from having a peaceful "ordinary life" threatened, and of being caught up in something "extraordinary" called war, might be one of the things that motivated the young people of SEALDs to protest. That being said, those who volunteered after the Great East Japan earthquake, and those who participated in protests against nuclear power and the security bill, account for just one segment of "young people" as a whole.

183. This expression was put forward in Noritoshi Furuichi's *Kibō nanmin goikkō sama* (A party of hope refugees; Kobunsha, 2010), but it was splendidly ignored by everyone and never became topical. It's no exaggeration to say that this chapter was written for the sole purpose of emphasizing this expression.[★63]

★63. But I now see that such a phrase could never become popular. I wonder what drove me to lean on it so heavily four years ago. Every time I'm told, during an interview for example, something along the lines of "The phrase *muramura* [clannish] youths appears in your book…" I cry out in my heart, "Stop! You're embarrassing me."

the assertion itself that young people were happy was perhaps reflective of something close to a kind of moral panic.[★64]

For someone championing a line of thought like "Young people are unhappy, that's why social reform is necessary," the claim that young people are happy must have been an inconvenience. However, as mentioned many times in this book, the fact that young people's level of subjective satisfaction is high doesn't in any way contradict the fact that they are relatively miserable in society.

I myself can't count the number of times I was approached by the media with the question, "Are young people really happy?" The science of happiness, or eudemonics, must have been an easy theme to cover. It was also a time when the government had set up the *Kōfukudo ni kansuru kenkyūkai* (commission on measuring well-being), drawing attention to the world's happiest country, Bhutan.

But I am against supporting the building of one kind of social system over another on the grounds of whether people are "happy" or "unhappy." For example, there is a study that shows that people can be happy even in poverty, as long as human relations are favorable.[★65] But would applying this finding to a governmental policy really be an appropriate step to take? For instance, wouldn't there be something terribly dystopic about the government providing a welfare recipient not with money, but a friend instead?

Whenever monetary wealth disappears, the state often begins to toss around words like "happiness." Even Bhutan, the world's happiest country, is a far cry from being a utopia, having, in fact, produced many refugees.[★66]

I have tried as much as possible to take a look at texts that were critical of this book;[★67] the most controversial ones I came across addressed the passages I wrote in reference to Masachi Ōsawa's theory: "When people can no longer imagine a future that sees them happier than they are now, that's when the level of happiness goes up"; "When people lose hope for the future, they find happiness."[★68]

★64. "Moral panic" is a concept proposed by the British sociologist Stanley Cohen (thirty-one years old, Johannesburg); it refers to agitations arising from a rejection of any phenomenon appearing to disturb the existing social order. Initially the word was coined to describe the overreaction of the media against out-of-control youths.

★65. Hiroshi Hamada, "Mazushikutemo kōfuku o kanjiru koto ga dekiruka" (Can you feel happy even if you're poor?) in *Sōsharu kyapitaru to kakusa shakai* (Social capital and the gap-widening society) edited by Ryūhei Tsuji and Yoshimichi Satō, University of Tokyo Press, 2014.

★66. Kaoru Nemoto, *Būtan "kōfukuna kuni" no futsugō na shinjitsu* (The inconvenient truth about Bhutan, the "land of happiness"), Kawade Shobo Shinsha, 2012.

★67. But I rarely get contacted, so I can't say that I've checked everything. I wonder how my colleagues go about checking—or whether they do it in the first place.

The criticisms made by the psychiatrist Tamaki Saitō (fifty-two years old, Iwate) struck me as worthy of heeding closely.[*69] Saitō's criticisms mainly rested on the following three points: 1. It is normal to think that the state of being able to have hope is happiness itself, with the concepts of "hope" and "happiness" being difficult to distinguish; 2. The research on unhappy youth in this book falls short; and 3. To begin with, for young people, the meaning of the words "happiness" and "hope" are qualitatively changing.

It is true that this book contains only a few references to unhappy youth.[*70] Admittedly, in the short term the rate of suicides among young people has seen a rising trend,[*71] and the unemployment rate, compared to other generations, is high.

However, what does Saitō mean when he says "happiness" and "hope" are qualitatively changing? According to Saitō's experience as a clinician, the vocabulary of young people nowadays for talking about themselves is poor. And that's why, he says, they're terrible at talking about unhappiness. While you don't need reasons to explain happiness, you do need reasons to explain unhappiness. Thus, he says, young people end up answering that they're "happy for the time being."

According to Saitō, young people don't answer that they're "happy at the present time" out of any sense of despair, but rather because they have given up on change. Saitō's claim, in effect, is that the true character of happiness—its real nature—is grounded in the sense that one can't see oneself becoming happier or unhappier in the future.

While I can't agree that young people are terrible at talking about unhappiness, I can understand the assertion that, to young people, happiness and a sense of unchanging constancy are two sides of the same coin. In this book, whenever I touched on the idea of losing hope, I was implying a state of mind that dismissed the need to be conscious of hope itself.[*72] If "hope" is too strong a word, it might be better to restate the premise: resignation—rather than hope—is what makes people happy.

★68.   For example, as a critique against my argument, the sociologist Kunisuke Hamada put to me the assertion that the level of happiness falls as a person's ability to have hope for the future declines. However, in his study, as a substitute index for "hope," the following question is used: "In current Japanese society, how many opportunities are available to improve your and your family's standard of living?" I believe responding that there's "no hope" in this sense is not the same thing as saying there's "no hope" in my book. Nonetheless, I'm glad to receive such an analysis. For specifics, refer to Kunisuke Hamada's "Wakamono-tachi no shōrai fuan to kōfukukan" (Young people's angst and sense of well-being regarding their future) in *Gendai o ikiru wakamono-tachi* (Youth living in the modern age) edited by Masafumi Kimura, Gakubunsha, 2013.

★69.   Tamaki Saitō, *Shōnin o meguru yamai* (Illnesses that seek approval), Nippon Hyoron sha, 2013.

★70.   That's because this book was written to counter the "unhappy youth theories" popular in those days.

★71.   While the rate of youth suicides has increased relative to the bubble period, seen from a long-term perspective, it is on a downward trend. Prewar Japan was notorious for being a country with a high rate of youth suicides.

★72.   As a matter of fact, in this book, I never say that young people are in "despair."

If we take this discussion one step further, perhaps it can be said that the high level of life satisfaction seen among modern Japanese youth is symbolic of a kind of "culture of poverty."

At one time, the anthropologist Oscar Lewis (fifty-two years old, New York), while investigating slum areas, presented a concept he called the culture of poverty.[73] According to him, the culture of poverty is something like a defense mechanism used by poor people to survive. The term "poverty," in this context, rather than referring just to material poverty, refers to a sense of resignation to existing circumstances and to adapting to those circumstances.

The people within this culture of poverty have no hope, and live for the present, not the future. Without an international outlook, they accept fatalism, having given up on the future. In the same way, it can perhaps be said that the high level of life satisfaction among Japanese youths is attributable to the "culture of poverty."

Where Saitō's opinions and mine align is on the point that peers play an extremely important role in the analysis of the happiness and unhappiness of young people.

Truth be told, "hope" and "peers" are themes from my debut work, *Kibō nanmin goikkō sama* (A party of hope refugees).[74] Backed by the research I carried out on Peace Boat passengers, in this work I described the process of how "purposiveness" was tempered by the spirit of cooperation.[75] To sum up, I assume the following framework: When a "collective of approval" gets established, thereby enabling mutual approval among friends, people can go on living even if they lose hope.

If we interpret along the lines of this framework, the reason a person can be happy as long as they have friends is because the presence of friends allows them to give up hope. What I basically want to say here is that even when I was writing this book, I had been working from the tacit premise of this "cooperation" and "purposiveness" framework.[76]

One critic who has understood such a continuity from my previous work while writing a detailed review of this book is the sociologist Naoto Mori.[77] Mori, too, casts

---

★73. Oscar Lewis, author; Akio Namekata, Kenkichi Kamijima, translators, *Ra bīda* (original title: *La Vida; A Puerto Rican Family in the Culture of Poverty: San Juan and New York*), Misuzu Shobo, 1970.

★74. Noritoshi Furuichi, *Kibō nanmin goikkō sama* (A party of hope refugees), Kobunsha, 2010. This work feels more "youthful" than *Zetsubō no kuni no kōfuku na wakamono-tachi* (The Happy Youth of a Desperate Country). Really, I now feel that I should have just titled the book *"Kibō nanmin"* (Hope refugees).

★75. For a critique of this schema, you can turn to *Shōnin yokubō no shakai henkaku* (Social reform led by the desire to be recognized) by Takeshi Nishio, Ken'ichi Yamaguchi, and Wataru Kusaka (Kyoto University Press, 2015).

★76. I wondered what was the use of writing such a pointless thing, but anyone who got this far in the book must be a dedicated reader, so I wrote it down, just in case.

★77. http://d.hatena.ne.jp/morinaoto/20120307/p1—It was a superb review, mixed with irony, in the best tradition of a sociologist.

suspicion on the interpretation of this chapter as suggesting that when people are no longer able to picture a future in which they are happier than at present, the level of happiness, the sense of well-being, goes up.

As far as we can tell from the *Public Opinion Survey Concerning People's Lifestyles*, the level of life satisfaction of twenty-somethings is certainly seeing an upward trend. However, this fluctuation in satisfaction level is occurring in parallel with fluctuations seen across all generations. In particular, until the mid-1990s, the levels of satisfaction of the "twenty-something bracket" and "all generations" were the same (figure 2.14).

The life satisfaction level of "twenty-somethings" has indisputably risen since the mid-1990s, but according to Mori, there are two reasons that greatly influence this outcome, negating the apparent progress: namely, the postponement of milestone life events and changes in research methodology.

After the 1990s, the percentage of students in Japan pursuing higher education rose, and more and more people began to put off milestones such as employment and marriage until later in life. This change proved to have a great impact on the twenty-somethings of Japan.

Many of the twenty-somethings of earlier times considered being steadily employed as a matter of course, as well as getting married, having babies, and worrying over the purchase of a house and the educational expenses for their children. Rather than being "young people," they were, in effect, full-fledged adults.

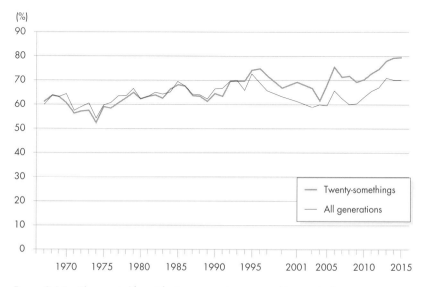

Figure 2.14   Changes in life satisfaction among twenty-somethings and all generations

In contrast, among the current twenty-somethings, there are those who continue to be students for a long time,[78] and experiencing childbirth and child care in one's thirties is steadily becoming the norm.

In other words, the meaning of "twenty-somethings" changed drastically over the course of these several decades.

In addition, the stance of the *Public Opinion Survey Concerning People's Lifestyles*, in asking about life satisfaction, had changed after 1992. The survey used to place the inquiry about how satisfied a respondent was with respect to his or her current life after highly detailed questions about the standard of living in their household. But after 1992, the question concerning life satisfaction appeared as the second item in the questionnaire. In other words, there is a subtle difference, it has been said, in the findings found between the surveys conducted after 1992 and those before 1992, when respondents had been describing their satisfaction in view of their various existing circumstances.[79]

Mori's explanation is extremely persuasive as a hypothesis explaining the rise in life satisfaction among twenty-somethings.[80]

Mori says that he had read *The Happy Youth of a Desperate Country* as a parody of *Shin chūkan taishū no jidai* (Era of new intermediate masses) by Yasusuke Murakami (fifty-three years old, Tokyo). Frankly, my intention didn't go as far as that. However, as Mori pointed out, I did certainly intend to show in this book, more than the concept of generationalism, the recognition that the problems of social divisions and poverty will grow in importance.

Such critical thinking has been inherited by my other work *Hoikuen gimukyōikuka* (Making nursery schools compulsory), published by Shogakukan in 2015.

★78. There are humanities scholars who spend the first half of their twenties in college, and the latter half in graduate school.

★79. However, in that case, the difference should influence the responses of all generations, but since the timing overlaps with the collapse of the bubble economy, after which began the two Lost Decades, the question of just how much impact the research approach would have had is a moot point.

★80. On the other hand, what I found the most attractive at the time of writing this book was Ōsawa's explanation, which I found to be the most convincing; and the hypothesis of the "renunciation of change" put forward by Saitō. At the present time, though, I don't have any data or grounds for concluding that one particular theory is absolutely correct, so I'll refrain from backing any interpretation.

Chapter 3

The "Collapse" of "Japan"?

The FIFA World Cup is a festival that takes place once every four years. And when it does, youths waving the Japanese flag begin to appear all across Japan, creating such a lively scene that at one time it made adults worry whether nationalism was in the air again. In this chapter, I will turn to young diehard fans of the World Cup event for clues, and consider the makeup of Japan—the nation we live in—and the magic called "nationalism."

1. Exclusive World Cup Nation

Resisting World Cup fever in Shibuya

On the night of June 24, 2010, at 11:00 p.m., the scramble intersection in front of Shibuya station was enveloped in a different kind of din and bustle than usual. Crowds of people in blue clothes were standing in front of the statue of Hachikō, along with other groups holding up the Japanese flag and blowing plastic vuvuzela horns.

The Japan vs. Denmark match of the FIFA World Cup tournament, which represented the Japan team's chance to advance to the final round, was going to be broadcast in the wee hours of the 24th, from 3:30 a.m. People in the crowd said they were planning to live it up in Shibuya while watching this game. As far as I could tell, the majority of them were young people in their twenties, including college students.

When it came to soccer, I was so clueless that I even had to ask, after receiving this thing called a yellow card, where I should put it away.[184/★81] Still, to observe the surge of excitement that happens only once every four years, I shamelessly went over to Shibuya on the night of the match.

At the scramble intersection, I stumbled upon some college friends of mine. These girls, who were third-year students at Keio University, said they were on their way to a sports bar to watch the game. Michiko (twenty-one years old, female) said, "I'm not usually interested in soccer; I'm not even very familiar with the rules." But today her friends had invited her, so she had decided to watch the game together with them. She also said that various people—mainly her friends from the same campus—were getting together.

To Michiko, the World Cup was "no different at all from a Waseda-Keio match." As it happened, the soccer match between Waseda and Keio universities was going to be held on the following night of the 25th, and the girls were planning to attend that match as well. Both of these events were apparently something like parties to them. "It's like fun, all of us having a blast together."

The lively scene around Shibuya station peaked at the scramble intersection, and its buzz faded the further you got from there. In the distance ahead, past the popular Center Gai street, I also found many young people dressed in the uniform of the Japanese team, but unlike the youths by the station, they weren't living it up, raising their voices while blowing through vuvuzelas.

A quiet queue had formed in front of a certain sports bar. When I approached Shōta, a twenty-five-year-old man who was standing in line, to ask his story, I learned that he was apparently going to watch the game with five pals he'd gotten to know at the sports bar during the previous game. He said that they were all job-hopping part-timers working in the restaurant industry.

I also approached a group of seven who were sitting in a parking lot and inquired after their stories. Apparently, they were fellow members of the soccer circle at Komazawa University. Two of them were active university students, while the remaining five had graduated and were full-fledged working members of society. To them, today was something like a class reunion. For these alumni who were too busy to find the time to meet up, the World Cup had become a suitable opportunity to do just that.

Once the game began, groups began to form in local areas of Shibuya. Since the area around Shibuya station didn't have any large-scale public viewing going on, the people who couldn't get into a sports bar gathered around small television sets in *izakaya* pubs.

In one such venue, coming to life, were these groups who reminded me of the

184.   Just in case I'm not the only one who had no idea about this, let me offer an explanation. The yellow card is just shown by the umpire. The players have no need to keep it on their person throughout the game.
★81.   I remain clueless about soccer to this day. No matter how many times people explain to me what this thing called "offsides" is, I can't get my head around it.

Early morning of June 25, 2010

clusters of people who used to form around street-side TVs of yore; the TV in the *izakaya* was so small you couldn't satisfactorily make out how the game was progressing. Which is why the people in the back had pulled out their cell phones to keep track of the game on their mobile displays.★82

Whenever there was a development in the game, the crowd would come alive with loud cheers, crying "Japan, Japan!" with arms around each other's shoulders, even

---

★82.　The most salient difference between the time when this book was written and the present is the degree to which smartphones have penetrated the market. You might skim through this account, but the cell phones carried by the young people who would gather in Shibuya in those days were mostly still flip phones. According to the *Communications Usage Trend Survey* conducted by the Ministry of Internal Affairs and Communications, the penetration of smartphones at the end of 2010 was 9.7 percent. By the end of 2014, it had risen to 64.2 percent.

though they'd only met that day.

The climax definitely happened the
moment the Japan team achieved victory, when everyone, all at once, began to
dash toward the scramble intersection.
With sports-bar spectators also joining
in, a high-five storm raged across the
area, as people continued to celebrate
"Japan's" victory until first light began
to brighten the city.

But the young people gathered in
Shibuya weren't the only ones celebrating Japan's victory. Though the game
was aired during late-night hours, the
audience rating for the latter half of the
match reached 40.9 percent. This meant

Late at night on June 29, 2010

that nearly half of the households in Japan had watched the World Cup, despite the
fact that the next day was a weekday.★83

"Ahhhhh, that felt good!"

The Japan team made its way into the finals. The opponent in the match held on June
29th was Paraguay. The game was scheduled for the same midnight time slot scheduled
for the game with Denmark.185 Once again, even though I remained clueless about the
rules, I brazenly ventured forth to Shibuya.

The city was sizzling with even more energy than last time. At the center of the
scramble intersection, people were exchanging high-fives and making "Japan" calls
even before the game kicked off. There were also many groups waving huge Japanese
national flags. It was beginning to drizzle, but everyone remained upbeat.186

But a closer look at the liveliness revealed that the actual crowd making the noise

★83.   The 2014 Japan vs. Cote d'Ivoire World Cup match was a daytime game held on a Sunday, so the
       audience share for the latter half of the game reached 46.6 percent. In addition, Shibuya once again saw
       a sudden influx soccer fans; in fact, the crush of people was so tremendous that a commotion involving
       sexual molestation ensued.
185.   To be sure, the timing of this game proved more troublesome than the timing of the game with Denmark.
       The Denmark game began at three a.m., so when it ended, the trains and the city were already getting
       started. But in the game against Paraguay, the match started at eleven at night and ended after one a.m.,
       which is just when the last trains of the night leave the station. So there you are, stranded in Shibuya at
       two in the morning. What are you supposed to do?

wasn't that huge. Firstly, at the core of the assembled group were around fifteen people who were the "festive type" of youths brimming with tremendous excitement. Even during the game, they were making so much noise all the time that they obviously weren't watching the match at all. It was likely that the crowd who appeared on TV were mainly these "festive types."

Surrounding them were the "observer types," such as the reporters and bloggers. Making remarks like, "This is serious blog material," they took pictures of the "festive types" with their cell phone cameras. In numbers, the "observer types" were far greater, without a doubt.

And further removed from the "observer types" were the "spectator types." They were diligently following the developments of the game with their cell phones. A twenty-year old male college student, Kazuya, was one of the "spectator types." He said he came to Shibuya because he had been getting lonely watching the game at home alone, and thought it would be better to join a buzzing crowd and share the excitement.

Gathered in front of the Tsutaya video rental shop just across the scramble intersection were around twenty "spectator types." They were basically looking into their cell phones, either individually or in pairs, but whenever there was some development in the game, they would all shout and yell together.

Taiga, a nineteen-year old male, and Jun, a twenty-year old male, were both following the game on the same cell phone screen. Jun said, laughing, "We came to Shibuya with the intention of checking out the spectacle up close, but instead we just ended up looking on."★84

However, all that die-hard support from the youngsters through their cell phone screens ended in vain, as Japan was defeated by Paraguay. The young people had supported "Japan" to such a maniacal extent that I expected they might turn into a rowdy mob, but no such thing occurred.

The moment it came to light that the Japan team had lost, all I heard everywhere were pleasant voices saying, "Good job!" Wait, what? "Good job"?

The youth who had come together in Shibuya parted company amid high-fives

---

186.   My friend made this suggestion of hurling the Paraguayan national flag into the crowd just to see what might happen. I thought it was a good idea, but unfortunately, there was no Paraguayan national flag to be found in nighttime Shibuya. Or rather, I should say that I couldn't go to such lengths, since I'm no modern artist.

★84.   Back then, I used to enjoy taking jaunts with my friends downtown and striking up conversations with young people to listen to their stories. Of course, I knew that this kind of "vox populi" (voice of the people) approach was nonsense as far as statistics went, but I did think that it was necessary as a slice-of-life glimpse into the times. Since those interviews weren't very interesting, I left them all out. But an early draft of this book contained a chapter titled "Young People Who Came Together at Power Spots," featuring a total of several dozen interviews with young people. I don't know what came over me.

and exclamations of, "Good job"; "Man, that felt good!"; "See you again in four years!" They didn't seem particularly annoyed about the fact that "Japan" had lost. On the contrary, many of them had bright smiles on their faces, as if they had followed through on some task and were feeling a sense of accomplishment.[187]

The emergence of a nation, for a limited time only

When you look at the way young people come to life at the World Cup, it's as if "Japan" the nation is a thing that appears only during that event, or more specifically, only for the limited time the game lasts. Symbolic of this is the remark made by the youths while high-fiving each other: "See you again in four years!" It was a statement that was heard at the 2006 World Cup, too.

The twenty-two-year-old medical student from Hyogo, Kōta Hada, who had built a school in Cambodia, planned a charity event that would coincide with the 2006 World Cup.[★85] A question suddenly struck him as he rode the train to the event. He wondered what on earth "Japan" the nation was about—the nation that he and his friends were about to root for.

The event came to an end amid such tumult that such concerns vanished in an instant. Hada, together with his pals, rooted for the country called "Japan." Hand in hand, fellow strangers prayed for the victory of a nation called "Japan." They shouted, "Japan! Japan!" like there was no tomorrow. And when the soccer match was over, the assembled crowd dispersed and each went their merry way home.

> On the way to Shibuya, inside the train, I saw many young people who, like me, were decked out in the uniform of the national team. While gazing at their backs, I gave some thought to the nation called Japan: even if we cry, "Japan! Japan!," do we truly love the nation called Japan? Do we truly cheer for the nation called Japan—we who usually aren't conscious of the nation called "Japan"?[188]

---

187. After the game, when the last trains had already left the station, I had an awful time trying to catch a cab in Shibuya. I tried walking a little, but I still couldn't find a vacant taxi. In the end, I ended up walking all the way past Ebisu before I finally got a ride. The moment I heard people saying "*otsukare*" (Thank you for your hard work), I looked down on them, thinking "Really? You guys didn't even play in the game. What's up with that remark?" But the word "*otsukare*," I realized then, was also intended for someone like me who, after the match, had ended up in the tough situation of not being able to catch a cab and having to race-walk in the middle of the night.

★85. After that, Hada reportedly went on to complete clinical training before traveling around the world to investigate areas afflicted by child prostitution and juvenile labor.

188. Kōta Hada, *Boku-tachi wa sekai o kaeru koto ga dekinai* (We can't change the world), Shogakukan, 2010. In 2011, this book was made into a film starring Osamu Mukai. The author's style is so restrained and decently self-effacing that many will find the book to be an enjoyable read. I'm envious. What's so original is that a group building schools in Cambodia was setting up events to collect money for providing relief to Japan.

It's a typical college-student concern, but if you think about it, certainly in everyday life, we don't find that many opportunities to be conscious of the nation called "Japan." Other than the World Cup and the Olympics,★86 the only other times we have the chance is when we travel abroad and whenever we suffer from a calamity, such as a devastating earthquake disaster (see chapter 5).

"Japan" as infrastructure

Awareness of the thing called "Japan" doesn't come easily, unless something other than "Japan" appears.

That's because, to many people, modern-day Japan smacks of an infrastructure. That is to say, we're all so totally immersed in this entity called "Japan" that we take it for granted, never becoming actively aware of its presence.

Many in "Japan" have been in "Japan" ever since they were born. In this way, it's slightly different from other collectives. In the case of high schools, universities, and companies, people usually take some kind of a test before they finally receive permission to join the collective. But the question of whether one can enter Japan or not is, in most cases, settled prior to birth.[189]

And that's why there is no need to be conscious about "Japan"; the whole notion of it is absolutely commonplace.

Of course, this doesn't mean that we're free from "Japan"; that we don't have any ties to it. "Japan as an infrastructure" prevails around and over our lives like air. For example, in addition to the electricity, gas, water supply, and roads—literally the infrastructure—we receive from "Japan" various material and immaterial services, including the protection of peace and order by the police, the education public schools provide, and the social security we need at times of sickness and unemployment.

But why does "Japan" provide such services to us? It's because we're all being coerced to buy them. In the form of such things as income taxes, residence taxes, and consumption taxes, we are being made to buy an entire set of services—the full lineup—obtainable by living in Japan.

Ordinarily, when we purchase goods and services, multiple options are available.

★86. After the publication of this book, the city of Tokyo was announced as the host of the 2020 Olympics. Ahead of the event, though, controversy over the reconstruction of the National Stadium and the rip-off furor over the Tokyo Olympics logo have been making headlines in Japan.

189. While there are cases of people being admitted into "Japan" after birth, they have to undergo a far more involved ordeal than that required for applying for a credit card, such as being required to be a resident for more than five years, and having to prepare an overwhelming number of procedural documents. Until then, among people who aren't "Japanese," only around 15,000 are allowed to become "Japanese" annually.

So if we're talking about, say, home security, then you can choose between SECOM or ALSOK; in the case of sportswear, you can choose between Nike or Adidas. However, in the case of the services provided by "Japan," there are no competing suppliers. Consequently, as long as we're in "Japan," we have no choice but to routinely buy—with no questions asked—the full lineup of services offered by "Japan."[190]

What's more, most people aren't that conscious of the fact that they're purchasing services. Why? Because "the full lineup of services obtainable by living in Japan" often ends up being paid for by money deducted from salaries (which is what taxes are). The taxes of salaried employees, who account for most of the Japanese population, are, as a rule, withheld from their pay. Students working in the current system, still remain dependent on parental support, and are therefore exempt from paying taxes in general, as long as their annual income doesn't exceed 1,030,000 yen. For this reason, the only tax they actually pay is the consumption tax.

Inside the magic called "Japan"

I have ended up describing "Japan" as if it were just a corporation providing infrastructure, like Tokyo Gas or Tokyo Electric Power (TEPCO), but obviously "Japan" isn't simply just infrastructure. It's much greater than that.

In the 2010 World Cup, the athlete named Keisuke Honda (twenty-four years old, Osaka) became an overnight hero all across Japan. Even someone like me who has no interest in soccer at least knows Honda. But why was it that we were able to root for him?

The many who supported Honda weren't related to him in any way; Honda wasn't their blood relative, nor was he supposedly someone whom they had ever directly spoken to. In many cases, the only thing in common shaping the relationship between Honda and those who supported him was the fact that they were all "Japanese."

Perhaps you're thinking at this point, why is this guy stating the obvious? But if you stop to ponder about this, I think you'll see that it's odd.

Why is it that we can cheer for a person whom we have never personally met?

If you dislike Honda, just recall the face of another player; it won't make any difference. Did you—as someone who rooted for Japan in the World Cup—actually

---

190.   One difference between the state and capitalism is that, in the case of the state, you're forced to buy what it sells. That's because only the state has exclusive rights regarding carrying out violence and collecting taxes. To borrow the words of Toshihito Kayano, taxes are essentially no different from protection money given to gangsters (Toshihito Kayano, *Kane to bōryoku no keifugaku* [The genealogy of money and violence], Kawade Shobo Shinsha, 2006). However, since the sovereign authority of the democratic nation of Japan rests in the hands of its constituency—its citizens with the power to vote—those who are supporting and maintaining, at least in form, this power structure are none other than "we" Japanese citizens.

know anyone on the Japan team as a personal acquaintance? Isn't it true that the majority of fans, in fact, knew no one on the team as a family relation, nor as a lover, nor as an old friend, nor as a childhood friend, nor as a classmate?

If so, why were you able to root for the Japan team—a team absent of any single member you can count as an acquaintance?

Let me put it to you in another way. Let's take the case of, say, a college student residing in Kanagawa. Let's say that he happens to be looking at a story currently appearing on a news website concerning a train accident that occurred in Shikoku, involving the Shikoku Railway Company. His heart breaks. He feels sorry for the victims. But does this incident really have anything to do with him? He wasn't born in Shikoku, he has never been to Shikoku, and he has never met any of the victims.

Let's consider another example: the case of a few drunken businessmen arguing at a bar over "the ideal form of Japan" and "the regeneration of the Japanese economy." They're passionately debating deflation and the strong yen, politics and the economy, drawing on a smattering of information they've recently come across on TV and in magazines. However, they're neither politicians nor bureaucrats. Nor do they have the power to get involved in any kind of intervention in foreign-currency markets. Regardless of what they talk about tonight, come tomorrow, not a single thing about the Japanese economy will have changed.

What makes it possible for a person to frantically root for the victory of a team composed of people they've never met? Why does a college student in Kanagawa get distressed about an incident occurring in Shikoku? Why do those elderly-types, who are neither politicians nor bureaucrats, fret over the Japanese economy? That's because, they are—or rather, we all are—under the spell of a certain magic.

The magic of considering someone "Japanese" when you've never met that person; and the magic of believing some locale to be "Japan" when you've never even visited the place, not even once. It's the magic spell that has lasted for more than 140 years, ever since it was first cast in the Meiji period (1868–1912) by the nation called "Japan." This magic is called nationalism.

2. The Magic Called Nationalism

The Edo period: a time of peace and stability

Nationalism can be said to be one of the greatest gimmicks devised by humankind in the past several hundred years. Thanks to the magic of nationalism, the country called

Japan saw the rise of its education level, the advancement of industrialization, the establishment of a sound infrastructure, and the loss of many lives.

To affirm what a tremendous magic nationalism is, let's make some comparisons to the Edo period (1603–1868).[191]

But why talk about nationalism in a book that's mainly about young people? I reached the conclusion that in contemplating Japanese youth, it was necessary to consider an overview of Japan as a nation, which is, after all, home to those young people.[★87] Though "Japan" has already become ubiquitous as the infrastructure and air, for this very reason, there remain structures and mechanisms unseen, veiled underneath its omnipresence.

For example, since Japan is an island nation, we tend to instinctively think that this country has been around since several thousand years ago, or even tens of thousands of years ago. But until the Edo period, many people didn't process reality through the lens of "Japan." Back then "country" meant one's feudal clan or village, and many people spent their entire lives in the place of their birth, never venturing beyond it.[192]

And with the class system in place, just because someone was born in Japan, it didn't necessarily mean that he or she automatically became Japanese. Basically, the child of a peasant could only become a peasant, and the child of a merchant could only become a merchant. In the eyes of the samurai, the peasant must not have appeared to be "Japanese" in the same way he was.

In other words, until the Edo period, you could safely say that the "Japanese" were nonexistent. Of course, if we look back on the Edo period from the vantage point of the present, the merchants of Edo, the traders of Sakai, and the peasants of Kishū cannot be conceived as anything other than Japanese, but whether these individuals at that time were aware of themselves as being Japanese is highly doubtful.[193] This is be-

191.   With regard to nationalism, I have referred to Eiji Oguma's *Nihon to iu kuni* (A nation called Japan; Rironsha, 2006) as a main source. As this book is intended for junior high students, it's very easy to understand. Its standard, too, is as high as that of Mr. Oguma's "Modern History" class, which he was in charge of at Keio University's Shonan Fujisawa Campus (Keio University SFC). —Wait, what?

★87.   More than any other part of this book, I wished to rewrite this section on modernization and nationalism the most, as it turned out to be one in which my understanding changed the most, compared to any other section. For a more detailed discussion, refer to this chapter's postscript.

192.   The Edo shogunate carried out mapping projects, including the *Shōhō Nihon-zu* (Japanese map in the Shōhō era) in an attempt to gain an understanding of the shape of the land of Japan, but the only ones who could obtain this map were members of the ruling classes and the small segment of the merchant class that had the means to do so.

193.   In the eighteenth century, as ships from America and Europe began to frequently arrive near the shores of Japan, not only the rulers and intelligentsia but even prominent peasants began to sense that "Japan was in danger" at times. (Norio Makihara, "Nihon wa itsu nēshon ni natta ka" [When did Japan become a nation?] in *Nashonarizumu-ron, nyūmon* [An introduction to the theory of nationalism] edited by Masachi Ōsawa and Kang Sang-jung, Yuhikaku Publishing, 2009.)

cause as long as there was no common mass media, nor a common education system, there was nothing there to tell them that they were "Japanese," nor did they have any need to see themselves as such.

The Edo period was an extremely stable time, because your entire life was determined by where you were born and the social status of your parents. If you were born a farmer's son in a farming village, you had no choice, for the most part, but to go on living as a farmer in the village in which you were born. In the first place, you wouldn't know that there were other options available to you; you would, in fact, live through your whole life without ever coming to know that. You had no need to embark on a soul-searching voyage of discovery, either. Competition was scarce. Conflicts rarely happened. The line between rich and poor was fixed and impermeable.

Even for a ruler (an Edo shogun), there was no better setup than this—it was superbly comfortable; there were no elections, which meant no recalls. Nobody knew anything about the state or politics. And that's why a handful of rulers were able to rule over the country as they pleased.

But it wasn't that the political practices of the Edo shogunate were so terrible.[194] In particular, during the late Edo period, the economy was favorable, and the standard of living was rising, too.

So what was the problem, then? If society at that time was enjoying peace and stability, what more could you ask for? Even now, in the present age, you find people saying that the Edo period was a good time, despite never having experienced the life and times of that era for themselves.[★88]

The Achilles' heel of the Edo period

A fatal flaw was discovered when this "stable" society was jolted by an external event. The society of Edo, like all societies with regional differences and social divisions, was ill-equipped to wage war.

---

194. In the past, the people of the Edo period, in particular the peasantry who accounted for most of the population, were often depicted as subjugated victims tormented by various burdens, including the need to pay tributes. For example, in Kōta Kodama's *Kinsei nōmin seikatsu-shi* (The life histories of the peasants of early modern times; Yoshikawa Kobunkan, 2006)—a work that first came out in 1947—the peasants are depicted as people who are strictly governed by various rules. On the other hand, these past thirty years have seen a flood of works depicting the people of the Edo period as being independent-minded and diverse, including the series of studies authored by Yoshihiko Amino.

★88. The Edo period lasted approximately three hundred years, and evaluations of it vary by which part of which decade you focus on. However, unlike the Sengoku Jidai (age of civil strife), when low rice yields led to annual famines, there doesn't seem to be any doubt that the Edo period saw the rise of a society that managed to sufficiently feed its populace of commoners, thanks to the spread of rice farming. (Jun Yonaha, *Chūgokuka suru Nihon,* zōhoban [The changing of Japan into a China-like nation, augmented edition], Bungeishunju, 2014.)

For example, in the battle waged between the feudal domain of Chōshū and the joint naval forces of European nations and the United States, neither peasants nor merchants were seen to be cooperating in the war.[195] In the case of the Boshin War (the conflict that ended the Edo period), even though it wasn't a foreign war, the people of various places, including the merchants and artisans of the castle town of Aizu Waka-matsu, are said to have fled the battlefield posthaste.

The late Edo period was a time of uncertainty, when people didn't know whether they were going to get invaded by the great powers of the West. The fact that only the samurai would fight in times of war engendered even more anxiety and instability. The population of Japan in the late years of the Edo period was around thirty-three mil-lion, but the proportion of samurai, even when counting their families, was less than ten percent. This meant that, in the event of a war against a foreign power, the military would only be three million strong.

What's more, the setup that allowed some rulers to monopolize politics by keeping the masses in a state of ignorance could not be sustained unless Japan remained a "closed world." In early 2011, a large-scale demonstration took place in Egypt to pro-test against the dictatorship of the Mubarak regime; the Internet is said to have played both a direct and indirect role in catalyzing this event (see chapter 4). In a time when the every person can easily obtain information from the world outside his own coun-try, maintaining a despotic government proves to be extremely difficult.

This situation was slightly similar to the one seen in Japan in the nineteenth cen-tury, when Japan was pressed to open its borders to the world, and when people in Europe and America, through commerce and innovation, were enjoying an unprece-dented degree of affluence.

It was a time that saw an increase in steamship traffic, which made it possible to have people, goods, and money come and go across borders at an unprecedented speed. In 1858, the transatlantic undersea telegraph cable was laid across the floor of the Atlantic, enabling the transmission of messages between the United States and Europe. With the advancement of improvements in undersea cable technology, the world was about to become one under the auspices of a "nineteenth-century version of the World Wide Web."[196] European nations and the United States, aided by the respec-tive national power they had elevated through "commerce" and "innovation," began to colonize countries in Asia and Africa, one after another.

---

195.   Far from cooperating, people had complained, as "victims," saying such things as, "I was terribly inconvenienced and bothered" and "It was a terrible experience." (Kaoru Furukawa, *Bakumatsu Chōshū-han no jōi senso* [Chōshū domain's war to oust foreigners in the late Edo period], Chuokoron-Shinsha, 1996.) War is, strictly speaking, not something you can call "ours."

And then the black ships, finally, arrived on the shores of Japan. If Japan continued to maintain the Edo-period system of governance, it would suffer defeat in the event of war—or, worse, Japan would get invaded and turned into a colony, a prospect that inspired a sense of impending crisis in the elites of the time. Thus, Japan chose to mimic Europe and America, and become a modern nation-state that would carry out economic growth and invasions, all under the banner of a strong, centralized government.

"Japan" and "the Japanese" are the creations of the Meiji government

Captured in the annals of history are these words left behind by a government official of the Ministry of Religious Education, which used to often express the policies of the Meiji government.[197]

> While we have been ruling by making a fool out of the little man, from now on, we must make him study and let him become intelligent as we rule. The same applies to the farmer and the merchant, as it does to the samurai. This is a welcome development for all of us.

Essentially, what the official was saying was this: until the Edo period, it was fine that only a handful of ruling-class elites were running the country, but moving forward, it would be imperative to turn Japan into a country where everyone, including peasants, would get educated, so that everyone could run the country together. For everyone to be able to run the country together, there were a few things that needed to be abolished. First of all, regional differences and social divisions needed to go out the door. In the Edo period, the language and food culture greatly varied by region. And the social status into which you were born had a decisive influence on your life. Under these circumstances, there was no way people could identify themselves as citizens of the same country. Unless *everyone* had the sense of relating to each other as equal citizens, no one would fight for "Japan" in a war.

Consequently, community registers that had been compiled by social status were abolished, and each and every citizen came to be collectively administered with the aid of their family register. Though a handful of the privileged classes remained, in princi-

---

196.   William Bernstein looks for the reasons behind the explosive period of innovation, and the improvement in the standard of living of common people, which took place between 1730 and 1850, including property rights, scientific rationalism, refined capital markets, and the expansion of transportation and communication technology. For a detailed discussion, refer to *Yutakasa no tanjō* (original title: *The Birth of Plenty* by William Bernstein), translated by Iehiro Tokugawa, *Nihon Keizai Shimbun*, 2006.

197.   Norio Makihara, *Nihon no rekishi 13: Bunmei-koku o mezashite* (The history of Japan 13: Toward a civilized nation), Shogakukan, 2008.

ple, the four classes—the warriors, peasants, craftsmen, and tradesmen of the Edo period—became equal.

This represented a drastic change, since, unlike in the Edo period, when one's life was largely determined by the place of birth and station in life, it now became possible for anyone—from any out-of-the-way village, and from any kind of home they might have been born into—to become prime minister.[198]

The homogenous "everyone" is created by a nationwide compulsory education program. Basically, the powers that be decreed that the same things be taught to everyone in every city and rural area. Furthermore, with strides made in media technology, it became possible to deliver uniform information to everyone.[199]

To educate everyone who was called "Japanese," a Japanese language and a Japanese culture and a Japanese history became necessary.

Until the Edo period, glaring regional differences and social divisions were evident even in the language. Naturally, though, the ruling classes, since they used to travel back and forth between Edo and the provinces, must have shared some kind of common language. They also had good command of written classical Chinese, a common language of East Asia.

However, since the movements of the populace at large were severely restricted, local dialects developed, rendering any communication between commoners of different locales pretty much impossible.[200] In these circumstances, the powers that be had no way of creating a homogenous mass of "Japanese." Thus, a Japanese language, which would serve as a common language, was designed and taught at schools all across the nation.[201]

---

198. That being said, the granting of eligibility to run for office occurred in incremental steps, with the abolishment in 1925 of the requirement to pay a special tax to be eligible for elections, and the eligibility of women to run for office being recognized in 1945. Furthermore, it's safe to say that, even to this day, it remains all but impossible for anyone from a truly impoverished class to become prime minister. To become a politician, such things as an extensive network of human contacts and abundant financial resources are necessary; the availability of such assets largely depends on the domestic circumstances you were born into.

199. The elementary school in particular was a base for turning not only school kids, but the people living nearby into "Japanese." Events and ceremonies that involved the people of villages to participate en masse were held, leading to the reorganization of premodern collectives. (Hiroshi Watanabe, *Utau kokumin* [The singing nation], Chuokoron-Shinsha, 2010.)

200. I mean, dialects still remain to this day. The last time I went to a rural village in Kagoshima, I couldn't understand 90 percent of the conversation taking place between two elderly folks, but they understood the words I spoke. That, dear reader, is the fruit of 140 years of modernization.

201. The commonly accepted theory is that standard Japanese was built on the foundations of the patois spoken in the Yamanote area of Tokyo. However, one historian believes that a common language already existed among the ruling classes in the Edo period, and that the Yamanote dialect was built on the foundations of this vernacular. (Takashi Nomura, *Hanashi kotoba no Nihon-shi* [The history of Japan's spoken language], Yoshikawa Kobunkan, 2010.)

A made-up story[★89]

To have everyone regard themselves as Japanese, a common story, or narrative, is also necessary. To that end, a Japanese history was created.

At school, we learn—as "Japanese history"—about a fairly large village (the Yoshi-nogari site) that existed in Saga 2,000 years ago, and the sibling rivalry (the Jinshin War) that occurred in Nara 1,300 years ago, and the story about an old man who was betrayed by his subordinate 400 years ago (the Honnō-ji incident). In effect, disparate events, unrelated to each other in terms of both social status and region, were roughly packaged into one presentation and slapped with the label "Stories of Japan," based on what constituted the territory of Japan at the time.

A "Japanese culture" also needed to be constructed. We here in the present age think of the early anthology of the waka form of Japanese poetry known as the *Kokin Wakashū*, along with noh drama and kabuki drama, as products of Japanese culture, but the *Kokin Wakashū* is the private anthology of imperial families, noh theater came out of the samurai culture of the Muromachi period, and kabuki arose from the culture of the commoners of early modern times. The decision was made to lump all these disparate art forms together into one bundle and call them "Japanese culture."

However, if ordinary people are simply given education, they will end up becoming a threat to the ruling class, since the people, with their acquired intelligence, may revolt. Consequently, it was decided that everyone should have a sense of loyalty toward the nation called "Japan."

So the subject of *shūshin* (ethics) was incorporated into the curriculum of compulsory education in an attempt to convince "everyone" to say to themselves, "We are the honorable Japanese!" and "Let's dedicate ourselves, as Japanese people, to the cause of His Majesty the Emperor, to the cause of the nation!" Thus, royal visits made by the emperor, along with education, came to demonstrate authority. The emperor would tour all over the country, and the people, by beholding him, would become conscious of the notion that they were the "subjects" of the emperor.[202]

"Imagined Communities" is the classy way to put it

No matter where you were born, and no matter what family you were born into, at school you learn Japanese history and Japanese culture in Japanese. This practice began in the Meiji period, all across Japan. Although, relatively speaking, the ancestors of

---

★89.   I had the editor come up with some of the subheadings at the time of publishing this book. I think most of them turned out well, but this expression feels rushed.

202.   Takeshi Hara, *Kashika sareta teikoku* (Visualized empire), Misuzu Shobo, 2001.

most Japanese should be peasants or commoners, it was the Meiji government that overlooked this fact and induced the people to adopt the "We are all the same Japanese" mindset.

In sociology, we use the classy expression "imagined communities" to describe this situation. Even without ever having met someone before, you can perceive him as a friend, just on account of being told that he's "Japanese." Even without ever having visited a place before, you can consider that place your country, just on account of being told that that place, too, is "Japan." "Japan" and "the Japanese" are constructs that become valid only when everybody consensually imagines, "We are Japanese."[203]

The time when this concept of imagined communities flowers most extravagantly is, as expected, at the time of war—when a young schoolchild faces a soldier to bluntly tell him, "Please die for our country," and when a mother encourages her son leaving for the battlefront with the words, "Die magnificently for our country, you hear?" It becomes—as history shows—a time when the future of "Japan" the nation is valued more than an individual life or the continuation of the family.

Having said that, though, it wasn't as if the "Japanese" were born instantly overnight. It is impossible to suddenly change tens of millions of people in all respects, from their ways of thinking to their ways of living. A case in point was the way they walked; correcting the posture of Japanese people was no mean feat.

Almost all modern Japanese have no problem walking in a straight line with their back fully erect. However, for a person of the Meiji period, this was extremely difficult. Incidentally, I doubt whether all of us today, too, would be walking with our back fully erect if we hadn't practiced marching when we were in elementary school.

In the Edo period, it is said that everybody used to walk frivolously, even in a feudal lord's procession. It wasn't customary to swing the arms while walking; rather, people commonly adopted the *namba* gait, which involved sticking out the right foot simultaneously with the right shoulder.[204] Although "exercises for walking in file" had been introduced as far back as the 1880s, an extant record shows an army school grumbling about the fact that, even though it was already the 1920s, many people couldn't walk in a straight line yet.[205]

---

203.   To take an example from the present age, we experience this when returning home from abroad when we land in an airplane at Narita Airport. At that time, many people probably think, "I'm back in Japan." They might even feel a little relieved. A person returning from studying abroad after a long time may even end up in tears. Most people, though, except for those who are originally from Narita, don't have any human ties or other connections to Narita.

204.   Masakazu Nomura, *Miburi to shigusa no jinruigaku* (The anthropology of gestures and mannerisms), Chuokoron-Shinsha, 1996.

The bumpy road to "imperialization"

The ever-important plan of inculcating in the masses the sense of "serving for His Majesty the Emperor and the nation" also appears to have taken quite some time to realize.

It was only in the early days of the Shōwa era (1926–89) that the recitation of the Imperial Rescript on Education—often painted as a contemptible part of the prewar landscape—came to be broadly enforced in the educational front; plans to have the emperor's portrait installed in all schools didn't go smoothly either.

Though the military draft was enforced in the sixth year of the Meiji period (1873), there were various exemptions at the time, so only a mere 3.5 percent of those targeted by the draft actually ended up becoming soldiers. In the days of the Sino-Japanese War, the overall figure was 5 percent, and even during the period spanning the end of the Meiji era to the Taishō era (the early 1900s), the figure was approximately 20 percent. Thus, it wasn't as if every single person was entering the military.[206]

Furthermore, it's unclear to just what degree soldiers had sworn their loyalty to the "emperor" and the "nation." For example, there is research showing that, in the letters written by the soldiers at the time of the Russo-Japanese War—at least in their personal letters—the words "emperor" and "nation" did not appear, leaving behind the lingering question, to what extent was the imperial institution of Japan actually working?

Also unclear is to what extent the people at large understood that this was a war being waged by a nation called "Japan." A record survives of an old woman living in Minamitsugaru-gun, Aomori, who, in 1939, asked an elementary school principal, "What time will the war end? Where on earth are they doing this war thing anyway?"[207] Seventy-one years had passed since the Meiji Restoration, yet "national consciousness" still had a long way to go to achieve ubiquity and reach every Japanese person.

Still, steadily and with certainty, the number of people willing to serve the nation called Japan in a concrete way went on to increase. In particular, from the late 1930s when the second Sino-Japanese War broke out, temporary exemption from conscrip-

205. Chikamatsu Oka, *Kokka oyobi kokumin no taiiku shidō* (Physical education instructions for the nation and its citizens), Rikugun Toyama Gakkō Shōkō Shūkaijo (Toyama army school community center), 1922. You can read this work in its entirety at Google Books.

206. This is because the armed forces at that time had adopted elitism (Yōko Katō, *Chōheisei to kindai Nihon* [The conscription system and modern Japan], Yoshikawa Kobunkan, 1996). What's more, when the young men who had become soldiers returned to their villages, they apparently could no longer readjust to life there and became public nuisances, or encumbrances.

207. At the time the Japan-China war was in full swing. This story appears in a discussion found in *Jūgo Aomori-ken o kataru* (On the home front, Aomori prefecture), a 1939 magazine circulated on the front lines to console soldiers. (Toshiya Ichinose, *Kokyō wa naze heishi o koroshita ka* [Why did the homeland kill the soldiers?], KADOKAWA, 2010).

tion began to get rejected, and people started to get caught up in wars waged by the country called "Japan."

Nationalism 2.0

If the period spanning from the Meiji Restoration to the 1930s is "Nationalism 1.0," then from around 1940, a phenomenon began that could be called "Nationalism 2.0."

The first factor was the full-fledged spread of a new medium called the radio. Radio broadcasts had already begun by 1925, and in 1936 the penetration in urban areas was above 40 percent, whereas the penetration in rural districts was still only 10 percent. But in 1941, the penetration in urban areas exceeded 60 percent, while in rural districts it exceeded 30 percent. It was at this time that the information gap between cities and rural villages closed.[208]

Through the radio, people throughout Japan would come to know, more or less in real time, of the attack on Pearl Harbor in December 8, 1941. Such a thing would have been unimaginable in times when newspapers were the only mass-media source of news available. The radio conveyed Japan's victories every day. Many citizens rejoiced. The war was the greatest entertainment in a time when there was no such thing as a World Cup. During the Pacific War, the penetration level of radio soared.

When you think about war, the image that comes to mind is that of a "dark time" when the state is regulating everything with an iron grip, and when everybody is going hungry with the rationing system in place, but this scenario took place after 1944 when the war situation took a turn for the worse. Prior to that period, in fact, the economy of Japan during the early period of the war was good, and leisurely pursuits such as swimming in the ocean and sightseeing around the country flourished. The war had brought about a sense of euphoria for leading vibrant, affluent lives.[209]

In this period in time various systems were devised that have lasted to the present age. Firstly, for instance, the "Japanese company," which prioritizes joint profits for employees, was a model that spread because the rights of shareholders were limited by the National Mobilization Act that took effect in 1938. Secondly, the financial system came to mainly revolve around indirect financing for the purpose of realizing a distribution system oriented toward the military industry. Thirdly, it was around this time

---

208. Masakatsu Ōkado, *Nihon no rekishi 15: Sensō to sengo o ikiru* (The history of Japan 15: Surviving the war and postwar period), Shogakukan, 2009. Incidentally, the radio in those days was something people listened to at such loud volumes that even their neighbors could hear, so in reality, the actual number of listeners must have been greater than penetration levels, or ownership rates, suggest. (Yōko Katō, *Soredemo Nihonjin wa "sensō" o eranda* [Nevertheless, Japan chose "war"], Asahi Press, 2009).

209. NHK *Shuzaihan, Nihonjin wa naze sensō e to mukatta no ka (Ge)* (Why did the Japanese go to war? [part II]), NHK Publishing, 2011.

that the character of governmental bureaucracy changed, giving bureaucrats complete control over the economy.[210]

What's more, many agricultural and fishing villages, whose only industries were those that could be called primary or light industries, went on to become full-scale subcontracting entities of the state. The light industries of certain villages were converted into munitions industries, while certain villages were turned into coal-mining operations to serve as sources of electricity. Acting as the "home front" supporting the war effort, many villages became sources of food supply and manpower. The people of agricultural and fishing villages, who, unlike those in urban areas, did not suffer from seeing their areas turned into scorched-earth battlefields, began to sense that they were in a position to be resourceful to the central areas of the nation.[211]

These were all elements of the system called for by an all-out-war effort that saw as its mandate the winning of the war through national solidarity. The project to build the nation called "Japan," which had begun in the Meiji period, had reached a milestone. The various jobs and businesses throughout the country, along with the entire populace, were reorganized for the sole purpose of executing the war.

In reality, this 1940 "power structure" or system was preserved even after the war, which was exactly why Japan was able to accomplish the unprecedented economic growth it did. If you replace the objective of "winning the war" with "becoming a major economic power," the all-out-war system proves to be just as effective for waging economic war.[212/★90]

If the people who were intoxicated with Japan's economic affluence, declaring the slogan, "Japan as number one," had been born during wartime, they would, without a doubt, have been equally delighted by Japan's steady advance.

That's how potent the magic of nationalism is.

---

210. Yukio Noguchi, *Zōhoban: 1940-nen taisei* (The Established Order in 1940 [augmented edition]), Toyo Keizai Inc., 2010.

211. After the war, many villages continued to do their part as the "home front" by supplying agricultural commodities and electric power to help Japan subsequently fight an economic war. A remarkable case in point is the nuclear power plant (Hiroshi Kainuma, *"Fukushima" ron* [The "Fukushima" theory], Seidosha, 2011). See also chapter 5 of this book.

212. Regarding the thread of continuity running from prewar days through the postwar period, refer, for example, to *Sōryoku-sen to gendaika* (All-out war and modernization) edited by Yasushi Yamanouchi et al. (Kashiwa Shobo, 1995) and *Shōwa* (original title: *Japan in War and Peace: Selected Essays*) by John W. Dower, translation supervised by Tōru Aketagawa (Misuzu Shobo, 2010).

3. Who Needs "Japan"?

And then the magic unraveled

The magic of nationalism enchanted Japan for more than a hundred years, but its effect appears to be gradually fading.

For example, for companies, the state is on the verge of losing its significance. As might be expected, what's important for multinationals such as Toyota and Sony is not Japan's national interest, but their corporate earnings. Although the corporate tax rate in Japan is basically 40 percent, in some cases—such as for Sony, which allocates its profits to overseas corporations—the actual corporate tax rate borne is 10 percent.[213/★91]

Meanwhile, even companies running their operations in Japan will take flight if the potential for business is found abroad. For example, the Japanese boy band W-inds (stylized as "w-inds.") is making waves in the markets of China and Taiwan. Pricing for a live concert held in Shanghai in the autumn of 2010 was aggressive, with a ticket for an arena seat costing 1,600 yuan, or around 20,000 yen, which is approximately the starting salary of a college graduate in Shanghai.

Similarly, even if a company is a Japanese company, if the profit margins are deemed to be unfavorable, the company will downplay the Japanese market. For example, the gaming company KONAMI, due to "various reasons," canceled the Japan-market release of a horror game titled *Silent Hill Homecoming*.

It's unclear as to whether the "various reasons" referred to the depiction of violence in the game or to a rights issue, but either way the problems weren't insurmountable. Any depiction of violence could have been modified to meet any censorial guidelines,

---

★90.   A theory as simple as the *1940-nen taisei-ron* (theory of the established order of 1940) has been criticized for underestimating the impact of the reforms carried out by the General Headquarters of the Allied Forces (GHQ) after the war. Certainly, when contemplating the postwar order, you cannot ignore the importance of the Antitrust Law, the zaibatsu dissolution, the Labor Union Law, the Purge, and agrarian reform. Many segments of the controlled economy of the wartime period simply fizzled out (Takemaro Mori, "Sōryoku-sen, fashizumu, sengo kaikaku" [All-out war, fascism, postwar reform] in *Naze ima Ajia, Taiheiyō sensō ka* [The Asia-Pacific War, why now?] edited by Aiko Kurasawa et al., Iwanami Shoten, 2005). Nonetheless, there is no doubt that a thread of continuity runs from prewar days through the postwar period, including the long-term employment agreement and the seniority pay system, which became firmly established in the wartime economy.

213.   In the *Shimbun Akahata* (June 24, 2010), there is an investigative piece covering the burden rates of corporate taxation for the top one-hundred companies in terms of ordinary profits for the period between 2003 and 2009.

★91.   The star economist Thomas Piketty points out the need for a progressive global tax on companies and the wealthy.

and any rights issue could have been resolved, since the company was able to release the game in both Europe and America. But what it most likely boiled down to was that the company didn't see enough merit in the Japanese market to justify going to extra lengths to release the game there. The Japanese company KONAMI prioritizes selling in Europe and America, where the markets are large and the conditions are favorable in terms of both distribution and trade regulations.[214/★92]

This attitude isn't surprising, if your position is that the corporation belongs not to its employees, nor to the people of the region where it's located, but to investors.[★93]

Of course, the flight of capital in pursuit of profits across borders isn't anything new, and it certainly didn't begin in the present age. Globalization and the "flattening" of the world didn't happen overnight in the wake of the communication and transportation revolution that took place at the end of the twentieth century. Their history is as old as the history of humankind.[215]

But there's no denying that the hurdle to cross borders has become less daunting than before. Rising economic standards in various countries, including China and Russia, also means a rise in the number of consumers sharing similar interests. The market scale attainable by crossing borders is steadily expanding, and the cost for doing so is steadily dropping.

With the global financial crisis of 1929, the world began to see the rise of block economies as nations leaned toward protectionism. Such tense relations were one of the key factors contributing to the outbreak of the Second World War, and out of the soul-searching that this recognition provoked came the active building—after the war—of multilateral economic relations championing the principles of liberalism. The nation-state paradigm attempted to disrupt the undercurrents of "globalization" that had been flowing throughout all of history, and divided the world into areas defined by "national borders." However, by the end of the 20th century the inadequacies of the nation-state were becoming exposed.

214.　However, this is not a major problem, since consumers can just buy overseas editions from Amazon.

★92.　Hideo Kojima (forty-seven years old, Tokyo), a game creator at KONAMI, the company famous for the "Metal Gear Solid" series, said in an interview, "To be blunt, Americans like games that involve shooting aliens with handguns. If you can't appreciate what's fun about that, you shouldn't be in the business of creating for the world." (*Famitsu* [Famicom news], July 7, 2011 issue).

★93.　The PlayStation 4 game console, which Sony put out in 2014, was released in Japan more than three months after it was released in the United States. There are still only a few games available for the Japanese market, clearly showing the manufacturer's awareness of European and American markets. For this reason, there have been criticisms raised against the company for being "neglectful of Japan"; this move, however, is a very rational corporate strategy for a global enterprise like Sony.

215.　William J. Bernstein, author; Shinobu Onizawa, translator, *Kareinaru kōeki* (original title: *A Splendid Exchange*), Nikkei Publishing, 2010.

There are political scientists who call the present age the "new Middle Ages."[216/★94] They say that the arena of international politics is no longer the domain of only sovereign states, but also of various other actors, such as multinational businesses, superwealthy individuals, international NGOs, and even terrorists—all well endowed with technology and money and carrying out aggressive diplomacy.[217]

Live anywhere in the world, with your "hometown"

Even at the personal level, if you meet specific requirements, the significance of national borders is waning. As long as you have your credit card, passport, and smartphone with you, you will no longer run into inconveniences in any part of the world you travel to, especially in urban areas; as long as you have a smart phone with a built-in GPS, you will rarely lose your way, and as long as you resolve the problem of packet fees, you can search for and download, on the spot, an app containing a tourist guide for the country you're visiting.[★95]

The hurdles to studying and finding employment abroad have also fallen. Access to information has become extremely easy with the Internet, and the number of intermediary sellers, who arrange everything from A to Z, has also increased. And after reaching an overseas destination,[★96] as long as Internet access is available, contacting your friends is a breeze, not to mention checking the news coming out of Japan. And if you have the Skype app installed on your smartphone, you can place a phone call to virtually anywhere in the world while spending very little money.

This means that, no matter where in the world you may be, you can live in sync with the place of your origin, your "hometown." From 2005 through 2006, I was studying in Norway, but I was nonetheless able to catch up on Japanese news in real time, for the most part.

I would simply open my web browser and go to Yahoo! JAPAN, which was completely identical to the website I used to access in Japan. I would also go to a vid-

---

216.   Akihiko Tanaka, *Atarashii chūsei* (The new Middle Ages), Nikkei Publishing, 2003.

★94.   Symbolic of this "New Middle Ages" is the spread of the influence of non-state actors such as the "Islamic State of Iraq and the Levant" (ISIL). In addition, it has been pointed out that areas such as Somaliland, where "nation-state" isn't a valid descriptor, bear a remarkable resemblance to Japan in the Middle Ages. (Hideyuki Takano and Katsuyuki Shimizu, *Sekai no henkyō to hādo boirudo Muromachi jidai* [The remote regions of the world and the hardboiled Muromachi era], Shueisha International, 2015.)

217.   Parag Khanna, author; Haruhiko Furumura, translator, *Nekusuto runesansu* (original title: *How to Run the World: Charting a Course to the Next Renaissance*), Kodansha, 2011.

★95.   To me, an issue that's becoming increasingly more important than the question of which country I'm in is the question of whether or not Internet connectivity is available.

★96.   Lately, thanks to the growing number of airplanes equipped with Wi-Fi access, it's become possible to stay connected even while you're on the move.

eo-sharing site, where I could watch a Japanese drama that had aired the day before. As for shipments from Japan, my packages would arrive in a matter of three days, thanks to the EMS express international delivery service. As long as I was sitting in front of my PC, averting my gaze from the freezing-cold, snowy view outside, I was in a place that was no different from Japan.

Such was the status quo five years ago—in a small country at the edge of Europe, no less. Early this year (January of 2011), before visiting Shanghai to see a friend studying there, I asked him via Twitter if there was anything he'd like me to bring for him from Japan. He told me, "Nothing in particular, everything's available here."[218]

Being able to live anywhere in the world as though you're living in "Japan" is also evidence of the emergence of a new nationalism. Being able to imagine your mother country even when you're abroad, continuing to hold on to your identity as a member of your mother country, is known as "long-distance nationalism."[219]

The so-called permanent or lifetime travelers who travel for tax-shelter purposes are also attracting attention, especially among the wealthy class. The idea is to become a "non-resident" by meeting certain conditions like spending only a certain number of days in a given country, without having a permanent address or dependents there, so as to avoid paying income or inheritance taxes.

There are courageous people who, by wandering from country to country, maintain non-resident status in any country they stay in order to evade taxation; there are also capitalists who live in countries with lower tax rates than those in Japan, such as Hong Kong and Singapore, in order to evade large amounts of taxes.[220]

Do we need nations anymore?

Lately, more and more economic experts have been telling me that nations have become

---

218. I mean this pre-travel exchange itself was unimaginable until twenty years ago. As long as you make use of virtually cost-free means of communications such as Twitter, email, or Skype, it has no longer become necessary, for the most part, to be conscious of whether the party at the other end of the line is in the same country as you or not.

219. Benedict Anderson, author; Masami Sekine, translator, "Enkakuchi nashonarizumu no shutsugen" (The emergence of long-distance nationalism) in *Sekai*, September 1993. However, Anderson's argument places emphasis on the point of continuing to retain one's birthplace identity even while living in a foreign country.

220. The definition of "non-resident" is also often disputed at trials. One such trial that reached the Supreme Court was the case concerning the gift tax levied on the former managing director of Takefuji for inheriting a substantial portion of the shares of an affiliated company from the former president. The former managing director had been in Hong Kong for more than 65 percent of the three-and-a-half year period before and after receiving the gift. But the point at issue was whether Japan could levy the tax on this gift. In the end, the court ruled that Japan had no legal right to do so. However, with the amended Special Taxation Measures Law passed in 2000, such a gift would be deemed taxable in a similar case today.

unnecessary. For instance, in the book titled *Mō kuni ni wa tayoranai* (I don't depend on the state anymore), Miki Watanabe of the Watami chain of Japanese-style pubs (forty-seven years old, Kanagawa) asserts, "There's nothing a private enterprise can't do."[221] After bragging about the fact that his company has, in the capacity of a private enterprise, entered into public domains such as education, medical care, welfare, nursing care, agriculture, and environment-related areas, he insists that there is no future for this country if we continue to rely solely on the old-fashioned "logic of the bureaucrats.★[97]

So what should we do? Watanabe says that we should open up public services to free competition based on free-market principles. Currently, various public institutions are just organizations set up to protect rights. To reset this modus operandi, it will be crucial to introduce the idea of the customer's viewpoint into the public services, including education and medical care. In other words, even the nation, too, must be "managed" like a private enterprise. This is Watanabe's idea.

At the same time, though, he keeps excusing himself by saying over and over, "I'm not a market fundamentalist." He maintains that the nation should be responsible for building a framework to prevent the collapse of the market platform, in the event that free-market principles go too far, and for providing oversight to check for any underhandedness in the market, and for the creation of a safety net to help those who have fallen through the cracks of free competition.

Internet portal Livedoor founder Takafumi Horie (thirty-eight years old, Fukuoka) took a similar stance. Prior to his incarceration on fraud charges, he had been appealing, at various places, for the introduction of a universal basic income.★[98] Universal basic income is a system for providing a fixed sum of money to everyone, regardless of their age or gender, whether they're rich or poor, or whether they're employed or not. While this idea was originally conceived as a safeguard to ensure the right to live and as a countermeasure against poverty, many advocates have also recently come to assess it from the standpoint of freedom from work.[222]

However, Horie's argument belongs in another school of thought. The reason he's in favor of basic income is because it promises to reduce "waste." According to the conceptual framework of Horiemon (as Horie is popularly known), the nation should

221.   Miki Watanabe, *Mō kuni ni wa tayoranai* (I don't depend on the state anymore), Nikkei Business Publications, 2007.

★97.   After that, Watami became synonymous with a "black company," and went into the red—for the first time since being listed—for the fiscal year ending March 2015. Ironically, the existence of the "black company" made people reaffirm the importance of the role of the "state" in enforcing laws such as the Labor Standards Law.

★98.   Horie was imprisoned in June 2011, and released on parole in March 2013. At present, he is happily carrying out a media business, working on his space development project, and playing "Jinroh" (Werewolf).

function as an organ specializing in the collection of consumption taxes. The collected taxes should then just be used as a financial resource to fund the universal basic income scheme; other affairs such as employment and welfare should be taken care of by private enterprises.

At the heart of his argument lies the conviction that the nation "should just disappear."[223]

The anarchy of the strong

While both Watanabe and Horie add a modern touch to their arguments with the mitigating claim that they are in favor of securing a minimum level of welfare through the establishment of a "safety net" and provision of a "universal basic income," the idea that private enterprise can entirely replace the role of the government approaches the stance of anarcho-capitalism.[224]

"If the country's not going to do it, I will" is what Watanabe would declare,[225] while Horie would say, "Who cares whether the nation exists or not!" In any case, they both harbor a deep mistrust of Japan's various institutions and organs, which, in their eyes, appear bloated.

But the view that the nation is unnecessary is slightly biased toward the strong man—that is to say, toward the powerful and privileged. While the nation may be unnecessary for a capable person, or a person of means, for the incapable person who has no means, the "safety net" and "basic income" stand to become convenient excuses.

In other words, with the reasoning that goes, "Hey, we've got basic income; that's good enough," it isn't difficult to imagine various employment regulations being abolished, along with welfare systems and insurance regimes. While certainly everyone can

---

222.   For example, the sociologist Satoshi Kotani advocates basic income from the viewpoint of championing "the right to be lazy," and finds the possibility of guaranteeing political freedom in this. (Satoshi Kotani, "'Namakeru kenri' no hō e" [Progressing toward "the right to be lazy"], *Wakamono no genzai: Rōdō* [Young people at present: Labor], Nihon Tosho Center, 2010). (Oh, that reminds me, whenever I meet Professor Kotani, I'm always told that his hair isn't white because of his age, but because he once suffered from leukemia. So if you ever run into him on the train, no matter how grandfatherly he may appear, don't ever give up your seat for him. Isn't that right, Professor?)

223.   Regarding the above discussion on Horiemon's ideas, I referred to Toshihito Kayano and Takafumi Horie's "Bēshikku inkamu wa zero seichō shakai no kyūseishu ka?" (Is basic income the salvation of zero-growth society?) in *Kotoba* no. 2, 2010.

224.   In contrast to anarchism, which seeks to completely abolish centralized power, anarcho-capitalism is a political order that seeks not only to abolish state power, but to subsequently establish full credence and faith in capitalism.

225.   In fact, Watanabe ran in the Tokyo gubernatorial race in 2011. If he had become the governor of Tokyo, I wonder whether, even at the ward office, people would have been greeted with, "Welcome, dear taxpayers," in the kind of loud voice that you hear when you walk into a bar. Sadly, he lost the race, so this remains anyone's guess.

still sustain a minimum standard of living, if we adopted the Horiemon plan, the nation would be abandoning its wealth distribution function, possibly bringing about, as a result, a society riddled with social disparities.

As for freely traveling around the world, only a limited few can actually do this. As we confirmed in chapter 2, the number of Japanese students studying abroad was less than 70,000, or about one in two hundred. The view of the world's common language, English, as being difficult is also deep-rooted. In scores for the TOEFL English test, which is used all over the world to screen for candidates seeking to study abroad, Japan ranks at second from the bottom among Asian countries, registering at sixty-seven points. Even if you looked all over the world, you would only find a handful of countries with test scores lower than Japan's.[226/★99]

In other words, many Japanese, it is expected, don't physically leave "Japan," and many Japanese communicate mainly in Japanese when they're on the Internet.

However, in this case, the attenuation of "Japan" is occurring on a different trajectory from the "strong man" one—and it is especially conspicuous among young people.

The collapse of "Japan" from the bottom up

Take, for instance, young people's disconnect with TV. According to the *Kokumin seikatsu jikan chōsa* (National time budget survey) conducted by the NHK, the number of young people who don't watch TV is continuing to increase.[227] The percentage of males aged ten to nineteen who don't watch TV on Sundays was merely 4 percent in 1980, but rose to 20 percent in 2010. Among males in their twenties, the number has increased from 6 percent to 31 percent. For females from ten to nineteen this number rose from 5 percent in 1980 to 19 percent in 2010, and among females in their twenties, from 6 percent to 23 percent.[228/★100]

---

226. ETS TOEFL (2009)—Test and Score Data Summary for TOEFL iBT and PBT. However, since Japan has a large number of examinees, the scores here tend to be lower than in countries where only the elite take the exam.

★99. According to a 2014 survey, the average TOEFL score among people whose native language was Japanese was seventy points. Out of 114 language groups, the Japanese language group ranked a dismal 105th place. Incidentally, among those whose native language was in the Germanic linguistic group, the average score was high, registering at 97 points, but the average for Chinese speakers also was 77 points; for Korean speakers, it was 84 points.

227. NHK Broadcasting Culture Research Institute, *Kokumin seikatsu jikan chōsa hōkokusho* (National time budget survey report).

228. In July, 2011, as announced previously, analog broadcasting was terminated on schedule. Consequently, upon this occasion, many young people likely stopped watching television. ("Chidejika made hantoshi desuga...wakamono wa terebi banare?" [Only six months to go before the complete switch to terrestrial digital TV takes place, but are young people disengaged from TV?], *Tokyo Shimbun*, January 24, 2011, morning edition.)

An examination of the survey carried out by the Agency for Cultural Affairs reveals that, in response to the question, "Where do you obtain your necessary information every day?" the percentage of young people answering, "TV and newspapers" has declined, while the percentage answering, "the Internet," has increased. In 2001, 93.9 percent of twenty-somethings said TV was their source of information, but by 2008, this figure had fallen to 81 percent.[229]

We shouldn't place too much weight on these findings, though. After all that's been said, around 80 percent of young people are watching TV, while even answering that TV is their information source of choice. So to talk of the "collapse of the masses" or "the extinction of TV" is a huge exaggeration. The TV and newspapers aren't going to disappear overnight. In fact, at the time of the Great East Japan Earthquake in particular, it became clear that the impact of the mass media was still huge. (See chapter 5.)

However, for postwar Japan, this trend may turn out to define its epoch. From the 1960s onward, even from a global perspective, TV had spread throughout Japan at an extraordinarily speedy pace. In addition, the TV viewing time was longer by far compared to that in foreign countries. It is no exaggeration, even, to say that TV played a key role in creating postwar "Japan"; with nationwide broadcasts of only a handful of programs, culture and fashion naturally spread throughout the country at an unprecedented pace.

You might say that this was TV nationalism, which would have taken the Meiji government by surprise. Transcending gaps imposed by cultural hierarchies and generational differences, the TV delivered common programs to the whole country, promising each and every viewer that they could acquire, before they knew it, a minimum level of education and a "Japanese consciousness," a Japanese mindset. The TV, in other words, was a cultural safety net that promoted the ideal of *ichi-oku sō-hakuchika* (the enlightenment of a hundred million) in Japan.[230]

★100. According to NHK's 2015 survey *Nihonjin to terebi* (The Japanese and television), among twenty-somethings, only 8 percent responded, "I almost never watch TV" in 2010, but by 2015 this figure had doubled to 16 percent. In addition, the percentage of those watching TV less than two hours a day has also gone up, from 40 percent to 51 percent. While TV's frequency of contact still remains high relative to newspapers, books, and magazines, the "disengagement from TV" among young people certainly seems to be advancing.

229. Agency for Cultural Affairs, *Kokugo ni kansuru yoron chōsa* (Public opinion poll on the Japanese language). Incidentally, the percentage for newspapers has seen a drop from 73.5 percent to 41.8 percent. On the other hand, the percentage for the Internet has risen from 24.7 percent to 48.1 percent.

People who want to think that the Internet will change society

Of course, with a good command of the Internet, even without watching the TV or reading newspapers, you can obtain more information than the mass media alone can ever provide. There are even people who watch foreign-language broadcasts of the news from abroad—which the Japanese media don't cover that much—and even evaluate multiple sources before releasing, on their blog, their own articles that are on par with a researcher's report.

However, regrettably, such information-savvy one-person powerhouses are a rare breed. Unlike TV, in the case of the Internet, the quality of information you can acquire varies greatly by the site you access or by your level of literacy. With TV, however, if you press the button, the screen switches on, and the number of channels is limited, so everyone accesses the TV in a more or less similar way; people don't have that many options to choose from. On the other hand, the Internet is a mass medium that offers an inexhaustible number of choices. With it, you're free to follow current events or have a chat about an old "Doraemon" movie.

The Internet has been characterized as a dream medium that can empower citizens to change society.[231] In fact, however, the Internet is a medium that relativizes "Japan" from the top to bottom, and from the bottom up as well.

To explain what I mean by this, let's take a look at what the medium-specific coverage of the news was like on February 12, 2011, the morning after the resignation of President Mubarak, the ruler who had maintained a thirty-year dictatorship in Egypt.

At 1:00 a.m. Japan time, when the news broke across the world that President Mubarak had resigned and transferred plenary powers to the military supreme council, news-related sites on the Internet reported the "collapse of the Mubarak regime" in a breaking-news format.

In sync with this, on media platforms such as Twitter and Facebook, which apparently accommodate many people who are highly responsive to news and information, there was a lot of buzz around Egypt-related news, with tweet after tweet criticizing Japanese TV. This was because, in stark contrast to the global news media such as

---

230. Takumi Satō, *Terebiteki kyōyō* (Television education), NTT Publishing, 2008. "Young people's disengagement from TV" isn't some new phenomenon that has suddenly attracted attention in recent times. For example, in the 1980s, there was a lot of buzz around the rise in the number of children who stopped watching TV, thanks to the increased presence of videos and the Nintendo Entertainment System.

231. While I don't know whether the Internet or Twitter will transform society or not, every time a new technology appears, it's said that "society will change," and whenever a major incident occurs, it's often attributed to a technology that is new at that moment in time. For example, when the Berlin Wall destroyed in 1989, it was said that "satellite broadcasting" had played a key role.

CNN and BBC, which were reporting the collapse of the Mubarak regime as breaking news, Japanese TV stations were carrying on with their normal programming.[232]

Now, that's the Internet for you. No wonder it's called the "citizen's media." It enables citizens around the world to transcend borders and connect.

I choose a bowl of egg rice over a revolution in a distant land

But that's just one aspect of the Internet. I looked into Japan's largest online social networking service, mixi [ミクシィ]. There, I saw a lineup of lighthearted pieces ranked at the top of the list of the most accessed news stories, such as "How to tell people not to chew audibly," "Ingredients to add to your *tamago kake gohan*" (raw egg mixed with white rice), "Masterpiece anime cartoons you'd want your children to watch," and so on and so forth.[233] In the top-twenty ranking, there was no news at all concerning the resignation of the Egyptian president.

However, in the list that ranks journal entries based on mixi's newsfeed, the story titled "Egyptian President Mubarak resigns" was beautifully ranked among the top ten. Among these entries were a series of wry, tongue-in-cheek wordplays, such as *Mubaraku shibaraku iidesu* (Mubarak, we've had enough of you); *Mubachan, sayonara* (Goodbye, Muba-baby); and *Otsukaresama deshita, yoku gambarimashita* (Thank you for your hard work. Well done, sir).[234]

On the Ameba news service, too, the news access ranking at the top only showed stories with titles like "Hottest men without girlfriends"; "Ranking of the most puzzling women's fashion arrangements and items,"; "Valentine confessions men are most paranoid about." There was no Egypt-related news to be found in the top fifty items.[235]

The news ranking, though, was even more eyebrow-raising; the types of stories you could actually call "news" were, for the most part, missing in action. What came close

---

232. Incidentally, NHK was rebroadcasting an episode of the documentary program *Purofesshonaru shigoto no ryūgi* (The way of the professional) that featured a close-up account of the comedian Hitoshi Matsumoto. I suppose, as far as Japanese TV went, this was fair—at least it wasn't news about "Japan."

233. Incidentally, there seems to be no effective solution to the problem of people who tend to chew audibly. As for ingredients you might want to add to your bowl of egg-and-rice, minced cooked chicken and dried bonito are recommended. The anime masterpieces recommended for children were *Anpan-Man* and *Doraemon.*

234. The tabulation of the ranking takes place every twenty-four hours, and this one was confirmed on February 12 in the middle of the night around 24:00. To the credit of mixi users, there were many earnest comments, including those on blogs that contrasted Egypt's situation to Japan's and considered the possibility that a people's revolt would never occur in Japan, and entries that analyzed the process of the disintegration of the Mubarak regime alongside historical precedents.

235. Apparently, one characteristic of a boy without a girlfriend was "being unable to call a female classmate by her nickname"; baffling trends in women's fashion included leopardskin patterns and huge sunglasses; and what men wished to experience on Valentine's Day was to be ambushed by a woman on their way back home and hear her confess, "I've always liked you."

to actual news—albeit barely—were celebrity gossip pieces such as "[identical sisters] Mana and Kana dine with Ichirō, their friend of fifteen years" and "Tsubasa Masu-waka releases photos of herself when she was twenty and tanned."[236]

This doesn't mean, however, that mixi users and readers of Ameba news are simply uninterested in the news. After all, both sites have news stories displayed at the top of their respective pages in a format that highlights them as timely pieces making waves, and so access to these stories naturally, of necessity, increases.[237]

But let's say that there are people who choose to get by without watching TV and reading the newspapers, and instead turn only to mixi's or Ameba's newsfeeds in-stead—what happens then? These people could spend their days without ever learning about the kinds of murder cases covered on the front page of newspapers, let alone a revolution in a distant nation.[★102]

Though both groups live in Japan and are similarly connected to the Internet, on the one hand there are people who, while following foreign news, have acquired a perspective that relativizes Japan (that is, one that helps them see Japan in relation to other countries); on the other hand, there are those who only look at Ameba's news-feed and end up missing out on the news of incidents occurring in Japan, never mind any news from abroad.[238] This is quite striking.

I'm not really complaining here. Just because you're living in Japan, you aren't obligated to have knowledge of any news about "Japan" in which not a single acquain-tance of yours appears. Conversely, if you wish to contemplate not only "Japan," but also the global situation of politics and economics, you're absolutely free to do so. What it boils down to is the fact that the national borders collectively defining "Japan"—those constructs the Meiji government had forcibly established—are col-lapsing. And that's what this story is all about in the end.

I do like Japan, but…

I may have gotten carried away here. It might have been a slight stretch, on my part, to argue that "Japan" was collapsing, using just the examples of the TV and Internet.

So let me now turn to hard statistical data, as we return to the story of the nation-

---

236.   However, when the Great East Japan Earthquake occurred on March 11, 2011, even on mixi News and Ameba News websites, earthquake-related news accounted for all the top-ranking headlines (see chapter 5).

237.   I contacted mixi and Ameba to inquire about their respective criteria for selecting headline news stories, but mixi was completely unresponsive, while Ameba let me know that they would be "checking with the relevant department." Since then, it's been over a month, but I have yet to hear from them.[★101]

★101. Of course, I still haven't had any response from them.

★102. The statements in this chapter still remain basically relevant today, but compared with 2011, the decline of mixi as an SNS is striking. So I'd like you to read "mixi News" as "LINE News."

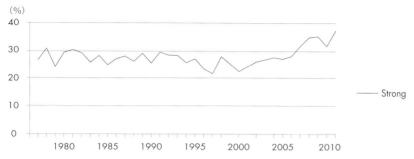

Figure 3.1   Changes in "Love for the country" (respondents in their twenties)
Source: *Public Opinion Survey on Social Awareness*

alism of Japanese youths. When we take a look at the *Public Opinion Survey on Social Awareness*, we see that the level of "love for the country" has been seeing an upward trend these past ten years (figure 3.1). While the proportion of young people with a strong "love for the country" had, for a time, dropped all the way down to 22 percent, the figure has surpassed 30 percent in the past several years. In 2011, in particular, the figure reached 37 percent, a record high.[239/★103]

In addition, the number of youths who feel they have been "fortunate to have been born in Japan" is also on the rise. In particular, if you look at the data available for those aged between twenty and twenty-four, the figure, which was 82 percent in 1973, rose to 93 percent in 1983; in 2008 it soared to a whopping 98 percent. Similarly, the number of youths who "wish to be helpful for Japan in my own way" is also on the rise. So it appears that, after all is said and done, everyone loves Japan at heart.

Seen in this light, the manic enthusiasm among young people witnessed at the

---

238.   Of course, even in the case of a TV addict, it would be the same thing if he or she only watched variety programs, but compared to TV, where viewing options are limited by the number of available channels, on the Internet the probability of missing out on information gets markedly higher. Although Twitter users poured scorn on the TV media, TV news programs nonetheless treated the Mubarak story as a top news item and gave it considerable coverage. National newspapers like the *Asahi Shimbun* and the *Yomiuri Shimbun* were running large headlines that read "Mubarak Regime Collapses" at the top of their front page, along with photographs showing throngs of people surging against the executive office of the president. For some reason, though, the *Sankei Shimbun*'s top front-page story was about a tentative plan for pension reform that the paper itself was proposing. Even then, however, the story on the Mubarak government appeared on the front page as well. As for the space for the story on the front page, *Asahi* allocated 550 cm^2, *Yomiuri* 1,017 cm^2, and *Sankei* 446 cm^2.

239.   Since the 2011 survey was carried out in January, it hasn't been influenced by the "Japan explosion" (chapter 5) that occurred in the immediate aftermath of the Great East Japan Earthquake.

★103. The "love for country" among twenty-somethings was 37 percent in the survey carried out in January 2012, indicating no change from the previous year. As the survey was carried out nearly a year after the Great East Japan Earthquake, the impact of the earthquake disaster was perhaps not large. But in the 2015 survey, the patriotism of twenty-somethings registered a record high of 42.3 percent.

World Cup becomes perfectly understandable. How can the level of support for the team called Japan, a country they love so much, not get lively?

At one time, though, Rika Kayama, a forty-two year old psychiatrist from Hokkaido, worried that the World Cup craze was a sign of "petit nationalism"—that an easygoing love affair with the country would, before long, turn into an exclusionary nationalism characterized by jingoistic tendencies.[240]

However, it's rather pointless to use the lens of nationalism to analyze young people who wave the Japanese flag while loudly and exuberantly cheering, "Japan!" As long as they continue to remain in a state of mob mania, as opposed to being mobilized to form an organization, there is no serious risk.[241]

As Atsushi Miura (fifty-two years old, Niigata) also points out, the Japan-centrism and love for the country exhibited by young people need to be distinctly set apart from political nationalism.[242]

Young people like Japan—but not necessarily just Japan. They visit Shinto shrines during the New Years' holidays, enjoy wearing the *yukata* (an informal summer kimono), and love ancient cities like Kyoto. But they love Apple products, too, and wear H&M clothes, and even travel abroad if they have the money and a friend who'll accompany them.

It's closer to the truth to say that this fondness for Japan, rather than being a sign of nationalism, is a sign of a "Japan boom." The magic spell of nationalism cast by the Meiji government was, it can be said, an altogether different variety of nationalism.

If war breaks out, I'm running away, of course

There's data that embodies this claim. According to the *World Values Survey* carried out in 2005, 15.1 percent of Japanese answered "yes" to the question, "If war breaks out, will you fight for your country?"[243] This figure was the lowest among the twenty-four countries targeted by the survey. Incidentally, the value was 80.1 percent in Sweden,

---

240. Rika Kayama, *Puchi nashonarizumu shōkōgun* (The petit-nationalism syndrome), Chuokoron-Shinsha, 2002.

241. As I pointed out in my book *Kibō nanmin goikkō sama* (A party of hope refugees; Kobunsha, 2010), though, there remains the danger of the facilitators who mobilize them being cunning. However, insofar as this present day and age are concerned, when we're seeing explosive growth in the number of collectives to which one can commit to besides the "nation," I feel we don't need to worry about any mobilization or recruitment occurring for the cause of nationalism. Rather, nationalism is likely just a secondary problem; the primary task at hand is to seriously respond to the lack of endorsements.

242. Akira Miura, *Aikoku shōhi* (Patriotic consumption), Tokuma Shoten, 2010.

243. This is based on the *World Values Survey*. A part of the data is compiled in *Sekai shuyō-koku, kachikan dēta bukku* (The data book of values in major countries) edited by Dentsu Soken and the Nippon Research Center (Doyukan, 2008).

75.5 percent in China, and 63.2 percent in the United States. You can tell how low the level of awareness concerning national defense is among the Japanese.[★104]

The younger the age group, the lower the willingness to protect the country became. While 21.1 percent of Japanese age fifty and above answered "I will fight for my country," the percentage of people between fifteen and twenty-nine giving the same answer fell to as low as 7.7 percent.[244/★105] Even in comparison with foreign countries, this is an overwhelmingly low level of national-defense awareness.

Running away when a war happens is exactly what the people of the feudal Chōshū domain did in the late Edo period. Fukuzawa Yukichi (forty-five years old, Osaka), in referring to the people of the Edo period, was pessimistic, saying "*Ichimei o sutsuru wa kabun naritote nigehashiru mono ōkaru beshi*" (Many of them would flee, believing the sacrifice of their lives was excessive). And that's why he went on to appeal for people to be educated, to have them turned into "citizens."[245]

Sadly, though, a span of 130 years has already passed since Fukuzawa said those words, and his hopes have come to nothing; the situation today appears unchanged.

All of which reminds me of the time I was cheering along with my friends at the World Cup event. We were all exchanging remarks like, "Thanks for your hard work!" and "Man, that felt good!" even though we weren't the ones who had been playing. Now that I think about it, though, that entire episode, strictly speaking, was a customer experience: we were living it up as spectators, using Japan as grist. In the context of the World Cup, this "Japan" was indistinguishable from an instantly consumed disposable consumer product.

But still, I think this situation should be welcomed with open arms. I'm sorry, Mr. Fukuzawa.

★104. According to the Cabinet Office's *Jieitai, bōei mondai ni kansuru yoron chōsa* (Public opinion poll concerning the issues of Self-Defense Forces and national defense; 2015), as expected, only 5.1 percent responded, "I will not resist at all" in the event of a foreign invasion. However, the combined percentage of people who would consider resisting the enemy country through some military means—e.g., joining the Self-Defense Forces (6.8 percent) or becoming a guerilla fighter (1.9 percent)—amounted to only 8.7 percent.

244. Even in foreign countries, in general, the percentage responding "I will fight for the country" was lower the younger the age group, but even among this international dataset, the percentage in Japan was notably low.

★105. According to the 2010 *World Values Survey*, the percentage of Japanese people answering that they would "fight for the country if war occurred" was 15.2 percent; among people aged fifteen to twenty-nine, the percentage answering the same was 9.5 percent. This is a slight increase from 2005.

245. Fukuzawa Yukichi, *Gakumon no susume* (*An Encouragement of Learning*). This was published as a book in 1880. Incidentally, when students enter Keio University they receive, as a gift, to this day, the original version of *Fukuōjiden* (*The Autobiography of Fukuzawa Yukichi*). This book can often be found on Yahoo Auctions.

What's the worst murder case in Japanese history?

It's not the Tsuyama incident. Nor is it the Aum Shinrikyō affair. In terms of the number of lives lost, the time span endured, and the scale realized, the worst murder in Japanese history was carried out during the Asia-Pacific War. The defendant's name was "Japan"—or the "Great Japanese Empire," if you prefer using the former title.

The Asia-Pacific War was a case of mass murder, in which Japan alone suffered approximately 3.1 million casualties. The combined total of World War II casualties is said to surpass 50 million. If you look at it in terms of numbers alone, individual murder cases are no match. In fact, making such a comparison is sheer nonsense.[246]

With that in mind, however, if we look at the numbers anyway, we see that in the Aum Shinrikyō case, the death toll amounted to twenty-seven. The Tsuyama case had thirty victims. In 2010 alone, the combined total of murder victims amounted to just 465.[247] So this nation called "Japan" has, ultimately, killed more people than any murderer to have appeared in the history of Japan. The warlord Oda Nobunaga pales in comparison, and relative to those "impenetrable" juvenile crimes or abnormal and bizarre murders, cross-national wars are considerably more ill-natured.[248/★106]

This story isn't unique to Japan, though. A look at any modern nation reveals that there have never been as many people who have fought for their nation, and lost their lives for their nation, than there were in the twentieth century. Even in Europe, until the eighteenth century the greatest threat to humanity was natural disasters such as floods.

However, battles that pitted kings against kings gave way to cross-national wars, which ultimately led to two all-out wars waged in the twentieth century: the World Wars. Thus, the war waged by soldiers (or mercenaries) hired by kings ended up becoming, under the authority of the modern nation-state, a massive undertaking that

---

246. Even compared with natural disasters, the toll is immense. The number of dead the Asia-Pacific War produced was one hundred times greater than the fatalities caused by the Great East Japan Earthquake.

247. National Police Agency, *Heisei 22-nen no hanzai jōsei* (The state of crime in 2010). The death toll due to murder has continued to decline; the number of recognized murder cases in 2010 was 1,067, a postwar record-low. Could this also be a gift of the emergent "herbivorous men?"

248. However, compared with mediated cross-national wars, conflicts involving multiple actors have the possibility of bringing about an even more tragic situation. For instance, in the Democratic Republic of Congo (formerly Zaire), a conflict over natural resources has been dragging on. Casualties are estimated at 5.4 million people for the period from 1998 through 2008 alone (Masako Yonekawa, *Sekai saiaku no funsō, "Kongo"* [The world's worst conflict: "Congo"], Soseisha, 2010).

★106. I raised the case of Congo in the book, but back then, in 2011, I downplayed the role of the "nation" even more than I do now. While there's no denying that nationalism has been responsible for many fatalities, historically the state of anarchy has produced even more victims. To dig deeper, see the postscript to this chapter and Noritoshi Furuichi's *Daremo sensō o oshierarenai* (Nobody can teach war; Kodansha, 2015).

entangled all citizens.[249]

This is the greatest failing of the magic of nationalism.

It is, in fact, a fatal flaw.

The dual dynamic of the modern nation-state and nationalism functions effectively during times when objectives are concrete and clear—objectives such as "Achieve victory in war by enhancing the wealth and military strength of the nation" or "Become the world's most affluent nation through economic growth." Owing to this, the infrastructure of Japan became complete, and the standard of living rose to the level the nation enjoys today. It was a dream collaboration—but one that required many sacrifices.

So why not let such a magic disappear? Why not just be done with it?

But of course, Japan, as a nation, won't disappear. At the very least, it will continue to survive as a supplier of infrastructure. Consequently, it will inherit the role of the nation-state, monopolizing violence and collecting taxes.

However, come World Cup time, though young people may audibly support this nation-state, as soon as the game ends, they'll say, "Thanks for your hard work!" and promptly forget their momentary passion. They'll access the Ameba newsfeed and read, say, a news story titled, "Points of interest about the opposite sex," live it up with friends, and plan on running away the moment a war breaks out. If such young people are on the rise, then, at least in terms of their attitude, I think it's a very positive thing, as the chances of an international war occurring decrease, even if by only a small margin.

Postscript: When Did "Japan" Begin?

Frankly, the part of the book I wanted to rework the most was this chapter. My understanding of two points has changed greatly.

The first is modernization and nationalism. In the book I had depicted the Edo period, in contrast with the Meiji period and beyond, as a time when social positions were fixed, freedom of movement was restricted, and when people didn't have a "Japanese" mindset. However, I subsequently met the sociologist Hidetoshi Katō (eighty-five years old, Tokyo), and in the course of reading his book, I came to question my

---

249. Yōichi Kibata, ed., *Kōza sensō to gendai 2: Nijusseiki no sensō to wa nandeatta ka* (Lecture wars and modernity 2: What were the wars of the twentieth century about?), Otsuki Shoten, 2004.

textbook understanding.★107

According to Katō, the Edo era should be grasped as not "premodern," but "early modern," given that by the mid-eighteenth century, changes considered to be the hall-marks of "modern times" were already underway.

Firstly, he says, the notion that the freedom of movement was severely restricted in the Edo period is incorrect. During this time in Japan, surprisingly, mass tourism had taken root. The most popular tourist attraction was the Ise Grand Shrine. In the year 1705 alone, a total of ten million people had visited the shrine on what's known as an *Okage Mairi* pilgrimage to offer thanks for blessings.

Even in years that weren't as special as 1705, in the late eighteenth century, the Tōkaidō road alone reportedly saw annual traffic of a million people. Guidebooks such as the *Tōkaidō meishoki* (A record of noted places along the Tōkaidō road) and maps of Japan were published, and during the agricultural off-season, when farmers had time for leisure, many Japanese used to take jaunts similar to the "farm co-op tours" of the Shōwa period.

Why did this age of grand tours arrive in Japan? It was because of the establish-ment of post towns in various parts of the country owing to the *sankin-kōtai*, the sys-tem in which feudal lords were compelled to take turns attending on the shogun at the capital in Edo. By the eighteenth century, roads had been completed, along with cities and settlements replete with accommodations.

In addition, in the eighteenth century, even educational facilities, including the *terakoya* (a kind of primary school for the children of commoners), had become wide-spread. Abandoned children had been a common sight in Japan before then, but by the eighteenth century the sense that infants were "children worthy of being treasured" gained popularity, and even among commoners, interest in education for children heightened.★108

In 1710, when the Confucianist scholar Kaibara Ekiken (eighty years old, Chiku-zen province) preached the need for common education in the pages of *Wazoku dōji kun* (Precepts for education), *terakoyas* were coming into existence. In addition, Okayama domain established *terakoyas* of its own, giving rise to what we know today as the public school. Of course, there was no such thing as a national curriculum yet, but there were apparently textbooks that were "fixtures," such as the *Keitenyoshi* (Chi-

---

★107. Hidetoshi Katō, *Media no tenkai* (The development of media), Chuokoron-Shinsha, 2015. See also Hidetoshi Katō's *Media no hassei* (The birth of media; Chuokoron-Shinsha, 2009) for a lively description of the Middle Ages. These two books have proved vital in my writing of the postscript.

★108. Jun Shibata, *Nihon yōjishi* (The history of Japanese children), Yoshikawa Kobunkan, 2012.

nese classics) and the *Jinkōki* (the first Japanese textbook on arithmetic).★109

Furthermore, with the flowering of the publishing culture in the Edo period, according to the *Zōeki shojaku mokuroku taizen* (Complete catalog of publications) published in 1696, nearly 8,000 books were circulating the market in those days. Even collections of book reviews were available for readers seeking recommendations.

In addition, as can be plainly seen by the presence of *kabunakama* (merchant guilds), the precursors of the Japanese corporate organization existed at this time, too. And the so-called *shinōkōshō* class system was, as claimed by a number of books of the time, just a rough classification of occupations, having no association with any sense of hierarchy. The status of samurai itself, to begin with, was a commodity that could be bought and sold.

Taking into account such circumstances, I cannot help but now believe that the binary approach I took in this chapter, of demarcating "modern times" from the past, with the turning point of the Meiji Restoration serving as the dividing line, was overly dogmatic.

According to Katō, such a "theory of modernization" itself might have been part of a hidden agenda—that of the historians who had established the national history department at Tokyo Imperial University. To justify the Meiji Restoration, the Edo and Meiji periods needed to be cut off and made distinct from each other; a discontinuity between them had to be created.

To be sure, it goes without saying that the Meiji government's attempt to turn the people living in Japan into Nihonjin (Japanese) through the implementation of nationwide education and military conscription is a seriously demanding project. However, when contemplating Japan's modernization, it's safer to find its germination in the mid-Edo period than to state that it suddenly sprouted, full-blown, in the Meiji period.

The other point I couldn't help but rethink is my point of view on the "nation-state." In this chapter, I wrote that "there have never been as many people who have fought for their nation, and have lost their lives for their nation, than there were in the twentieth century." That statement per se isn't wrong, as World War II proved to be the worst mass-murder incident in the history of humanity, causing the loss of the lives of

---

★109. The *Keitenyoshi* is a Confucianist work, and the *Jinkōki* is a mathematics textbook. They were both huge bestsellers published in the Edo period and cherished for three centuries until the Meiji era. The *Keitenyoshi*, it is said, is very likely the book in Ninomiya Kinjirō's hands in the well-known bronze statues depicting him reading.

20 million soldiers and 46 million civilians for a total of 66 million lives lost.[110]

However, prior to the formation of the nation-state, 15 to 60 percent of men in hunter-gatherer societies, according to some estimates, lost their lives in battle. If humanity had reached the twentieth century with such a society still intact, the number of people killed in action would have amounted to two billion.

While the modern state has certainly been guilty of repeating horrifying wars over and over again, compared with tribal warfare, cross-national wars have a lower death rate, and the rate of active duty among men tends to be low.[111] Furthermore, at times a state of anarchy can produce even more victims than war.[112]

With such figures before me, I became convinced that it was no longer easy to simply consider the "state" a villain. In addition, ever since the war ended, Japan has been a nation of "corporate welfare," turning to companies to meet social-security needs, and amid the heightening mobility of employment, the role of the state as a driving force behind social security can only go on to elevate in prominence. Furthermore, the state is most likely the only entity that can genuinely grapple with the issue of the dwindling birthrate and aging population that Japan faces.

But make no mistake. I'm not in any way saying here that it would be ideal to have everyone in Japan fall in love with Japan and enjoy a World Cup–like situation all year round. What's more, as I have emphasized many times throughout the book, I continue to believe that the age of depending on the state to be responsible for everything is over.

Recently, companies like Axelspace, which specializes in the development of ultra-compact satellites, have appeared in Japan, too, demonstrating that we now live in a time when even an individual company can enter into the field of "space"—one that has hitherto been the prerogative of the state.

Going forward, the shape of the nation called "Japan" will likely go on changing.

---

[110]. Matthew White, author; Susumu Sumitomo, translator, *Satsuriku no sekaishi* (original title: *The Great Big Book of Horrible Things: The Definitive Chronicle of History's 100 Worst Atrocities*), Hayakawa Publishing, 2013.

[111]. Steven Pinker, author; Sachiko Ikushima et al., translator, *Bōryoku no jinruishi* (original title: *The Better Angels of Our Nature: Why Violence Has Declined*), Seidosha, 2015.

[112]. For example, in the civil war in Russia that took place from 1918 through 1920, 9 million people were killed; in the two civil wars fought in China—one from 1926 to 1937, and the other from 1945 through 1949—a total of 7 million people fell victim. In recent times, the Syrian civil war, which was triggered by the Arab Spring, has produced, at minimum, more than 200,000 fatalities, while giving rise to more than four million refugees.

Chapter 4
The Youths Who Stand Up for Japan

In chapter 3, we saw how nationalism has slackened. However, you can still find some young people today raising the Japanese flag and announcing their love for this country called Japan. In this chapter, we will first of all see what these youths look like—the young people who stand up for "Japan," who have taken action in the name of "Japan." With that in mind, we will also consider what it means to start a protest demonstration, and what it means to change society.

1. Japanese Flags Raised on Bright, Sunny Holidays

Japanese flags appear in Aoyama Park

It was a fine autumn Saturday, or to put it in the style of a weather forecast, an "ideal day for an outing." In the early afternoon the atmosphere was calm in Roppongi as I was exiting Nogizaka station—a stop on the Chiyoda subway line—and then I heard some strange cheering coming from Aoyama Park. I turned toward the park and spotted a massive number of Japanese flags fluttering in the wind.

On October 16, 2010, a protest rally against the Chinese government was being held. It was sponsored by several groups, including Gambare Nippon! Zenkoku kōdō iinkai (Persevere Japan! All Japan action committee, hereafter referred to as Gambare Nippon!). Launched in February 2010, Gambare Nippon! is a conservative citizen's group chaired by Toshio Tamogami (sixty-three years old, Fukushima).[250/★113]

The group says their purpose is to think about Japan, which is facing a crisis of national dissolution and destruction today, by turning a gaze on Japan and the Japanese from the down-to-earth vantage point of grassroots citizens—individuals with

October 16, 2010

their feet firmly planted on the ground. It seemed to me that this group was aligning itself with the words of Yoshida Shōin (then twenty-eight years old, Chōshū domain): *Sōmō kukki* or "Arise, everyday people!"[251]

---

250. You might feel like saying to these people something like, "If you're going to say *Gambare* [try hard, persevere], tell it to yourself, not Japan." But that's too harsh, so just don't. You might also want to lash out in the same way at the political party of elderly people, Tachiagare Nippon (the Sunrise Party of Japan, or literally the "Stand up Japan" party), but keep in mind that on their own they don't even have the ability to *gambaru*—or to stand up, for that matter.

★113. Tamogami resigned as chairperson of Gambare Nippon! in August, 2014; in December of the same year he ran as a candidate for Jisedai no Tō (the Party for Future Generations) in the general elections held for the House of Representatives, representing the twelfth district of Tokyo. He lost, coming in last.

251. The source of *Sōmō kukki* (Rise with determination from the grass-roots) is the writings of the Chinese thinker Mencius. The declaration, "Arise, everyday people!" is reminiscent of Karl Marx's famous quote, "Workers of the world, unite!" in *The Communist Manifesto*. Now, that's Toshio Tamogami's organization for you; an outfit with affinities to China and Marx.

While they're basically opposed to the proposed bill granting foreigners the right to vote, after the development of the Senkaku Islands issue, they have been criticizing the Democratic Party for continuing a "weak-kneed diplomacy" vis-à-vis China.★114 The participants in the demonstration that day, according to the Metropolitan Police Department, amounted to 2,800 people.252 This turnout was apparently similar to the one for the demonstration held in Shibuya on October 2, in which 2,600 people participated in response to the appeal made by several groups—including, once again, Gambare Nippon!—to protest the Chinese foray into the Senkaku Islands; the demonstration was officially called "Citizens united nationwide against the Chinese invasion of the Senkaku Islands!"

Aoyama Park and its environs were thrown into such an uproar that the scene resembled a festival. Sadly, though, there were no stalls to be found, but there was a woman—she reminded me of a P.T.A. parent in charge of managing the proceedings of a bazaar—who was handing out a newspaper called *Sakura Shimbun*, a Gambare Nippon! publication. The front page showed a news story declaring that the Senkaku Islands were in danger of being occupied by China, while content on the second page criticized the "cowardly Democratic Party," asserting that "If the government can't do it, then it's up to us citizens to bear the burdens of national defense."253

Safe for even beginners!

There didn't seem to be any particular age bracket that stood out among the participants. Apparently, the demonstration succeeded in mobilizing a wide range of people, from high school students to the elderly. While many speeches were made at the gathering, the people listening to them in the front were mainly elderly; many young people, on the other hand, were talking to their friends further away.

I approached Megumi, a twenty-seven-year-old female office worker who was holding a gigantic Japanese flag. The huge flag seemed so heavy that I became concerned, but she willingly agreed to be interviewed, and in the course of our exchange she frequently emphasized that she herself was a "moderate conservative."

She said she had learned about today's event through an online community on the social networking service mixi calling itself "Who the hell voted for the Democratic

---

★114. The Democratic Party was in power in Japan from September 2009 to December 2012.
252. There's even news coverage reporting that six thousand people participated. I doubt it was that many, though.
253. Yet what was written in the paper were appeals to the government and to the United States to help out, as evidenced in headlines like, "The government is being urged to prepare to defend territorial waters," and "Make major U.S. oil companies participate in deep-sea mining projects."

Party?"★115 In addition, she herself had recently set up an online community called "Conservative Men. Conservative Women."254 According to Megumi, conservative youths, unlike "left-wing youngsters," don't have places to gather. Apparently, this is why she wanted to expand their circle by simply bonding through fun events like karaoke parties or cherry-blossom picnics.255

For many young people, it seemed, this demonstration was their first, or the second after the Shibuya protest. One such person was Keiji, my next interviewee, a twenty-nine-year-old male office worker. He was a *moteishiki-kei* (the girl-conscious, fashionable type)256 who was having a delightful exchange with other young people. He told me today was the first time he had taken part in a demonstration or social movement like this.

He had learned about the demonstration through the conservative social networking site called "my Nihon" (my Japan).★116 The mood of the scene, he said, was just as he'd imagined. "There's nobody around wearing any kind of military uniform…" Apparently, prior to today's demonstration, there had been news circulating that there weren't going to be any "rugged, shady types" in attendance.

While affirming he was in favor of coexisting with such people, saying, "Of course, I believe right-wing types have a place in the grand scheme of things," Keiji admitted that he himself wouldn't take part in the "right-wing" type of demonstration. Apparently, for him, this demonstration didn't seem to be a right-wing type, somehow or other.

Other young people at the protest called themselves liberal. Keita, a thirty-five-year-old male teacher, said, "I want Chinese and Korean people to find happiness." He was a young man with longish hair and a melancholic air, with the look of a bass player in a band.

What he felt was problematic was the "biased news coverage" of the Japanese me-

---

★115. I checked, just to be sure, and found out that as of September 2015, the "Who the hell voted for the Democratic Party" community still existed, with its members aggressively exchanging conspiracy theories.

254. These days you hear various labels describe various types of people, from the *sōshoku-kei danshi* (herbivorous men, or grass-eaters) to *bosatsu-kei danshi* (Bodhisattva men) and even *shakyō-kei joshi* (sutra-scribe women), but "conservative men" and "conservative women"? I mean, come on! My face hid my surprise, though, as I continued to listen to her.

255. In fact, these girls said they had held several events already, which involved meeting to engage in a study session first, and then holding a karaoke after-party.

256. But a failure at that. A bit too much.

★116. This was a community that began in 2009; by August 2010 it had a membership count of 30,000, and by July 2011, it had grown to 50,000 people. So this was a community that was just picking up momentum around the time I was conducting my interviews for this chapter. By August 2015, the membership was 78,000 strong. To sign in, only a username and an email address had to be registered; neither the entry of personal information nor any invitation to join was necessary.

dia. He was participating in the demonstration because, he said, "Rather than hoping to do this or that about China, or have the Democratic Party do this or that, I want other Japanese to become aware of how biased the news media really is." He went on to express concern over how demonstrations like this one tend to get written off as right-wing Internet activism. "Whatever you talk about, whatever claims you make, it all gets brushed off in the end as 'Net-based right-wing trash talk.'"

Incidentally, Keita was also part of the movement to legalize medical marijuana. While cannabis legalization seems to be a left-wing movement, in his mind, the two movements are seamlessly connected—that is, on the point that the "media is suspect." Interesting.

Mao Asada opened my eyes!

I approached Eri, a twenty-year-old female college student, to ask about her story, while she was having a pleasant chat in a four-person group. When I asked about their relationship to each other, it became clear that they weren't acquaintances from before, but apparently had just met for the first time, and were having a lively conversation about the incompetence of the Democratic Party.

It seems that Eri, who resembled a slightly thinner version of the writer and social activist Karin Amamiya, had become interested in the conservative movement because of the figure skater Mao Asada. Watching the news on figure skating to follow this idol of hers, she was surprised to see that Kim Yuna (a South Korean figure skater) was being flattered an awful lot, so she began searching the Internet. As a result, she stumbled upon all sorts of details that hadn't been reported in the media, including the lowdown on the relationship between the Dentsu advertising agency and Kim Yuna. From this story she just went on to follow the relevant links from one site to another, until she discovered the existence of conservative movements like Gambare Nippon!

Eri also took part in distributing Gambare Nippon! leaflets. She said, "It's easy to take part in Gambare Nippon! because there are many other women in the group, so it's not too scary." She, too, had a huge national flag, which she had purchased at Yasukuni shrine before today's demonstration. Yasukuni, she said, was a place she had "wanted to go to for quite some time now."

Whenever I inquire about someone's reason for becoming interested in politics, I often hear that the Internet was instrumental. For example, Aomori resident Susumu (twenty years old, manufacturing industry, male) came to know about "conservatism" and the presence of the "right wing" through Nico Nico Douga, a website that shares short videos. He told me, "There's nobody around my hometown who's interested in such [political] things."

Today, he said, he was traveling alone on his moped around the Kanto area, and his participation in the demonstration in Shibuya had marked his first offline, re-al-world event. "I found various kinds of information that you'd never be exposed to if you just relied on Nico Nico." With an expression of apparent satisfaction, he commented on the enthusiasm that can't be perceived online: "There's a feeling of tension, a sense of urgency."

What are the Senkaku Islands?

After being urged to fall into five lines by a supervisor type, the demonstration proceeded to move along its predetermined route in a well-behaved fashion. The chants were varied, from "The Senkaku Islands belong to Japan" to "Congratulations on the Nobel Peace Prize!" and even "We will liberate the Chinese worker!"

Although I had believed the protest demonstration was about the movement related to the Chinese Senkaku Islands, there didn't seem to be any particular consensus. Furthermore, perhaps because it was an ideal day for an outing, some were even protesting along with their families, pushing baby carriages.

It was a holiday demonstration parading around Roppongi. The passersby who stumbled upon it were rather surprised; we had suddenly appeared out of the blue, after all, with Japanese flags raised in the air. A person in charge called out to them to join the demonstration if they sympathized with the cause.

I wondered about the reception of this demonstration. Makoto, a twenty-year-old male who was standing in line in front of the "A-life" dance club[117] facing Roppongi-dori, was brusque, saying, "I'm not very interested. They're noisy, but, hey, what sort of people are they, anyway?" When I explained briefly, he asked, "Senkaku Islands? What's that?" Yūji (twenty-one years old, male), who was also standing in line, chimed in, "I'm not sure I understand what they're saying. It's too complicated."[118]

The ultimate destination of the march was the Chinese embassy, but Roppongi was surprisingly riddled with rising and falling roads, gradually draining everyone's spirit. Without even stopping to form a scrum, the demonstration advanced while people stopped at convenience stores along the way.

Finally, we arrived at the Chinese embassy. However, the cry that followed, "Okay,

---

★117. The club "alife" closed up shop in July, 2012. It had seen many dramas unfold, including the Asashōryū assault incident. A club called BRAND TOKYO opened in July 2013 on the same site.

★118. The Senkaku Islands are islands whose dominion is being claimed by both Japan and China; Japan nonetheless exercises effective control over them. From 2010, fishery patrol boats from China began to operate frequently around the periphery of the islands, heightening Japan-China tensions. Furthermore, a remark made by Shintarō Ishihara in 2012 made waves, resulting in Japan nationalizing a part of the Senkaku Islands, and a succession of anti-Japan demonstrations occurring in China.

everyone, we're going to encircle the embassy!" was in vain; the group no longer had enough people carry out such an action. Besides, the police had notified the group that, as a rule, no more than five people were allowed to stand in front of the embassy at one time.

So five by five, the demonstrators took turns standing in front of the embassy and protesting against China, after which they took commemorative photographs before going home. Ryōsuke (twenty-five years old, office worker, male) who had dropped by to observe the demonstration, wore a cynical smile while tweeting about the situation and wondering, "How are they ever going to surround the embassy with just five people?"

Even the police officer guarding the embassy had a smile on his face as he watched the protestors, saying, "It's Saturday today, so I doubt there's that many people inside the embassy. This demonstration is more for the media, don't you think? Let me tell you, demonstrations these days are tame, so my job as a security guard is a breeze."

The sun was going to set soon, bringing a clear and mild autumn day to an end.

2. Festive Demonstrations

"Ordinary citizens" dressed in kimono

A sea of Japanese flags flutters in the wind. Sprinkled amid them are some individuals in military uniforms. They appear to be loudly shouting out radical messages. A demonstration like this must appear strange in the eyes of many. Perhaps they're enjoying their day off, doing some shopping, and then they suddenly encounter, out of the blue, an odd-looking group they've never seen before.

However, as I have described in the preceding pages, modern demonstrations and movements are casual affairs for the most part—at least with respect to the participants' level of consciousness, regardless of any right- or left-wing connection. Now, let's take a look at another demonstration led by a conservative group. This is the refreshing-sounding *Soyokaze Demo* (Gentle Breeze Demonstration).

On May 22, 2010, covering the distance from Yoyogi Park to Shibuya, a political demonstration sponsored by the conservative women's group Nippon Josei no Kai—Soyokaze (Association of Japanese Women—Gentle Breeze) took place. It was titled "Gentle Breeze Demo—Part Three! At this rate, Japan will be destroyed!"★[119] By around half past one, the designated time, around 150 people had gathered.[257] As far as I could tell at this meeting held prior to the demonstration, young people in their twenties and thirties comprised up to 30 percent of the participants; around 40 percent were middle-aged people in their forties and fifties, and around 30 percent were in their sixties and above.

While the demonstration was hosted by a women's group, the male-to-female ratio was around seven to three. This was because members of several other conservative groups were gathered there too, starting with those of the nationalist Zainichi Tokken o Yurusanai Shimin no Kai (Zaitokukai) (Association of Citizens against the Special Privileges of Koreans in Japan [Zaitokukai]). While there were a good number of people whose protest positions—and looks—were radical, the atmosphere was nonetheless festive, with only a few people looking serious. While the group's name includes the term *soyokaze* (gentle breeze), when you take a look at the contents of their positions, you quickly realize that they're not moderate.

For instance, during the microphone relay carried out prior to the demonstration, the participants loudly appealed for "rejecting the extension of suffrage to foreigners," "crushing the child-care allowance," and "objecting to the dual-surname system," which permitted married couples to keep separate surnames. In addition, during the demonstration, banners written with anti-foreigner suffrage messages and national flags flashed everywhere. Although there were no loudspeaker vehicles, fierce-looking hard-faced men surrounded the gathering in place of security guards.

The demonstrators, however, unanimously emphasized that they were all "ordinary citizens." For Rika (late twenties, office worker, female), a member of Soyokaze, today was the second time she had taken part in this event.

As for why she came to be involved with such a movement, she said it was because of the change in government from the LDP to the Democratic Party that had taken place in the Lower House election of the summer of 2009, and because of the death of the former LDP politician Shōichi Nakagawa.

"Until then, even if I didn't take action, I felt safe leaving everything in the hands of the LDP, but after Mr. Nakagawa passed away, I began to sense that Japan was in danger, so I joined this movement." Saying that she intended to do whatever she could in her capacity as a citizen, she described the people of Soyokaze as "just normal people, unlike right-wing activists who cause trouble."

This comment is typical of the people here. They strictly define themselves as nor-

---

★ 119. Soyokaze continues to be active to this day, albeit in small ways. Still another of the women's conservative groups is the Aikoku Josei no Tsudoi Hanadokei ("flower clock" gathering of patriotic women).

257. On the same day, in pre-World Cup Yoyogi Park, a "Samurai Blue" (Japan national soccer team) event was held, mobilizing dozens of times more people than Soyokaze. Incidentally, nobody participating in the Soyokaze event I had interviewed was interested in soccer.

mal or ordinary citizens, drawing the line between themselves and the right wing. Incidentally, though, Rika was dressed in a kimono that day. She makes it a point, she said, to always go out in a kimono on holidays, but if you ask me, that's not exactly "normal" these days.

With the way things are going, Japan is in danger

Shigeru, a thirty-six-year-old electronics professional who was taking part in the event together with his wife, began participating in events like this after the change in government took place. With one of his parents involved in a political movement, he had been interested in politically related issues from the start, but didn't take part in any kind of politically oriented activities. That changed, though, around the autumn of 2009, when he began to sense that the Democratic Party was "dangerous." Consequently, he came to think he had to do something, and from that point on, he began to participate in demonstrations and attend meetings.

Shigeru's wife, Yukari (thirty-two years old, full-time housewife) said that this demonstration was her first. She had decided to drop in after hearing from Shigeru that "this place wasn't intense." She, too, had begun "to sense from around the time of the change in government that the Democratic Party government spelled trouble."

Among the participants, there were some who had no interest in so-called conservative positions. Daichi (nineteen years old, college student, male) had seen a TV program about foot-and-mouth disease. Keenly aware of how lax Japan's crisis control management was, he had felt the urge to take action and do something before joining this demonstration today. It was around this time that an outbreak of foot-and-mouth disease in Miyazaki prefecture was in the news, and one of the themes of the demonstration was to denounce the laxness in the Democratic Party's response to the issue.[258]

What I often heard from young participants there were comments infused with a sense of impending crisis, along the lines of, "With the way things are going, Japan is in danger." The LDP government, which they had taken for granted until then, had collapsed, and various Japanese institutions were changing and hanging in the balance. Thus, no longer able to take free rides on the back of the LDP, they began to think that they, too, must do something. And that "something" was to participate in an event like today's demonstration.

This insistence on considering themselves to be "ordinary, normal, or common"

---

258.   In Miyazaki, in the period between spring and summer of 2010, there was an outbreak of foot-and-mouth disease among cattle, swine, and water buffalo. The Democratic Party administration was criticized for the delay in carrying out its initial response, which was given as one of the reasons for the spread of the disease.

May 22, 2010

brings to mind the group called Atarashii Rekishi Kyōkasho o Tsukuru Kai (the Japanese Society for History Textbook Reform, henceforth referred to as the Tsukuru-kai).[259] According to research carried out by Eiji Oguma et al., those involved with the Tsukurukai are individualists; the only common code they share is their willingness to laugh at how weak-kneed Japan is.

In other words, he says, they're a vulnerable assemblage that remains valid insofar as it functions to exclude the left wing, which, in the eyes of its members, is not "ordinary or normal."[260]

Just as the Tsukurukai validates itself by rejecting the left wing, an entity they consider unusual, what connects the participants in the Soyokaze demonstrations to each other is their perception of themselves as "normal citizens" rejecting the dangerous thing named the "Democratic Party."[261] Certainly, various doctrines and positions can be linked to an awareness that says, "With the way things are going, we're in danger"—a line often uttered by Soyokaze demonstrators.

---

259.   Perhaps everyone has already forgotten about Tsukurunokai, but this group was saying that existing textbooks were running "the unadulterated propaganda of former enemy nations," and as such they were making the "Japanese lose their pride." For this reason, they had attempted to create new textbooks of their own making.

260.   Eiji Oguma and Yōko Ueno, *"Iyashi" no nashonarizumu* ("Healing" nationalism), Keio University Press, 2003.

261.   However, unlike Tsukurukai, which has made "history" and "Japan" its domain, the Soyokaze community is a relatively more casual and temporary affair, I feel.

Youths getting hooked on the "right wing"

However, among the demonstrators, there are those who become deeply committed to right-wing affiliated movements while engaging in activities as "normal citizens." Shingo (twenty-four years old, freelance professional, male), who was holding up a huge Japanese flag, said it has been nearly seven years now since he began to get involved in right-wing movements.

In college, he majored in political science, studying the national constitution and the United States' annexation of Hawaii. Although he had been interested in conservative ideas since junior high school, he didn't have like-minded friends, since he was residing in the countryside. However, after entering a university in Tokyo, he began to commit to political activities in earnest.

Shingo said he knew half of the people taking part in the demonstration that day, adding that most of his current friends were involved in some sort of conservative movement. When I asked why he continued being involved in these kinds of activities, he answered, "Because I want to."

When it gets busy, he ends up attending meetings and taking part in demonstrations every day. "But it's no different from going out to see a movie," he said. "I'm not particularly conscious about the act." While he declares he's a freelancer, much of his work involves the production of bulletins and banners for right-wing groups. "I'm borderline working poor," he says, laughing.

Kōsuke, a thirty-two-year old jobless male from Aichi, came to the conclusion that Japan is in a crisis after reading a book titled *Hannichi masukomi no shinjitsu* (The truth about the anti-Japan media). What he fears is the possibility of China and Korea taking over Japan.

"If China makes an incursion, it'll band together with the South Koreans residing in Japan and take over the country. If Japan gets conquered, there's a chance that we will end up in the same situation as the Tibetans and the Uyghur, leading to Japanese genocide." These are his pet theories.

Though Kōsuke is currently unemployed, he has no interest in what the left wing has to say in their critiques of the "gap-widening society" and of "temping." That's because he himself has a favorable assessment of how Japanese companies have been supported by irregular workers like job-hopping part-timers and temp staff. "They're necessary for companies to maintain their financial stability," he says. The old guys over at the Keidanren (Japan Business Federation) would shed tears of joy upon hearing this line, while the eminent educationalist Yuki Honda would die of indignation.

Kōsuke says his current life is "reasonably fun, with a job worth doing. Almost every day the Democratic Party drops material I can work with." He's a heavy user of the Nico Nico Douga website, but says that he never runs short of "material" like the issue of foot-and-mouth disease and the commotion surrounding the base relocation, adding, with a laugh, that "It's fun."

How interesting. So it's not all about just being fueled by resentment against the Democratic Party.

Shingo and Kōsuke differ in that Shingo is the one taking part in activities carried out by an actual right-wing organization, while Kōsuke carries out his activism via the Internet, leveraging such sites as Nico Nico Douga. But it's nonetheless clear that they both feel at home in the realm of "right-wing" discourses and spaces.

On the one hand, Shingo compares his activities to watching movies, while on the other, Kōsuke is happy to treat the policies of the Democratic Party as "material" or grist. In other words, their commitment is at once earnest and detached.

The citizens who the Internet connects

Just like the young people I interviewed about the Senkaku Islands issue, the ones I interviewed this time, too, had learned about today's demonstration via the Internet. There were many who found out about the event through the many conservative social networking sites that have been recently starting up one after another, like "FreeJapan" and "myNippon," not to mention the notification webpages of large-scale organizations such as the Zaitokukai.

Rika (late twenties, office worker, female) neither watches TV nor reads the newspaper, but she says she regularly checks myNippon. As someone who doesn't have much time, she says this medium helps her quickly "understand what the immediate threats are right now." She learned about today's demonstration from an online journal of a person she had "friended" on a social networking site.

The Internet is also a source of information for people who don't belong to any specific group, even though they may be taking part in demonstrations. To begin with, there are many like Kōsuke who don't watch TV or read newspapers very much; as he says, "Both the TV and newspaper are untrustworthy. They're full of lies."

Calling attention to an incident in which the TV show *Aru aru daijiten* (Encyclopedia of living) was caught forging test results and false testimonials for promoting *natto* fermented soybeans as a dieting aid, he talked about how the mass media really can't be trusted. The sources he trusts these days include "Channel Sakura," which actively airs on YouTube; websites on foreign-resident rights and anti-Japan movements, social network sites such as myNippon, and the comments and remarks of the journalist Shigeharu Aoyama (fifty-seven years old, Hyogo).

Shigeru, mentioned above, also keeps a cool distance from the news reported by the mass media. As for TV, even though he believes that everything it shows is biased, he nonetheless watches it "to see how wrong it is." For the most part, he doesn't read newspapers; predictably, he uses the FreeJapan social networking site for information-gathering. He often reads books by Shigeharu Aoyama and Yoshiko Sakurai, which have generated a huge buzz on FreeJapan.

The Soyokaze demonstration was a form of political activism made possible by the age of the Internet. Members of multiple organizations, people who didn't belong to any group, and participants from outlying districts all came together via website notifications or word-of-mouth communication circulating on social networking sites.

Among those present were Internet-based right-wingers; people who just had a vague sense that the Democratic Party was dangerous; people feeling a sense of crisis about foot-and-mouth disease; and people who were activists in earnest. It may be that a demonstration march is open and nonexclusive by nature, but the network of the Soyokaze demonstration protestors was certainly very easy-going and open.[262] Its members go so far as to object to the policy of permitting separate surnames for a married couple and are attempting to prevent "the dismantlement of the family unit." But Shingo feels at home in the conservative group, and the demonstrators, through their involvement in a short-lived collaboration, are trying to downplay their disaffection toward this dangerous thing called the Democratic Party. So in this sense, by creating an ersatz "new family" and "new community" for themselves, they appear to be contributing to the "dismantlement of the family unit" themselves.

Totally like the left wing

Unlike the Tsukurukai, which had no choice but to make use of "history" and "Japan" as resources to help forge connections among its members, the people mobilized for a Soyokaze demonstration are drawn together to cooperate by their array of resentments and anxieties over this dangerous thing called the Democratic Party. It is likely for this very reason—this common ground—that various groups and people, in response to a call for action, feel free to join demonstrations in a casual manner.

Furthermore, in the case of the Senkaku Islands demonstration, while at a glance it seemed to have the clear purpose of protesting against China, the attitudes and conduct

---

262.   Perhaps partly because Soyokaze was a moderate group, many of its members were open. Even with interviews, they were very gracious and cooperative. Many even dropped out of the demonstration for a few minutes to tell me their stories, and said things like, "What a tremendous undertaking! Good luck with your studies. Hang in there." Well, I did hang in there, and I came up with this kind of analysis in the end.

of the participants greatly varied. Some among them were even against regulating cannabis. I also found an affable young person there whose reason for joining the demonstration was to "beg China to stop using money from Japan to make chemical weapons."

Of course I'm not saying that all conservative movements are freewheeling as this, but nonetheless these people's actions call to mind the social movements of the former left wing. For example, it could be said that the easygoing, loose solidarity observable in the Senkaku and Soyokaze demonstrations is the realization of the non-hierarchical social movement dreamed of by the Beheiren, the former Japanese activist group that protested Japanese assistance to the United States during the Vietnam War. In addition, the occasional criticism leveled against the government is somewhat of a left-wing specialty.

According to the Soyokaze website, the association's motto is "Begin with the things that make the most of your special qualities." Since there are all kinds of people, including "people who wish to speak, people who do not wish to speak, people who would prefer to take action in modest ways, and those who like to take center stage," the website advises its readers to refrain from coercing anyone into taking action. What they value, they say, is, strictly speaking, "family life" and "everyday life."

Activities organized via the Internet enable the forging of loose, non-hierarchical connections. If you've signed up for a social networking account, you can stay in touch with your contacts easily; and since related groups carry out some kind of event almost every week nowadays, it's not difficult to make new acquaintances. Unlike the days before the spread of the Internet, it's extremely easy to find out what kind of events will take place and where they will take place.

By taking full advantage of new tools in this way, and by identifying with the spirit of a new social movement, young people are attempting to "conserve" Japan.

3. When Do We Rise Up?

An age when there's no right or left wing

We have been looking at the big picture of young people who stand up for "Japan" in times when nationalism is supposed to have completely eased up.

Raising the national flag of Japan, they criticize the abuse of rights perpetrated by other countries and proclaim their love for Japan. Ordinarily, such people are called "right-wingers." But in reality, taking action for "Japan" has nothing to do with whether a person is oriented to the right wing or the left. For example, even those who are classified as "left-wingers" for the most part aren't interested in breaking up the nation, nor are they aiming to instigate a socialist revolution. In fact, when it comes to their intent to make this country called "Japan" better, they are no different from the right wing.

But what's unfortunate for Japan is that before anyone knew it, expressions like "making the country better" and "for the country" became the exclusive province of the right wing. For some reason, in Japan, the moment you say, "for Japan," you'll be branded a nationalist.[263] And that's why the left wing has been evasive, making use of vague expressions like "to create a better society," instead of specifically mentioning the word "nation."[264]

However, such fussiness over the right wing-left wing divide may be already becoming a thing of the past.[265] This seems especially true when I listen to the stories of young people. At such times, I often feel that the vain and futile opposition between the right wing and the left wing no longer exists.

For instance, there was this one time when I was researching the young passengers on board the Peace Boat.[266] Founded by Kiyomi Tsujimoto, the Peace Boat is a non-governmental organization whose main business is operating around-the-world cruises in the name of world peace and for the cause of protecting the constitution. But it's often labeled as being "left wing."

On the cruise ship I boarded, there was even a novel dance called the "Article Nine Dance," celebrating the idea of pacifism enshrined in Article Nine of the Japanese Constitution, to the rhythm of a hip-hop beat. But when I talked to the youngsters doing this "Article Nine Dance," they unanimously talked about their "pride in being a Japanese citizen" and about "offering thanks to ancestors."

Apparently, you can't simply classify a person as either right wing or left wing sole-

---

263. There was a time in Japan, prior to the period of high economic growth, when the "left wing" was affirmative about the Constitution of Japan, based on their nationalism. (Eiji Oguma, *"Minshu" to "aikoku"* ["Democracy" and "patriotism"], Shin-yo-sha, 2002). In addition, it has become popular these days for "left-wingers," as nationalists, to demand the redistribution of income (Toshihito Kayano, "Aete sayoku to nashonarizumu o yōgo suru?" [Boldly defend the left wing and nationalism?] in *Wakamono no genzai seiji* [Current politics of the young] edited by Satoshi Kotani et al., Nihon Tosho Center, 2011].

264. Well, the distinction, I feel, is quite meaningless, as the term "Japanese society" is in many people's sights. I myself keep using the vague word "society" in this book, but basically think of it as referring to "Japanese society." If by any chance you're someone who wishes to seriously contemplate "society" at the conceptual level, you should read Yasutaka Ichinokawa's *Shakai* (Society; Iwanami Shoten, 2006).

265. Even the sociologist Motoaki Takahara, who can easily go on and on for several hours, drawing just from self-deprecating material, emphasizes the futility of the existing right-left dualism. ("'Wakamono no ukeiku' ron no haikei to atarashii nashonarizumu-ron" [The background of the theory of "young people's conservative shift" and the new theory of nationalism] in *Wakamono no genzai: Seiji* [Young people at present: politics] edited by Satoshi Kotani et al., Nihon Tosho Center, 2011.)

266. Noritoshi Furuichi, *Kibō nanmin goikkō sama* (A party of hope refugees), Kobunsha, 2010.

ly on account of superficial characteristics like proclaiming a "patriotic love for country" or "waving the Japanese flag." Especially given that, ever since the change of government, the actions of the right wing and those of the left wing have become difficult to tell apart.

Criticizing the nation out of love for the nation is a beautifully left-wing sentiment. And at the Senkaku Islands demonstration, there were young people like Keita who, while raising the national flag of Japan, said, "I want the Chinese to find happiness."

So let's put aside, for the time being, the matter of differentiating between the "right wing" and "left wing."[267] What I'd like to consider is the question of when young people take action.

Dissatisfaction is not enough to get people to take a stand

When do people rise up and take a stand? When do they start a movement? These are the kinds of questions that have been asked for a long time in the field of social-movement theory.[268]

One early premise in this area is the collective behavior theory, which explains social movements through the lens of a capitalist society's contradictions. Specifically, this theory says the structural tensions and grievances produced by social change lead people to take action.

However, as can be seen in present-day Japan, people don't necessarily rush into starting movements just because they happen to be dissatisfied. Of course, "dissatisfaction" or "discontentment" can certainly be one of the leading factors causing people to start social movements, I feel. But that in and of itself is not enough to trigger a social movement.[269]

Enter the "resource mobilization theory"—the heir to the collective behavior the-

---

267. Of course, whether these categories have any meaning depends on the definition and purpose. Since the purpose of this chapter is not to look at ways of thinking, but to touch on the motives of people who get involved in movements, I'm basically not particular about the right-wing – left-wing divide.

268. For those of you who wish to dig deeper into the field of social-movement theories, you will find well-rounded discussions in Masa'aki Itō's *Furasshu Mobuzu* (Flash mobs; NTT Publishing, 2011) and in *Shigen dōin to soshiki senryaku* (Resource mobilization and organizational strategy) edited by Tsutomu Shiobara (Shin-yo-sha, 1989).

269. Even today, many continue to argue that "dissatisfaction" and "lack of approval" drive people toward movements. For example, German philosopher Axel Honneth makes much of problems related to "approval," such as humiliation and lack of pride, in the act of group resistance (Axel Honneth, author; Hiraku Yamamoto and Kiyotaka Naoe, translators, *Shōnin o meguru tōsō* [translated English title, *The Struggle for Recognition*; original German title, *Kampf um Anerkennung*], Hosei University Press, 2003). When Honneth visited Japan, I got him to autograph this book. Nobody has been jealous about it yet, though.

ory—which gives weight to resources such as people, money, and networks. According to this theory, a social movement happens only after the acquisition of available resources.

For example, let's say there's a person harboring a grudge against society. To this person, the nicest thing that could happen would be to see society change through someone else's efforts. That way, he or she can enjoy a free ride on the back of another person's efforts and live in a better world. The resource mobilization theory anticipates such "rational" people.

How to get everyone involved

But if everybody waited around for someone else to change society, believing that such a person should appear, society will never change. For this reason, the resource mobilization theory depends greatly on strategy.

When a movement acquires resources, what then becomes key is the skill of framing. In other words, the success of a movement will hinge on what kind of presentation and branding it's capable of carrying out.

A successful case in point is the American civil rights movement. When the struggle—which was originally a movement by African Americans demanding civil rights—activated the polysemic, or lexically ambiguous, framing of "human rights and equal opportunity," it became possible to involve various other minorities, including women, disabled people, Native Americans, and the elderly.

But even the civil rights movement hit a brick wall; participation was limited to those minorities, or in other words, only to the "concerned parties." So in recent times another kind of movement has begun to catch on; a new kind that aims to involve not just stakeholders, but other people outside their circle. To that end, this new type of movement is set up to have people participate in a festive fashion—a change from the kinds of protests where people rally to save the earth with a hard, dour look on their faces.

For example, take the event known as "Earth Day."[270] Its aim is to interest people in environmental issues, and yet on the actual "Earth Day" held every year in Tokyo, the event would be more suitably described as a festival or fiesta. The attractions include live concerts, talk shows, and even happenings like the one in which people are encouraged to take up the challenge of producing naturally fermented sake. Such social movements are becoming prevalent lately; the kind of movements that urge people

---

270.   See the following website for up-to-date information on the "Earth Day" event in Japan.
        http://www.earthday-tokyo.org/

to take part in a "festival," rather than have them get seriously interested in environmental issues.[271]

In such movements, whether you are a concerned party or not isn't called into question. Rather, they try to draw people in by having them affirm their motivation to "have fun" or to "meet with friends." Even in the field of social movement theory, the theories that are on the rise are rooted in studies attaching great importance to participants' pleasure and cultural aspects, unlike those that, like the resource mobilization theory, anticipate "rational" people.[272] These movements are collectively referred to as "new social movements" or "network organizations."

The rival is Disneyland

At any rate, movements attempting to involve everyone, or to be all-inclusive, are on the right track if their aim is to achieve maximum mobilization. According to official estimates, in Yoyogi Park in 2010, 135,000 people gathered to attend the Earth Day event titled "Ai to heiwa no chikyū no matsuri" (The earth festival for love and peace).[★120]

We don't start movements after making an objective assessment of the state of society. Environmental issues are supposedly a "remote" problem for people living in Japan. Should global warming get worse, the Japanese islands will still remain afloat tomorrow. No matter how much noise is made about the risk of environmental hormones, it's not as if the distinction between males and females of all species will suddenly disappear completely.

Nor will it be us—the men and women living today—who will be critically damaged by environmental problems; it will be our descendants, those living in the world a hundred years from now. Let's also recognize the position that, during our times, the North-South divide merits even more serious attention.

Thus, we who live in present-day Japan are most likely not the direct "concerned party" in today's environmental problems.[273] Still, the reason 130,000 people come to-

---

271.   Social movements that let people participate in a lighthearted manner are not a recent development. For example, with regard to the protest movement in 1960 against the U.S.-Japan Security Treaty, there were demonstrations that encouraged people to join with a lighthearted feeling, as if they were "going on a picnic," and various groups that had gathered from all over the country were made the leading figures of the movement. (Eiji Oguma, *"Minshu" to "aikoku"* ["Democracy" and "patriotism"], Shin-yo-sha, 2002). But the modern Earth Day movement is more refined, and even its "political color" evinced at first glance is lighter in comparison.

272.   Makoto Nishikido, *Aragai no jōken* (The requirements of resistance), Jimbun Shoin, 2008.

★120. Approximately 110,000 people gathered on the Earth Day event held in 2015. It's amazing how, for these past ten years, the event has been able to mobilize some 100,000 people every year.

273.   As long as we're living on the planet called Earth, though, we are likely the peripheral "beneficiaries" of the environmental problem.

gether on an event like Earth Day is because a wide variety of people are able to join the gathering in a lighthearted fashion, expecting to have some fun. The event, in effect, is a festival held in Yoyogi Park on a holiday; but on top of that, attending this festival makes you feel slightly good, in an ethical sense. The threshold to going there is quite low.

In other words, unless the threshold is lowered by this much and the entertainment value heightened, mobilizing a sizeable crowd to social movements will prove quite a considerable challenge. (By the way, I don't know if you can call Earth Day a social movement anymore.)

The present age is teeming with entertainment. You can play games at home or visit a Costco or an outlet store with your friends or take a date to a movie theater or Disneyland. So getting people to engage in a "social movement" in the face of such innumerable alternatives is no easy task.[274] It therefore is essential for a movement to be as easygoing and casual as Earth Day.

However, if you look into whether everyone used to join social movements in a lighthearted spirit back when there were fewer amusements than today, you'll find that wasn't the case at all.

The moral economy

All through the ages, a large gap has existed between intellectuals and the common people. For example, although many have a painful and terrible image of the Public Security Preservation Law enforced in 1925, the question remains how much impact this ordinance really had on the general public.[275]

On February 11, 1925, at Arimagahara, in Shiba, Tokyo, a gathering was held by thirty-five groups, including the Japanese Confederation of Labor Unions, to protest the Public Security Preservation Law. There were reportedly only 3,000 participants in

---

274.   Incidentally, the combined annual traffic to Disneyland and DisneySea was approximately 25 million. That works out to 68,000 people per day if you simply divide the figure by 365 days. Since Earth Day was only held for two days, you can clearly see that it put up a surprisingly good fight. [★121]

★121. The attendance figure of 25 million that appears in footnote 274 is data from around 2010. By 2014, this figure had increased to 31,380,000 people. As usual, in the land of dreams, both people and money are concentrated.

275.   The Public Security Preservation Law prohibited movements, and support for movements, that renounced capitalism and the "national polity"—in other words, the emperor system of Japan. In 1928, the maximum punishment became the death penalty, which is now considered to be symbolic of the prewar clampdown on free speech. Of course, I don't condone the Public Security Preservation Law, either. Without a doubt, actions such as the mass arrests of influential antiwar elements found to be in violation of the Public Security Preservation Law were one of the factors that led Japan to war (Yōko Katō, *Soredemo Nihonjin wa "sensō" o eranda* [Nevertheless, Japan chose "war"], Asahi Press, 2009). But the point I'm making here is that it's questionable that the rank and file had any significant interest in, or were affected to a considerable degree by, the Public Security Preservation Law.

all,[276] so it wasn't as if the whole of Japan had gathered to protest this law.

At that time in history, consumer society had begun to flower around Tokyo, and in Ginza, so-called *moga* (modern girls) and *mobo* (modern boys) were seen swaggering along the streets.[277] At a movie-star photo shoot titled "Asahigraph Day," held at the Shinjuku-en entertainment complex on February 9—two days prior to the gathering protesting the Public Security Preservation Law—30,000 visitors reportedly past through.[278] Many people were absorbed with consumption and leisure activities, and the Peace Preservation Law was the furthest thing from their mind.

Studies examining the annals of the general public—common, ordinary people—reveal that people often tend to rise up and take a stand only when they perceive their deep-rooted rules have been violated;[279] rules rooted in a social norm of their own called the "moral economy." A case in point in Japan is the rice riots of the Edo period (1603–1868) that were triggered by price manipulations. According to these studies, the rice riots, which led to incidents of *uchi-kowashi* (the tearing down of houses), attest to the fact that when the moral economy is violated, people begin to rise up.★[122]

But the rice riots were something close to a festival, as remaining archival records of personal accounts of the people who had taken part in the 1918 incident show—their tone betraying a slight sense of bemusement. One person said, "I tried acting violent just for fun," while another said, "I joined thoughtlessly after someone invited me." There was even a person who had been dancing at the Bon festival and just seamlessly drifted toward the riot scene.[280] It sure sounds like it was fun.

I believe this "moral economy" argument is still valid today. To illustrate, let me

---

276. Hiroshi Komatsu, *Nihon no rekishi 14: "Inochi" to teikoku Nippon* (The history of Japan 14: "Life" and the Empire of Japan), Shogakukan, 2009. In the February 12, 1925, evening edition of the *Asahi Shimbun*, the figure is said to be 5,000.

277. Toshikazu Inoue, *Senzen Shōwa no shakai, 1926–1945* (Prewar Shōwa society, 1926–1945), Kodansha, 2011.

278. Kōichirō Aoki, *Taishō roman* (Taishō Romance), Chuokoron-Shinsha, 2005.

279. Michio Shibata et al., eds., *Sekaishi e no toi 6: Minshū bunka* (Questions of world history 6: Folk culture), Iwanami Shoten, 1990.

★122. Sometimes the usage and definition of "moral economy" varies with the researcher. An account that approaches this book's explanation is, in addition to the source mentioned in footnote 279, Eiji Oguma's *Shakai o kaeru ni wa* (To change society; Kodansha, 2012).

280. However, such a grassroots movement did not necessarily target *okami* (government); i.e., the administration in power. In the *yonaoshi sōdō* (world-reformation riot) seen in the late Edo period, conflicts among commoners were occurring; the world-reformation group was threatening villages in order to coerce people to join their movement, while on the other hand, on the village side, the rural folk prepared columns of agrarian soldiers and killed off the world-reformation group. In effect, the people inflicted violence on themselves (Tsutomu Suda, *Bakumatsu no yonaoshi* [World reformation in the late Edo period], Yoshikawa Kobunkan, 2010).

switch the scene to China and fast-forward to autumn of 2010, when the news of the Nobel Peace Prize being awarded to the Chinese human rights campaigner Liu Xiaobo was making waves around the world. What consequently came to international light was the state of censorship practiced by the Chinese government. The news of Liu didn't get broadcast on TV in China, nor did an Internet search there of Liu Xiaobo retrieve any results. These restrictions on freedom of speech in China enraged Japanese intellectuals, too.

But what was popular on the Chinese Internet at that time, except among some intellectuals and free-speech advocates, was the "My dad is Li Gang!" incident,[281] a pathetic case involving an imbecilic spoiled brat. Having killed someone in an accident while driving under the influence of alcohol, the young assailant declared to the people that surrounded him at the scene of the crime, "Do you know who my father is? My dad is Li Gang!" (Li Gang was the name of a well-known police official in the local area.)

This case was heavily censored by the government, but the young assailant instantly became the talk of the town, condemned and accused over the Internet. Juicy bits of his private life were revealed one after another, leading in the end to a press conference in which the father, Li Gang, apologized.

It's safe to say that this incident blew up to the extent it did because it had offended the "moral economy" of the Chinese people.

Rising up and resisting even when you're consummatory

When people take action, when do their actions morph into a large movement? Apparently, it's when their sense of values and moral standards are violated.[282]

But as I mentioned in chapter 2, young people's sense of values is becoming more and more consummatory—that is to say, more young people are treasuring the personal world around them, such as the world of close friends, instead of striving hard to achieve some goal.

Consequently, no matter how much noise you make about the "gap-widening society" or about exploitative companies (called "black companies" in Japan), as long as young people think these aren't problems, it is highly unlikely that a large movement will ever occur.

By the same token, though, if young people perceive a trespass has been made into

---

281. Shino Nishimoto, *Mono iu chūgokujin* (The assertive Chinese), Shueisha, 2011.
282. Recent times saw a flourishing of signature-collecting campaigns demanding local governments to carry out measurements of radiation dosage and to release data. The leading figures in these campaigns were mothers who were concerned about protecting their children.

their own self-contained world—their own bubble—or if outsiders find fault with their social norms, some kind of movement will probably result.[283]

To illustrate, let me call your attention to the movement opposing the "nonexistent youth" bill, which occurred in 2010. The Tokyo Metropolitan Government, through a proposed amendment to the Ordinance Regarding the Healthy Development of Youth, attempted to restrict the depiction of fictional characters appearing in manga and anime if they were deemed to look eighteen or younger. The term "nonexistent youth" alludes to the fact that, unlike with child pornography, there was no real victim. With this rather novel naming, the reform bill went viral across social networking sites such as Twitter.

The telephones in the office of the Tokyo chapter of the Democratic Party rang ceaselessly; their inbox, at times, was flooded with approximately seven hundred emails a day. The secretariat of the Tokyo Metropolitan Assembly received more than five thousand messages expressing opposition to the bill.[284] The number of signatures collected, in just one month after May, during a campaign by the Committee for Rethinking the Amendment to the Ordinance Regarding the Healthy Development of Youths, amounted to approximately twenty thousand.[285] Even though in the end the reform bill went on to be approved in December after its text was altered, it should be noted that the opposition movement persisted with fervor for nearly a year.

This movement, which was triggered by a sense of impending crisis among young people—arising from the potential threat to "my world," the threat that "my world might change"—consequently went on to blossom into a public crusade aiming to prevent the reform of the Tokyo Metropolitan Government's Ordinance in the name of protecting freedom of expression.

So even a cozy, self-contained sphere has the seeds of transforming into something much bigger, something much more public.

The restless *aitai-kei*

The sociologist Tomohiko Asano (forty-six years old, Miyagi) points out that "an earnest desire to maintain a distance" may be spreading among youth.[286]

---

283. I hit upon this idea when I heard a remark made by Tomohiko Asano in a talk session held at the Ikebukuro branch of the Junkudo bookstore on November 11, 2010. The talk was titled, "How are the young people living their present?"

284. "Sendō shakai 2: Netto jō zōfukusuru fushin" (Agitation society 2: The growing mistrust on the Internet), *Asahi Shimbun*, April 30, 2010, morning edition.

285. http://yama-ben.cocolog-nifty.com/ooinikataru/2010/05/post-6e5c.html

286. Tomohiko Asano, "Kyori o katsubō suru wakamono-tachi" (Young people yearning for distance), *Shūkan Dokushojin*, November 5, 2010.

A case in point he submits is the rising trend of *aitai-kei*. *Aitai-kei* is a general reference to recent J-pop songs that express the sentiment, "I want to see you, but I can't."[287] The queen of *aitai-kei* is Kana Nishino (twenty-two years old, Mie). Her song titled "Aitakute, Aitakute," with lyrics like "I want to see you so much I'm shaking," was the number-one full-song ringtone download in 2010, setting parts of the Internet abuzz.[★123]

Asano concludes that, if Kana Nishino's song manages to tug at the heartstrings of the young, it's because in modern society it's actually difficult to truthfully say, "I want to reach you, but I can't"—in other words, today it has become difficult to be technically incommunicado. With a cell phone, you can communicate with a lover or a friend from anywhere, at any time. For this reason, Asano says, in the modern day it's impossible to be in a situation where you want to reach someone, but you can't.[288]

In fact, in this day and age, not being able to be in touch with someone when you want to is, counterintuitively, a romantic notion.[★124] The young are finding too much gratification in intimate relations, which has given them an enormous thirst for grandiose ideals like "community" and "society." To put it in the language of this book, what I'm talking about here are cliquish young people who are consummatory—that is to say, self-contained—while being "society-centric" at the same time.

---

287. J-pop songs with lyrics like "I want to see you" didn't suddenly erupt out of the blue in the 2010s. In the 1990s, at least, there were a good number of songs expressing the sentiment of not being able to see someone despite longing to do so; these tunes include the song "Aitakute—Lover Soul—" by LINDBERG (1993), and "DEPARTURES" by globe (1996). But none of them went to the extent of singing about a yearning so strong that it made you shiver, as Kana Nishino did.

★123. Sales in the paid music download market are going down, as evidenced in services like Chaku-uta Furu. The sales, which amounted to 86 billion yen in 2010, were reduced by half to 43,700 million yen in 2014. The peak was 91 billion yen in 2009. This is attributed to the spread of free music apps and the perception that music is "something you watch on YouTube with your friends"—which has gained currency thanks to the spread of smartphones. From 2015, all-you-can-listen subscription services, such as AWA and LINE MUSIC, also began to start up in Japan in rapid succession.

288. In Japan, Willcom had introduced flat-rate voice-call subscriptions, and my younger sister, along with a regular cell phone, immediately bought a Willcom plan for the exclusive purpose of communicating with her boyfriend. For a fixed sum of several thousand yen, she could keep talking for as many hours as she liked. What I was truly impressed with, though, was that this plan allowed her to keep watching the same TV program while leaving her phone on telephone mode all the time. Not much conversation took place; just the occasional "Ha, ha." Certainly, given these kinds of amenities, I can't imagine a situation where girls can truthfully say, "I want to meet you, but I can't."

★124. Many tunes in the repertoire of globe, a pop band that was predominant in the late 1990s, are about "the loneliness of being alone," such as the 1995 tune, "Feel Like Dance." In those days, although there were cell phones and PHS phones, without the availability of SNS, whenever people parted company from friends in the city, they would become physically alone; they would literally be just by themselves. In the present age, on the other hand, when we have LINE and Facebook, it is rather difficult for anyone to be alone—to be just by themselves. These days, what's catching on in the world of girls' comics are works that depict the state of being alone as a fantasy, such as Aya Asano's *Koi desuga koi janai* (It's willful, but it's not love; Shogakukan, 2015).

Connecting the close-knit familiar sphere to the public sphere

Herein lies the clue to helping young people's interests shift toward "community," "society," and "politics."

If you ask why the number of young people taking action—that is to say, playing active roles in society—has dwindled to so few, even when public opinion polls are showing that the number of young people interested in "society" are on the rise, you will see that this is because the circuitry connecting young people to "society" has been missing.

A young person might say, "I'd love to do something for society, but no matter how much I want to, I don't know what I can do, especially when I'm preoccupied with other things every day. In the first place, I have no clue about what things I can do to benefit society. Should I volunteer? I don't even know how to go about searching for volunteer work I'm suited to take on, and, besides, it seems difficult to approach. Should I vote? I keep telling myself that I need to go to the polls and vote, but it really won't make a difference anyway who I vote for, since they're all the same; I don't feel like my vote's going to change anything."

In response to such sentiments, all we need to do is to connect their world— the familiar sphere; the close-knit, intimate world young people live in—to the public sphere; the larger world called "society."

To that end, we can deploy an effective framing device, like the civil rights movement did, or make young people participate in an event like Earth Day, and connect the two worlds in the process. Social movements and volunteer groups that have managed to attract a reasonably large number of people are adept at connecting the familiar sphere to the public sphere. In other words, with an outstanding facilitator, mobilizing young people, even in modern society, is well within the realm of the possible.

With the use of technology, it is becoming easier to link the intimate world (the close-knit, familiar sphere), where young people live, to the bigger world called "society" (the public sphere).

For example, many people, upon being suddenly informed of the exploitation of migrant workers in Chinese factories, will not become automatically interested in the topic. But what if you were to present this information in a different way—say, by telling iPhone users that in the factories producing their iPhones, a series of suicides have become a problem?[289]

---

289.   At a factory in China operated by Foxconn, the manufacturing company which has produced 90 million iPhone units, seventeen suicides have occurred. ("Boku no iPhone ga 17-nin o koroshitanoka?" [Did my iPhone kill seventeen people?], *WIRED* vol. 1, 2011.)

Furthermore, what if these iPhone users were sent a document containing this news, along with a photograph stating, "The person who died yesterday was a young person aged nineteen like you"—or "twenty like you," or some other age, depending on the age of the targeted recipient? These iPhone users might imagine a little bit about this young person, a worker in another country whom they have never met.

Matching user attributes in this way to recommend "news you should be interested in" or "news you should be aware of" is a forte of Web service.[290/★125]

4. A Society that Won't Change with a Revolution

Is being public-spirited a good thing?

The question remains, however, whether "public-spirited" and "sociable" attitudes deserve unreserved appreciation. Should everyone really be public-spirited and social?

I cannot simply say that everybody should be interested in society.

First, let me unpack the "everybody" part. I may be stating the obvious here, but a "good society" doesn't get perfected automatically when "everybody" takes an interest in it, contemplating it at a deep level.

For instance, take the case of the project called the Jukugi Kakeai (an online forum for educators), run by the Ministry of Education, Culture, Sports, Science and Technology.[291/★126] The term *jukugi* apparently refers to the process of shaping policies out of "mature deliberations" and "discussions" among concerned parties who have come together. The discussions you can find on the website include threads started by Kan Suzuki, the senior vice minister of education, culture, sports, science and technology (forty-seven years old, Hyogo), titled "Issues of the National University Corporation and Approaches Toward Their Resolution" and "How to Solve Job-Hunting Prob-

---

290. In fact, services like LinkedIn Today, which recommend news stories based on the networks and professional communities to which users belong, are on the rise. They still lack precision, though.

★125. From around 2013, news-curation apps, such as SmartNews and Gunosy, began to get buzzworthy. Drawing from multiple news sources, users can read stories optimized for them.

291. The official web site (http://www.mext.go.jp/jukugi/) even has a feature created by a volunteer titled *Manga de wakaru jukugi* (Understanding *Jukugi* through manga), which conveys the story of a family that settles on a dinner menu after repeated deliberations, and another about a class that ended up running a yakisoba noodle shop at the school festival because they neglected to carry out a discussion. After going through them, I'm absolutely sure you'll still be clueless about *jukugi* in the end, and even wonder "What do the Ministry of Education, Culture, Sports, Science and Technology think they're doing?"

★126. *Jukugi* began as a project under the Democratic Party administration, but the website has been shut down, leaving part of its contents behind.

lems." Anyone can join the discussions, as long as they register.

Frankly, the forum is something like a class meeting, with everyone just saying whatever they please. And so far, this process has failed to produce any epoch-making ideas hitherto unthought-of by experts. The Jukugi's conviction that "if you talk, you will understand," to the contrary, rejects participation by people who aren't well versed in the art of conversation.[292] The level of aspiration it expects people to have is too high. To my eyes, at least, the current Jukugi Kakeai is suitable for only those who are expressive and fond of debating.[293]

What's more challenging to grasp, though, are the attributes of "public-spiritedness" and "sociability"—just what on earth are they?

For instance, take uber-exclusive groups like online right-wingers and the Zaitokukai; just how should we think about such people? Compared to the young person in Roppongi who asked, "What are the Senkaku Islands?" these extremists are considerably more interested in "public" and "social" matters. But their idea of a public-spirited and social attitude contains the latent possibility of hurting others, and even harassing them.[294]

If it were just online right-wing activists and the Zaitokukai, I wouldn't be that concerned. For the moment, no actual harm has ever come about from them.[★127] But how about Aum Shinrikyō? Having waited eagerly for an apocalyptic war, this cult's members planned a revolution of their own. But, in their own way, they were "public-spirited" and "sociable."[295]

---

292.   Ikuo Gonoi, "Gurōbaru demokurashī-ron kokkyō o koeru seiji no kōsō" (Global democracy theory: Framework of a politics that transcends national borders) in *Kokusaiseiji tetsugaku* (International political philosophy) edited by Daisuke Odagawa et al., Nakanishiya Shuppan, 2011.

293.   Of course, there might be nothing wrong with that. Perhaps this is the way it should be. After all, it's only natural that a service provider called "the state" listens to the voices of its customers called "the citizens." At the least, it's not a mistake to exhibit an attitude of concern—a willingness to listen. In that case, rather than arguing over major issues like "problems of the National University Corporation and approaches toward their resolution," the state, I feel, should be listening to more quotidian concerns and proposals. Nonetheless, discussing major issues leads to a greater sense of accomplishment, raising customer satisfaction levels as a result, so it's not a mistake.

294.   However, at the present time, in the wake of the stable growth period—a period when elitism's merits exceeded its drawbacks—my opinion is losing its legitimacy. The payback of having left decisionmaking in the hands of elites with an ivy-league educational background is indeed epitomized by the manmade disaster of the nuclear plant accident, which was caused by the lax responses of the government and Tokyo Electric Power.

★127.   Later on, part of the demonstration became radicalized, stirring up trouble with hate speeches like those that called for "killing Koreans." "Hate speech" refers to the kind of speech and behavior that expresses hate for and discrimination against certain groups or individuals. In particular, the term applies to discrimination against attributes of an individual that cannot be changed, such as race or ethnicity. In 2013, the phrase became so popular it was nominated for the *Shingo/Ryūkōgo taishō* (best new vogue-word award).

Of course, it's easy to denounce the "public-spiritedness" and "sociability" of groups like the Zaitokukai and Aum Shinrikyō as not being "genuine" public-spiritedness, and as not being a "good" kind of sociability. But who should decide, and in what way should it be decided, what's "genuine" and what's "good?"

I'd like to consult with Professor Michael J. Sandel (fifty-eight years old, Minnesota) on this matter, but it wouldn't be decent of me to turn to him every time such a question occurs.

The social movement as a place of belonging

While Aum Shinrikyō may be emblematic, it is not universal. I'm convinced that many collectives, before they ever go rogue like Aum Shinrikyō, just end up becoming a "place of belonging."

According to the reportage by Kōichi Yasuda (forty-six years old, Shizuoka), the young people associating with the Zaitokukai don't seem that different from those in the other conservative groups examined in this chapter.[296] By and large, they tend to be young people who lead lives of desperation every day, feeling a sense of hopelessness and alienation, when they come across one of the works of animation the Zaitokukai broadcasts. At that juncture, they have a moment of revelation about the "real nature" of foreign residents and are seized with a sense of mission to tell the truth.

Eriyasu Hoshi, a twenty-four-year-old youth of mixed Iranian-Japanese descent who had started to keep a distance from the Zaitokukai, said, "Most of the members of the Zaitokukai seemed like the friendless type."[297] On the other hand, when asked by Yasuda if anything good came of joining the Zaitokukai, one female member said, "I'm having so much fun I can't help it. It's like I've finally found my true friends." In short, everyone in the group was satisfied because they had made new "friends" and felt

---

295. That democracy can convert to fascism is a lesson prewar history also teaches. Recent studies have pointed out that the lowest classes of the generation that experienced Taishō democracy in the 1920s came to raise their voices in society because of that experience, before eventually becoming leading figures in the fascist movement of the 1930s. (Toshiya Ichinose, *Kokyō wa naze heishi o koroshita ka* [Why did the homeland kill the soldiers?], KADOKAWA, 2010.)

296. Kōichi Yasuda, "'Zaitokukai' no shōtai" (The real nature of the "Zaitokukai") in *G2* no. 6, 2010.

297. Kōichi Yasuda, "Zaitokukai to netto uyoku" (The Zaitokukai and the Internet right wing) in *G2* no. 7, 2011.[*128]

★128. These studies have been put together in Kōichi Yasuda's *Netto to aikoku* (The Internet and patriotism; Kodansha, 2012). Regarding the Zaitokukai, refer also to Naoto Higuchi's *Nihon-gata haigaishugi* (Japanese-style xenophobia; The University of Nagoya Press, 2014). Unlike Yasuda's study, which saw the Zaitokukai as a gathering of people "who are apparently leading tough lives," this work analyzes them as an extension of grassroots conservatism. According to Higuchi, it's a mistake to consider the leader of a xenophobic movement a person of low-class origin. This distinctively different analysis is believed to be the result of a different interview approach taken; in contrast to Yasuda's coverage involving "on-the-spot," candid interviews, Higuchi mainly interviewed the management after being formally introduced to the subjects of his research by the Zaitokukai.

that they were a part of a circle, or were among "peers."

The same situation is also found in groups whose political stances are at the polar opposite end. There exists a recording of an interview with the leftist Zenshinsha, the greatest bastion of the radical Marxist group known as the Middle Core Faction.[298] Conducted by the TV director Ryōsuke Tanaka (thirty-five years old, Tokyo), this interview shows approximately one hundred people living together in Zenshinsha, with thirteen young people living in a space they call "the student room." These youths are individuals of such conviction that they declare, "The history of humanity promises us a revolution."

But when Tanaka asked about what they found attractive about Zenshinsha, all of them unanimously said, "This place is where I belong," "If we unite, we can fight!" "We have nothing to lose but our friends." So at the end of the day, even these radical revolutionaries apparently just want to connect with everybody.[299]

Even in the slightly more moderate labor movement, the key phrase proves to be "A place of belonging."[300] Moreover, as organizations, their function isn't so different from that of the Zaitokukai—to get people involved in demonstrations.

A thirty-year-old woman involved with Part-timer, Arbeiter, Freeter & Foreign Worker, a union which organizes the annual "May Day of Freedom and Survival" demonstration, said that her first impression of May Day, an event she had been invited to attend, was negative; she had found it "scary." However, she gradually realized the pleasure of "building a demonstration together" and began to get interested in the role of the community again, feeling that she didn't need to give up, that she could take a stand and address her grievances about her company, her job.

Many of the other participants, too, praised what the labor movement had provided them with—namely "a place of belonging" and "friends." They made statements like, "I've been looking for a place like this to call my *ibasho* [place of belonging]," and, "Friends are friends, after all." Thus, even for people who were involved in serious

---

298.   Ryōsuke Tanaka, "Rupo: Hatachi no kakumei shōjo" (Reportage: Twenty-year-old girls of the revolution) in *G2* no. 5, 2010. As you can see, *G2* regularly features heavy news stories. [*129]

★129.   *G2* was a nonfiction magazine launched by Kodansha in September 2009 as the successor to *Gekkan gendai*. It was discontinued in May 2015. My book *Daremo sensō o oshierarenai* (Nobody can teach war) was created from this magazine.

299.   In the past, this type of edgy juvenile tribe would have had no choice but to morph into a political movement. (Noritoshi Furuichi, "Chippoke na otoko-tachi no monogatari" [The story of small men], *Eureka*, June 2011.)

300.   The example of the labor movement was sourced from Shōji Hashiguchi's *Wakamono no rōdō undō* (The labor movement of youth; Seikatsushoin, 2011). Apparently written by a scholar, this work enumerates a tremendous number of references over the course of fifteen pages, so I recommend it to anyone working on a graduation thesis on labor issues.

movements like those related to the labor problem—movements solidly focused on principled ideas about society—what proved important were basic human longings, like a "sense of belonging" and "mutual acceptance."

In my previous study covering the young passengers on board the Peace Boat, I concluded that cooperation had a "cooling effect" on purposiveness.[301] In other words, even people who appeared to be unified in their hard work to serve a common purpose as a group would, at the end of the day, abandon their original purpose after seeing their group turn into an *ibasho*—a place of belonging.

No matter how radical an organization may be, if that organization turns into a "place of belonging," the motivation—that is to say, the initial radical purpose—will be "cooled" or dampened. And even if it doesn't turn out to be the "place of belonging" that people have been looking for, the organization will only function as an outlet to re-enact short-lived "festivals," and will never develop into a serious threat to society.

In the first place, what does it mean to change society?

When you use the expression "change society," you can't help but recall revolutions and large-scale demonstrations. For example, the Arab Spring, which took place between 2010 and 2011, was visually remarkable in showing how a society was undergoing change.

The catalyst was the attempted self-immolation of a twenty-six-year-old youth in Tunisia on December 17, 2010.[302] Mohamed Bouazizi, a poor street vendor, set himself on fire in front of a prefectural office building to protest the oppressive acts of a law-enforcement official. His death sparked a people's revolt in the capital, Tunis, forcing President Ben Ali, who had been running a dictatorial regime for twenty-three years, to flee abroad. On January 14, 2011, the government would virtually collapse. It was a revolution-drama that spanned just several weeks.

This revolution in Tunisia, also known as the Jasmine Revolution, went on to spread throughout other Arab countries. Anti-government demonstrations ensued one after another in nations such as Jordan, Egypt, and Libya. In particular, the Egyptian revolution, which took place from January through February, was given extensive me-

---

301. In Japan the term *reikyaku* (cooling) is often used as a technical term in the context of educational sociology (Hiroshi Takeuchi, *Nippon no meritokurashī* [Japan's meritocracy], University of Tokyo Press, 1995), but in the context of this book, I wouldn't mind if you interpret it to mean the same thing as "resignation" or "giving up."

302. While he survived for eighteen days in the hospital, he died on January 4, 2011. With regard to the Arab Spring, the April, 2011 extra edition of the magazine *Gendai shisō* (Modern thought) contains a comprehensive summary, ranging from translated studies of overseas writers to running blow-by-blow coverage of the protest demonstrations.

dia coverage in Japan. With a million participants taking part in the demonstration of February 11, the Mubarak-led dictatorial regime that had been ruling the country for thirty years collapsed like Tunisia's under the pressure of the people's revolt.

However, the chances of something like the Jasmine Revolution taking place in Japan are virtually zero. In Tunisia and Egypt, the scene was adequately set—including the presence of necessary, principal actors—for a revolution to take place. The straight-forward enemy—the dictatorial regime—had no compunctions about carrying out everything from censorship to torture. The youths who lived under this regime literally had trouble eating, because of rising prices and a high rate of youth unemployment.[303] It was all like a B-movie with a predictable plotline.

On the other hand, in Japan, there is no clear-cut villain like Mubarak. Instead, there's such a huge pile of "social issues" that listing even just some of them here would wear me out; issues such as the recovery from the devastation of the Great East Japan Earthquake, corrupt politicians, the vested interests of government officials, the abuse of legal authority by the police, youth unemployment, the suicide rate failing to go down, and the problem of low birthrate and aging. But there are no unambiguous cut-and-dried problems like censorship and torture. Nor are there, broadly speaking, any people who will go hungry tomorrow and starve to death.[★130]

"Society" won't change dramatically

Your average Japanese today, including the younger generation, are probably leading richer lives than Louis XIV ever did in his lifetime.[304] While today's young people don't have a personal chef, they can enjoy dishes from all over the world at a restaurant found in their neighborhood. While today's young people don't have exclusive carriages to ride in, they can travel around the world by purchasing a discount air ticket or boarding the Peace Boat.

Young people can also get away with murder for a long time, if they disguise their identity. Tatsuya Ichihashi (twenty-eight years old, Gifu), who was put on a nation-wide wanted list for the murder in Chiba of a woman who was an English conversation

---

303.   In addition, there are middle classes with a high level of education, since their countries are no longer categorized as either the Least Developed Countries or Most Seriously Affected Countries. Media such as Facebook and the satellite broadcaster Al Jazeera have helped them connect with each other.

★130.   According to the international survey conducted by the PEW Research Center, the percentage of people in Japan who "experienced such dire poverty that they were unable to buy daily necessities" is, compared with the rest of the world, extremely low. In the 2013 survey, 53 percent in Mexico, 24 percent in the U.S., 15 percent in the U.K. had answered that, in the past year, there were times when they were so poverty-stricken they couldn't afford to buy food. But in Japan, this number was just 2 percent.

304.   Matt Ridley, author; Naoko Ōta et al., translators, *Han'ei* (original title: *The Rational Optimist: How Prosperity Evolves*), Hayakawa Publishing, 2010.

teacher, was working at construction and demolition sites after finding job notices in free circulars and on the Internet, which he accessed through a PC in a public library. In the two years and seven months he spent as a fugitive from justice, he accumulated a sum of nearly a million yen.[305]

In such an affluent society, you'll be hard pressed to find any clear-cut problems that everyone can list as common concerns to solve.

As for such problems as youth employment and generational disparities, relatively speaking, "young people" should be the ones bearing the brunt of these issues, but the very youths in question say they're happy; furthermore, due to the declining birthrate, the absolute number of "young people" is small. Additionally, young people are too diverse to be pigeonholed into the category called "youth" (see chapter 6).

Besides, just as we saw in the Arab countries, dramatic revolutions don't instantly lead to a sweeping transformation of society. A malfunctioning state structure, economic unrest, and the problem of the youth unemployment rate didn't get resolved as soon as a change of government took place. Steady efforts need to be sustained to bring about incremental changes in the system, one by one.

In addition, even after the change of government, demonstrations and gun battles ensued, producing a large number of casualties. Depending on the security scenario, further adverse effects on the economy are also feared. While revolution is a starting point for changing society, it is absolutely nothing more than just that.★[131]

But "society" can be changed

If your aim is to make a social impact, you don't always have to leverage the platform of a political movement, such as a street demonstration or parade. For example, the novelist Ryū Murakami (forty-eight years old, Nagasaki), in his novel titled *Kibō no kuni no ekusodasu* (Exodus to the land of hope), proposes an educational reform that could be carried out right this minute. The idea, as expressed in the novel, is to have 800,000 junior high school students collectively refuse to go to school.[306]

---

305.   Tatsuya Ichihashi, *Taiho sareru made* (Until I get arrested), Gentosha, 2011.
★131.   The Jasmine Revolution and the Arab Spring have demonstrated the complexity involved in not changing, but rebuilding a society. In Egypt, a coup d'état occurred in 2013, adding to the unease of the political situation. Relative to Egypt, Tunisia maintained public order, but 2015 saw the occurrence of large-scale terrorist attacks targeting sightseeing spots. In addition, a civil war is ensuing in Syria, giving rise to more than 4 million refugees.
306.   Ryū Murakami, *Kibō no kuni no ekusodasu* (Exodus to the land of hope), Bungeishunju, 2002. Among researchers, too, there are those who assess the phenomena of truancy and *hikikomori* (social withdrawal)—"collective actions" that can never turn into "collective organizations"—on the merits of how much they press society to pay attention and respond. (Seiji Soranaka et al., eds., *Shakai undō to iu kōkyō-kūkan* [The public space called social movement], Seibundoh, 2004.)

Specifically, these students, disillusioned by society and triggered by a certain event, would suddenly refuse to go to school, causing a flurry of panic among adults. The novel goes to the extent of depicting the establishment of a "country of hope," an autonomous and distinctly separate entity from Japan. However, in reality, even before going that far, a wave of junior high truants would have a huge impact on society.★132

The actual number of truants in Japan is a little under 130,000.307/★133 Certainly, unlike the Zaitokukai, truants don't shout their protests out on the streets, but the phenomenon of truancy is widely known in Japan, creating an impact on educational policies that is by no means small.

In modern Japan, you can't readily find an image of a "good society" with which all people sympathize, nor can you readily find a "bad human being" unanimously detested by all people. For this reason, measures to change society, or the actions you can take to that end, come in a variety of shapes.308

You can become a member of a municipal assembly and change the local regulations of a city; or you can become an entrepreneur and run a business that contributes to society; or you can become a bureaucrat and dedicate your entire life to reforming a terrible law; or you can aim to become a tycoon so powerful that you can change the course of politics. And in this day and age, you can even realize an international treaty as a member of a non-governmental organization—such an achievement is no longer the stuff of dreams.309

So then, are we to assume that the street protestors are useless? Not at all. Compared to entrepreneurs, their impact on society may be more or less zero, but if they

---

★132. Ryū Murakami (sixty-three years old, Nagasaki) subsequently went on to release what could be called a sequel to the *Kibō no kuni no ekusodasu* (Exodus to the land of hope) titled, *Ōrudo terorisuto* (Old terrorist; Bungeishunju, 2015). Set in Japan in 2018, the story is about elderly people between the ages of seventy and ninety who attempt to change Japan through committing acts of terrorism. Unlike "Exodus to the land of hope," which showed an alternative society, this story sees senior citizens trying to reduce Japan to ashes. Perhaps this was an expression of Murakami's exasperation at the fact that Japan hadn't changed.

307. In the *Gakkō kihon chōsa* (2010) (2010 School data survey), the number of primary- and secondary-school students whose "truancy" was classified as long-term absence—that is, those who were absent for more than thirty days a year—amounted to 125,637. When you include high school and university students, the actual figure is expected to be considerably higher.

★133. According to the *Gakkō kihon chōsa* (2015) (2015 School data survey), there were 122,655 long-term truants among primary and secondary students. While this number was roughly level with 2010, since the overall number of children had decreased, the rate of truancy (0.39 percent) was at a record high.

308. In the first place, in an intricate modern society it is more difficult to act in a way that won't benefit anyone at all. If you buy something, someone's purse will grow fat; even the mere act of carelessly tossing away garbage creates employment. By the same token, it is also difficult to act in such a way so as to cause no trouble to anybody at all.

309. Motoko Mekata, *Kōdō suru shimin ga sekai o kaeta* (Citizen activists have changed the world) Mainichi Shimbun, 2009.

can find happiness in what they're doing, even if only a little, we should watch over them from a cool distance.[310]

In this chapter we have looked at young people who have continued to carry out demonstrations to change Japan. Their activities were fueled by a desire to overcome their sense of entrapment and despair by taking part in expressive activities, or by the desire to find an *ibasho* (place of belonging) to seek acceptance and approval.

And there's nothing wrong with that.

It's probably better for their health, anyway, to walk along the streets outside under the sun rather than being cooped up inside their home. And on top of that, they get to make new friends who share common interests; now that's killing two birds with one stone.

But in my opinion there are slightly more constructive avenues young people can take, and in society, you can also find more enjoyable things to do.

Postscript: Will Protest Demonstrations Change Japan?

After 2011, demonstrations and conventions in this country became a part of everyday life.

And in 2012, protests against the reactivation of the Fukushima nuclear power plant were held every Friday in front of the prime minister's office, reportedly attracting a gathering of 200,000 people on June 29, according to the press release from the organizers of the protest. In an event held on July 16, titled "*Sayonara genpatsu jūmannin shūkai*" (Goodbye nuclear power plant—a gathering of 100,000 people), according to the press release from the organizers, approximately 170,000 participated.[★134]

The subject of the protests has changed depending on the period in time: in 2012 the keynote theme of the protests was phasing out nuclear power; in 2014, opposition to the State Secrecy Law was emphasized; and in 2015, the protest movement that stood out was the one opposing the 2015 Japanese military legislation approving the

---

310. In the end, if demonstrations serve as an outlet for people to let off steam and thereby prevent the occurrence of a bloody "revolution," society would be better off for it.

★134. The turnout numbers for demonstrations and gatherings greatly vary depending on whether the figures are provided by organizers, media reports, or police news releases. The protest that took place in front of the official residence, according to the press release from the police, had a turnout of 20,000 people, whereas the *Sayonara genpatsu jūmannin shūkai* (Goodbye nuclear power plant—a gathering of 100,000 people) had 75,000 participants. A demonstration is essentially a fluid assembly, making it difficult to determine an accurate headcount.

right to collective self-defense.★[135]

However, as I mention in chapter 5, the participants in these demonstrations were not necessarily just young people. Rather, the number of young participants wasn't necessarily considerable. In a conversation I had with him after the publication of this book, Eiji Oguma (forty-nine years old, Tokyo) said that young people were the segment of the population that stayed away from demonstrations the most.

Young people today don't see themselves as belonging to a privileged class, unlike the college students who led the demonstrations in the 1960s. In addition, young people today aren't experiencing austere lives, either. That such people are indifferent to politics isn't particularly surprising, Oguma says.★[136]

Meanwhile, a group that's suddenly attracting attention is the student group called Students Emergency Action for Liberal Democracy (SEALDs). As the name suggests, the group was set up to carry out urgent demonstrations in the name of freedom and democracy. The group formerly began in 2014 as Students Against the Secret Protection Law (SASPL), which was a student volunteer association set up to voice opposition to Prime Minister Abe's Special Secrecy Law. Since then, they have been carrying out demonstrations and have staged protest rallies in front of the official residence. Subsequently, in 2015, they drew huge attention while the discussions on the 2015 military legislation were taking place in the Diet.

On August 23, demonstrations and assemblies were held in over sixty places across the country; the event was called "*Zenkoku wakamono issei kōdō*" (A nationwide youth chain of action). Regional organizations emerged in various places all over the country—not just in major urban centers like Tokyo and Kansai. According to the SEALDs press release, approximately 6,500 people came together in Tokyo alone.

Probably the greatest reason their demonstrations attracted so much attention is because their appearance—the look of their movement—has a contemporary "youthful" vibe about it. The favorable media reception, I believe, is due to the perception that their movement is about ordinary "young people" coolly carrying out protest activities; so coolly, in fact, that people are saying their demonstrations are a gathering of *riajū* (people who have fulfilling real lives, as opposed to online ones). Instead of wearing a helmet, holding a wooden staff, and consequently projecting an anachronistic look, these protestors are dressed in reasonably stylish clothes, and they appeal for

★135. Regarding the series of protest demonstrations that took place in front of the official residence, refer to the 2015 documentary film directed by Eiji Oguma (fifty-two years old, Tokyo) titled *Shushō kantei no mae de* (In front of the prime minister's office).

★136. The conversation that took place rather accidentally at that time is recorded in Eiji Oguma's *Shinken ni hanashimashō* (Let's talk seriously; Shin-yo-sha, 2014).

peace to the rhythms of rap music. Even their placards and flyers have a touch of stylishness in their design. This kind of outward appearance is probably, in the eyes of adults, a refreshing sight.★137

Haunted by the image of the sixties, many players in the media have the image—or the preconception—that "demonstrations = young people." Meanwhile, "young people" today, whom many had written off as being apathetic toward politics, are, in fact, launching political movements, so it's not surprising to see that their movements are attracting so much attention.

But at the same time, to consider SEALDs as a typical "youth" movement in general is risky. Just for argument's sake, let's say the scale of the SEALDs movement numbers in the tens of thousands of people. However, the number of university students in the entire country amounts to approximately 2.9 million. So, as you can see, on no account can it be said that all young people are participating in demonstrations.

Rather, instead of being a representative of "youth," SEALDs is a group that survives by reaching out to the middle-aged and the elderly. I have written a book titled *Dakara Nippon wa zureteiru* (That's why Japan is off; published by Shinchosha), and I can say that the middle-aged men of this nation love to see their generation criticized by the young.★138

Nonetheless, it's certainly true that young people have come to play a key role in SEALD, at a time when they have been a rare presence in political movements in recent years. Just as not all fans of a musical artist show up at the artist's live performances, the number of youths whose sense of values resonate with SEALDs' values must be several times more than those who take part in the group's events.

This may very well be because the issues that came up in the discourses concerning the 2015 military legislation—issues such as war and the draft—may have ended up connecting the "close-knit, self-contained sphere" of the young to the "public, community sphere" of society. Another theory suggests that young people today have been driven to take action ever since the Great East Japan Earthquake, when mistrust of the government became rampant.

★137. That being said, there's nothing surprising about what they did. On the contrary, in a time when fast fashion had caught on, it would have been quite difficult to find extremely uncool, nerdy clothes. As for the flyers, they would have been already used to making them for school festivals and club or interest-group activities.

★138. According to the critic Tsunehira Furuya (thirty-two years old, Hokkaido), the SEALDs attract attention because they're perceived as people who "can tell apart truth from fiction, thanks to their innocence." In reality, they're speaking not to young people, but to the middle-aged and elderly, who in turn are the ones endorsing them. In other words, it's a stretch to consider the SEALDs as "spokespeople for the young generation." ("Wakamono no demo wa media no shōmōhin" [Youth demonstrations are media expendables], *WiLL*, September 2015).

While revisiting this chapter, I began to regret how much I had looked down on protest demonstrations; I really didn't have to sneer at them so much. As I got to know politicians and government officials in Kasumigaseki, my views on demonstrations changed; I came to realize that the paranoia these authority figures felt regarding demonstrations was greater than I had ever imagined.

For instance, the LDP's Shigeru Ishiba (fifty-six years old, Tottori) wrote on his blog in November 2013 that "Simple screaming tactics are not that different from terrorism in both act and intent." This triggered a flame war, having virtually equated the "protest demonstration" to an "act of terrorism." Such a remark is a likely sign that Ishiba, to a certain extent, considers demonstrations to be a threat.

Many of the other the bureaucrats of Kasumigaseki were concerned about demonstrations, too. But this is understandable; if demonstrations and gatherings were held almost every day in front of the building in which they worked, they'd naturally become conscious of their presence, even if they didn't want to. Thus, I could longer deny the influence that demonstrations can, to a certain extent, have over the state.

However, I personally have no intention of attending a demonstration myself,★139 and I'm not too pleased either by people who are thrilled when a demonstration attracts tens of thousands of people; their enthusiasm shows that the demonstration, to them, has become an end in itself.

At the risk of stating the obvious, the protest demonstration alone has no power to change society. We shouldn't be abandoning the tools of indirect democracy, such as elections and referendums, and as I emphasized in this chapter, we no longer live in times when only the state engages in "society-building." If you take a macro view, you can see that what you decide to buy, and where you decide to buy, is also connected to changing society. And that's why I think it's wrong to criticize people for going to demonstrations, as well as for not going to them.

On August 30, 2015, a demonstration was held before the Diet building to protest the 2015 military legislation. According to the organizers, 120,000 people had gathered, while the police said the number was 33,000. To give you context, this was a scale equal to AVEX's huge "a-nation" music festival held on the same day, which had a turnout of 50,000; and to the Sandaime J Soul Brothers musical group concert that was held at the Seibu Prince Dome with a turnout of 30,000; as well as to the free concert of singer-songwriter aiko (thirty-nine years old, Osaka), staged in Chigasaki,

★139. If there were a social institution I really wanted to change, I'd consult with my politician and bureaucrat friends. Also, I stopped going out to cover demonstrations—during the time I was writing this book—largely because they had become something I was used to seeing on a routine basis.

which drew a crowd of 36,000. So, as it turned out, a terribly large number of people had gathered before the Diet building that day, where—with a few exceptions—no well-known artists made an appearance.★140

At least the demonstration, without a doubt, was able to mobilize far more people than any demonstration staged by the Zaitokukai or net-based right-wingers.

In the end, whether you went to a-nation, or the Sandaime J Soul Brothers concert, or to see aiko, or whether you took part in the demonstration held in front of the Diet building, any one of them would have been a wonderful way to spend the last Sunday of August that year.

★140. Ryūichi Sakamoto (sixty-three years old, Tokyo) was making a speech in front of the Diet building.

Chapter 5

The Great East Japan Earthquake and the Young People Who Met Expectations

The Great East Japan Earthquake struck the Tohoku and Kanto regions on March 11, 2011, at 2:46 p.m. The magnitude-nine quake unleashed a savage tsunami that wiped out many towns and triggered an accident at a nuclear power plant; the full picture of the total devastation has not yet been brought to light.

In response to this unexpected mega-earthquake disaster, what kind of action did young people take?

1. Japan Erupts

The global spread of charitable fundraising activities

In the immediate aftermath of the earthquake disaster, charitable fundraising campaigns began to gain momentum above all else. Even as the logistics for dispatching volunteers and for accepting them were still in a state of disarray, young people who felt the urge to "take action no matter what," began collecting contributions.

On March 13, in front of Tokyo's Shinjuku station, more than fifty young people who had answered the appeal for help by the Global Change Makers Program (GCMP), a student group related to relief efforts for Bangladesh, were soliciting donations from passersby. While a "donation rush" eventually emerged after the disaster,[311]

---

311.   Up to a certain point, you can collect more money through donations than in an ordinary job. However, the number of groups calling for donations gradually increases with time, decreasing the amount of money that can be collected through fundraising. For now, I'd like to define the donation break-even point as the time when donating the hourly wage earned for a part-time job at McDonald's becomes greater than what a fundraising campaign can raise.

it was rare to see a fundraising campaign as large as this one take place just two days after the earthquake.[312]

Apparently the campaign began with an offer of assistance from the Bangladeshi side when, on the night of March 12, a Bangladeshi youth sent a message saying, "I love Japan, I want to repay Japan's kindness." Soon after, a meeting was held among the core members via Skype.

GCMP operates together with the Grameen Bank, the Nobel Peace Prize–winning microfinance organization which provides unsecured loans to the impoverished. This collaboration began when a college student found out about the bank while looking for something he could do that was so big and wonderful it would make the world a more interesting place. On their website is written the passionate message, "We want to turn this field into a runway from which young people of our generation can take flight toward their dreams."[313/★141]

Having mainly carried out study tours and surveys, the group had never engaged in a fundraising campaign before. Akane Miyajima (twenty-one years old, female), the person in charge on the Japan side, said, "As a fellow Japanese, I couldn't just turn a blind eye to the situation. While I briefly considered going to the affected areas myself, I came to the conclusion that at this stage I shouldn't, so I just thought about what I could do right now." Consequently, it was decided that Japan and Bangladesh would start soliciting monetary contributions simultaneously.

After calls for volunteers for the campaign were made via Twitter and Facebook, many young people responded. When I asked for some comments from college student Hirokazu (twenty-one years old, male), who had rushed over after hearing about the campaign from a friend, he answered, "I'm glad I was able to contribute to Japan," adding heatedly, "The earthquake this time has made me reaffirm my love for Japan."

Although he had never taken part in a fundraising campaign before, he said he wasn't at all ashamed of this. He then went on to report his impression of the day. "I know I look like kind of an airhead, you know, so when some people made donations I was really glad. But it was still sad to see quite a few people who, to my surprise, didn't even turn around to look at me." Nonetheless, his face was suffused with a sense

---

312. An account of that day was introduced in a story in the *Asahi Shimbun* titled "Tokyo to banguradeshu gakusei ga dōji bokin" (Students in Tokyo and Bangladesh simultaneously raise funds; March 18, 2011, morning edition). The remarks of the participants that appear in this book are excerpted from an interview carried out on March 13.

313. http://www.gcm-p.com/story.html

★141. GCMP became a limited liability company (LLC) in 2013. It continues to carry out goodwill exchanges with Bangladesh. The company's passion still remains, but its URL has changed as follows: http://www.gcm-p.com/about/story/

of accomplishment.

Job-hopping part-timer Ren (twenty-one years old, male) was initially pushing ahead with a project he had been working on with his friends—a movie depicting teens who had lost their families due to a falling-out with their parents. However, after the earthquake, he says, "I rescheduled everything."

The devastation wreaked by the earthquake, he said, "was beyond the scope of the local communities to manage on their own. Actually, I personally wanted to just storm into the disaster-stricken areas so badly I didn't even mind exposing myself to radiation. But I changed my mind and decided that now was the time to collect money, so I joined the fundraising campaign." Since then Ren has been continuing to carry out fundraising work almost every week.

The fundraising campaign lasted for only two hours, but in Shinjuku the group was able to collect approximately 400,000 yen, while in Bangladesh a total donation of 15,000 *taka* (18,000 yen) was collected. In the end, all the participants took commemorative photos, bringing the fundraising campaign to a close.[314] Without even drifting toward a drinking session to celebrate the completion of the project, everyone just parted company and went their own respective ways.

Now Japan can become one

The fundraising campaign even spread through regions that hadn't suffered any losses from the earthquake. One such campaign that took place in front of Hakata station succeeded in collecting, within just a five-day period spanning from March 12 through March 16, a total of 7 million yen in donations. In this campaign, the Fukuoka student group Soul Works[315/★142] played a key role.

The group was originally formed to "unite the students of Fukuoka." While Fukuoka has many student groups, they weren't interacting with each other effectively. For this reason, the founders of Soul Works wanted to set up a place that could help connect student groups to each other and "build a community, give rise to a common language."

Immediately after the earthquake, group representative Masashi Sagara (twenty-one years old, male) called for carrying out a fundraising campaign, believing that the

---

314.   There's nothing unusual about a student volunteer circle taking commemorative photographs before and after their activity. It's just that clueless passersby were murmuring, "What's this—a party? Tourists in a package tour?"

315.   Apparently, they have changed the group's name to SAU (Student Asian Representative Union).

★142.   At present, I couldn't confirm any signs of their current activities. According to the official web site, Masashi Sagara, the twenty-six-year-old group leader from Fukuoka, appears to be active as a "Human Relations Specialist" and "Total Vision Therapist" (*kanjutsu sesshon-shi*).

group should take prompt action in whatever way it was able to at that moment. He said, "Through the fundraising campaign, I want to unite Fukuoka, I want to unite Japan. Until now, there has never been any reason for Fukuoka to unite, nor for Japan to unite. But now we have a reason for everyone to unite."

For these students, who had originally intended to just connect the students of Fukuoka to each other, the earthquake disaster was something that produced a tangible objective. At a meeting, when Sagara addressed the members, saying, "Now is the time for us all to join forces and become one!" the members nodded enthusiastically.

Yūko (twenty years old, female), who says, "I like starting new things," found out about the fundraising campaign via mixi. "Watching TV just confused me, with all the reporting so full of technical jargon." And that's why, she said, she didn't feel right unless she did something that was within her means to do.

Fearless for a cause

What I frequently heard them say was, "At any rate, I wanted to do something."

For Takaaki (twenty-one years old, male), "watching TV wasn't enough. I wanted to take action. Unless I did it just didn't feel right." This was why he went on to join the fundraising campaign. He's currently busy looking for a job, but whenever he has time to spare, he takes part in the campaign.

He said he learned from the fundraising campaign that "If you're really sincere in what you do, others will pay back that sincerity to you. People notice your perseverance." He added, joyfully, "There's a sense of fulfillment in that."[316]

Shiho (twenty-one years old, female), who was also looking for a job, decided to join the fundraising campaign after being struck by the notion that she wanted to change herself. During Q&A sessions at company orientations, all the other students around her were actively speaking out, but she just couldn't raise her hand. However, thanks to her fundraising activities, she had the opportunity to hear the ideas of a great variety of people, and she began to enjoy meeting new people. She says that, as a result, "I was able to get back to job hunting with a positive, forward-looking attitude."[317]

After the fundraising campaign was over, a meeting was held in the group's office, which was decorated with colorful banners displaying words like "co-creation," "co-

---

316.   Job hunting, he says, "becomes a source of encouragement for you—even the rejections you experience. At interviews, you make new discoveries about yourself." It certainly sounds as though his days have been fulfilling. He added, "I want to work at a company that emphasizes the importance of gratitude."

317.   With regard to Shiho's remarks, I referred to the article "Daishinsai de kokoro hitotsu ni: Gaitō bokin ni mananda gakusei gurūpu SAU" (Solidarity of hearts in the face of the major earthquake disaster: Lessons learned from street fundraising by the student group SAU) in the *Nishinippon Shimbun* (April 10, 2011, morning edition). Remarks by others were made in the course of the interviews conducted on March 17.

existence," and "co-education." After the representative delivered a longish salutation, each person spoke in turn about the ways they wanted to see themselves change, and about what was on their minds right now.

Taishi (twenty years old, male) said he wanted to stare back at grownups who glared at him as if to say, "What the hell do you think you're doing, kid?" To do that, he said, "I have to be fearless."

Apparently the group had experienced some trouble getting the campaign underway, with the West Japan Railway company refusing to readily grant them permission to solicit donations in front of Hakata station. Upon hearing Taishi's remarks, some were moved to tears, and that day's meeting came to an end.

Youth rushing to disaster-stricken areas

Once the facilities and other arrangements had been set up for receiving volunteers, many people, including younger ones, rushed to the disaster sites.

According to the Japan National Council of Social Welfare, for the period between the occurrence of the earthquake disaster and just prior to the Golden Week holidays, 175,000 volunteers entered the three prefectures of Tohoku. Furthermore, within just the first half of the consecutive holidays between April 29 and May 3, an additional 43,000 were recorded arriving in those areas.[318]

Having had experience with the Great Hanshin-Awaji Earthquake, many non-profit and non-governmental organizations (NPOs and NGOs) swiftly began volunteer-based disaster-relief operations. For example, the international NGO Peace Boat dispatched advance staff to disaster-stricken areas on March 15; in addition to delivering relief supplies, they also began collecting information and carrying out feasibility studies for relief operations.

From March 25, the organization began to dispatch general volunteer applicants to the city of Ishinomaki in Miyagi prefecture. A hallmark of Peace Boat is its built-in flexibility that allows anyone to become an immediate asset to the group, even if they don't have any special expertise or experience. While the main work involved tasks such as preparing meals for soup kitchens and sludge removal, the tasks assigned to individuals could be carried out by practically anyone.

However, even though no special expertise or talent was required, motivation was a must. Volunteers had to be responsible for taking enough of their own water and

---

318.   "Borantia kyūgen: Seikyō no hisaichi, GW shūban itten: Higashi Nihon dai shinsai" (Rapid decrease in the number of volunteers: Disaster-stricken areas were bustling: final phase of Golden Week Thrown into upheaval by the Great East Japan Earthquake), *Asahi Shimbun*, May 8, 2011, morning edition.

food with them to last the whole one-week assignment, and they also needed to prepare a tent and sleeping bag for every group they were assigned to. Volunteers even had
to take care of the transportation expenses they incurred to get to an affected area.
Nevertheless, within about one month, a total of 1,500 volunteers (as of the end of
April) were reported to have joined.★143

Sari, a twenty-one-year-old college student who had joined Peace Boat in the beginning of May, explained her reason for becoming a volunteer. "I wanted to see the
actual place. To say that I was curious might be improper, but instead of cut-out images you see on TV, I wanted to see what the TV screen failed to capture."

She was interested in the subject of international contribution, to begin with,
majoring in peace studies in college. She also had experience as a passenger on board a
Peace Boat–sponsored cruise ship traveling around the world. "In Japan," she continued, "the whole idea of things like refugees was a remote issue until now. But now the
country is facing a crisis in which support and assistance for relief efforts is lacking."
She then explained, "When I heard there was a shortage of helping hands, I wanted to
do anything I could do to help."★144

Independently arriving at a disaster site and setting up a relief organization

Nanami (twenty-six years old, female, Saitama), a former Peace Boat passenger who
was currently in graduate school studying security, was heading for the coastal town of
Minamisanriku in Miyagi prefecture under the auspices of the project named Tsuna-
puro. Chiefly organized by the Nippon Foundation and the NPO ETIC, the group
aims to serve as an intermediary to NPOs specializing in various fields by investigating
local needs through interviews conducted in disaster-stricken areas.[319]

Nanami had decided to join as a volunteer because she was concerned about what
kind of situation these areas were in, and she wanted to actually see them for herself.
Since her entire day was spent making rounds to about five places, she said she was so
busy she didn't have the time to think about all kinds of other things. Looking back on
the activities she had carried out, she summed up, "I'm glad I was able to go to those
stricken areas. It was of great interest to me."★145

There were also some volunteer groups that young people had started up all by

---

★143. Even after that, the Peace Boat continued to carry out its volunteer activities, mainly around Ishinomaki
and Onagawa in Miyagi prefecture, and had dispatched 13,816 people by the end of March 2013. To this
day, they remain active, continuing to operate the "Peace Boat Center Ishinomaki."

★144. After graduating from university, Sari secured a position at Peace Boat, and currently works as an English
teacher at a private school.

319. The legal name is *Hisaisha o NPO to tsunaide sasaeru gōdō purojekuto* (Joint project to support victims by
connecting them to NPOs).

themselves.

The Student Emergency Task Force (SET) is a group formed by college students in Tokyo who have expressed their intent to "be of help to the people of disaster-stricken areas."[320]/[146] In the immediate aftermath of the earthquake, on the night of March 12, a meeting was held among the volunteers, after which the organization was established on March 13. The motive behind the group's establishment, I was told, was to convert the sympathies and the power of young people into hope for the people of the disaster-stricken areas.

At the heart of the activities was Yūsuke Yoshida (twenty-one years old, Tokyo), founder of the student group SWITCH, which carries out international exchange programs with Bangladesh. Yoshida is also involved with the group called Gakusei Ishin (Student Reformation), whose declared mission is "to make Earth more and more energetic."[147]

In March, Yoshida dedicated his time to providing logistical support for supplies and attending study sessions; in April he headed for the city of Rikuzentakata in Iwate, where he began carrying out volunteer activities with local NPOs through a tri-al-and-error process, as well as attempting to grasp local needs.

Upon arriving at the scene of disaster, Yoshida's impression was, "This can't be the same Japan I know."

The objective of SET is thus: "As the young generation that can shoulder the bur-dens of Japan, we will continue to be engaged in the affairs of Rikuzentakata as our second hometown, even after its reconstruction is complete."

From Cambodia to Tohoku

Hiroaki Ishimatsu, a twenty-seven-year old from Oita who launched the student vol-unteer group GRAPHIS (see chapter 2) and is currently working at a university hos-pital in Tokyo as a medical intern, headed for Kesennuma (a port city in Miyagi pre-fecture) in late April. He wanted to go to the affected areas immediately after the earthquake disaster struck, but as a doctor he had daily duties to attend to, and couldn't

★145. Nanami went on to acquire a master's degree, and, after graduating, found employment at a consultancy. She is currently involved in numerous international aid projects.

320. With regard to SET, refer to their official blog at http://ameblo.jp/set-japan/

★146. Currently, SET—as an NPO—is mainly active in Iwate prefecture, around Hirotacho, in the city of Rikuzentakata. I have been told that four young people have settled down in affected areas by the spring of 2015. As I write this footnote, I can't help but feel surprised that the project that started four years ago is still running to this day.

★147. SET is still active, but Yoshida himself appears to be working at a venture company handling wedding productions.

take action so quickly because he would have ended up neglecting his patients."[148]

He finally managed to find the time to travel to one of the affected areas. Upon arrival, he says, "No words came out." His blog contains an entry in which he puts into words the feelings he experienced at that time: "Is this place here really Japan? Isn't it Cambodia?" He also felt, he says, assaulted by the same helplessness—the same sense of futility—he'd experienced when he visited Cambodia for the first time.

Still, Ishimatsu searched for what he could do to help. To that end, upon being led to the meeting of the Oshima Recovery Committee by a local legislator, Ishimatsu would hear the local people expressing views like, "I want to work so badly I can't help myself!" and "I'll work for a daily wage of just 6,000 yen, or even 5,000 yen."

What then occurred to Ishimatsu was the idea of holding study tours of the remote island of Oshima. This study tour would attract students from all over the country who would perform field work under the guidance of the local islanders. The admission fees collected from these students would be used to pay the guides. It was a brilliant plan that applied Ishimatsu's knowledge about implementing study tours, which he had been running in Cambodia through GRAPHIS.

Ishimatsu realized, just as he did when providing international assistance to Cambodia, that "Everything starts from seeing." On the other hand, he doesn't forget to give due consideration to the participants, appreciating that it's necessary for them to attain some sense of accomplishment. One possible area of focus for the study tour is the maintenance of Oshima's beaches, which are among the top hundred swimming areas listed by the Ministry of the Environment. This is being considered because it's easier to achieve visible results through cleaning beaches than with simple debris elimination.

Incidentally, with some time set aside for enjoying barbecues and stargazing, an attempt is apparently being made to make the study tours more than just volunteer work.

The long-awaited "days of extraordinary living"
If I were to say that it seems like the World Cup has been going on all this time, I might be accused of being thoughtless, but what has occurred in the wake of the Great East Japan Earthquake was the explosion of the "Japan" trend. On heavy rotation for a time were the messages from the Advertising Council making frequent mentions of

---

★148. Since then, Ishimatsu went on to work as a doctor in Okinawa while launching a business, developing the service "Dr. Joy," an in-hospital SNS for medical institutions, in partnership with Mitsui & Co. and KDDI. He says that it's a system designed for smartphones that can reduce inefficiencies in healthcare settings. I guess everyone's really applying themselves in all sorts of different scenes.

Japan, such as through catchphrases like, "Japan is a powerful nation," or "I believe in the power of Japan," or "Japan is a single unified team."

Furthermore, as we have seen in this chapter, many young people made remarks along the lines of "Japan can bond as one through the earthquake disaster" and "I reaffirmed my love of Japan" (through participating in fundraising activities).

As long as we lead ordinary lives, the presence of "Japan" slips under the radar of consciousness; people fail to readily become aware of it unless something other than what we associate with normal "Japan" appears (chapter 3). In this sense, the natural disaster of the earthquake is indeed an externality appearing before the normality that is the nation of "Japan."

That student groups and young people performing overseas volunteer work swiftly reacted to the earthquake disaster this time is telling in a symbolic way. The founders of GRAPHIS and SWITCH, when discussing the purpose behind their establishment of these groups, cited the feelings of desperation, entrapment, and hopelessness they had felt in their everyday lives. So at that point, they discovered the platforms of Cambodia and Bangladesh as an antidote. To break through their sense of desperation, they probably needed something as extraordinary—to their eyes—as those foreign countries.

In the same vein, the Great East Japan Earthquake instantly changed the Tohoku region into the "extraordinary." Just as Ishimatsu openly expressed his feelings when he said, "Is this place here really Japan? Isn't it Cambodia?" the disaster-stricken areas of Tohoku had functionally become as "extraordinary" as Cambodia.

That many youths are attempting to get involved in the reconstruction of the affected areas isn't strange at all. To the contrary, if you have been reading up to this point, you should be feeling that the actions taken by young people were within the scope of expectations.

As we saw in chapter 3, young people today, while feeling satisfied with living in the "here and now," are at the same time slightly weighed down by a sense of despair at the unchanging, blandness of the everyday mundane. They're looking for an exit somewhere. This restless feeling of wanting to do something is driving them toward volunteerism.

But the problem is that, until now, the object of their commitment was unclear; in other words, a concrete connection to "society" was missing. For this reason, though many young people considered their country and society to be valuable, many of them weren't able to take action to actually act on those values.

However, when the earthquake disaster struck, an object of commitment appeared in the form of support for the stricken areas.

What I'm about to say may sound rather reckless, but it can be said that for society-minded youths, the earthquake disaster was an incident they had been looking forward to with anticipation. It was just as the people of the Fukuoka student group told me: "Now there's a reason for everybody to come together as one."

In that sense, the Japan trend that occurred in the wake of the earthquake disaster may have been a phenomenon that you couldn't even call nationalism. In other words, in the eyes of young people, if "Tohoku" is interchangeable with "Cambodia," then no matter how much emphasis is placed on "Japan," in the end, it's not about ourselves, but about problems outside ourselves.[321]

2. In the Midst of an Anti-Nuclear Power Festival

The ten-thousand-strong gathering in Koenji

On April 10 in Koenji, Tokyo, an anti-nuclear demonstration called the "Stop Nuclear Power Generation Demo" took place.[322] The group behind this protest was the Shirōto no Ran (Layman's Revolt), which runs a secondhand-goods shop and a used-clothing store in Koenji while staging occasional playful demonstrations and events.[323]

For example, at one point they ran for office in the ward-assembly elections and, under the pretext of a stump speech, threw a colossal party in front of Koenji station, calling out bands and DJs to perform. On another occasion, they had applied to the police for a license to stage a demonstration, but in reality this protest consisted of just three people walking, not even carrying any placards. Naturally, there were many times more police officers there, having been assigned to protect the protestors. The "Stop Nuclear Power Generation Demo" was infused with a carnival-like atmosphere, as might be expected of a Shirōto no Ran–sponsored event. On that day, after I stepped out of the south exit of Koenji station and headed for Koenji Chūō Park, the designat-

---

321.   If you think about it, messages like "Japan is a strong country" or "I believe in Japan's strength" sound somewhat detached and impersonal. If actual victims of the disaster said things like, "I believe in Japan's strength," you could appreciate the message as an SOS cry for help. But when you hear a celebrity in Tokyo saying, "I believe in Japan's strength," it fails to sink in; who are those words targeting?

322.   It appears that the official title is "*Chō kyodai hangenpatsu rokku fesu demo in kōenji—Hisaichi shien gienkin atsume & genpatsu iikagen ni shiro!*" (Super-ginormous anti-nuclear power rock festival demonstration in Koenji—Fundraising for supporting affected areas & for crying out loud, stop nuclear power generation!).

323.   To be precise, the group takes its name from the store they run. Incidentally, according to his Twitter account, Hajime Matsumoto, the thirty-six-year old Tokyoite kingpin of Shirōto no Ran, fled Tokyo after the nuclear plant accident, saying "Radiation's no joke, man."

ed meeting place, I found a tremendous number of people there.[324] At the center of this gathering spot were not only people giving speeches, but bands performing as well. The scene appeared to be a typical example of the "new social movement" mentioned in chapter 4.[★149]

The participants were across the board in terms of age, ranging from young people to the elderly, but there weren't that many who looked like forty-year veterans of the anti-nuclear movement. In general, most were clad in simple and unostentatious clothes—the type of people peculiar to neighborhoods found along the Chūō train line—and the naturalist types, the kind of people who seemed to be interested in all things organic. There were many who had brought along their children as well.

Yōsuke (twenty-two years old, male), who had been involved with the anti-nuclear movement even before the earthquake disaster, said, "At the demonstrations I usually attend, you don't see children around, and we engage in choral chanting of political slogans like, 'Say no to nuclear power!' Today's event is fun, though. I don't even feel like I'm in Japan." Even the placards testified as to how freewheeling and peppy everyone was at this demonstration, with messages like "We want to eat spinach!" and "The age of inner power generation."

The wide variety of viewpoints represented by the participants was another hallmark of that day's demonstration. For example, Ryōta (twenty-one years old, male), who is majoring in nuclear engineering at college, carries out research on breeder reactors. When it comes to the issue of nuclear power generation, he belongs in the "pro" camp, whose mission is fueled by the conviction that "without nuclear power generation, we're in trouble." Nevertheless, he says, he decided to pay a visit to today's demonstration was because he wanted to gauge public opinion on this matter.

Yasuo (twenty-two years old, male) and Nozomi (twenty-four years old, female) happened to be taking a walk in the neighborhood, and decided to drop by the demonstration to check it out. Yasuo said he's in favor of nuclear power generation, because "We're using a lot of electricity." As for his impression of the demonstration itself, he says, "It's fun in a festival kind of way. If it were serious, though, I'd be sympathetic and even have a favorable impression. But then again, if it were serious, I wouldn't be able to approach it."

324.　According to the organizer's press release, there were 15,000 participants there. It certainly seemed like there were around 10,000 people at least.

★149.　Shirōto no Ran dropped the pace of their activities as the demonstrations in front of the prime minister's office gained momentum. Even today, though, they continue to plan for new events around Koenji, such as the *Ajia hansen daisakusen* (Great Asian antiwar campaign).

April 10, 2011

Although Nozomi didn't have any views in particular about the issue of nuclear power generation, she said, while surveying the people gathered at the Koenji Chūō Park, "They all look happy. Is this demonstration for real? Aren't there any people seriously concerned with the cause of this movement? It all seems so casual." Since the atmosphere is reminiscent of a festival or bazaar held by a neighborhood association, anyone can drop by and observe the proceedings without hesitation, regardless of their political principles, positions, or viewpoints.

But many of the people there likely took a stance opposing nuclear power generation.

Kazuya, a twenty-two-year old male college student who had never been to a demonstration before, was stunned by the festive atmosphere, commenting, "Now, what's this mood all about?" Nonetheless, he added, "As a festival, it's fun!"

But there were also some people who were a little more serious. Sayuri, a twenty-nine year old female office worker, was part of a ten-person team carrying placards that read "Say no to nuclear power generation." She had gotten to know the other women in her group at a demonstration held in front of the Tokyo Electric Power building in the wake of the earthquake disaster. While she had had nothing to do with social movements prior to the earthquake, she said, "I realized that now was the time to take action; that now was the time to get angry."

The women in this group make it a point to take part in the demonstrations held in front of the Tokyo Electric Power building on their way home from work these days. Sayuri said, with enthusiasm, "We want to spread this activity among more young people and ordinary citizens. We aim to establish connections all across Japan until we finally achieve a demonstration that's one million strong."[325]/[★150]

Anti-nuclear power and pro-nuclear power are the same things

We have arrived at an understanding of how demonstrations advocating the abandonment of nuclear power plants can be fun, like a festival. But just how much of a social impact do such demonstrations have?

Naoya (twenty-six years old, male) came to the demonstration to find out "what the truth was." However, after beholding the festival-like spectacle, he seemed troubled, wondering, "What's the point of having a demonstration?"

Indeed, just how much of an impact that day's demonstration had on society remains unknown. For instance, on April 10, the day the demonstration was staged, the city of Tokyo was holding its gubernatorial elections. One of the issues at stake in the election was the question of whether nuclear power generation should be continued, and people were watching with interest the election results of the incumbent Shintarō Ishihara (seventy-eight years old, Hyogo), who had announced his pro-nuclear power policy. The other candidates, though they varied from each other in nuance, were all championing the abolition of nuclear power.

Since the people at the Stop Nuclear Power Generation Demo wouldn't have been there if they weren't environmentally and politically aware individuals, I naturally assumed that they must have gone to the polls to cast their votes before coming to Koenji; but that wasn't the case at all. In a country with a parliamentary democracy, rather than participating in demonstrations, declaring your anti-nuclear position through voting would get you closer to realizing the abolition of nuclear power,

---

325. Incidentally, by the middle of May 2011, no group resembling any kind of demonstration was to be seen in front of the Tokyo Electric Power building.

★150. The anti-nuclear power demonstrations were succeeded by the 2012 demonstrations that took place in front of the prime minister's official residence. According to the book *Genpatsu o tomeru hitobito* (The People aiming to stop nuclear power generation; Eiji Oguma, ed., Bungeishunju, 2013), the anti-nuclear power demonstration, which became galvanized in the wake of the earthquake disaster, reached a turning point in September 2011; at the *Genpatsu yamero demo* (Stop nuclear power generation demo) led by Shirōto no Ran, twelve participants were arrested. After that, Shirōto no Ran slowed down their activities. For a while, small-scale demonstrations were taking place across the country, but in March of 2012—around the first anniversary of the earthquake disaster—30,000 people encircled the Diet. Furthermore, at the end of March, people began protesting in front of the official residence; subsequently demonstrations went on to take place every Friday.

I feel.[326]/[★151]

"Stop nuclear power generation!" is, at first glance, an extremely easy-to-under-stand message. In a time when the Fukushima Daiichi Nuclear Power Station triggered an accident that led to the uncontained leakage of radioactive substances, many will sympathize with the concise appeal of this slogan.

But the faction for maintaining nuclear power and the faction for abolishing it aren't diametrically opposed to each other. For example, in Shibuya on April 17, the Zaitokukai led a protest march titled "Let's protect Japan's electric power supply! The demonstration for preventing the extinguishment of the nuclear fire!!"[327] Claims at this demonstration were, in fact, not that different from the ones made by the abolitionist faction, the "Stop nuclear power" group.

A representative of the Zaitokukai delivered a speech. In it, he said, "I personally feel that if there were no nuclear power, then that in and of itself wouldn't be such a bad thing. But there's no viable alternative energy source available, so we can't help it." How surprisingly plain. That is to say, his views seem to be close to those of people taking part in the "Stop nuclear power" demonstrations.

And even among the "Stop nuclear power" folk, there probably aren't that many insisting on the immediate shutdown of nuclear power plants all over Japan. That's because, as the Zaitokukai asserts, at this stage there are no viable alternative energy sources.

So, in that case, what on earth is the "Stop nuclear power" faction insisting on? While it does turn out that they are criticizing the faction "aggressively promoting nuclear power generation"—the faction that aims, by hook or by crook, to build even more nuclear power plants—in the end, the "Stop nuclear power" faction's view—that reliance on nuclear power generation for the time being is unavoidable—is not largely different from the stance of the faction in favor of maintaining nuclear power.[328]

Just about the only outstanding difference between the two demonstrations was in

---

326. Of course, there were many who had come to the demonstration after voting at the polls. Others who stood out were those who couldn't vote in the Tokyo gubernatorial election because, even though they were residing in Tokyo, they had left their resident card behind in their hometown.

★151. I don't think anyone remembers this, but at the Lower House election held at the end of 2012, the Nippon Mirai no Tō (Tomorrow Party of Japan), who were championing an anti-nuclear stance, had presented 121 candidates before suffering a crushing defeat. For an account of how elated intellectuals were at the time, refer to Noritoshi Furuichi's *Dakara Nippon wa zureteiru* (That's why Japan is off; Shinchosha, 2014).

327. This event name gives the impression that the Zaitokukai is, in fact, an organization that has no convictions, just a group that keeps criticizing for criticism's sake.

328. An examination of public opinion polls carried out after the disaster reveals that the "status quo" faction, even when seen in nationwide terms, accounts for the majority.

May 8, 2011

the number of people mobilized. The number of participants in the "Don't put out the nuclear fire demo" was approximately thirty. For demonstrations held in Tokyo by the Zaitokukai, this was said to be the lowest number to date.[329]

Puzzled by serious demonstrations

Although the Stop Nuclear Power Generation Demo held in Koenji managed to mobilize a more diverse crowd than any other anti-nuclear power demonstrations had ever managed to attract, there was no denying that all the participants had, as expected, similar political leanings.

However, the "Stop nuclear power demo" carried out in Shibuya and hosted by the Shirōto no Ran on May 8 was different. At that demonstration were plenty of seasoned, elderly men and women who appeared to have forty years of dedicated service to the leftist movement under their belts.

Many flyers were in circulation, displaying headlines like "Protecting the right to live in peace with security" and "Say no to building a military base in Henoko"; there

---

329. The venue was Shibuya, so the demonstration turned into a topic of conversation among fashionable girls passing by; you could hear them saying things like, "Ooh, who are these people, they're scary!" and "What? They're like what you might call the left wing, right?" Certainly, they're "left wing" in the sense that they keep doggedly criticizing the government, no matter what.

were even hand-drawn mini-comics.

In the center of Yoyogi Park, the designated meeting place, Shirōto no Ran was hosting a live musical performance, while in a corner an elderly left-wing man was starting to deliver a speech, giving the impression that there were several demonstrations going on at the same time.

Junji, a sixty-three-year-old former engineer who was holding up a placard, found out about today's demonstration via an online bulletin board. On the day of the previous demonstration in Koenji, he had gone to one that was "mainly comprised of old people," but he came to the one in Shibuya's Yoyogi Park today because "there wasn't anything else taking place today."

Kenta (twenty-nine years old, male), who was taking part in the demonstration while tricked out in cosplay gear, was puzzled by how different the atmosphere seemed compared to the one he had felt in Koenji, saying, "A lot of serious people around today, yeah? The age bracket is also high." He reminisced, "Koenji was fun, you know? It was like a festival."

Next to the elderly men and women earnestly protesting the risks of nuclear power, Kenta, in his original cosplay gear, surely looked out of place. Apparently, it's no easy task to get people of different age groups and social status to join forces, even though they may share the common goal of seeing nuclear power discontinued.

The limitations of the "Stop nuclear power demo"

While a demonstration belongs to its participants, as long as it parades through public streets, it also belongs to those who witness it. But it's doubtful that the "Stop nuclear power demo" had any significant impact on the passersby as it went through the scramble intersection in Shibuya and around the streets of Omotesando.

Though the people enjoying some holiday shopping in Omotesando would shift their attention to the demonstration, albeit just for an instant, most of them were indifferent. I even overheard exasperated voices saying, "Not another demonstration again," and "What's the point of doing it here?"

Ryō, a twenty-year-old male college student who was soliciting donations in Harajuku for the reconstruction of disaster-stricken areas, viewed the demonstration passing by before him with disdain. He said, "I'm a science and technology person, and I think being against nuclear power is reckless. We can't suddenly put an end to nuclear power generation." Yūto (twenty years old, male), who was also asking for donations, said, "Before complaining, they should be thinking about reconstruction first."

As you can see, it is not clear what kind of impact the "Stop nuclear power demo" had.[330/★152]

As of this writing, the memory of the accident in Fukushima is still fresh, and many are concerned about the problem of nuclear power generation. But the "festival" won't last for long. And the moment a rigid organization pops up to attempt to make the party last, things tend to end up getting dull. Given such a situation, how can the "Stop nuclear power" movement continue?

At any rate, as a way to spend the holidays in the wake of the earthquake disaster, going to a demonstration isn't a bad idea. People who are somewhat paranoid about nuclear power spot some demonstration, perhaps thanks to related information drifting down their Twitter stream, and upon taking part in the protest they find many other people there, and after circling Koenji in something of a festive mood, they find themselves quite tired, yet strangely fulfilled before going home.

At least their experience would serve as a way for them to vent their unease over nuclear power.[★153]

The spreading of good and evil across the Internet

As it turned out, in the immediate aftermath of the earthquake disaster we came to witness many "goodwill festivals" on the Internet.

For example, on March 12, a movement called Yashima Sakusen (Yashima Ops) spread, calling for people to save electricity. In response to the Tokyo Electric Power Company's announcement that a power shortage could occur, a movement demanding people to refrain from consuming electricity during peak periods caught fire on the Internet.

The name Yashima Sakusen came from the fictional tactical plan of action deployed in the anime *Neon Genesis Evangelion*, which involves channeling the power supply from all over Japan to defeat the enemy with long-range firepower. One of the

---

330. The demonstration held in Shibuya was given considerable coverage by the mass media. Which is perhaps why the event had some influence over the policymaking process and people's attitudes.

★152. Since 2011, after being subjected to demonstrations, the prime minister at that time, Naoto Kan (sixty-four years old, Yamaguchi), was aware that a groundswell of "movements and public opinion against nuclear power" had developed. (Eiji Oguma, ed., *Genpatsu o tomeru hitobito* [The people aiming to stop nuclear power generation], Bungeishunju, 2013). In addition, the former deputy chief cabinet secretary, Yoshito Sengoku (sixty-five years old, Tokushima), mentioned, after taking a hint from the anti-nuclear demonstrations held in Koenji, that he was beginning to feel that the reactivation of nuclear power could prove to be the death blow for the Democratic Party. (*Enerugī, genshiryoku daitenkan* [Great transformation of energy/nuclear power], Kodansha, 2013.)

★153. I really didn't have to be so emphatic and rub "sensible intellectuals" the wrong way.

central figures is a college student born in the 1990s.[331/★154] While the actual extent of this project's effect on power saving is unknown, at least on the Internet, many were sympathizing with Yashima Sakusen.

However, even the goodwill on the Internet spiraled out of control at times. For example, a chain mail that went viral menaced its readers with the claim, "An explosion at Cosmo Oil has spewed toxic substances into the clouds. From there, the poison will fall with the rain."[332]

I observed some Twitter users in situations where they were censured for failing to exercise self-restraint, being told, for example, that "tweeting about personal matters is imprudent."

And some, clearly out of malice, were disseminating the misinformation that foreigners, riding on the momentum of post-disaster chaos, were committing crimes. We don't seem to have changed very much from the time of the Great Kanto Earthquake some ninety years ago.

In addition, on the pretext of an "experiment," someone wrote the following (fake) message, which went viral on Twitter: "I got trapped inside a building when the earthquake struck. Help me!"

But in many cases, false rumors were immediately corrected, and their corrections were instantly circulated through the Internet. People also began to frequently express views like, "We shouldn't give a broad interpretation of the word 'imprudent,'" and "People leading their respective daily lives are not imprudent."

Even mixi and Ameba, which hitherto hadn't shown any interest at all in revolutions in distant lands (see chapter 3), were inundated with nothing but news of the earthquake at this time. Ameba News, which usually neglected to report any society-related news, ran at the top of its webpage a serious piece titled, "A summary of appropriate earthquake measures to prevent secondary casualties!"[333]

Is the mass media better?

However, what came to light in the wake of the earthquake disaster were the weak-

---

331.   http://nerv.evangelion.ne.jp/about.html

★154. This website no longer exists, but Daiki Ishimori (twenty-five years old, Miyagi), who launched the Yashima Sakusen, is serving as the CEO of Gehirn, a company focusing on disaster prevention and information security, apparently in addition to concentrating on disaster-prevention information, including the visualization of climatological data.

332.   This was an affair that was treated—soon after the earthquake disaster—as a typical "false rumor," with Cosmo Oil releasing a statement that denied the content of the chain mail. However, it subsequently became clear in the news that the adjacent facility for storing depleted uranium had also caught fire. ("Rekka uran hokan shisetsu mo enshō" [Depleted uranium storage facility also caught fire], *Chiba Nippo*, July 1, 2011).

nesses of the social media, and the fact that the conventional mass media still remained powerfully viable.

No matter how much the mass media is criticized for being arbitrary in its selection of the scenes and information it provides, no other outlet, with its sheer scale, could ever invest in such an enormous number of staff and televise local information in real time for twenty-four hours.

Meanwhile, on the Internet, information blossomed like so many flowers, bringing into relief the difficulty for the every person to distinguish correct pieces of information from the wrong ones. In this regard, the Internet went through a particularly terrible time after the accident at the Fukushima Daiichi Nuclear Power Station.

Now, if you were looking for some restaurant recommendations, you wouldn't run into any problems if you turned to the word-of-mouth reviews online. Even in the worst-case scenario, you might just end up complaining that the food was bad and overpriced. But when it comes to the question of the risks of radiation exposure, you can't really depend on online word of mouth, can you? What's more, ascertaining the risks of radiation exposure is markedly more complex than passing judgments on restaurant recommendations.

Several sharp-looking experts such as university professors appear, each of them expressing their own differing views. Then the following nugget of information circulates through the Internet: "Individuals holding down excellent positions are unprincipled, government-sponsored scholars." And then experts working at questionable laboratories and even experts with uncertain credentials enter the fray to chime in with the revelations of their own respective theories.

This situation in and of itself is not a problem in particular. After all, just as in the liberal arts, the discipline of science, to begin with, does not teach just one single truth. All that scientists can clarify through conducting experiments is a data-backed hypoth-

---

333.   As of March 12, 2011, in the middle of the night, the top-ranking news story on mixi was "Great East Japan Earthquake—the worst day in Japan—global community impacted." In second place was "Toward a complete power saving mode—Supporters of 'Yashima ops' grow in number on Twitter." In third place was "Has the 'earthquake' caused remotely triggered quakes in Nagano and Akita? Entire landmass of East Japan deformed." The most-viewed news story at Ameba News was "Voices pleading for rescue spreads across Twitter: 'I've been swept away by the tsunami and am now standing on top of a truck. Help.'" In second place was "Tomizawa and Date [the popular comedy duo Sandwichman] encounter the earthquake in Kesennuma and ride out the night with blankets." In third place was, "An appropriate summary of earthquake countermeasures for preventing secondary casualties." Not all the top-ranked news stories on Ameba News were solely about the earthquake, though; while earthquake-related stories accounted for the top twenty news items at mixi, in terms of both access rankings and blog post rankings, at Ameba News, the story ranked in fifth place was "Ai Kago reveals a *gyaru* hairstyle." Nonetheless, the fact that even Ameba News responded to support disaster-related news, made me realize, above all, just how great the impact of the earthquake disaster on Japanese society had been.

esis, which can be rejected by a group of their peers if the hypothesis turns out to be wrong. And in the process of having each peer criticize the other's hypothesis, as a group they manage to collectively build up a hypothesis containing as few errors as possible. This is the way of science; this is how it is practiced.

So in this vein, on the Internet, as it turns out, a democratic forum was spontaneously held; a scientific mega-conference that sought an understanding of the risks of nuclear energy and radioactivity. And it was a good thing.

But many people were not hoping to receive arguments for arriving at a hypothesis with the least number of errors. What they were after, in fact, was just one single "truth."

In times of emergency, media literacy is useless

The result: chaos.★[155]

Conscientious scientists don't readily say "absolutely" or "never." On the other hand, self-styled experts, who aren't scientists, thoughtlessly use the words "absolutely" or "never." The kind of information that was flooding the Internet was in the guise of "single facts," such as "Tokyo is absolutely safe," and "Kanto is already contaminated, so escape in a westerly direction."

Further complicating the problem was the fact that we all had to play the guessing game called the "incomplete information game."

While the experts advanced their arguments with assumptions based on the available, publicly disclosed information, in reality there may still have been other information that was hidden from public scrutiny, thereby clouding our understanding of the big picture. Amid this environment of partial disclosure of information, even people who were usually calm lapsed into a state of paranoia and suspicion.[334] In retrospect, I see now that even correct information was censured with remarks like, "Stop spreading false rumors, reveal your sources!"

In times of emergency, "media literacy" proves mostly useless.

It can be extremely challenging to sort out the wide array of information available from the conflicting opinions found even among experts. But it's hard to tell who the

---

★155. While the dispute over the issue of "radiation" has calmed down over time since the earthquake, some groups have become radicalized, and information thought to be rumors and opinions that are clearly false, as far as you can tell from consulting official statistics and surveys, are still in circulation, mainly around the Internet. What's more, there are even social scientists taking part in spreading these "false rumors." In this context, a book that attempts to clarify the existing circumstances in Fukushima through proper reference to objective information is Hiroshi Kainuma's *Hajimete no Fukushimagaku* (A Fukushima Studies Primer; Eastpress, 2015).

334. In fact, our lives are an "incomplete information game" in which "death" is always prepared as a worst-case scenario. Our lives are made up of a vast number of daily risks.

trustworthy "experts" are in the first place.

Besides, you can't afford to take too much time when it comes to critical information that could possibly mean the difference between life and death, such as information on nuclear power, radioactivity, and earthquakes.

Soon after the earthquake, Chiki Ogiue (thirty years old, Hyogo), a commentator who has been contemplating the role of media literacy in modern society, started to compile and fact-check on his blog false rumors spreading throughout the Internet. But on the issue of nuclear power, which was on everybody's mind, he pretty much stayed silent.[335]

3. Disaster Dystopia

Did the world change after 3/11, the day the calamity struck?

People who are referred to as intellectuals frequently claim that the world has changed since 3/11, and say that Japan can never go back to being the nation it was before 3/11.

Just when I was thinking that there was a ring of déjà vu about these sentiments, I was reminded of the commotion made by intellectuals in the wake of the September 11 terrorist attacks in the United States; their reactions were also in a similar vein. Under tensions similar to those that arose in the wake of the disaster in Japan, everyone in the U.S. was heatedly saying that the world had changed after 9/11.

But is it possible for the world to change overnight, with a certain day serving as the borderline between the status quo and the change?

Of course, there is no denying that drastic changes occurred in the lives of the people who suffered actual losses from the three-pronged disaster. The earthquake, the tsunami, and the nuclear-plant accident had, in the blink of an eye, transformed the lives of hundreds of thousands of individuals who had jobs, families, and daily routines to attend to.

With even the capital of Japan, Tokyo, at risk of being affected by airborne radioactive material, and the fact that Tokyo was also one of the areas that could face a power shortage, the impact of the earthquake disaster and nuclear-plant accident on

---

335. Concerning nuclear power related information, he only examined uncontroversial items, such as "Don't drink any disinfectant containing iodine." While he proposes to increase the number of people with "resistance" to rumors and misinformation, and to build a structure that hampers the spread of misinformation (Chiki Ogiue, *Kenshō Higashi Nihon daishinsai no ryūgen, dema* [A Study into the rumors and misinformation of the Great East Japan Earthquake], Kobunsha, 2011), how is the layman supposed to verify information that falls somewhere between "truth" and "misinformation"—the kind that cannot be validated even through discussions between experts?

the economy is, at present, certainly unfathomable.

But Japan is spacious. The combined population of the three prefectures of Iwate, Miyagi, and Fukushima—the main affected areas—is approximately 5,710,000, while the population of the entire northeastern area of Japan—the Tohoku region—is approximately 9,300,000. This comprises approximately 7 percent of Japan's total population.[336/★156] In terms of economic scale, the combined gross production within the three prefectures of Iwate, Miyagi, and Fukushima amounts to approximately 21 trillion yen, which is around 4 percent of the nationwide ratio, and less than 7 percent of the ratio of the entire Tohoku region.[★157] Furthermore, the shipment value of manufactured goods and sales in the retail industry there doesn't even amount to 7 percent of the nationwide total.[337]

Obviously, no matter how broadly you define the disaster, it did not turn all of Japan into a "stricken area."

In the end, "life went on endlessly"

After the earthquake I was in western Japan, where I was stunned by the completely different prevailing mood. On March 14, when people were still mourning in the streets in Tokyo, in western Japan the reception of the incident was so tepid it was as if the earthquake had taken place in some distant land.[338]

When I spoke with a local person in a Hiroshima café, the topic of the earthquake did come up, but it never moved beyond the level of a terrible disaster that had affected some far-off place. What this local person—an elderly man—asked me was whether it was the building that shook, or the ground that shook at the time of the earthquake. What? Didn't they shake together?

What I found in western Japan was endlessly vast stretches of daily existence. While there are scholars like me who often talk of being able—or of not being able—

---

336.   In deference to the name of the earthquake, even if we add the population of the Kanto area (approximately 42 million), it still doesn't reach half of Japan's total population.

★156. According to the October 2014 population estimate, the combined population of Iwate, Miyagi, and Fukushima prefectures was approximately 5,550,000 people, whereas the population of the entire northeastern region was approximately 9,040,000.

★157. The gross production within Iwate, Miyagi, and Fukushima prefectures was 19,500 billion yen, accounting for 3.9 percent of the national ratio. (Cabinet Office, *Heisei 24-nendo kenmin keizaikeisan ni tsuite* [On the 2012 economic calculations of the citizens of prefectures].)

337.   Ministry of Economy, Trade and Industry, Bureau of the Economic and Industrial Affairs of Tohoku, *Tohoku chiikikeizai dēta bukku* (The Tohoku Regional Economy Data Book).

338.   Of course, it could have been that I only felt that way; in reality there might have been people who were anxious and distressed over the loss or injuries of those who were close to them. But I do recall noticing an ad running across the electric signboard in the Tokaido Shinkansen and feeling unimpressed; it was a usual Chubu Electric Power ad that read, "We'll keep pushing forward with nuclear power generation."

to tolerate the mundane everyday without an end in sight, I reaffirmed that for many people, such an issue never comes to mind in the first place;[339] that whatever happens, they just go about coping with their daily lives.

To just what extent have the lifestyles of people changed, anyway, under the influence of the earthquake disaster? Other than the more than one hundred thousand people considered victims and refugees, haven't most people, without waiting for even a month to lapse since the earthquake, returned to their same old lives in their same old places?

Did Japan change in 1995?

Whenever a disaster or some sensational event occurs, sociologists and pundits immediately begin to say things like, "Society has changed." For instance, a significant number of people consider the year 1995 to be a turning point for Japan.

Sixty-year-old sociologist Shintarō Nakanishi asserts, "For Japanese society, 1995 was obviously a historic turning point."[340] According to Nakanishi, two calamities in that year—the Great Hanshin-Awaji Earthquake and the Aum Shinrikyō scandal—established the impression that the end of "postwar Japanese society" was imminent. And, he added, after 1995, due to structural reforms, the age of "social polarization and impoverishment" began.

However, whether you take a look at the several graphs in chapter 2, or whether you look for relevant statistics on the Internet, you will be hard pressed to find any evidence of a sudden, dramatic change, at least in the consciousness of the Japanese, including the country's youth, with 1995 as the cutoff point.

As Eiji Oguma (forty-eight years old, Tokyo) says, people tend to overestimate the significance of incidents and events they themselves have experienced in real time.[341]

---

339. Now that I think about it, the expression "everyday life went on endlessly" itself has perhaps been too compromised by Modernism, which presupposes a linear temporal axis. The ones who attached great importance to the reality that "everyday life" has neither a beginning nor an end were the philosophers of the early twentieth century. (Harry Harootunian, author; Takeshi Kimoto, translator, *Rekishi no fuon* [original title: *History's Disquiet: Modernity, Cultural Practice, and the Question of Everyday Life*], Kobushi Shobo, 2011.)

340. Shintarō Nakanishi, ed., *1995-nen* (The Year 1995), Otsuki Shoten, 2008. Rather than being a concept originally thought up by Nakanishi, this idea of 1995 being a turning point is often stressed in comments made by slightly pop sociologists and thinkers.

341. Eiji Oguma, "Posuto sengo no shisō wa ika ni kanō ka?" (In what ways is postwar thought possible?) in *Watashi-tachi wa ima doko ni iru no ka* (Where are we right now?), Mainichi Shimbun, 2011. As a cutoff point, 1991 is far more significant, given that it saw the reversal of Japan's economic growth, the end of the Cold War, and the outbreak of the Gulf War. With regard to this issue, I would like to eventually clarify it in another work.[★158]

★158. For the people who lived through 1991, it would have been difficult to see that year, too, as "a turning point of the times." With regard to "turning point," refer to the postscript of this chapter. Incidentally, I have no plans for "another work" for the time being.

The Lost Generation in particular were in their teens or twenties when they experienced the year 1995, so it may have left a huge impression in their minds. But college students today are no longer aware of "1995."

Well, then, am I saying that 3/11 didn't change society? No, I am not.

The forum for free discourse, including academia, is a small world occupying only a tiny part of Japan. Even a book in print that achieves super-bestseller status amounts to just two million copies; usually sales of tens of thousands of copies would be considered a triumphant blockbuster hit for the parties concerned. With regard to academic or scholarly books, a circulation of just a thousand copies isn't uncommon either. In other words, if we translated these numbers into TV ratings, a huge bestseller would be just 2 percent, while an ordinary hit wouldn't even amount to 0.1 percent. So this is a story about a small world that can't even hold a candle to late-night TV.

And that's why, if the people who speak and write on the issue of 3/11 insist that society has changed after 3/11, and if the several thousand to tens of thousands of people who agree with their views thereby come to believe that 3/11 has changed society, then among these people, 3/11 will have changed society. This is no different from the case of those people who became familiar with certain commentaries and reviews that led them to commonly bond around the idea that Japanese society definitively changed after 1995.

In novels, *shōjo manga* (comics for girls), and J-pop lyrics that belong to a genre called *sekai-kei* (world type), a change in an individual's consciousness is often expressed as a "change in the world." If we were to focus on not the macro dynamics of society or general attitudinal trends, but on individual awareness instead, then there may very well be many people for whom the world changed when 3/11 happened. And such people will likely go on to have many more "world-changing" experiences over the course of their lifetimes.

Of course, in every possible way, the impact on Japan of the Great East Japan Earthquake is larger than that of the Great Hanshin-Awaji Earthquake. As for how society and people's awareness will change as a result, we can only wait and see, as we follow those changes to come with great interest.[342/★159]

---

342.   For example, the numerical values related to patriotism might see a rise over the short term. In addition, the number of people feeling anxious about the future may also go up. However, whether these increases will translate into long-term trends is unclear.

★159.   According to the Cabinet Office's the *Public Opinion Survey on Social Awareness*, patriotism (for all generations), which registered at 56.8 percent in January 2011, slightly dropped to 55.4 percent in January 2012.

The disappointed, conservative elderly

We have yet to understand the full repercussions of the 3/11 disaster—just how much has Japan changed as a result, and how will Japan change further as a result? However, just like 9/11, such an incident can shed light on the world for an instant.

It brings to light things many people hadn't seen, or had turned away from. In this sense, 3/11 certainly exposed before our very eyes, in stark view, the various problems weighing Japanese society down.

Problems such as the absence of a leader; the laxness of the nation's crisis management; the evils of an inflexible, ossified bureaucracy; the troubled relations between outlying localities and the center; and the problems of contract labor didn't suddenly appear on March 11—rather, they are like time bombs that have been burdening Japan for a long time.

Among the things that emerged in the wake of 3/11 is the disappointment of conservative senior citizens. Since they were always declaring the importance of patriotism and civic responsibility, you'd expect they would have been the first to rush to the stricken areas to offer tremendous support; in reality, however, nothing was further from the truth.

The Catholic writer Ayako Sono (seventy-nine years old, Tokyo) says that the earthquake "…aroused in me a pride and dignity in the Japanese race, because the presence of mind, the spirit of give and take, the moderation and patience exhibited were wonderful."

But young people were apparently an exception. According to Sono, no other generation was as bereft of the ability to respond to extraordinary situations.[343] "Young people," she said, "are terribly out of touch with their instincts. They become clueless amid circumstances that deviate from the norm."[344]

What makes Sono truly radical, though, is her support for forming squads of senior citizens who "wouldn't mind dying anytime soon" in order to carry out the deactivation of the Fukushima Daiichi Nuclear Power Station. "I wouldn't mind being exposed to radiation at all," she said, declaring her intent to take part in such work herself.[345/★160]

Nonetheless, she is fully prepared to survive disasters with her anti-disaster mea-

---

343.   Ayako Sono, "Shōsetsuka no migatte dai 40-shō: Gerira no jikan" (The self-indulgence of the novelist, chapter 40: Time of the guerilla), *WiLL*, May 2011.

344.   As far as I could see, the young people who had gotten stranded in Tokyo were able to calmly go about their affairs with their smartphones in hand.

345.   At the time of writing, no news has been heard of Sono organizing "senior-citizen squads" and marching into the nuclear power plant with them.

★160. As of 2015, there still hasn't been any such news.

sures in place. Sono says that after the earthquake struck, she began carrying around a helmet with her wherever she went, and that she was also prepared with a 400-liter supply of water. How befitting of the author of *Oi no saikaku* (The resourcefulness of old age) who upholds the "spirit of restraint" as a virtue, exhorting the elderly to be "ready to die by the roadside."[346]

Tokyo governor Shintarō Ishihara (seventy-eight years old, Hyogo) was his usual self. Immediately after the earthquake, after making his standard claim that the national consciousness had "been hijacked by self-interests such as the lust for money, worldly desires, and sexual desires," he said, "We need to take advantage of this tsunami to wash away our self-interests for once. I believe this calamity is, after all, divine retribution." In effect, he had made the *tenbatsu* (wrath of Heaven) remark.[347]

At the same time, he urged young people to head for the stricken areas, saying that he had always been concerned about their rush to egocentrism. That was why, he said, he was urging many of them to "see the predicament of the earthquake this time as an opportunity to awaken and sweat for the reconstruction of the affected areas."[348]

In truth, there are a lot of elderly conservatives making similar "wrath of Heaven" remarks. The politician Shingo Nishimura (sixty-two years old, Osaka), who once even advocated the nuclear armament of Japan, used the expression *Tenmō kaikaisonishite morasazu* (the mesh of heaven's net is wide, but nothing escapes)[349] in reference to the earthquake disaster, inferring that those who commit evil deeds will suffer the wrath of Heaven.

Incidentally, at the time of the earthquake Nishimura was in his residence in Osaka, but he mistook the shaking for a break-in by a thief and went around searching inside the house for the intruder, yelling out warnings. Osaka should have registered a seismic intensity of three at that time, but the way Nishimura panicked was no half-hearted response. Indeed, you'd expect no less from a man calling for the nuclear

---

346.   Ayako Sono, *Oi no saikaku* (The resourcefulness of old age), KK Bestsellers, 2010. Incidentally, in this book the author also touches on how one should act at the time an earthquake disaster strikes: victims shouldn't just sit around waiting for help to arrive, but should cook rice instead, using scrap wood from collapsed houses.

347.   "Tsunami, Nihonjin no gayoku arau tenbatsu: Ishihara tochiji ga hatsugen" (The tsunami is divine retribution washing away the greed of the Japanese people: Governor Ishihara remarks), *Nihon Keizai Shimbun*, March 15, 2011, morning edition.

348.   Shintarō Ishihara, "Shiren ni taete, warera nao chikara ari" (Enduring the ordeal, we have even more strength), *Bungeishunjū*, May 2011. While Ishihara uttered words like, "divine retribution," young people were already taking action. In the first place, if youths were really "self-centered and greedy," the people in the disaster-stricken areas would only get annoyed if they came, since such areas aren't educational institutions.

349.   Shingo Nishimura, "Kokumin kyūjo no kokkasōdōin-teki ketsudan o" (We must resolve to realize a national mobilization effort for rescuing citizens), *WiLL*, May 2011.

armament of Japan.

Shōichi Watanabe (eighty years old, Yamagata), noting that the prime minister at the time of the Great Hanshin-Awaji Earthquake was the socialist Tomiichi Muraya-ma, asserted that the earthquake disaster this time was the result of the "fury aimed at the left-wing administration." And that was why, he said, going forward we needed to pay respect to the national flag and the nation by electing a politician who would go and worship at Yasukuni shrine.[350] These remarks appeared, by the way, not in the occult magazine *Mu*, but in the conservative magazine *WILL*.

Well, same difference, I guess.

Nuclear villages and local communities

There are people who are eager to see the recovery of local communities in affected areas.[351]

However, breaking up local communities to create "citizens" loyal and obedient to the center was a wish near and dear to Japan as a modern nation-state. Emblematic of this are the localities known as "nuclear villages," which tolerate the presence of nucle-ar power plants in their midst.

The sociologist Hiroshi Kainuma (twenty-six years old, Fukushima) describes how local governments were voluntarily "obedient"—that is to say, willingly showed their allegiance—to the central government when they welcomed the presence of nuclear power plants in their communities.[352] The provinces, which couldn't escape poverty even after the war ended, had set up local industries, government, and mass media to attract nuclear power plants in order to superimpose themselves onto the story of the economic miracle, which was the story of the central areas of Japan.

The localities that took in these nuclear power stations were revitalized. Jobs were created, eliminating the need for people to work away from their province. With cafés and bars and lodgings and hotels coming up, these localities became galvanized. Through subsidies granted by power-source siting laws (*dengensampō*, or three laws for power development) and the collection of property taxes, the localities began to see the construction of top-notch public facilities such as libraries and welfare institutions.

---

350. Shōichi Watanabe, "Ten mo ikatta shijō saitei no saishō" (The all-time worst prime minister who even enraged heaven), *WiLL*, May 2011.
351. For example, a concept called Cash for Work, for the purpose of realizing recovery, is attracting attention. The idea is to create local employment and support the autonomous revival of local economies. However, there is criticism that Cash for Work may undo the activities assumed by local communities, such as running shelters and looking out for the elderly. The significance and problems of this concept are skillfully laid out in *at+* magazine (no. 8, 2011).
352. Hiroshi Kainuma, *"Fukushima" ron* (The "Fukushima" theory), Seidosha, 2011).

However, with the depreciation of fixed assets, the finances for the provinces, in effect, became worse over time. A newly constructed nuclear power plant had a high asset value, assuring a large income for the local government from fixed-asset taxation. However, due to depreciation, the value of the nuclear power plant fell every year. Consequently, tax revenues decreased, making it impossible to even pay for the maintenance of the public facilities that had already been built.

Before long, the infamous accidents at Three Mile Island and Chernobyl occurred, bringing forth a global outcry against the risks of nuclear power generation.

But there was no turning back for the nuclear villages. So what solution did they come up with to improve their declining financial situation? —Enticements to attract even more nuclear power plants.

To borrow Kainuma's words, this was a sign of the perfection not of a spontaneous loyalty system, but of an automatic subordination system.

And this system isn't one that would be shaken by a mere nuclear-power-plant accident, either. On April 10, when the anti-nuclear power demonstration was held, nationwide local elections were also held, yet what was given coverage in the local media were the elections of the Diet members of the "pro-nuclear power" faction in the municipalities that had accepted nuclear facilities.

In spite of the fact that all kinds of other media outlets were continuing to cover the nuclear power plant accident when elections were held, local public opinion failed to budge.

The automatic subordination system of the "home front"

There are also people who haven't changed since 3/11: the people of the nuclear village.

A worker in his thirties who had been working at the Fukushima Daiichi Nuclear Power Station on March 11 said, in an interview conducted by Kainuma after the accident, "I can finally come back in May to carry out repair work on the first floor [of the Fukushima Daiichi Nuclear Power Station]. The company's going to set me up in a house they run." As you can infer from such a comment, shutting down the nuclear power plant would threaten the livelihood—the basis of survival—of the people of the nuclear village.[161]

This mechanism that prompts spontaneous and automatic subordination is not unique to the nuclear village. The entire Tohoku region has consistently served as Japan's

---

★161. The work of decommissioning is proceeding at the Fukushima Daiichi Nuclear Power Station. The everyday life of a worker there is detailed in a comic book by Kazuto Tatsuta titled *Ichiefu* (*Ichi-F: A Worker's Graphic Memoir of the Fukushima Nuclear Power Plant*; Kodansha, 2015).

"home front" since prewar times as a source of supply for electricity, food, and labor.

The framework of the "home front," which has been enabling the support of Japan from the shadows, as it were, should have been overcome and done away with a long time ago. For example, in 1972, Kakuei Tanaka (fifty-four years old, Niigata) published *Nihonrettō kaizō-ron* (The theory of remodeling the Japanese archipelago), aiming to annul the disparities existing between the Pacific side of Japan and the districts along the Sea of Japan, and also to overcome the problems of overpopulation in the capital and under-population in the provinces.[353] In addition, the government had repeatedly devised plans for comprehensive infrastructure improvement, aiming for "well-balanced development."

The result: a network of highways was set up throughout the country; the Kyushu Shinkansen service opened a new route connecting Tohoku and Kyushu while quietly resuming operations on March 12, 2011, the day after the earthquake;[354] and approximately one hundred airports were built, scattered throughout the Japanese islands.[355]

However, there was no way the provinces would achieve a "well-balanced development" on the basis of infrastructure alone, no matter how sound and well-positioned it was.[356]

The function of the Tohoku area, a "home front" region, as a local community had gradually eroded. For this reason, a significant number of local areas had said, in response to hopes for the revival of local communities, "We have had no such thing as local communities, even before the earthquake disaster."

Like programmed robots, people clamor for a "revival," but what would constitute a "revival" in Tohoku in the first place? Restoring Tohoku to what it was prior to the earthquake—in other words, a rural settlement without any major industry, where depopulation was advancing—wouldn't ensure a bright future for the region. What

---

353. Kakuei Tanaka, *Nihonrettō kaizō-ron* (The theory of remodeling the Japanese archipelago), Nikkan Kogyo Shimbun, 1972.

354. To be precise, due to the impact of the earthquake disaster, the Tohoku Shinkansen was suspended, and on April 29, Shin-amori and Kagoshima Chuo were finally linked via shinkansen. If you were to travel across the Japanese archipelago by shinkansen only, your trip would last more than ten hours, requiring you to make connections with the Hayate, Nozomi, and Sakura train services.

355. There are airports that follow their own path, such as the Noto Airport, which has adopted a system in which the local government compensates the airport for any loss arising from failing to meet a predetermined passenger load factor guarantee. The airport also established a government building within the airport terminal; realized a collaboration with Kagaya, a well-established hot-spring hotel; and is offering aggressive enticements to attract international charter flights. However, many provincial airports are in the red. (Toshiyuki Uemura and Sayuri Hirai, *Kūkō no daimondai ga yoku wakaru* [Understanding the major problems faced in airports], Kobunsha, 2010.)

356. These days, the concept of the "compact city" has come into vogue; namely, this idea proposes to put a halt to flawed exurban developments and scale down urban areas. (Hiroshi Yahagi, *Toshi shukushō no jidai* [The age of scaled-down cities], KADOKAWA, 2009.)

will resurface, after the cleanup of the debris and rubble, will likely be a mere shadow of Tohoku's former identity as a "home front," but I can't see any future in that.★[162]

Rather, owing to the nuclear power issue, it may become necessary to proceed with the migration of entire settlements of displaced inhabitants and execute an "aggressive withdrawal" that would merge these separate settlements.[357] Even prior to 3/11, it had been anticipated that in Tohoku the challenges posed by critically declining birthrates and a rapidly aging population would only get worse going forward.

In this age of globalization, there are, in fact, no longer many reasons left for Tohoku to take on the role of "home front."[358]

Are the people who speak of "hope" thinking about "revival"?

There are people who find hope in the post-3/11 world. For example, they say this tragedy may turn into an opportunity for the Japanese to sustain Japan all by themselves.

Hiroki Azuma (thirty-nine years old, Tokyo) says that the Japanese are, to his surprise, beginning to take pride in being Japanese. They earnestly wish to support their own nation and government. Clearly, Azuma is trying to find hope in this phenomenon of wanting to support one's own nation and government. At the least, he says, a public-minded, patriotic character exists among the Japanese people, and the experience of discovering this character will never fade away.[359]

Even Hidetoshi Nakata (thirty-four years old, Yamanashi), while recognizing that Japan is currently standing at a turning point, asserts that the earthquake disaster this time has turned into "an opportunity to rethink human emotions and person-to-person connections, which were apt to be tenuous."[360]

Whenever I hear such talk, I'm reminded of the last scene in the animated film *Doraemon: Nobita to buriki no rabirinsu* (Doraemon: Nobita and the tin labyrinth).

★162. Subsequently, the "Masuda report" was released, creating a large buzz by threatening that by 2040, the population of women aged between twenty and thirty-nine will decrease by more than 50 percent, giving rise to the fear that as many as 896 cities and districts and municipalities across the entire nation could potentially become extinct. (Hiroya Masuda, *Chihō shōmetsu* [The extinction of provinces], Chuokoron-Shinsha, 2014.)

357.   Hiroshi Kitō, *2100-nen, jinkō san bun no ichi no Nihon* (The year 2100: Japan with only a third of its population), KADOKAWA, 2011.

358.   Eiji Oguma, "Tohoku to Tokyo no bundan kukkiri" (The clear gap between Tohoku and Tokyo), *Asahi Shimbun*, April 28, 2011, morning edition.

359.   See Hiroki Azuma, "For a Change, Proud to be Japanese" (*New York Times*, March 16, 2011). The original Japanese version of this piece can be found at http://d.hatena.ne.jp/hazuma/20110322

360.   Hidetoshi Nakata, "Donna seikatsu o suru no ka mukashi no Nihon ni wa hinto ga aru" (Japan of old has hints to help you determine what kind of life to lead), Special emergency *AERA* issue: The great east Japan earthquake: The testimonies of 100 people, April 10, 2011.

The planet of Chamocha is in ruins, its people having left the task of running their society entirely in the hands of robots. "We have lost everything. This is the end," despairs the king. In response, a nobleman delivers a speech, saying, "This is not the end. It's the beginning. Let's start anew. Let's build a society in which we no longer have to depend on machines anymore—in which humans can live like humans."

The movie doesn't show what happens to the planet of Chamocha after that. But as far as you can tell from the last scene, since Doraemon seemed to be willing to lend a helping hand, the planet of Chamocha probably went on to achieve a recovery, borrowing the scientific powers of the twenty-second century.[361]

Doraemon doesn't exist yet

What about Japan?

Will this earthquake disaster turn out to be not the end, but the beginning?

If we look at history, in the interval between the old order and the new, we can, it is said, see the emergence of the "disaster utopia."[362] This alludes to situations like the one in which many people rushed to volunteer soon after the earthquake disaster, and different people in various countries pulled for Japan. Rebecca Solnit, the author of *A Paradise Built in Hell: The Extraordinary Communities That Arise in Disaster* (translated into Japanese with the title *Sainan yutopia* [Disaster utopia]) claims that such actions will play a key role in the formation of a new society.

But what's really challenging is the process of building this society, this new order. Many sacrifices will be made during this process,[363] so I believe we shouldn't delude ourselves by using words like "hope" to sugarcoat what will turn out to be a long-term period of trials and tribulations. After all, a recovery isn't achieved in just a matter of one or two years; and just months after the earthquake disaster the number of volunteers saw a sharp decline. Furthermore, in twenty-first-century Japan, Doraemon still doesn't exist.

---

361. Using better science to solve problems arising from tragedies produced by overconfidence in science is a recurring thematic pattern often seen in *Doraemon*. The manga artist Fujiko F. Fujio believed in a benevolent future made possible through science. By the way, Doraemon has a small nuclear reactor installed in his body, but this must be an advanced version of a meltdown-proof next-generation reactor like the pebble-bed nuclear reactor. In his pocket, though, there's an "A-bomb" (which was revised to *chikyū hakai bakudan* [earth-buster bomb] when the stories were collected into a book).

362. Rebecca Solnit, author; Sonoko Takatsuki, translator, *Sainan yūtopia* (original title: *A Paradise Built in Hell: The Extraordinary Communities That Arise in Disaster*), Akishobo, 2010. There are some who spoke of the absence of panic in the wake of the earthquake disaster as a sign of the "virtue of Japanese people," but according to this book, in the case of most disasters, people simply don't panic. Rather, what commonly becomes a problem is the so-called "elite panic," which is the excessive self-defense exhibited by the elites of society who mistrust the populace.

363. For example, it is known that, after the French Revolution, the government carried out a massive purge.

For a time, this country may lose the part of the northeastern region that has Fukushima at its center, along with other things subjected to harmful rumors. In a country with such a small territory, that's a crying shame. If I were working for a foreign company in Japan, I would seriously consider disengaging from or reducing the size of my business here, riddled as it is with serious national risks.★163

The people who appeal for hope in the aftermath of 3/11 are, of course, proud Japanese citizens. Surely they're not under any delusions that their experiences in Tohoku or the disaster areas are grist for the mill of their self-actualization, nor are they lost in a form of self-congratulatory narcissism for having witnessed the "historic" event of an unprecedented mega-earthquake disaster. Nor are they confusing the recovery of the northeastern region with "national talk."364

And that's why the idea of "hope after 3/11" is less a critique or analysis than it is a declaration.

So if those advocating for "hope" are saying they're going to create hope in this country in a responsible manner, then we cannot help but watch them with a nodding acknowledgment, as detached observers.

Postscript: Did the Great East Japan Earthquake Change Japan?

Four years have passed since the Great East Japan Earthquake struck.

While the book *Zetsubō no kuni no kōfuku na wakamono-tachi* (The Happy Youth of a Desperate Country) was published on September 5, 2011, the manuscript itself had been ready by the end of June. Thus, this chapter was written between March and June. What occurred to me in retrospect as I was reading this section again was that I had been writing this prose at a time when I had yet to grasp the overall significance of the Great East Japan Earthquake, and, as such, my writing reflects how upset I was.

Of course, just like in the other chapters, I assume an air of cool objectivity here, but this one sentence clearly betrays how hyperbolic my grasp of the impact of the

---

★163. You can see that I have overestimated the impact of the Great East Japan Earthquake. The areas that still remain off-limits (zones which are difficult to return to) to this day constitute only about 2.4 percent of the whole of Fukushima. In addition, only about 2.5 percent of the people who were living in Fukushima prior to the occurrence of the earthquake disaster now live outside the prefecture (Hiroshi Kainuma, *Hajimete no Fukushimagaku* [A Fukushima studies Primer], Eastpress, 2015). This country hasn't lost "Fukushima."

364. Hideshi Ōtsuka, "'Sengo' bungakuron: Kōyō to sōshitsu" ("Postwar" literary theory: Exaltation and loss) in *at+* no. 8, 2011.

earthquake disaster was: "For a time, this country may lose the part of the northeastern region that has Fukushima at its center, along with other things subjected to harmful rumors."

This probably had a lot to do with the fact that the place where I live—Tokyo—was one of the areas that was directly affected by the Great East Japan Earthquake; even in the summer the city was dimly lit due to the power-saving campaign. Soon after that, however, the everyday seemed to have returned immediately to this country.

Hiroki Azuma proposed turning the Fukushima Daiichi Nuclear Power Station into a tourist destination, and even put in a lot of effort toward creating a "mook" (a magazine-book) to that end, but sales were poor.[★164] Society's interest, including the gaze of the so-called culturati, gradually shifted toward the Tokyo Olympics.

Certainly, the notion that a particular event could change society completely, even though it may appear to do just that, is nothing more than a kind of fantasy. Each and every person in this country has their share of "daily life" to cope with, after all.

But at the same time, to search for the turning point of an era is also an attractive endeavor. With 2015 also happening to fall on the seventieth anniversary of the end of the Second World War, the year saw experts being consulted about when the postwar turning point had occurred in Japan, as if they were contestants vying against each other to give the wittiest answer in a quiz game show.

In my case, in the course of my conversation with the dramatist Masakazu Yamazaki (eighty-one years old, Kyoto), I answered 1990.[★165] This was the year in which the average number of births per woman was announced to be 1.57, setting Japan abuzz with talk of the declining birthrate. This average was less than that registered in 1966, the year of *hinoeuma* (fire horse), making it the worst rate on record to date for the postwar era.

It was also a time when the population dividend was approaching its end. If, at that time, Japan had begun working seriously on measures to buck the declining birthrate, the low birthrate and aging problem of this nation might now be a slightly more manageable issue. At any rate, it was with such implications that I chose "1990" as my answer, but of course, there are more ways than one to answer the turning-point question.

Let's reflect on the year 1995, for instance, which is a year this chapter has also covered. That year is often considered to be a turning point in the history of postwar Japanese society.

★164. Hiroki Azuma, ed., *Fukushima daiichi genpatsu kankōchika keikaku* (The Fukushima Daiichi Nuclear Power Station tourist destination project), Genron, 2013.

★165. "Sengo 70-nen Nihon no tenkaiten wa" (The Turning Point for Japan seventy years after the war), *Asahi Shimbun*, August 9, 2015, morning edition.

While 1995 saw the Great Hanshin-Awaji Earthquake on January 17 and the sarin subway attacks in Tokyo on March 20, it was also the year when the *amurer*—diehard fans of singer Namie Amuro—strutted along the streets of Shibuya; and when plenty of hit products, like *purikura* (photo stickers), emerged from the trends of high school girls; and when the game Virtua Fighter became popular.

In particular, just prior to the sarin incident, the song "WOW WAR TONIGHT" by H Jungle With t sold more than two million copies, making it cool to sing "*Tama-ni wa kata o narabete nomōyo*" (Let's drink shoulder-to-shoulder sometimes) at karaoke bars.

So for some people, the greatest turning point in their lives turned out to be the year 1995, while for others it turned out to be 2011, but there is no need for any of them to impose their views by forcibly entangling the whole of Japan in their discussion.

But while I was adding footnotes, I came across something surprising. I was searching online to find updates on the figures and student groups appearing in this chapter—to see what had become of them since I met them last—and I found out that a lot of them were still carrying out activities for the cause of "society." There were some who had moved to Tohoku, and the central figure of the Yashima Sakusen continued to hold a strong interest in disaster prevention.

Though they weren't taking part in activities that were directly related to the Great East Japan Earthquake, for those who had attempted to get involved with relief efforts at the time of the disaster, the impact may have been greater than initially imagined. And when, for the magazine *Sotokoto*, I interviewed young people working at a social company, I found out that it was the earthquake disaster that had motivated many of them, too, to become interested in philanthropy or contributing to society.★[166]

The Great East Japan Earthquake Disaster did not give rise to the kind of great big hope that could transform Japan. But still, it has certainly left behind small sprouts of hope in this country.★[167]

★166. I was running a column titled "Shakai-kei wakamono hakusho" (White paper on society-oriented youths), which first appeared in the April 2012 issue and ended in the May 2014 issue of *Sotokoto*, a magazine that was clearly attempting to change society. I interviewed a total of thirty-five young individuals, some of whom were working at MOTHERHOUSE, some at Teach for Japan, and the rest at Katariba. You may be surprised, but I do carry out such monotonous work, too.

★167. I'm concerned about whether I should have concluded in such a nice, pat textbook fashion, but what to do? I've become adult enough to stop finding faults with people who strive.

Chapter 6
The Happy Youth of a Desperate Country

Japan is weighed down by a pileup of issues, such as the financial deficit and the problem of the declining birth rate and a rapidly aging population. As if this set of circumstances weren't hopeless enough, the country was beset by an unprecedented earthquake. Young people nonetheless appear to be surprisingly upbeat. But why? Why are they able to remain happy in the face of a situation which is, by all objective measures, hopeless? In this final chapter, let's look back on the existing circumstances young people find themselves in today before we go on to contemplate the future.

1. To Live in a Desperate Country

A 100 million-yen intergenerational disparity

It's easy to paint the future of Japan as hopeless or desperate.[365] The country is teeming with endless fodder for anxiety: Japan's budget deficit, which is indicated in multiple references to be the worst among major countries; the swelling of the social-security budget due to low birthrates and aging; the evils caused by inflexible organizations and labor markets.

These issues, when seen from the perspective of young people, could be labeled "inter-generational disparities."

When thinking about the future of social security, the most important determin-

---

365. To borrow the pessimistic words of Yuki Honda (forty-six years old, Tokushima), in present-day Japan, "society's frictions—the disparities and poverty, the divisions and isolation, the nihilism and despair—are starting to stand out." (*Wakamono no kibun: Gakkō no "kūki"* [The mood of young people: The school "atmosphere"], Iwanami Shoten, 2011.)

ing factor is population composition. Japan's social-security system (pensions, medical care, nursing care) basically adopts a pay-as-you-go financing plan, whereby the generation of active, working adults supports the elderly of the time by paying insurance premiums and taxes. And that's why, if you look at the ratio of the working age bracket—the productive population between the ages of fifteen and sixty-four—to the elderly group (those aged sixty-five and above), you can see how risky Japan's future is.[366]

With its population declining at the fastest pace in the world, Japan has entered an era of depopulation of people in the productive age range, which peaked at 87 million in 1995. Forecasts warn that by 2030 this figure will decrease to 67 million, and by 2050, to 49 million.

If Japan's total population were to decline in exactly this fashion, there wouldn't be any problem. Tokyo's trains are overcrowded anyway, and there are too many houses in the first place.

The problem is that while the active, working generation, whose members pay insurance premiums and taxes, continues to decline in number, the population of elderly people isn't decreasing at the same pace.

In fact, the ratio of the elderly, dependent population to the economically active working population has risen considerably; in 1980 one elderly person was being supported by 7.5 members of the working generation, but by 2000, this had changed to four workers per elderly person, and by 2008, it became three workers per elderly person.

Furthermore, in approximately ten years from now, in the year 2023, one elderly person will be supported by just two members of the active, working generation.[★168] Unless there's a sudden miraculous rise in the birth rate, or the elderly mysteriously disappear on a massive scale, the proportion of elderly people to active, working adults will continue to rise until 2072.[367] So what will be the consequences of that? Existing elderly persons will receive welfare benefits worth several times more than what they paid when they were young; as for young people, the younger they are, the more

---

366. You will find a skillful organization of the topics of social security and the generation gap in Wataru Suzuki's *Shakai hoshō no "futsugō na shinjitsu"* (Social security's "inconvenient truth"; Nikkei Publishing, 2010). I took into account the figures presented in Suzuki's book for the population forecasts appearing throughout the current volume.

★168. According to the latest provisional estimates, 2020 will be a time when every two people will be supporting one elderly person. (Cabinet Office, *Heisei 27-nen ban kōreishakai hakusho* [2015 white paper on aging society]).

367. As long as there is no sudden rise in the number of children, for the time being, we'll have to proceed with a social design that presupposes a dwindling birthrate and an aging population. It will become necessary to review our compulsory retirement plans and spousal deductions and transform society into one in which everybody works, including the elderly and women. (Kaku Sechiyama, *Owarai jendā-ron* [Comedy gender theory], Keiso Shobo, 2001).

losses they will suffer.

Just how much of a loss will young people suffer? If it were just a minor loss, it would be okay, wouldn't it? Grandfathers and grandmothers give out allowances, after all.

According to a certain provisional estimate, the correlation between costs and benefits received through the public sector, including pensions and medical care, will be such that the generation currently composed of the elderly age sixty and above stands to pocket a profit of 65 million yen, while the generation of those under twenty will be burdened with a liability in excess of approximately 52 million yen.

In effect, the above figures say that the generation of grandchildren is suffering a loss of 100 million yen more than the generation of grandparents.[368] However you look at it, this is more than allowances will cover.

Young people unable to become "regular employees"

Apparently, social security isn't the only thing young people are losing out on.

What Shigeyuki Jō (thirty-seven years old, Yamaguchi) views as a problem in particular is the Japanese employment system;[369] namely, its lifetime employment feature, which makes it extremely difficult to lay off anyone once they are hired as a regular full-time employee. Under this system, while you're young, you're made to work more than your remuneration warrants, but since it's seniority based, you can expect future payback.

This setup, referred to as the "Japanese business model," functioned effectively in the period of high economic growth, when companies continued to show growth and business performance improved year after year. However, after the bubble economy went bust, a reexamination of this model was urged. After all, management preferred to fire employees if business results became risky, and they no longer had enough flexibility to guarantee cushy positions with high pay for individuals who didn't seem to be doing anything other than just showing up to the office and hanging around.

But companies couldn't fire regular full-time employees once they had been hired.[370] Consequently, they attempted to reduce the number of college-graduate hires, and began using contract labor and temporary workers to make up for the shortage in their workforce. This, in effect, was Japan after the 1990s. Even in big compa-

---

368.   A provisional estimate from the Cabinet Office's *Annual Report on the Japanese Economy and Public Finance* released in 2005. For details, refer to Manabu Shimasawa and Tsutomu Yamashita's *Mago wa sofu yori ichi-oku en son o suru* (The grandchild will be 100 million yen worse off than his grandfather; Asahi Shimbun Publications, 2009). This book brims with righteousness.

369.   Shigeyuki Jō, "Rōdō biggu ban ga wakamono o sukū" (A labor "big bang" will save young people) in *Sedaikan kakusatte nanda* (Generational difference—what's that?) by Shigeyuki Jō et al., PHP Institute, 2010.

nies, it became far more difficult for young employees to be promoted than in the past.[371]

In other words, due to generational disparities, young people were getting the short end of the stick even where work was concerned. For this reason, Jō made the case for what he calls a labor "big bang" to bring about employment fluidity. With this, he proposes not to protect the vested interests of regular full-time employees, but to get rid of the distinction between "regular employment" and "irregular employment."

In coming up with this proposal, he likely took the European system into account. In places like Denmark, laying workers off is easy; however, arrangements for vocational training and unemployment insurance are firmly in place and maintained, providing labor market flexibility and social security in tandem.[372]

In Europe in general, youth measures as public policy are substantial; a reallocation of resources is put into effect to create a safety net that includes features such as unemployment and employment measures for young people.

In Japan, too, the standard of annuity insurance and medical insurance reaches levels comparable to that in Europe. However, with the aging of society, the ratio of pension and medical expenses to national income is seeing a sudden increase. And yet when it comes to safeguards for the active, working generation—such as unemployment policies and housing measures—the level continues to remain at a 1970s standard.[373]

So, as it turns out, the elderly enjoy European-standard guarantees, while the active, working generation is stuck with disappointing, subpar measures.

Back when there was a "youth culture"

The elderly profit more from social security than young people do. Essentially, by leaning on their vested interests, the elderly are quitting while they're ahead.

So if you see the situation in this way—that is, if you separate social security and the employment system along a generational axis– you'll begin to see just how com-

---

370. Even from a global perspective, Japan is known as a country with tough regulations that make firing regular employees difficult. This is also evident in manuals for executives on how to discharge workers, which include "How to Dismiss Office Staff Correctly" and "How to Decrease an Employee's Salary" (Nippon Jitsugyo Publishing, 2009).

371. Masahiro Watanabe, "Kigyō nai no sedaikan kakusa wa 'mondai' de wa nai" (The generational disparities within a company are not a "problem"), *Voice*, April 2011.

372. Such a system is called "flexicurity," a portmanteau of "flexible" and "security." It's a tongue-twister. To dig deeper, refer to Tarō Miyamoto's *Seikatsu hoshō* (Life security; Iwanami Shoten, 2009).

373. Norihiro Nihei, "Sedai-ron o aminaosu tameni: Shakai, shōnin, jiyū" (Reworking generationalism: Society/approval/freedom) in *Wakamono to hinkon* (Young people and poverty) edited by Makoto Yuasa et al., Akashi Shoten, 2009.

fortable an experience the elderly have been enjoying, and how coldly young people are being treated.

Certainly there's a lot to agree with in the claims and proposed solutions of those who make the inter-generational disparity argument. But how valid is this argument? Is it really correct to zero in on the point of intergenerational disparity? To me, the "youth vs. the elderly" dichotomy doesn't seem to have widespread currency, either in writing or in movements.

This is because, first of all, as I discuss in chapter 1, the category of "young people" has become so diffuse that it cannot, I believe, become a defining basis of any political movement. Just as Satoshi Kotani (fifty-five years old, Tottori) pointed out, the world-famous youth "rebellion" of the late 1960s was only possible because of the existence of the huge group of young people known as the baby-boom generation.[374]

The youth of that time, being members of the "postwar generation" who had never experienced war, were able to easily discover differences between adults and themselves. The commonly accepted theory is that they were not interested in the culture being arbitrarily forced upon them by the preceding generation, and so went on to form a distinctive "youth culture" of their own, anchored in the spirit of rebellion;[375] their solidarity as a generation was apparently so powerful that they referred to themselves as "We young people."

An age when even Chizuko Ueno tweets

While it is not clear exactly how many youths identified so strongly with their generation that they would refer to themselves as "We young people,"[376] it is a fact that today's youth are finding it difficult to be conscious of themselves as "young people." Thanks to longer periods spent in education and the emergence of employment fluidity, the period of young adulthood continues to extend itself. If you visit a graduate school, you can meet many "students" around the age of thirty.

As for the worlds of fashion, hobby, and tastes; here, too, there no longer exists any culture you can describe as being peculiar to young people. For example, the main

---

374. Satoshi Kotani, "*Wakamono wa futatabi seijika suru ka*" (Will young people become political again?) in *Wakamono no genzai: Seiji* (Young people at present: Politics) edited by Satoshi Kotani et al., Nihon Tosho Center, 2011.

375. Mamoru Yamada, "*Futsū" to iu kibō* (A hope called "normal"), Seikyusha, 2009. However, it's not that the entire nation of Japan was homogenously tainted with the "youth culture." Although agriculturalists were rapidly decreasing in number during the period of high economic growth, a significant number of young people were continuing to live in the provinces and rural districts. So, to give you a rough idea, it would be rather more appropriate to say that the new culture which had attracted attention in the central parts of the country, such as "Tokyo," was delivered to the provinces via the mass media such as TV, which was rapidly spreading at that time.

target demographic for the Lowry's Farm fashion brand[377] is supposedly women in their twenties and thirties, but you often spot women in their fifties dressed in this brand's attire, too.

Even comics, before anyone knew it, and anime and games, too, had become the crowning glories of "Japanese culture" that make all generations proud, and not just the youth. The baby boomers, who were in elementary school when the first issues of *Shōnen Magazine* and *Shōnen Sunday* came out in 1959, are now over sixty. These days, probably the only parent forbidding their children to read manga is *Doraemon* character Nobita Nobi's mom (thirty-eight years old).[378]

In reality, it's more enjoyable to talk with someone who is not of the same age, but shares the same interests with you, than to talk with someone who is of the same age but doesn't share any of your interests. The development of the Internet has greatly expanded our opportunities to meet new people. This is the age when even sociologist Chizuko Ueno (sixty-three years old, Toyama), has exchanges with her former students via Twitter.

A look at the data also reveals that differences in attitude and perception between generations are disappearing. Sociologist Munesuke Mita (seventy years old, Tokyo), drawing on the *Nihonjin no ishiki chōsa* (Survey of Japanese attitudes), confirms that differences in attitude and perception between generations get smaller the younger the generation.[379] According to Mita, such differences have been dwindling in particular since the emergence of the *shinjinrui* (new species) generation, the demographic born between 1954 and 1968.

In an age when you can't draw distinctions between attitudes and mindsets along generational lines, you can't expect a young person to identify him or herself with an entire "youth generation"—or to be conscious of being part of such a generation—just

---

376. For example, the number of young people who joined student movements accounted for around 5 percent of the population of their generation. While Tadashi Yanai, the founder of UNIQLO, entered Waseda when student movements were in full swing, he said those four years of his student life were days of "wandering around, watching movies and playing pachinko and mahjong." (*Isshō kyūhai* [One win, nine losses], Shinchosha, 2006). In addition, an examination of an attitude survey targeting youths between fifteen and twenty-four years of age at the time also reveals that only 2 percent of respondents indicated that they would "support the claims and approaches" of student movements. (Cabinet Office, *Seishōnen no ishiki* 1970 [1970 Survey on the Attitudes of Youth]). Well, the generation was populous enough to begin with, so even a small percentage would have had a considerable impact, I believe. As many as 10,390,000 people were born between 1947 and 1950. (Ministry of Health, Labour and Welfare, *Vital Statistics*).

377. A female-oriented brand run by POINT INC. Apparently the brand is for "women who have a normal sensibility toward life."

378. As far as I could tell from reading the original works, Nobita's parents were born during wartime.

379. Munesuke Mita, "Kindai no mujun no 'kaitō': Datsu kōdoseichōki no seishin hen'yō" (The "thawing" of the contradictions of modern times: A shift in the ethos of the post-high economic growth period), *Shisō* no. 1002, 2007.

because he or she happens to be young.

To put it differently, people all over Japan are rapidly becoming young people. We are, in effect, living in the "age of 100 million youths."

Would you like to be a baby boomer?

If we were to define a category called "youth" based on some kind of criteria, would those "youth" themselves still perceive the disparities between generations to be a problem? I doubt it.

For example, no matter how much you emphasize the point that young people are losing out on social welfare funds, this is, strictly speaking, a financial matter. The question of just how much "loss" is being suffered is slightly more subjective. That's because the infrastructure and technology we are currently using were built by the preceding generation.

In the immediate aftermath of the war, many places in Japan were literally burned to ashes; it can be said that the preceding generation dedicated their lives to the reconstruction of those areas.[380] Whether it was because of that generation, or whether it was because of the times, or whether we just got lucky, modern Japan is in the midst of a historically unprecedented state of affluence.

And that's why I wouldn't want to be a baby boomer, no matter how many times I was told that I stand to make a profit of 100 million yen. Back in the old days, injections were more painful, the level of pollution was terrible, you couldn't easily buy chocolate from overseas, and there were no cell phones. Economic growth may be promised moving forward, but I'd much rather prefer the affluence of the present.

As for Jō's proposal regarding employment fluidity, while I feel it's reasonable, I doubt whether there truly exist "inter-generational disparities" with respect to work. For example, even before the bubble economy burst, only a small handful of people were able to become regular full-time employees at well-established major firms that offered employee benefits and welfare schemes. Furthermore, as Tsuguo Ebihara (for-

---

380. The economic growth of Japan after the war is also called the "East Asia Miracle." However, rather than being the result of their "perseverance," this was made possible through a series of fortunate coincidences—a run of luck—including the fact that Japan had the opportunity to imitate other countries due to becoming an economic backwater in the wake of the defeat it suffered, and the fact that the victorious nation, the United States, prioritized Japan's economic development as a part of its Japan strategy. In addition, by the time the people who were born after 1945—including the baby-boom generation—were old enough to understand things, the clearing of the wartime debris was mostly finished, and in 1969 Japan had become the second-greatest economic power on a GDP basis. In this sense, the ones who were at the core of the economic revitalization were not the baby-boom generation, who were ridiculed as the *senmuha* (the war-ignorant pack) but the generation before them. (Taijirō Hayasaka, *Gendai no wakamono-tachi* [The youth of modern times], Nikkei Publishing, 1971.)

ty-six years old, Tokyo) has repeatedly pointed out, the reason the youth-job shortage seen since the 1990s has come to attract so much attention is because the percentage of students pursuing higher education suddenly soared.[381]

Ebihara also says that young people need to think about whether they need to force themselves to join major companies built by the preceding generation. The more historical a large firm is, the older the people in the firm will be, making it obviously difficult, in a sense, for young people to enter.

Even Toyota (established in 1937) and Sony (established in 1946) were once young companies. If anything, Ebihara suggests that young people should join young companies with promising futures, like Rakuten (established in 1997) and Cyber Agent (established in 1998), and stop being biased toward large firms and long-established brands.

Which brings me to this question: Is it really a problem of inter-generational disparities or differences to be unable to enter into the machinery of a large company, or the "Japanese business-management model," a creation of the preceding generation?

The elderly generation supporting young people? You're kidding

How happy do you think the people who once supported the "Japanese business-management model" were? Personally, I doubt that they were that happy. In their time, lifelong stability was promised if you made it into a big company. Yet to the people of that time, doing so was, to a certain extent, suffocating. The married couple of the time consisted of a full-time, regular employee and a full-time homemaker—occupations that people yearn for these days. But in reality, the regular employee was actually a "wage slave" chained to the company, and the homemaker was actually a "housekeeper" chained to the modern family; it was the worst pairing imaginable.

The labor circumstances were sometimes even worse than those found today, given that prior to the 1970s there were very few companies that had adopted the five-day work week (as opposed to six); regulatory compliance was nonexistent.[382] The "Japanese business-management model" was, in effect, founded on the sacrifices of many workaholics and a lot of *karōshi* (death from overwork).

Thus, after the bubble economy burst, young people were able to lead relatively freer lives, whether they wanted to or not.[383] So the story isn't as simple as the past

---

381.   Tsuguo Ebihara, *"Wakamono wa kawaisō" ron no uso* (The lie of the "pitiful young people" theory), Fusosha, 2010.

382.   It was 1962 when Hitoshi Ueki first sang that the job of a salaryman was "carefree." Eight years later, *Shokuba sabaku* (Workplace desert), a series of stories running in the *Yomiuri Shimbun* about the tragic life of the office worker—the salaryman—became popular.

being a happy time and the present being an unhappy one.

I feel that those who are enraged by generational differences and are calling for the gaps to be addressed tend to be "old guys" of around forty.

For example, magazines like *Voice*, which target conservative old folk, come out with one special feature after another about "generational differences," but the commentators are mostly in their forties or above. Kōsuke Motani, who pushed for income transfers from the elderly to young people in his book *Defure no shōtai* (The truth about deflation), was forty-six years old at the time of his book's release.[384/★169]

The co-authors of the fittingly titled *Sedaikan kakusatte nanda* (Generational difference—what's that?) are rather young, but the three of them—Shigeyuki Jō (thirty-seven years old, Yamaguchi), Kazumasa Oguro (thirty-six years old, Tokyo), and Ryōhei Takahashi (thirty-four years old, Chiba)—can, in terms of age, be considered "old guys."

"Wait, what? Old guys are thinking about young people? You mean they actually care?" you might say to yourself, moved to tears for an instant. But the more these old guys fan the flames of "generational differences," the further they will probably get from resolving the issue. This is because in Japan, where parliamentary democracy has been adopted, as long as a social issue is treated as a generational problem, the young group has no chance of winning.

Within Japan, 45 percent of the population is under forty, but since those under twenty have no right to vote, the combined total percentage of voters in their twenties and thirties is just 33 percent. The percentage of voters in their twenties alone is only 14 percent.[385/★170] In addition, there's the problem of the gap in the value of individual votes—that is, the fact that the value per vote is low in urban areas, where the population of young people is relatively large.

Furthermore, no group has lower voter turnout than the young (see chapter 2). If young people, whose population is negligible to begin with, don't even show up at the polls to vote, is it any wonder that they end up getting politically neglected?[★171]

---

383.   In the end, this ended up giving birth to "hope refugees" who lead lives of an endless search for the self, believing, "There must be a more shining version of myself than myself now."

384.   Kōsuke Motani, *Defure no shōtai* (The truth about deflation), *KADOKAWA*, 2010.

★169.   In the meantime, Kōsuke Motani has gone on to once again score a smash hit with the release of *Satoyama shihonshugi* (Satoyama capitalism; *KADOKAWA*, 2013).

385.   http://d.hatena.ne.jp/longlow/20090725/p1

★170.   In 2015, the Revised Public Officers' Election Act was passed, effectively lowering the franchise age from twenty and above to eighteen and above. However, simply lowering the voting age by two years won't lead to a sudden increase in the number of "youth" voters.

★171.   However, the second-generation baby boomers must also be taken into account, so at the juncture of 2015, the population of people in their thirties and forties put together (34,230,000) was more than that of people in their sixties and seventies (32,330,000). Though "young people" can't win against the "elderly" when it comes to numbers, the "middle-aged" can.

This is how young people stay away from politics

There must be all sorts of reasons young people don't go to the polls. For example, college student Yūsuke (twenty-one years old, male) says he would feel guilty for voting. He thinks that the world of elections is not his world; it's not where he belongs; in his view, elections are arbitrarily carried out by "great, distinguished" people.

Statistically speaking, relative to other nations, Japan's sense of political powerlessness is strong. The percentage of high school students who believe that they're incapable of influencing the decisions of the government by themselves is as large as 80 percent.[386] This is twice the corresponding value found in the United States.

While many young people are interested in "changing society" (see chapters 2 and 5), this interest doesn't readily lead to voting behavior or political participation. Perhaps young people are too society-oriented, or too "other-people" oriented, so much so that they lose interest in dealing with politics related to their "own" problems. After all, even though they can build schools in Cambodia and become passionate about giving aid to Africa, they don't think about taking any kind of action for the municipality they belong to.[387]

What good boys and girls they are!

In addition, a public opinion poll confirms that 58.3 percent of twenty-somethings seek social security services such as medical care and pensions from the government. In addition, 45.7 percent of twenty-somethings (a ratio that is, alas, lower than the average for all ages) seek the adoption of "measures to counter the problems arising from the silvering of society."[388]/[★172]

Thus, if you consider the political impact of young people, the possibility that they will rectify generational differences or disparities within the framework of a parliamentary democracy is extremely low.

---

386.   With regard to the question of why young people don't take issue, the answer can mostly be found in employment-related discussions. Nevertheless, refer to Yuki Honda's "Wakamono ni totte hataraku koto wa ikanaru imi o motte iru no ka" (What significance does work hold for young people?) in *Wakamono no genzai: Rōdō* (Young people at present: Labor) edited by Satoshi Kotani et al., Nihon Tosho Center, 2010.

387.   The reason many volunteers gathered at the time of the Great East Japan Earthquake may have been because it wasn't about "themselves," but about "others." In this sense also, it may be a phenomenon that's the polar opposite of the surge in nationalism.

388.   Cabinet Office, the *Public Opinion Survey on the Life of the People*, 2010. Among people nationwide, 69.9 percent sought improvements in social security, while 56.5 percent sought the adoption of measures to respond to the challenges of the aging society.

★172.   In the 2015 survey also, 56.1 percent of twenty-somethings sought improvements in components of social security, such as medical care and pensions, while 43.5 percent sought the adoption of measures for dealing with issues of the aging of society. On the other hand, those seeking the adoption of measures for dealing with the issue of the "declining birthrate" amounted to 42.4 percent. Perhaps they find it difficult to see the problem of the declining birthrate as having any bearing on themselves.

Is it really a "generational" problem?

In fact, however, it is not just young people who are the victims of so-called generational disparities. For example, with regard to employment, maintaining a system that's unattractive to young people will actually affect Japan as a nation more than it will those young people.

In a *New York Times* story on the subject of "generational barriers," there is an account of a promising automobile engineer who has left Japan to work in Taiwan.[389] He says that, despite having been praised highly for his work when he was working for a Japanese carmaker, he was only able to work as a contract employee there, at just half the salary of a regular employee. While the outflow of talented professionals like this engineer may not take place all at once, it will happen bit by bit, chipping away at the growth potential of Japanese companies.

In addition, the current social security system is taxing not just young people, but to the entire nation, when it ignores employment measures and restricts public expenditures for families and children for the sake of reinforcing the social security scheme for the elderly.

When the working population dwindles because of the declining birthrate, the economy falls into a labor shortage and tax revenues decrease. If many young people continued to be low-paid workers, tax revenues would still go down. In reality, many young people have already left the pension plan on their own account; approximately half of the population under thirty-five is not paying national pension premiums.

Then there's the problem of public security. While Japanese youths are said to be "tame and averse to causing riots," if the underclass of the poor—those people who can't even plan their meals—increases in size, deterioration of the public peace and order appears very likely.[390]

The improvement of employment measures and social security is necessary not because we feel sorry for "young people." It's simply necessary for the Japanese nation. And that's why I believe that if you're a nationalist, you should actually be out there demanding measures that promote employment, deal with the problem of the declining birth rate, and improve social security.[391]

---

389. "In Japan, Young Face Generational Roadblocks," *New York Times*, January 28, 2011.
390. In Europe, a rise in the unemployment rate has led to the deterioration of the public peace and the prevalence of drugs. For details, see publications such as *Youth Unemployment and Society* (Anne C. Petersen and Jeylan T. Mortimer, eds., Cambridge University Press, 1994).
391. Incidentally, I'm not a nationalist, as I intend to promptly flee abroad the moment some major problem occurs in Japan, but I am a nationalist in that I would write endlessly about Japan's problems, as I have demonstrated in this book.

The truth about the elderly

Even the elderly—the designated enemy in the context of the "generational barrier" problem—don't all have money. As it is well known, wealth inequalities among the elderly are greater than in any other generation. Furthermore, elderly people account for a higher percentage of poor households, welfare beneficiaries, and suicides.

The number of households on welfare has surpassed 1.4 million, of which elderly households account for approximately 40 percent.[392/★173] In addition, adults in their fifties accounted for 18.8 percent of the 31,690 suicides that took place in 2010. They were followed by those in their sixties, which accounted for 18.6 percent.[393/★174] The rate of suicides committed by those in their sixties and above amounted to as much as 37.8 percent, while those committed by people in their twenties and under was just 11.9 percent of the overall total.

I'm beginning to feel that I should be working on a theory about the elderly instead of a theory about youth. Nonetheless, it seems clear that the young are not the only ones finding themselves in a quandary. It is the elderly, not the young, who are facing the urgent problems of poverty and suicide.

When you filter society through the lens of the variable called "generation"—that is to say, if you look at society only in generational terms—I think it's clear that you end up overlooking a multitude of things.[394]

Back in the 1970s, when Japan was just entering the age of the corporate society—in other words, when there was no pay gap, and when "young people" constituted a group of significant size—it may have been meaningful to label them as "young people" or "youth." However, at present, in their old age, they prove to be so diverse that they defy easy one-size-fits-all categorization as "elderly." Their walks of life are varied, as are their fortunes.

But of course, we can still denounce the "elderly" generation. We can say that, in a

---

392.   Ministry of Health, Labour and Welfare, *Report on Social Welfare Administration and Services* (Approximate Figures for December 2010).
★173. In February 2015, the number of households receiving social relief exceeded 1,600,000, with elderly households accounting for 45.5 percent. The terms *karyū rōjin* (the low-class elderly) and *hyōryū rōjin* (the drifting, homeless elderly) have become buzzwords.
393.   *Keisatsuchō seikatsu anzenkyoku seikatsu anzen kikaku-ka* (National Police Agency: Bureau of community safety of the community safety planning division), *Heisei 22-nen chū ni okeru jisatsu no gaiyō shiryō* (Overview data on suicides in 2010).
★174. The number of suicides in 2014 had fallen to 25,427. People in their sixties accounted for the highest percentage of suicides, at 17 percent, while twenty-somethings accounted for 10.6 percent.
394.   There's also the point of view that says that when you see an issue as a "generational" problem," you end up overlooking the responsibilities of policy decision-makers and business organizations. ("Sedaikan tairitsu to iu wana" [The trap of intergenerational strife], Chizuko Ueno interview, *Shisō chizu* vol. 2, 2008).

nation of parliamentary democracy upholding the sovereignty of the people, the cumulative effect of the voting decisions of the "elderly" is the mess we find ourselves in today.

And we can also say that, as Taichi Sakaiya (forty-one years old, Osaka) predicted as early as 1976, we were already aware of the likelihood that Japan would end up in this mess, that it would be facing financial problems caused by a declining birth rate and social security programs for the elderly.[395]

With regard to measures for dealing with the declining birth rate, Japan falls completely behind European countries. While there is no universal theory regarding the causal factors driving the declining birth rate and the measures that need to be adopted to deal with them,[396] Japan is sorely lacking in the arrangements to ensure a suitable environment for giving birth and bringing up children.

Few workplaces allow employees to work while also taking care of children, and there is also a scarcity of nursery schools and kindergartens. The government's lack of serious willingness to proactively engage with the problem of the declining birth rate is patently transparent in the fact that the issue of children on waiting lists for nursery schools remains utterly unresolved. There are many young people, too, who can't take the step toward marriage and childbirth amid the precarious job climate. As a short-term trend at least, the birth rate tends to rise with the health of the economy.

But if we really wish to do something about the declining birth rate, discriminating against "love children"—those conceived outside the bounds of marriage—is out of the question.[397/★175] We're at the point where I wouldn't mind endorsing single mothers.[398] In Japan, only about 2 percent of children are conceived outside of marriage, whereas in Sweden and France, the ratio exceeds 50 percent.[399] Whatever the circumstances, it's easy to imagine that a sufficiently dependable birthing environment to ensure that infants will be taken care of, even if their births happen to be unexpect-

---

395. Taichi Sakaiya, *Dankai no sedai* (Baby-boom generation), Bungeishunju, 2005. Originally released in 1976, this work of fiction portrays the future of the baby-boom generation. The final story, which is set in 2000, depicts a fifty-two-year old elite bureaucrat who earnestly engages in a "business catering to the elderly" while grappling with the "energy problem."

396. There is data backing the claim that a country's birthrate tends to fall as its public expenditures for the elderly rise relative to its public expenditures for families and children. (Yutaka Honkawa, *Tōkei dēta wa omoshiroi!* [Statistical data are interesting!], Gijutsu-Hyohron, 2010).

397. In Japan, the succession to property, or inheritance, for children of unmarried couples is determined to be half the inheritance children of married couples receive. Courts continue to deem this constitutional. In 2010, the Supreme Court decided to send a trial to the Grand Bench, triggering an uproar over whether an unconstitutional verdict would be passed, but the parties concerned settled, after which the lawsuit was dropped. ("Kongaishi soshō o kyakka, Saikōsai" [Supreme court dismisses love-child lawsuit], *Asahi Shimbun*, March 12, 2011, morning edition.)

★175. In 2013, upon accepting the Supreme Court's decision, the Diet passed the Civil Law Amendment, which annulled discrimination against children born out of wedlock with regard to inheritance.

ed, is what contributes to a rise in the fertility rate.

At any rate, the future is beyond hope

Well, at any rate, the number of children will not rise immediately, and criticizing past policies won't do anything to change the present state of affairs in Japan. And even if generational disparities aren't at the heart of the problem, the fact remains that Japan's future will be one of despair and desperation.

In the end, though, without a doubt, the ones who will have to live through and endure this future for a long while will be the youth and children.

In 2012, the baby-boom generation reached the age of sixty-five, making them eligible to receive pensions. This is all well and good, since the market today still gets energized by targeting "baby-boomers," but unless some dramatic development in medical technology occurs, many of them will be leaving the consumer market in twenty years' time.

In 2030, the group known as Japan's "lost generation" will begin reaching the age of sixty. Around that time, problems such as *hikikomori* (withdrawal from society) and "NEET" (Not in Education, Employment, or Training), despite being youth issues, will also become problems of the elderly. When the baby-boom generation has disappeared, taking their healthy appetite for consumption along with them, will the active, working generation of the time really be able to support and sustain a society with a growing number of aging "lost gen-ers"?

I suppose I've laid out a paranoid vision of a pretty miserable future here, but Japan as of 2011 is still in a state of blissful, laid-back apathy.[400/★176] In the face of such a dire situation, how can young people remain happy?

---

398.   The standard of living of children growing up in single-female-parent households is lower than that of other children. In addition, even though among families of mother and child the employment rate is high—even relative to other countries—economic circumstances are grim, and support from the government and father is minimal. The situation is terrible. (Aya Abe, *Kodomo no hinkon* [The poverty of children], Iwanami Shoten, 2008). What are the nationalists thinking—they who are supposed to be seriously concerned with the future of this nation? How do they see these people who have given birth to the next generation of Japan?

399.   Though the number of children born out of wedlock is on the rise, in many cases, children are still brought up in the presence of a parent. For this reason, the growing number of such children rather reinforces the bond between mother and child, and does not lead to the "dismantling of the family." (Chizuko Ueno, "Kazoku no rinkai Kea no bunpai kōsei o megutte" [The critical parameter of the family: In search of a fair allocation of care] in *Kazoku o koeru shakaigaku* [Sociology that goes beyond the family] edited by Kazue Muta, Shin-yo-sha, 2009). In addition, single-parent households comprise 20 percent of all households in both Sweden and France, so in most cases, both parents—even if they aren't married—are taking care of their children.

2. A Somewhat Happy Society

The minimum standards for wholesome and cultured living?

In Article 25 of the Constitution of Japan, it is established that "All people shall have the right to maintain the minimum standards of wholesome and cultured living." While the exact interpretation of "the minimum standards of wholesome and cultured living" greatly depends on the times and social circumstances, I used to think for a time that this meant the kind of life in which there would be a lover or friend with whom I could play Wii together, or enjoy Monster Hunter together.★177

I thought that, as long as your financial circumstances allowed you to purchase a Wii or PSP game console, while having sufficient social capital (relationships) to enjoy games together, then most people in general would be happy.

To put it in another way, I was considering happiness—or its condition—by splitting it into two distinct issues—namely, the issue of finance and the issue of social approval.

Exactly how difficult is this? Let's first consider the financial issue. There's no denying that young people are finding themselves in the midst of severe social circumstances, just as various individuals have been saying with solemn looks on their faces. However, in Japan, no matter how much you talk about the problem of poverty affecting youth, it somehow doesn't seem to ring true.

That's because you can't find any young people who can be clearly identified as being poor. Even when they walk around town, young people are dressed neatly and appear happy. Everyone, from entertainers to college students and even young road construction workers, carries a smartphone, which by no means is cheap.

With statistics, you will be hard pressed to find any evidence of "straightforward poverty." For example, in 2009, 1,656 people in Japan died of starvation, but among them only four were in their twenties, and just fifteen were in their thirties.[401/★178] Most likely, the reason why the net-café refugees attracted so much media attention had

---

400. In the wake of the Great East Japan Earthquake, the atmosphere across the whole of Japan was that of mourning, as expected, but people are creatures who go on to forget. The mood in many cities has returned to an apparently downright blissful one.

★176. What about Japan in 2015? Though it probably varies by one's living environment, as far as I can tell from the crime rates, the era of barbarity has not yet arrived.

★177. The Wii's presence has become completely weak, thanks to the failure of its successor, the Wii U. The times are changing in that more and more people are enjoying games on smartphones, instead of on dedicated gaming machines.

nothing to do with their actual number; rather, the media were drawn to them precisely because they were the exceptional face of an uncomplicated, straightforward manifestation of poverty.

Our society appears, at first glance, to be too affluent. Young people appear, at first glance, to be too happy.

The youth aren't poor, for now

It's doubtful, though, just how long this affluence and happiness will last. The reason the issue of youth poverty is opaque to young people is because, to them, "poverty" is a problem of the distant future, not of the present time.

The younger the generation, the less wealth disparity exists within it.[402] This is because, regardless of whether you're a regular employee or a job-hopping part-timer, while you're in your twenties, there's not much difference between your salaries. In major Japanese firms, where payrolls continue to be based on seniority and lifetime employment policies to this day, the annual income of the young is curbed, no matter how much they work. On the other hand, those with part-time jobs can earn even more money than regular employees of the same generation, just by working more days or at odd hours.

For example, a part-timer working at an *izakaya* pub could, by increasing the number of his late-night shifts, easily make a monthly income of anywhere from around 300,000 to 400,000 yen. While there may be programs that allow for a part-time job to lead to a full-time position as a regular employee at a company, crucially, young people often aren't attracted to such programs. Kenji (twenty-one years old, male), a job-hopping part-timer who currently works at a major *izakaya* chain, says the reason he isn't inclined to become a regular employee is because he would have to show up on fixed days; furthermore, the pay is low.

However, workers realize the difference between regular and irregular employees, and the difference between employees of a blue-chip company and employees of a "black" company, when something happens to them; for example, when they get sick, or when they think about marriage or parental care, or when nursing care becomes

---

401.   These figures represent people whose causes of death were filed under "malnutrition" and "food deficiency" in the *2009 Vital Statistics* released by the Ministry of Health, Labour and Welfare. However, since a food deficiency could lead a person to waste away and die of other causes, it should be noted that these figures are, strictly speaking, just one set of reference values.

★178.   In 2014, twenty-four people died due to "food deficiency," and 1,697 due to "malnutrition." Among those who died from "food deficiency," there were no twenty-somethings and just two thirty-somethings. As for "malnutrition," the numbers were eight and eighteen respectively. (2014 *Vital Statistics*).

402.   Ministry of Health, Labour and Welfare, *Survey on the Redistribution of Income* in 2008, released in 2010.

necessary for their parents. The options available to them will vary depending on whether they have enrolled in social insurance, and whether they have savings.

Family—the most powerful infrastructure

One of the major factors that keep the reality of poverty from surfacing is "family welfare."[403] No matter how low a young person's income may be, and no matter how unstable the job market may be, if he or she is living together with parents who are, to a certain extent, well-off, this person won't have any problems.

The parents of those who are currently in their twenties and thirties are in their fifties and sixties.[404] Many of them still work regularly and haven't yet reached the age when nursing care becomes necessary. What's more, in general, they also have money and a home of their own. The average savings of households whose head of family is in their fifties is 15,930,000 yen, while for households whose head is in their sixties, the average savings is 19,520,000 yen. In addition, the average rate of home ownership for people in their fifties is 86.7 percent, while for people in their sixties it is 91.3 percent.[405]

I've been talking about generational disparities, but this generation of parents indeed comprises the "winners" who have been reaping the benefits of the period of high economic growth known as the Japanese economic miracle. That's why what appear to be generational differences when viewed from a macro perspective are, in fact, when seen from a micro perspective, not really differences. Instead, in many cases various resources are being shifted among the family members.[406]

For example, among single individuals between eighteen and thirty-four, approximately 70 percent of males and approximately 80 percent of females live together with their parents. In particular, the percentage is high among those who are irregularly employed, such as short-term workers and part-timers.[407]

Some working offspring add money to the family coffers, but in most cases, this

---

403.   A classic treating the subject of "family welfare" is Masahiro Yamada's *Parasaito, shinguru no jidai* (The era of the parasite single; Chikumashobo, 1999).

404.   For example, the average age of parents in 1986—the parents of those who are twenty-five as of the present writing in 2011—was 29.7 years old in the case of fathers, and was 26.8 years old in the case of mothers (Ministry of Health, Labour and Welfare, *Vital Statistics*).

405.   Wage-earning households among households of more than two inhabitants (Ministry of Internal Affairs and Communications, *Family Income and Expenditure Survey*, 2010). Survey period was 2009.

406.   Here, too, the difficulty of the problem of intergenerational inequity is apparent. This is because the burdens forced upon the elderly, due to the annulment of intergenerational inequity, also become, in the end, the burdens of their children.

407.   National Institute of Population and Social Security Research, *Dai-13-kai shusshō dōkō kihon chōsa* (Thirteenth data survey on childbirth trends).

isn't enough to support the family. In many cases they rarely help with the house-work.[408] Additionally, there are studies showing higher life-satisfaction levels among singles who live together with their parents than among those who do not.[409]

In the high-growth period, there were many cases of young people leaving their hometowns for jobs in the city due to a lack of available work in their area. However, the development of local or provincial cities made the "localization" of young people possible (see chapter 2).

"Localization," in other words, was the enablement of the young generation to sponge off the parental generation who had established their wealth in sync with the growth of the economy.

However, even those young people currently receiving the benefits of family wel-fare—as "children"—will, in twenty to thirty years' time, be facing the problem of parental-generation nursing care. Furthermore, by that time, their homes will require maintenance, too.

Poverty is a future issue, approval is a current issue

Yūji, a twenty-two-year old male contract employee who lives alone in Tokyo, hasn't been paying residence taxes and national health insurance. The amounts aren't so high that he can't afford to make those payments. However, he goes to concerts featuring his favorite artists, hangs out with his friends until morning, and in general leads a decent-ly pleasant life. To live such a life, he asserts, he can't pay taxes and health insurance fees.

This might not be a problem in particular when you're young and healthy, but the chances of running into health problems grows the older you get. Compared to people in their twenties, 1.4 times more people in their thirties are hospitalized—and twice as many people in their forties. In addition, compared to people in their twenties, 1.3 times more people in their thirties, and 1.5 times more in their forties, become outpa-tients.[410] Thus, the problem of "youth poverty" truly becomes a problem after the passage of ten, twenty years; when the young are no longer young.

The reason researchers are making so much noise about the "youth poverty" prob-lem today is that they are concerned that young people will never cease to be an underclass.

---

408. Mami Iwakami, ed., *Wakamono to oya no shakaigaku* (The sociology of young people and parents), Seikyusha, 2010.
409. *White Paper on the National Life*, 2003.
410. Calculations based on rates for care received found in the *Patient Survey 2008* conducted by the Ministry of Health, Labour and Welfare, released in 2010.

As it is commonly understood, in Japan, once people get off the truck called "Good school, good company," it becomes difficult to hop on board again. No matter how motivated they may be, people who don't have a decent educational background, or those who have continued to work as *freeters* (job-hopping part-timers) don't readily come by opportunities to work at a "good company."[411] In effect, there is no career ladder for them to climb.

Herein lies the difference between the current "youth poverty" problem and the former "youth poverty" problem.

Without a doubt, the old guy is right when he says things like, "In my time we were leading poorer lives," or "Poor people have been around since the old days." But back in those days, young people also had many opportunities to escape poverty.[412]

Nowadays, though, it's doubly difficult to escape the life of a *freeter*. Firstly, there are still many companies that hesitate to recruit people with *freeter* experience.[413] And secondly, it's not as if the young in question necessarily wish to become regular full-time employees anyway.[414]

Society's attitude toward *freeters* has softened somewhat, leaning toward lukewarm acceptance, and even if you don't become a regular full-time worker, you can enjoy a certain level of affluence in your life, so there is no need, while you're young, to force yourself to become one. And that's why the seriousness of the "youth poverty" problem has failed to materialize.

Of course, not every young person needs to aim to become a regular full-time employee at a large company. Nor is there any need for a young person to take the plunge into a world where his or her social standing will be that of what was formerly known as a *shachiku*, or wage slave. However, with the existing social institutions, there's no denying that the *freeter* stands to face comparably more risks in his or her old age.★[179]

As many debaters have pointed out, there is a need to restructure Japan's social

411. Of course, this is just a schematic explanation; in reality, it's often the case that occupational matching simply isn't carried out. For example, companies located in provincial areas, particularly small business enterprises, frequently and actively accept job hoppers (Takao Nakazawa, *Shigoto o tōshite hito ga seichō suru kaisha* [Companies in which people grow through their work], PHP Institute, 2010).
412. Kenji Hashimoto, "Sengoshi ni okeru wakamono no hinkon" (Youth poverty in postwar history) in *Gendai no riron* no. 26, 2011.
413. According to a survey conducted by the Ministry of Health, Labour and Welfare targeting people between fifteen and thirty-four, businesses that hired job-hopping part-timers as regular staff in the past three years only amounted to 11.6 percent of all companies (2009 *Survey on Employment of Young People*, released in 2010). However, the percentage of businesses answering that they made "negative assessments" of people who were *freeters* (job-hopping part-time workers) had declined from the previous survey to 18.5 percent.
414. Yukie Hori, *Furītā ni tairyū suru wakamono-tachi* (Young people who remain job-hopping part-timers), Keiso Shobo, 2007.

system, which currently leans heavily toward corporate-mediated welfare, so that it provides life security instead.

Only 30 percent of young people have a romantic partner

To young people, unlike financial poverty, which is a problem of the distant future, matters related to social approval and acceptance manifest in relatively plain, straightforward form. For many people, after all, what's far more acute than the prospect of meeting a fate of poverty in an unforeseeable future is the problem of facing loneliness in the lucid here and now.

The simplest way to satisfy this craving for approval is to have a lover. The lover who gives total personal approval can, at least temporarily, solve most of the problems troubling a person. Well, because anybody, by having just one person love him or her, can become an "irreplaceable somebody."

However, not everyone can easily find a person to be their sweetheart. According to a survey conducted by the National Institute of Population and Social Security Research, among singles aged between eighteen and thirty-four, only 27.2 percent of men, and only 38.7 percent of women, have a lover of the opposite gender.[415/★180]

In addition, the same survey was thoughtful enough to inquire about whether respondents have had sexual intercourse with the opposite sex. According to the findings, the rate of virginity among men between twenty and twenty-four was 33.6 percent, while among women in the same age range it was 36.3 percent. Among those between twenty-five and twenty-nine, the rate for men was 23.2 percent; for women it was 25.1 percent. So, as you can see, the number of people without any experience

---

★179. Lately, there has been a rise in the number of companies, including IKEA, that turn job-hopping part-timers into regular staff. According to the *Heisei 25-nen jakunensha koyō jittai chōsa no gaikyō* (2013 General survey on employment of young people), 46.6 percent of businesses responded, "There have been times, in the past three years, when we converted young people who were non-regular employees into regular employees."

415. These percentages are the sum of the following responses found in the *Dai 13 kai shusshō dōkō kihon chōsa* (Thirteenth data survey on childbirth trends), a 2006 survey on singles conducted by the National Institute of Population and Social Security Research: "I have a fiancé" and "I'm associating with someone of the opposite sex as a lover." Since the term "opposite sex" is used here on purpose, these statistics might provoke the ire of those researching gender studies, who might complain, "What about homosexuals?" Even in the 2011-released Cabinet Office's *Kekkon, kazoku keisei ni kansuru chōsa* (Survey concerning marriages and family formation) (The chairperson was, of course, none other than Masahiro Yamada, who is known for coining the word *konkatsu* [marriage-partner hunting]), the percentage of bachelors in their twenties and thirties who had romantic partners was 36 percent; conversely, the percentage without any dating experience was 26 percent. In particular, there were many men residing in provincial areas who had never had a lover, and among those in the latter half of their thirties, this described 31.8 percent of them.

★180. Note that this was a survey covering single people. Approximately 20 percent of men and women aged eighteen to thirty-four were married.

of having coitus with the opposite sex is not insignificant.★181

When studying the problem of approval, the friend, like the lover, proves essential. Just as we saw in chapter 2, the importance of friendships to the happiness of young people has greatly increased.★182 Additionally, one survey shows that the No. 1 thing that would make young people unhappy if it were missing in their lives is "a friend."416/★183

Responding to the results of that survey, the writer Kikuko Tsumura (thirty-two years old, Osaka), made the following analysis: "If you're ugly, you can use makeup to disguise your blemishes; and if you don't have a job, you can make the excuse that times are bad. But if you don't have any friends, you can't make any excuses. Your entire personality—formed since your childhood phase—would seem to have been rejected."

You certainly can laugh while telling people, "I don't have a lover," but that's not so easy to do when you say, "I don't have a friend." However, in modern Japan, innumerable resources are available for meeting our need for social approval in forms that don't rely on having a lover or friend. But what's more, these resources, in the end, can serve as tools to help you gain "friends," in the broad sense of the word.

Handy approval society

On Twitter, even if you're anonymous or an obscure figure, if you tweet something interesting, hundreds of others will "retweet" your remark. And if you continue to tweet interesting things regularly, your number of followers will steadily keep rising. What used to be the exclusive province of authors and celebrities—the thrill of having several thousand, even tens of thousands of people read what you say—has become a privilege that many people enjoy.417

★181. Note, too, that this figure is also a finding in a survey for single people. Incidentally, in the same survey carried out in 2010, there was no major variation in the rates of male and female virginity.

★182. Among the songs produced by the Sandaime J Soul Brothers, who won the Japan Record Award in 2014, many have the theme of not love, but friendship. In the hit tune, "R.Y.U.S.E.I.," the lyrics contain the phrases, "The friends I want to live together with" and "You get only one life" and "I want to catch a dream."

416. "Shiawase to fukō no sakaime wa doko ni? Nijū, sanjūdai 300-nin chōsa" (Where is the borderline separating happiness from misery? A survey of 300 people in their twenties and thirties), *AERA*, October 4, 2010.

★183. In the past several years, Halloween has become lively in Tokyo as an event to enjoy with friends. The festive, exhilarating atmosphere seen on Halloween night in Roppongi and Shibuya is reminiscent of the day of the World Cup match with Japan.

417. The readership for a celebrity on Twitter is far more than that of a baffling book on young people like this one. With reactions or feedback directly received, Twitter is an indispensable tool for self-styled *hyōgenshi* (expressors).

The Nico Nico Douga video-sharing website is a perfect source of social approval. While a person may gain a sense of "connection" with others by simply submitting a comment on a favorite movie or animation, at times a person, hitherto an obscure presence on the site, can end up with several thousand followers by just uploading a video of his or her own making.

These videos come in various genres; for example, those in the "I tried dancing" genre feature many youths actually dancing to music. The twenty-six-year-old male *freeter* Tsubasa has been uploading "I tried dancing" videos since around 2008, and has also held events with friends in Yoyogi Park. The number of views for some of his videos exceeds the tens of thousands, and his community of fans, which he set up on the mixi platform, is several hundred people strong. As far as you can tell from reading the comments posted by these fans, the way they treat Tsubasa is no different from the way a well-known artist, singer, or actor would be treated.

Another popular genre is "let's play," which features videos of people playing games while chatting.[418] Tarochin (twenty-five years old, male) is gaining popularity with his videos that show him sluggishly playing games while drunk. The videos in which he costars with another popular broadcaster in the "let's play" genre have more than 500,000 views.

The Internet has produced plenty of "small celebrities" like Tsubasa and Tarochin. In a time when "everyone" doesn't necessarily mean "every Japanese" the way it once did, the Internet is helping to bring together a smaller, more modest-sized "everyone." Of course, small-name celebrities have been around since before the advent of the Internet, but with the Internet, anyone can taste the thrill of mass-media empowerment.[419/★184]

Just as those business magazines for old guys have been insisting, though, I can't see social media like Twitter ever becoming suitable for large-scale businesses and commercial enterprises. For example, only twenty people attended an event announced by a big-name Twitter celebrity who has approximately 200,000 followers. What's more, instead of being upset about the low turnout, this celebrity was delighted, saying, "I'm

418. The number of people who have uploaded game videos with running commentary amounted to 10,000, and dozens of videos have registered a playback count of more than one million. The sensation of faceless commentators connecting through Nico Nico Douga might be something akin to the late-night radio experience of the past (Fan club for game commentaries, ed., *Tsumoru hanashi mo arukeredo, toriaezu minna gēmu jikkyō miyōze!* [Hey, dudes, we need to catch up, but let's all just watch game commentaries for the time being!], harvest-inc, 2011).

419. Toshiki Satō, *Kakusa gēmu no jidai* (The age of the disparity game), Chuokoron-Shinsha, 2009. While the Internet theory found in this book made its first appearance in the late 1990s, it still doesn't feel that outdated today. One of the reasons for this is the fact that the world of the Internet, at least at the level of how we talk about it, hasn't changed at all, for all this time.

glad there are actually people who take the trouble to come."[420] That's about how limited the reach of the celebrity is on Twitter.

Similarly, I don't think that Twitter and other social media can become tools for changing society. Their function is rather the opposite, given that they readily help meet the desire for personal approval. For instance, many people end up attaining a sense of fulfillment simply by scoring a huge number of retweets and being praised by followers for tweeting arbitrary remarks that smack of social consciousness.

My thinking is that, in the end, the purposefulness of "changing society" is co-opted by the "spirit of cooperation" Twitter provides.[421]

Living in a happy, relationship-free society

Indeed, it's easy to see why we young people are satisfied with life; poverty is a problem that lies in the distant future, so it's hard to grasp; and the means for meeting our desire for social approval are available in droves. Since, according to a study investigating levels of happiness, achieving a sense of happiness hinges on how aware one is of social issues, rather than on actual income levels, obviously no other group should be happier than the members of the younger generation who are living in the "here and now."[422]

However, regrettably, in modern society, every relationship, and every place of belonging, is very fragile. Relationships between friends and lovers, in the absence of institutional guarantees, immediately break when they break. Units of human relations bound via social institutions—that is, units of human relations such as the corporation and family—tend to be more durable and endure for a long time, but even they aren't absolute.

With the impact of the earthquake disaster, we have forgotten that from 2010 through 2011, Japan was seeing a lot of hype about the *muen shakai* (no-relationship society). This coinage refers to a society without personal connections or relationships. When NHK aired a special which sensationally reported the fact that the annual total of unclaimed bodies of people dying in solitude had reached 32,000, the word *muen* became a buzzword. (*Muen*, which literally means "no relationships," alludes to the growing number of people who refuse to take care of their own family members or

---

★184. In the eyes of children, people who are called YouTubers, like HIKAKIN (twenty-six years old, Niigata), are as wildly popular as well-known entertainers. Since the playback count of their videos directly translates to a revenue stream for them, they continue to upload their videos day and night for the purpose of doing "business," rather than for "approval."

420. Masato Kogure and Masaki Ishitani, *Maki komi no gijutsu* (Techniques of entrainment), Impress Japan, 2010.

421. In the first place, though, there probably aren't many people who use Twitter with social awareness.

422. Fumio Ōtake et al., eds., *Nihon no kōfukudo* (Japan's level of happiness), Nippon Hyoron Sha, 2010.

relatives.)

The *muen shakai* is described as a society that emerged in the aftermath of a number of losses; namely, the loss of "blood relations" in the form of family connections, the loss of "shared territorial bonding" as experienced in one's connection to their hometown, and the loss of "relationships with work colleagues" which constitute one's connection to a company.[423] However, these ties were once criticized for being relationships you couldn't choose.

In the project of "modernization," which has been aiming to convert people into individualists, these types of ties were considered obstacles that needed to be overcome. In particular, familial and territorial ties were considered symbolic of suffocating relationships.

Chizuko Ueno (forty-five years old, Toyama), in criticizing "relationships that aren't of one's own choosing," referred to *muen* as *sentakuen* (selective relations, or relationships of one's own choosing).[424] When the term *muen shakai* (no-relationship society) is rephrased as *sentakuen shakai* (selective-relationship society), it doesn't sound so bad, does it?

In the worst-case scenario, such a society may make us bereft of obligatory relationships, but we will still retain the freedom to choose the people we keep company with and the communities we wish to belong to. We will also be free to belong to multiple communities, joining and leaving them at will. In effect, we will have relationships that continue loosely and noncommittally, unrestricted by any rules.

With the increase of such communities—that is, communities not based on utility and profit—the outlets of approval get dispersed, while also serving to guarantee our identities.[425] Thanks to the warm and mutual approval offered by those communities, young people can go on living without having to deal with any of the various problems of society.[426]

This is because, no matter how bad their working environment is, and no matter how terrible the anxieties they harbor are, all they have to do to make things right is return to their community of friends. Whether they are suffering from dissatisfaction with the economy or restlessness about the future, various types of communities are

---

423.   NHK "No-Relationship Society Project" news crew, eds., *Muen shakai* (No-relationship society), Bungeishunju, 2010.

424.   Chizuko Ueno, "'Onna en' no kanōsei" (The possibilities of "female relationships") in *Kindai kazoku no seiritsu to shūen* (The modern family in Japan: Its rise and fall), Iwanami Shoten, 1994.

425.   Tadao Umesao, *Watashi no ikigai-ron* (My theory of fulfillment), Kodansha, 1985. On the subject of communities, the ideas of journalists and writers didn't see much progress for thirty years, apparently.

426.   Noritoshi Furuichi, *Kibō nanmin goikkō sama* (A party of hope refugees), Kobunsha, 2010.

there for the young person seeking relief and healing from all types of angst.

This is one of the very reasons young people aren't rebelling or launching insurgencies (see chapter 4). Then again, young people don't have other options, so it can't be helped.

3. Where Are We Going?

China: a society structured around social status

From a micro perspective, no matter how serious disparities between and within generations are, these gaps don't necessarily indicate that society as a whole is "unhappy." As I have repeatedly emphasized throughout this book, this is because even when a situation is, objectively speaking, hopeless, people may nonetheless consider themselves to be happy.

Curiously, in fact, if Japan were to become an extremely socially polarized society marked by even greater disparities than those that exist today, or if it were to become a class-based society in which those disparities became entrenched, we might end up seeing the number of happy youth rise even further.

For example, even before China became a socially polarized society marked by inequalities, the "family register for city dwellers" and the "family register for provincial commoners" always served as barriers to upward mobility. Family registers for cities are maintained separately from those for rural villages, and people born in rural villages are barred from living in cities.

In reality, there are many workers from agricultural villages in urban areas; they are called *nōminkō* (rural migrant workers),[427] but they aren't entitled to receive any social-security benefits, nor do many public schools accept their children, if they happen to have any.

Modern Chinese society can no longer do without these rural migrant workers. They can be found working in many sectors of the economy, including as waiters in restaurants, not to mention in factories and public-works facilities.

Their minimum hourly wage in urban areas has risen every year, but it's still just 11

---

427.   Assuming rural migrant workers to be people who worked outside of their birthplace for more than half a year, the number in 2009 amounted to 145,330,000 (National Bureau of Statistics of the People's Republic of China, *The Population, Structure and Characteristics of the New-generation of Migrant Workers*, 2011).

yuan in Shanghai.[428]/[★185] In China, due to tariffs, prices of brand-name products are higher than those in Japan. As a result, in cities where a Burberry Prorsum coat sells for more than 200,000 yen, there are rural migrant workers who willingly work for an hourly wage of just 140 yen.

On top of underpaying them, employers don't need to think about providing these workers social security. Furthermore, since the idea of migrant workers—or seasonal workers—is based on the workers returning to their agricultural villages, slums generally don't form in urban areas, which is yet another convenient boon for the city. These workers are like modern-day slaves.

Satisfaction level of migrant workers: 80 percent; satisfaction level of the "ant tribe": 1 percent

What do those very migrant workers think about this social paradigm—which is, in a substantial sense, a class system?

According to a survey of migrant workers hailing from agricultural villages, their satisfaction level was 85.6 percent. In effect, 80 percent of this so-called "floating population," whose members are supposedly situated in poor working environments, are satisfied with their lives. This is higher than the 75.5 percent life satisfaction level reported by permanent urban residents.[429]

This is because, though their lives may lack a safety net or amenities, compared with the standard of living in their agricultural villages, the migrant workers lead better lives. In rural communities of China, to this day, a good number of people are still living in houses made of bricks or stone, with hardly any household appliances inside.[430]

In addition, the possibility exists that the migrant workers' resignation to an inferior social status, as dictated by their different family registry, helps raise their satisfac-

---

428.   Approximately 140 Japanese yen (as of April 2011).

★185.   The minimum hourly wage in Shanghai was raised to 18 yuan in 2015. With the influence of the weak yen, this converts to approximately 340 yen (as of September 2015). On the other hand, the minimum hourly wage in Tokyo, which was 837 yen in 2011, went up to 907 yen in October 2015. Shanghai saw a speedier upturn.

429.   Findings of the survey carried out by Shigeto Sonoda in 2004 in the city of Tianjin, covering 1,200 migrant workers and 600 urban residents (*Fubyōdō kokka chūgoku* [China, an unequal nation], Chuokoron-Shinsha, 2008). However, since each city in China is like a different country, the question of whether the data for Tianjin can be treated as typical of all other cities in China should be considered carefully.

430.   But with an infrastructure-maintenance project that began in the late 1990s to spread telephones all across agricultural villages, rural regions reportedly saw rapid development. Of late, thanks to the "Subsidy Program for Electronic Appliances for Homes in Rural Areas," penetration of household appliances in rural communities is rising.

tion level. As I mentioned in passing in chapter 2, this is what is called "relative depri-vation" in sociology. People gauge their happiness in the context of the group they belong to. So, as long as they view the gorgeous lifestyles of people living in urban areas as stories about another world—a world different from theirs—those lifestyles will fail to serve as criteria for measuring their own happiness. This is the same logic operating behind the rise of life satisfaction levels during recessionary periods in Japan.

Now, in contrast to the rural migrant workers, there is the group known as the "ant tribe," the Chinese version of the highly educated poor. At one point, reforms to China's educational system made it easy to acquire university diplomas, contributing to the social problem of professional mismatches. While public-works projects pushed forward by the Chinese government had generated massive employment in the prov-inces, the actual jobs created were not jobs the members of the ant tribe aspired to have as knowledge workers. They would say things like, "I took the trouble to graduate from a university, so why should I accept a blue-collar job?"

Among the ant tribe, a mere 1 percent say that they're satisfied with life, and one study even found that 84 percent harbor some form of dissatisfaction with their lives.[431] It's likely that their desire to achieve upward mobility or their aspiration to become elites is contributing to their unhappiness.

In truth, it would be ideal to generate enough white-collar, knowledge-based, or creative jobs that would satisfy the ant tribe, but, at least in the short term, this doesn't seem possible.

Turning Japanese youths into "migrant workers"

Based on the high level of life satisfaction among China's migrant workers, and the low level of life satisfaction within the ant tribe, we arrive at a certain regrettable conclu-sion: if Japan were to become a class society with fixed disparities among its citizens, or if it were to become a hierarchically oriented society where identity and social posi-tion played a more central role, many people would likely become happy.

In an objective sense, the migrant workers, who remain happy amid inferior living circumstances, and the ant tribe, who are miserable because they are unwilling to abandon their drive toward achieving self-actualization and upward mobility, are sym-bolic when considering Japan's future. Young Japanese are already on their way to be-

---

431. Lian Si, ed., Ken Sekine, translation supervisor, *Arizoku* (Ant Tribe), Bensei Shuppan, 2010. Because the research method differs, this work cannot be indiscriminately compared with the survey on rural migrant workers, but still, the 1 percent satisfaction level is abnormal.

Street stalls of "rural migrant workers" in Shanghai

coming *nōminkō* (rural migrant workers), as the continuing rise in life-satisfaction levels among twenty-somethings appears to indicate. Believing themselves to be different from the generation who were the privileged beneficiaries of economic growth, the youth of today find whatever happiness they can in their immediate surroundings, relating more closely to their friends in the process. Moving away from the age when people were focused on winning and dressing themselves up, they live contented with small, mutual approvals they can enjoy inside their communities.

This way of living is a wise one suited to the times. For example, the goal of becoming a "wealthy person," is hardly ever achieved, because, in this capitalist society, there's hardly any limit to what money can buy; the accumulation of wealth knows no bounds. Promptly dropping out of such an endless "race to the top" is also a way to be happy in an energy-efficient way, a path of least resistance to a state of well-being.

No matter how much of a social issue altruistic adults make "youth poverty" out to be, or how often they exclaim that they feel sorry for young people, the young themselves fail to feel that such claims are real. This could be symbolic of the fact that the times we call the "modern age"—when anyone could aim to become "number one" regardless of where they were born, or the kind of household they were born into—is finally reaching a tipping point.

The revenge of our former selves

Modernization was a project that aimed to elevate villagers, who lived through their entire lifetime without ever imagining the world beyond their village, to the level of independent presences called "citizens" and "individuals." Our society has been attempting to create moderners—the kind of people who would determine their own lives with their own decisions, without ever turning to God or being influenced by tradition (see chapter 3).

In Japan, the class system was abolished and suffrage was progressively granted to all citizens. This was the birth of the democratic nation of "Japan," whose citizens have sovereign rights as moderners.

However, perhaps Japan the nation may have failed in the construction of the system we call democracy. The modernization of Japan began when it witnessed the Industrial Revolution taking place in Europe in the late nineteenth century and attempted to transplant that phenomenon to Japan. But what if Japan's Meiji Restoration had happened fifty years earlier—around the year 1810? What kind of society would have consequently taken shape?[432]

In the early nineteenth century, before the U.K. became the world's factory, Europe was still embroiled in the maelstrom of the people's revolution. If the Iwakura Mission had visited Europe around that time, would they have then attempted to establish "democracy" and "freedom and human rights" at the core of the formation of Japan? In Latin American countries, where modernization took place earlier than in Japan, politicians considered the creation of a democracy to be critical as they aimed to build their nations.

The result, however, was that Japan developed economically, while Latin America didn't. Of course, democracy—or the lack thereof—wasn't the only reason, but the industrial revolution was easier to crib than the people's revolution. In addition, by making light of the value of democracy, Japan was able to disregard the interests of its people for a time and make economic growth its national priority.

Basically, the nation had been faring well in this way for a long time. In effect, Japan, a small Asian country, had repeatedly carried out wars to expand its territory, and for a time ended up colonizing the whole of East Asia. Although it had lost in the Pacific War, in the end, after a run of good fortune, it came out victorious in the economic war. It was a time when nothing mattered, as long as the wheels of the nation-led economy kept turning.

However, clouds were gathering over this machinery. In a country where many believed that the nation would manage to get by somehow as long as economic growth was achieved, that very economic growth came to a standstill. What's more, in a coun-

---

432.   Yōsuke Kōtō, *Gurōbarizēshon inpakuto* (Impact of globalization), Minerva Shobo, 2011.

try without a democratic tradition, everyone was at a loss, as if paralyzed with horror.★[186] Japan became one of the world's greatest economic powers by having prioritized economic growth at the expense of democracy. Perhaps we are now making amends for this sin.

For Japan, a nation whose road to modernization differed from the one taken by Europe, there was no longer any other nation to look to for precedent in short order.

And then we moved toward a happy, class-based society

Even while declaring equality for its citizens, every modern society has required the presence of "second-class citizens." For example, modern nations—including Japan—have always imposed the role of "second-class citizens" on women. This generally involves the breadwinner model in which the man, working energetically, serves as the central pillar of his family, while the woman supports him by taking on household burdens like child and elder care.

However, amid cries for equality between the sexes and the emergence of labor shortages, European countries started to support the advancement of women in society, while aggressively employing immigrants as a cheap source of labor.[433]

However, in Japan, a nation that has continued to reject immigrant labor, young people, in addition to women, have come to be treated as second-class citizens.

In fact, the campaign to turn Japanese youth into full-fledged second-class citizens has already made headway. It is a well-known fact that if employers irresponsibly deceive them with expressions like "dream" and "worth doing," young people can become a cheap and expendable source of labor.

At this rate, Japan will turn itself into a moderately class-based society. The gap between first-class and second-class citizens will go on to widen, little by little, with the arrangement being such that a segment of first-class citizens will be busy making decisions for corporations and the country, while many second-class citizens will be leading hand-to-mouth lives of apathy.

★186. In this country, since 2011, two phenomena—the seemingly sudden rise of "democracy," as evidenced by demonstrations becoming common; and the idea of regressing back to the Shōwa period, as evidenced in the attempts to restore Japan to its former glory through staging the Olympics and creating the maglev train—have been gaining ground at the same time.

433. For example, the rise in the number of working women in Northern Europe—rather than being something that the government aimed to achieve—is primarily due to the creation of a massive number of jobs in the public sector, which accompanied the expansion of the welfare state. In addition, commodity prices soared during the same period, making it impossible to continue the model of the man alone supporting the family budget. To provide relief in these circumstances, nursery schools and parental leave programs were established. For further details, refer to Arnlaug Leira, *Welfare States and Working Mothers: The Scandinavian Experience* (Cambridge University Press, 1992).

However, for these people, this will not be tantamount to living in an unhappy society. For example, even if the minimum hourly wage rises to around three hundred yen, if Wii or PSP★187 gaming consoles are provided as a means of guaranteeing the "minimum standards of wholesome and cultured living," we could most likely prevent riots from happening.

At the same time, technological developments will change the shape of society, little by little. For example, as of 2011, Google doesn't tell us what we should be googling on Google. Additionally, we need to choose the "right" information by ourselves from a vast sea of search results displayed.

But there may come a time when the search window will altogether disappear from Google.★188 Based on the record of your behavioral patterns, Google will, instead, make all sorts of recommendations. Amazon might even end up recommending not just books, but specific places in a book for you to read.

By that time, "national news" may have become meaningless to many people. While some elites may continue to watch esoteric news programs aired by the NHK public broadcasting service, many will turn to whatever news stories have been recommended to them—for example, ones with headlines like, "Self-introductions that create a lasting impression at mixers."

Once society reaches this stage, it won't be that different from living in the Edo period (1603–1868).434

The age of 100 million youths

We are now living in an era that is moving toward the age of 100 million youths; that is, the age when everyone is basically considered young. The generation gap is continuing to diminish, and if more and more young people are barred from becoming "regular employees" or "full-time homemakers"—in other words, from being "adults" as defined by existing society—they will have no choice but to remain "young people,"

★187. I'd like you to read "PS Vita" as "smartphone." As for Wii, nobody thinks about getting one nowadays, right?

★188. In fact, the "decline of the online search" is becoming a reality. This is probably because the time spent on reading information via social networking services such as Facebook, and the time spent using apps on smartphones without going through search engines is increasing. However, if you think about it, prior to the emergence of the Internet, all that people ever did, when it came to the act of searching, was to "search" or "look up" terms in dictionaries once in a while, so they—that is, the people of the 2000s—may have had a peculiar fondness for searching.

434. Of course, once "second-class citizens" can no longer remain nonchalant, the situation will change. Just as history shows, when the "moral economy" is infringed upon, and when it becomes difficult to even eat, the people will revolt. Lately, in the urban areas of China also, riots caused by rural migrant workers have become a problem.

regardless of their age.

Indeed, we are in the midst of a transitional period in which people throughout Japan are turning into "young people." Even this book, while raising the subject of "youth theory," has ended up as a window into this picture of Japan. This is because "young people" can now be found everywhere, regardless of their age, and also because no one can be considered real young people.

And that's why this book has been hesitant in actively defining "young people." Ever since the collapse of the bubble economy in 1991—when we saw the demise of the "middle-class dream" of everyone owning a home, of Daddy working in a company until retirement age, of Mommy the full-time housewife warmly watching over her children—the number of "young people" has been rising.

This book has been mainly focused on portraying the stories of people in their twenties as the ultimate embodiment of the characteristics of "young people" in this sense. But these stories should resonate with many other "young people," regardless of age. In other words, these stories are the stories of this nation.

So where, then, is this nation headed, home to such large numbers of "young people?"

If anything, one fact is certain: "those days" to which we should return no longer exist.

Would we want to return to the postwar period, when material wealth was lacking, but not spiritual wealth? When the nation had taken the lives of millions of people, and when everyone had lost someone, and when poverty, crime, and unsanitary conditions were rampant throughout Japan?

How about going back to the period of high economic growth, when Japan rose to the heights of greatness as one of the leading economic superpowers of the world, when ordinary people suffered inflation, and when pollution became so serious that cities were smothered in photochemical smog?

How about going back to the bubble period when Japan was enveloped in a bafflingly festive mood? When it was all the rage to eat what was, judging by today's standards, bad French cuisine in shabby "city hotels" while land and commodity prices were soaring?

But in the first place, no matter how much you yearn to go back to "those days," they will never return. The postwar economic growth was only possible because of a run of good fortune that included the United States' Japan policy, which sought to keep Japan in the democratic camp; a population bonus that allowed the country to leverage the abundant supply of a young workforce; the fact that all Japan had to do, after becoming an economic backwater in the wake of its defeat in the war, was copy other countries.

There was a five-person dance troupe that was once the biggest act around, but doesn't sell at all anymore. Ten years after their heyday, we are left with the following lyrics to one of their songs.[435/★189]

> I know, days like that will never come back again
> But I lose if I say so

We are living in the future of "those days"

We can no longer return to those days. But at the same time we're living in a future that people of those days longed for.

For example, students in 1960 were concerned that the whole story of their lives was clearly visible from an early stage. They were troubled by the fact that as soon as they found employment, they were able to estimate, with considerable accuracy, how much their retirement bonus would be.[436] In the present day, though, we can't even estimate the amount of next year's salary, let alone the retirement bonus. Ours is certainly a time of uncertainty. But it can be said that there's pleasure in that, too—that is, in not being able to foresee what lies ahead.

The rosy society of the future, as depicted in a 1969 news story, has been realized to a considerable degree.[437] "If you suddenly wish to see an archival photograph of the Tokyo Olympics, you can call the central computer and, if necessary, print the image on the printer attached to a terminal unit to acquire a hard copy. Without leaving your room, you will be able to watch programs airing on televisions everywhere around the world. With the 'telephone' and 'typewriter,' your car will become a 'mobile office.'" While such talk must have seemed like pie in the sky back then, today, with just one iPad, the whole world can become your "mobile office."

The shape of education, as hoped for by a thirty-year-old housewife in Tokyo in 1979, has become a reality. Concerned about the overheated exam wars, she prayed for the day when "a great number of children would be able to play in towns while shout-

---

435. TRF, "As it is," from *Lif-e-Motions*, 2006.
★189. TRF scored a huge hit with their release of an exercise video in 2012, attaining sales of more than one million copies. I stated that they weren't selling at all anymore, but this was a complete misapprehension on my part. I'm so sorry.
436. Tadao Umesao, *Watashi no ikigai-ron* (My theory of fulfillment), Kodansha, 1985. The original lecture was delivered in 1960.
437. "Jōhō sangyō no yoake: Enkakushindan, terebi denwa bara iro no 'mirai shakai'" (The dawn of the information industry: Rosy videophone "future society"), *Yomiuri Shimbun*, February 11, 1969, morning edition.

ing freely and cheerfully in loud voices, and that at schools, students would be able to receive an education catering to their individual personality."[438]

Today, in towns, children with PSP or DS gaming devices are having fun playing in battles against each other over Wi-Fi. The intensity of the exam wars, too, has eased considerably.

On Seijin no Hi (Coming-of-Age Day) in 1991, one newspaper exhorted young people to be "stingy."[439] An editorial in this paper expressed discomfort at the fact that people were frantically spending lavish amounts of money on overseas travel to commemorate their graduation, on luxurious wedding ceremonies, and on the new cars and electronic products that kept coming out one after another. Consequently, they hoped that young people, whom they believed to be brimming with great sensibility, would "spearhead the revolution to reform waste-nation Japan."

Today, without a doubt, young people are starting to distance themselves from overseas trips, automobiles, and electrical goods. The person who wrote this editorial twenty years ago must certainly be overjoyed.

Financial collapse? We're going to get invaded? So what?

"There was a time when the mass media made a big issue out of the decline in academic ability. Right now, however, human resources and self-reliance have also declined, not to mention scholastic ability. Problems are beginning to occur one after another today, as if the bottom has dropped out of the bucket. This is already an extremely alarming situation for our nation."[440]

Above are the words of the education pundit Naoki Ogi (sixty-four years old, Shiga), which appeared in a 2011 piece titled "Arenaku natta seijinshiki" (The no-longer-wild coming-of-age ceremony). The adults had been denouncing coming-of-age ceremonies, which tended to get out of control every year, but in 2011, the ceremonies were apparently subdued nationwide. There shouldn't have been anything wrong with that, but once young people became quiet and accommodating, the grownups launched another round of youth bashing, this time revolving around the complaint that young people have "lost their zest for life."

---

438.   "Kiryū: Nichiyō hiroba" (Air stream: Sunday plaza), *Yomiuri Shimbun*, January 21, 1979, morning edition.
439.   "Shin-seijin e 'Kechi' no susume" (Toward becoming a new adult: Recommendations of a "cheapskate,") *Asahi Shimbun*, January 14, 1991, morning edition.
440.   "Nihon wa donzoko o jikkan suru: 'Shin seijin' wa shijō saitei ka" (Japan will hit rock bottom: Are "new adults" an all-time low?), *Shūkan Shincho*, January 20, 2011.

Fanning the fears of an impending crisis, Ogi furthermore asserts, "Japan has ended." If you have read this book, you can see that this is such a groundless paranoid fantasy that it doesn't even merit a counterargument. Such comments as "Japan is finished" or "Japan is on the brink of collapse" are not limited to Ogi, however; whenever something happens, someone always starts saying things like this.★[190]

But exactly what kind of situation do declarations like "Japan is finished" truly point to?

For example, we cannot say, with absolute certainty, that in Japan there is zero possibility of a financial crash occurring, triggered by a sharp decline in the value of Japanese government bonds.[441] If Japan were to fall under IMF management, the social-security budget would be greatly reduced, and a decline in the quality of public services like medical care and education would likely follow. A series of bankruptcies would also occur, while the unemployment rate would rise. Japanese companies and real estate properties might be bought up at low, undervalued prices by foreign capital.★[191]

But even if such a situation where to arise, it's not as if Japanese citizens are going to die out and become extinct. Rather, such a situation would prove to be an opportunity for young people, who don't have a lot of material possessions to lose in the first place. The ossified, inflexible employment system would collapse and give way to an age in which one might prove one's mettle by dint of ability and talent. Just as young people in the provinces once used to dream about Tokyo and left their homes for the big city, young people today can travel to China or India for work, with the dream of making a sudden fortune, of getting rich quick.

On the other hand, though, if they wish to stay in Japan, they can spend their days with their friends, living on low wages like Chinese migrant workers. Young people today, after all, have enough knowhow to lead decently pleasant lives without much money.

The possibility exists, too, of a military invasion from a foreign country. Although I have seemingly praised, with keen relish, the way young people have abandoned antagonistic violence (see chapter 3), I have failed to present a sufficient account of just

---

★190. I believe it wasn't necessary to criticize a mere magazine interview to this extent. Mother Ogi, I went a little too far.

441. "Nijūdai no tame no Nippon kaizō keikaku" (A project for twenty-somethings for remodeling Japan), *Shūkan Pureibōi*, May 23, 2011.

★191. Given the scale of the GDP, the prospect of the current IMF giving relief to Japan is an impossibility. With Japan's GDP being twenty-five times that of Greece, Japan, even if it were just on the brink of bankruptcy, would be helpless with only the IMF's assets. Even before support from IMF would be considered, though, the international financial market would very likely have fallen into a state of panic.

how many policy avenues are available as alternatives to the use of armed force, with respect to the problem of the so-called Lesson of Munich and Nazi Germany.[442]

Despite the arrival of the "new Middle Ages," even though the role of the nation-state has declined, we are still living to this day in modern nation-states that go hand in hand with wars—in systems that Anthony Giddens refers to as "military societies."[443]

As a matter of fact, the idea of a "just war" can be found in the Charter of the United Nations. In addition to the just war authorized by the United Nations Security Council (Article 42), the Charter of the United Nations legalizes any war carried out in the name of self-defense (Article 51). Indeed, the Gulf War and aerial raids on Yugoslavia were settled in international courts as "lawful wars." Furthermore, many nations—outside countries like Iceland and Costa Rica—possess armed forces, proving that realpolitik, as evidenced in the existing security power structure, is still valid to this day in international relations.[444] On the other hand, however, new types of wars—those that go beyond the framework of the nation-state, referred to as "terrorism" or "conflicts"—are also occurring frequently all over the world.

At the foundation supporting all of us who are living through the ennui of "late modern times," can be found the turbulent currents of "modern times"—which go hand in hand with wars. These currents continue to flow, while the threat of wars that take place beyond the framework of "modern times" is spreading.

It's OK if Japan ends

Even if the government were to make a declaration of war, however, I believe that if we all ran away together, there wouldn't be any war.[445/★192] Let me elaborate: should a war break out, and Japan the nation suffer defeat, I would be okay with that if it meant that the people living in the country—that is, in the country that was once "Japan"—

---

442. A work discussing the abandonment of antagonistic violence from a feminist perspective is Chizuko Ueno's *Ikinobiru tame no shisō* (Concepts for survival; Iwanami Shoten, 2006). While Ueno was discussing "ideas associated with becoming refugees," as evinced in phrases like, "Let's escape, let's survive!" in retrospect she said, "Those words were mostly something like prayers." (Yuki Senda, ed., *Ueno Chizuko ni idomu* [Challenging Chizuko Ueno], Keiso Shobo, 2011.)

443. Anthony Giddens, author; Kiyobumi Matsuo et al., translators, *Kokumin kokka to bōryoku* (original title: *The Nation-State and Violence*), Jiritsu Shobo, 1999.

444. Kiichi Fujiwara, *"Tadashii sensō" wa hontō ni aru no ka* (Is there really such a thing as a "just war?"), rockin'on, 2003.

445. However, many youths, including those who were irregular workers, faithfully handled their duties in the immediate aftermath of the earthquake disaster, with some losing their lives in the process. These incidents were reported as "moving stories." In other words, not because of "nationalism," but due to a noble sense of "professional ethics," I believe the possibility of Japan's youth engaging in war is conceivable.

★192. At that time, my concept of "war" involved an all-out war like World War II. However, wars in recent times revolve around local conflicts and terrorism, and it is said that the chances of an all-out-war breaking out are extremely low.

would end up surviving.

War, as originally conceived, doesn't aim to bring about genocide; rather, it's a tool of diplomacy that aims to destroy government structures while keeping as much infrastructure and human life intact as possible. Even without carrying out the large-scale aerial attacks as seen in wars of the twentieth century, there are other ways that "Japan," could be conquered, including blocking the power and water supplies and destroying communication networks.

But even if "Japan" were to disappear, what would be the problem with that, if the people living in what was once "Japan" remained happy? More than the survival of the nation, more than the history of the nation, and even more than the honor of the nation, what should be vital is how each and every person can live.[446]

If each and every one can live more happily, "Japan" should be protected, but if not, there is no need to be particular about "Japan." And that's why I don't understand the feelings of someone who panics and says, "Japan is going to end"; I just end up shrugging and saying, "So what?" As history teaches us, people—surprisingly—can survive in almost any kind of situation.

At any rate, it's hard to imagine that the Japanese economy will suddenly break down all at once tomorrow, or that Japan will be invaded by a foreign power. We still have time; though it seems inevitable that this country will go on sinking little by little, we still have enough time to contemplate the future. The "strange" and "warped" kind of happiness will still endure.

Will we continue to be particular about "Japan," or will we become the kind of people who could live anywhere in the world, or will we just go on living day-to-day without bothering to wrap our heads around complex matters?

Fortunately, there are innumerable options available to us. We also have our inheritance as a great economic superpower, as well as the lack of foresight of a nation in decline. From a historical standpoint, it's not such a bad time.

We no longer have "those days" we should be returning to, and we face problems that are stacked up before us, and we have no such thing as "hope" for the future. But we aren't that dissatisfied with our existing circumstances.

We're somewhat happy, and somewhat anxious. Such are the times we live in, and will be living through—as the happy "youth" of a nation in despair.

---

446. I'm not insisting here that Japan should be ruled by any country but Japan. If there is something we can do within the framework of "Japan," and if "Japan" remains valid for the purpose of achieving this objective, we should actively make use of "Japan." In addition, significant sacrifices are expected to occur during the transitional period of a social system, so we shouldn't hope for an easy revolution or the end of "Japan."

Supplementary Chapter

A Conversation with Takeru Satō

Takeru strolled into the agreed-upon place alone. He was dressed casually in a shirt and sarouel pants, but his fashion was still in good taste, albeit not so good that it was perfect. It was very natural.

"Takeru Satō here," he said bobbing his head.

Although I had read his interviews and heard stories about him from mutual friends, I was meeting him for the first time that day. Nevertheless, he turned out to be just as I had imagined.

He was clever and had the ability to reflect on things from a bird's-eye view, but never in an aloof, detached manner. And he would respond to whatever you asked him with deliberation, choosing his words carefully so as not to hurt anybody. I could hardly believe he was twenty-two years old.

It's no wonder, I thought, that he was such a superstar.

For example, without a doubt, the Takeru who appears on the screen, be it in *Q10* (Kyūto), *Ryomaden/The Legend of Ryoma Sakamoto*, or in the "Fits" chewing-gum commercial, is a star, but Takeru as an individual never advertises, or shows off, this aspect of himself at all. He's truly a natural and nice young man.

I had been interested in listening to his story ever since I read the interview that appeared when *Ryomaden/The Legend of Ryoma Sakamoto* was airing—the very interview I cite in this book. Takeru asserted that if he had the choice to be reborn either into the late Edo period or the present age, he would definitely choose the latter. The present age, he says, is more likely to let you savor the "happiness of taking an overnight trip to Chiba with your friends to enjoy a barbecue party."

It occurred to me then that this was symbolic of a new type of "happiness" that was spreading among young people. Instead of seeking happiness, say, in the revolution of the late Edo period, young people these days pursue happiness in daily life. In the dialogue of *Q10*—the show Takeru stars in—the closest expression describing this type of happiness is *kirakirashita mono* (glittering, shiny things). While young people can't bear to lead endlessly unchanging everyday lives, they're not lusting after anything transcendental either.

I have no intention of having the entity called "Takeru Satō" represent young people. As I have repeatedly mentioned in this book, you cannot talk about "young people" as if they were a monolithic presence. But we need to recognize the small slivers of happiness Takeru shares and cherishes with his friends, and appreciate the fact that this sense of values is spreading among young people. Such things may be petty, but I believe they're also precious seeds of hope.

I used to say every day that school was dull

Furuichi: You went to the same high school I did, although we weren't there at the same time. What kind of a high school life did you have back then? I understand that, in a magazine interview you gave once, you said that you were a high school student who didn't know what to do…

Satō: I used to say every day how bored I was with school, you know [laughs].

Furuichi: In the show Q10, the main character you played, Heita, was tormented by a sense of hopelessness until he came across Q10 [a robot played by Atsuko Maeda], right? The character was leading an ordinary existence in which he hadn't met anyone more important than himself, and in which nothing life-changing was happening.

Satō: I felt a lot of empathy for my character in *Q10*, so it was easy to play my role.

Furuichi: Wasn't there anything interesting about high school?

Satō: I don't know. I might have been having fun, actually, but at the same time, I was probably dissatisfied with how things were the same day after day. Before I knew it, I'd be mouthing the words, "I don't know why, but I'm bored." Now that I think about it, that line was as natural as breathing to me.

Furuichi: You used to dance when you were in high school, right? Didn't dancing become an outlet for venting this sense of despair you had in your everyday life?

Satō: I took up dancing in a place outside high school. It was like I'd go there for dance lessons after school, and since I'd practice until quite late, by the time I got home I would be so exhausted that I'd be asleep in school the next day.

Furuichi: Did you want to take up dancing as a future profession?

Satō: Never—not even once.

Furuichi: Why not?

Satō: Simply because my experience in dancing led me to believe that it was impossible to make it in the dance world. If there had been more money in the dance world, though, I might have wanted to dance for a living in the future.

Furuichi: So then, even while pursuing dancing, you were thinking about going the normal route of taking an entrance exam and entering a university?

Satō: Yes, that's right. But, frankly, I wasn't sure about entering a college-prep school either. Since I didn't have any particular ambition I wanted to pursue, I thought, at one time, that it would be better if I just went to a local high school I knew I could get into without studying hard.

Furuichi: High schools in Japan basically just get ranked by T-scores, so even if you get into one, you can't really map out your future. The percentage of regular high schools in Japan stands at more than 70 percent, which is an abnormally high rate compared with other countries. In Europe, the percentage of regular high schools is about 40 percent; the rest are vocational high schools.

Satō: Is that right? How interesting. In my case, I was recommended by various people, like the teacher at my *juku* (private supplementary school) and the teacher at my school, so I ended up somehow veering toward the decision of entering a prep school to go on to college.

One day the world changed

Furuichi: You were scouted on the streets of Harajuku when you were in the eleventh grade, is that right?

Satō: I got scouted and entered the world of show business. After that, once every two weeks, I would get on a train and go to Shibuya for lessons. I remember how I used to really look forward to the days when I would go to Shibuya, and because of those days, I was happy and excited every day.

Furuichi: So it was like your dull days suddenly began to *kirakira* (sparkle)?

Satō: Now that I look back, it wasn't as if it was boring every day; it was actually fun, but school itself was tedious.

Furuichi: So you were continuing to carry out your activities as an entertainer, while still thinking about taking college entrance exams. At what point did you stop thinking about going to college?

Satō: At the last minute allowed by the center exams (the National Center Test for University Admissions).

Furuichi: Were you studying for the exams until that time?

Satō: No, I wasn't, which is why I thought about going somewhere that didn't require me to take exams.

Furuichi: How about the people around you? Did they encourage you to go ahead and take the entrance exams anyway?

Satō: Some did, it was fifty-fifty.

Furuichi: Despite that, you had made up your mind about making a living as an actor, right?

Satō: Emotionally, to make a living as an actor was a major premise in my life. But I also had this hesitation that I should be going to college because I might not be able to continue being an actor throughout my life. So my true ambition, actually, was set from quite early on.

Furuichi: So you were going to a school where almost everyone goes on to enter universities, or otherwise goes on to become a *rōnin* (a student who studies again for another attempt at the entrance exams if they fail to enter the university of their choice). How did you ultimately arrive at your decision to forgo the entrance exams?

Satō: Well, I told myself I'd just go to college if I ended up not making it. So it was sort of this assurance that made it possible for me to take that final step forward.

Furuichi: In Japan, university is somewhere you go immediately after graduating high school, right? But in the United States and Europe, it's not uncommon at all to see people attending college in their later years, and people in their twenties tend to go back and forth between academia and the world of work. It's not like in Japan where people look for a job and then find employment immediately after graduation. Over in those countries, after graduating, people become interns or, after finding a job, they return to university, and in the process of doing so, they finally settle—when they're around thirty years old—on a lifetime pursuit or permanent life work. That's the pattern you often see overseas. But in the case of Japan, it's binary—it's either zero or one—particularly in the case of a profession like acting.

Satō: Yes, you're quite right. It's a kind of gamble…

Furuichi: Yes, a gamble! That's what it ends up being, right? So how did you arrive at the decision to go through with this gamble?

Satō: Ultimately it was decided from the beginning, you see; I wanted to do it from the get-go.

The world that changes every three months

Furuichi: Did you want to become an actor even before you got scouted?

Satō: Yeah, I guess so, ever since I was in junior high.

Furuichi: Was there anything that triggered that ambition in you?

Satō: When I watched those "making-of" documentaries of movies or programs that show deleted scenes, I was shocked to see how fabricated all of it really was. I was like, "Really? Are you serious?" It was so amazing to realize that the filmmakers were shooting dialogue, cut by cut, before they could create a world that everyone gets drawn into so powerfully. This sense of amazed wonder gradually turned into admiration and longing.

Furuichi: And now you, Satō-san, have fulfilled this longing. Was the world of your dreams as you imagined it to be?

Satō: You know, it's—how should I put it—all down to habit…

Furuichi: Habit?

Satō: Frankly, even though I wanted to become an actor, I personally never thought I could act in a dramatic production. I know that sounds strange. But once I got scouted and began to take lessons and act in productions—though of course I didn't perform well—I had so much fun. I looked forward to the lessons, and with steady practice, my shyness disappeared completely. And then, before I knew it, I'd forgotten about that fear I had, of thinking that I was incapable of acting. So I came to believe that it all comes down to habit, or practice—to getting accustomed to something. You can get accustomed to anything if you work toward it gradually, bit by bit.

Furuichi: So it's a matter of habit or practice, but also growth, right? But are there times when your occupation as an actor becomes so routine in the course of your everyday life that you end up getting bored in spite of this?

Satō: What I really like about the acting profession is the fact that your workplace changes once every three months. After the shooting for a film or TV show is over, the scene totally changes. All the people working with you change, and the role you play also changes. Truth be told, in the course of the three months when we're on the same location, there are times during the latter half of that period when I get too used to the surroundings and get a little bored as a result.

Furuichi: Just within three months, huh? Do you ever feel like staying in one place?

Satō: No, I don't.

Furuichi: Generally speaking, it's not rare to see people staying in the same company for ten, twenty years; at the very least, people tend to remain for two to three years. Even if you get transferred, it still doesn't happen every three months.

Satō: It struck me that I could never handle a normal job… And that's why I'm seriously amazed by office workers—those salarymen. My profession has irregular holidays, which is why weekends are meaningless in my line of work; there are times when I can hardly get any sleep, and I have to work without a single day off for a period of one or two months, but at other times, bam, I get an entire month off all at once. But office workers, apart from their summer vacations and paid vacations, they work from Mondays through Fridays.

Furuichi: This spring is exactly the time when your classmates in high school would become newly hired employees.

Satō: A friend of mine told me that he was going to travel overseas on a graduation trip for around two weeks. I said, "Wow! That's great. Where did you get the money from?" He answered, "Once I find a job, I won't be able to do anything like this until I hit retirement age, so I tried hard." When you work for a company, until you reach retirement age—which is around sixty years old—you can't take long vacations. I was surprised to find this out.

Furuichi: Yeah, that's something, isn't it? That's the price you pay for stability, I suppose. In other words, you get stability in your life if you become a proper regular employee of a corporation, but while you're young, you work for tremendously low pay, with only a few days off.

Satō: I was like, Wow! That's amazing. In my line of work, people work like crazy for stretches of time, but we also get days off for stretches of time. And so that's why I have a lot of respect for office workers.

Furuichi: In Japan, around 1960, society first started to see college graduates finding lifetime employment at companies. Students of that time were troubled by the fact they could calculate all the money they would earn up to their retirement bonuses; they said it was even painful to see all that. Everything worked in accordance with a seniority system, so the rest of your entire life was transparent.

Satō: Transparent! That's painful, for sure.

The vista from the place where dreams came true

Furuichi: In this day and age—although, of course, some can still clearly see what lies ahead—the future is getting fuzzier and fuzzier. If you look on the bright side of this, you can say there's joy in not knowing what lies ahead, but the flip side is that this fear of uncertainty is always looming, right? For instance, you, Satō-san, in the role of Morioka, the character in the film, *MW dai-0-shō: Akuma no gēmu* (MW [mu'u] chapter zero: The devil's game) are suddenly fired from the factory you've been working in and end up getting lost on the roadside.

Satō: Uh-huh, that's right.

Furuichi: Apart from actors like you, who have achieved the level of success you have, the occupation of acting is, for most actors, in essence a worrisome profession where the future is extremely uncertain, right? So when you made up your mind about not going to college, were you more excited, or were you more anxious?

Satō: Hmm, I have to say I was more excited. Of course I was also anxious, as I am even to this day, but if you asked me which emotion was bigger, I'd have to say the excitement was bigger by far.

Furuichi: What do you think about office workers who handle ordinary tasks? Are there any words you can convey to them, as a message?

Satō: I'd say they're admirable.

Furuichi: That they may be, but there are people who aren't suited to such a lifestyle.

Satō: I have this friend who works and complains about it all the time. But I caught a brief glimpse of some unfulfilled ambition inside this person, so I handed them Ayumu Takahashi's book, *Jinsei no chizu* (Life map), and told them to read it.

Furuichi: It's the kind of book that makes you want to quit your day job of being an office worker, a salaryman [laughs]. You, Satō-san, are someone who was able to make it in an occupation many people dream about. In effect, you're someone who made his dream come true. But not everyone can do that; that is, make their dreams come true.

Satō: Oh yeah, that would be difficult. What can you say to people like that?

Furuicihi: Yes, well, what's difficult from your standpoint is that you're someone who made his dream come true, and yet that doesn't mean everyone can make their dreams come true.

Satō: It's incredibly difficult. But all kinds of people keep saying, "Dreams can absolutely come true." I think that's a really wonderful thing. But it's not always the case, is it? Still, various kinds of people say dreams absolutely do come true, and actually, I suppose I'm in a position where I should be telling people that—but I can't do that easily.

Furuichi: Even on your blog, you've been careful with your word choices in your writing, haven't you? You don't offer any easy encouragement.

Satō: I hesitate a great deal about that, but there are people who hold on and persevere because of others who say dreams can absolutely come true, right? And that's why I think it's truly a wonderful thing if people can hang in there and try to do their best just by being told, "Your dream can absolutely come true," regardless of whether it's true or not. Still, I, for one, can't say things like that. . .

Furuichi: Satō-san, you're a good person.

Satō: Ah, ha, ha. Yes, I'm a good person [laughs].

Furuichi: I'm a good person, too [laughs], but I can't say, "Don't give up on your dreams." While such words might inspire for an instant, they may also lead some to suffer from the gap between dream and reality in their lives.

Satō: Exactly! That's why I have second thoughts about saying things like that. You and I, we're probably on the side of thinking like that. But there are those cool guys out there, stuff like that doesn't matter to them, and so they say without hesitation, "You go, dude!"

Furuichi: Surely, the world needs people like that too.

Satō: Yes. I admire people like that, too, but I personally can't be like them.

The real nature of happy youths

Furuichi: Do you have friends who have part-time jobs?

Satō: Yes, I do, like people who are still freelancing in their thirties and leading unstable lives, working part-time. But they seem somehow happy whenever I get together with them for fun.

Furuichi: One of this book's themes was that the happiness and unhappiness of modern times is being able to lead decently happy and pleasant lives without having to spend that much money.

Satō: But you know, last time, I got together with a friend from my dancing days. She's the same age as me and currently works as a hairdresser. It was only recently, though, that she began to cut hair professionally, once she finished her training period. When I asked her, "What do you want to be in the future?" she told me, "I want to become someone who's capable of making money." So, even though I myself may tend to overlook such things, I can say that even in our generation, when I see people living alone and working every day…

Furuichi: I see, so you're saying that even youngsters have the desire to chase after money or material wealth.

Satō: Yes, that's right. I didn't notice it that much while I was hanging out with the people I usually socialize with, but when I meet my former junior high and high school classmates, I get the impression that a lot of them want to become capable of earning terrific amounts of money before anything else.

Furuichi: Happiness is a state of mind that arises when a certain level of economic affluence is achieved, and unless people meet that level, they can't readily feel they're happy. . .

Satō: I agree.

Furuichi: I quoted this in the book, but roughly 70 percent of twenty-somethings today say they're satisfied with life. Although at first glance we appear to be living in unhappy times, 70 percent of youths nonetheless responded that they were "satisfied with life." I doubt the wisdom of a twenty-something to be asking another twenty-something, but, tell me, what do you think about this figure?

Satō: I think young people today would answer that they're "satisfied." But while saying so, they're also griping every day, dissatisfied with one thing or another.

Furuichi: You've got a good point there.

Satō: I have all sorts of things I want, too, but if you ask me whether I'm satisfied, my answer would be yes, I am.

Furuichi: If I asked whether you have any worries, what would your answer be?

Satō: My answer would be, yes I do.

Furuichi: So, by that you mean, you're in a situation where you do have worries, but you're still satisfied.

Satō: Yes, that's right. But another thing I can say about those people who say they're satisfied is that I believe they're surrounded by others who are in a similar state of mind. Perhaps if someone clearly richer than themselves happened to be living very nearby, they would be answering that they're not satisfied.

Furuichi: Yes, even if they had answered that they were satisfied, they certainly might not actually be a hundred percent satisfied. I probably shouldn't be saying this after finishing this book, but perhaps my interpretation of the words "happiness" and "satisfaction" was too broad.

On friends and solitude

Furuichi: You were saying that in your job everything changes once every three months, but is there some kind of anchor in your life? Some unchanging base you can turn to as you live through the instability of your days?

Satō: What first comes to mind right now is friends.

Furuichi: When you say friends, are many of them actors like you, as one might expect?

Satō: Some of them are. Some are singers, ordinary office workers, or comedians.

Furuichi: Are these friends of yours people you can confide in about anything?

Satō: Well, I might be changing the subject slightly here, but frankly, I came to the realization recently that I am, in a sense, very lonely. I have a lot of friends, and I have a lot of fun as well, but in a certain sense I'm absolutely lonely, and I'm beginning to think that the number of people who completely understand me is, in fact, extremely small.

Furuichi: So what you're saying is that you have friends or intimates who you can talk to or confide in, but no one who understands you perfectly?

Satō: I feel like I hardly ever had anyone who understood me, even looking back on my junior high and high school days. Back then, I didn't really care about anything, but when I turned out to be that way, it occurred to me that I was all alone.

I was having fun; a lot of fun, in fact. But then again, in retrospect, I see now that there was nobody, really. Still, it's not necessarily true that someone who understands you is someone who's close to you, so in the end, I do feel that as long as you're having fun, then that's all that matters in the end.

Furuichi: Do you have someone who understands you now?

Satō: Yes. I met someone like that after I started this work. But a complete understanding is impossible, with anybody, don't you think?

Furuichi: Uh huh. Both sides might be convinced that there is a mutual understanding of each other, but that kind of thinking itself might just be a one-sided belief or prejudice. Even if both of you can share the present together, you can't both share the future together.

Satō: That's why I sort of thought that everyone, in a sense, is on their own, that we're all lonely throughout our lifetime.

Furuichi: When you're highly sensitive, doesn't life become uncomfortable? For example, if you were too dull to be aware that you're lonely, you might be far happier. But the moment you realize you're lonely, the shape and form of the world might, wham, suddenly change completely.

Satō: Right. But it's not just me that's lonely—it's you and him and her and everyone else; I think there's that understanding too, that I'm not the only one who's lonely.

Furuichi: But usually, most people will turn a deaf ear to that kind of talk.

Satō: Yeah, they probably don't get it. I don't think they understand.

Furuichi: Maybe I don't either. While I'm sitting here with an understanding look on my face, in reality, no one can tell exactly to what extent I've truly understood, right?

You'd end up dead if you were born in the late Edo period

Furuichi: When I read your interview about *Ryomaden/The Legend of Ryoma Sakamoto*, I liked what you said about your attitude towards happiness—that it was something to be found in daily life. I thought this was very natural; it struck a chord in me.

Satō: I know, right? That's absolutely true, don't you think? [Laughs]

Furuichi: I agree. But among the people who watched *Ryomaden/The Legend of Ryoma Sakamoto*, I believe some fantasized about being born in the late Edo period and taking part in political intrigues and plots like Ryōma did, or about just living in turbulent and fiery times.

Satō: You think? Because they'd just end up dead.

Furuichi: Ha, ha, that's certainly true. Well, the late Edo period might be an extreme case, but I believe there are people who would have liked to have been born in, say, the period of high economic growth shown in *Ōru'ueizu: San-chōme no yūhi* (ALWAYS: Sunset on third street). Did you think that the characters in "ALWAYS" looked happy? Would you want to be born in that time?

Satō: No, not at all.

Furuichi: Why not?

Satō: I don't know, but probably because I'm happy in the present. I'd be lying if I said I was completely satisfied now, but I'm happy living in this present time. Perhaps people longing for the world of the late Edo period or the world of "ALWAYS" don't see the present time as being that much of a happy time for them. If that's the case, those other times would naturally seem better.

Furuichi: That's true. I feel like it's the ones who aren't satisfied with their lives who tend to say big things like, "I want to change the country." People like that bother me. I mean, where do they get the nerve to talk about the entire country when they can't even get along with a single person in their immediate surroundings, when they can't even manage a single personal relationship?

Satō: Yes, yes.

Furuichi: You know there's this song by Mr. Children called "HERO"? Well, the protagonist in the song values the intimate ties of love over saving the lives of everyone around the world. The running theme is protecting a "small world" where the ones you love are found, rather than the whole wide-open world. Do you appreciate this song, too, Satō-san? Do you sympathize with its sentiments?

Satō: Yes, well, it's absolutely true, isn't it? But if there really was someone who could truly value the world over close personal relationships, I'd have huge respect for him or her. I don't know if such a person exists, but most likely they don't, don't you think?

Furuichi: It's impossible, right?

Satō: I'd be surprised. It would be amazing.

Will you follow an illusion?

Furuichi: What would you do if war broke out?

Satō: [Pauses to think for a while] I believe I'd go to some place that was as unrelated to the war as possible.

Furuichi: You mean like you'd escape together with someone important to you?

Satō: Yes, probably.

Furuichi: I'd also be thinking about running away promptly if war broke out. But actually, that kind of attitude appears to be rare, when seen from an international perspective. Compared to other countries, the percentage of people in Japan who say they'd fight for their country if war occurred is extremely low.

Satō: Oh.

Furuichi: Among those between the ages of fifteen and twenty-nine, it's 7.7 percent. I personally think that's a very positive thing. For example, even if you might not end up becoming a legendary hero, if you ended up dying, you'd get absolutely nothing out it. In that case, I believe you should first and foremost think about protecting yourself and those around you who you cherish. But there are people who say that such an attitude is "outrageous."

Satō: Yeah, I bet. It sure feels like there would be folks like that. Incidentally, I happen to be acting in a film that's currently being shot called *Saigo no kizuna* (The final bond), and this story is indeed about war. I play the role of a junior high student who gets roped into battle as a member of the Tekketsu Kinnōtai, a military unit of child soldiers. It's set in a time when everyone thought that it was natural and "good" to throw away your life for Japan.

Furuichi: Are you uncomfortable with that sense of values?

Satō: It's complicated. And by that I mean that, even though we ourselves in this day and age can't understand those values, at the time that way of thinking was commonplace for everybody, right? Today everyone thinks war is absolutely useless, because we were all taught growing up that "war is no good," but if I was living at that time, since the prevailing wisdom back then considered dying for your country to be a good thing, I might have thought that it was good thing too.

Furuichi: That's interesting. For instance, we all think that the earth is round, don't we? But most people haven't gone to the trouble of verifying this claim for themselves; they're just convinced the earth is round. Seeing that you're adept at physics, though, maybe you might be able to verify.

Satō: Conventional wisdom or common sense varies by the country and the time period, doesn't it? For instance, in China it's considered a good thing to drink hot water as soon as you step out of the bath. As a Japanese, you would think, what?

Furuichi: Many aspects of the world are founded on delusions and illusions—that is to say, claims you personally haven't verified for yourself. As I wrote in this book, I believe that "Japan" and the "Japanese people" are also a kind of illusion.

In between the World Cup and war

Furuichi: Satō-san, your sense of values is always relative, isn't it? By that I mean you don't thoughtlessly judge others or the past on the basis of your values or the values of modern times. That's extremely wise.

Satō: No, no, but you see, I have to play the roles of all kinds of people from all sorts of time periods, so…

Furuichi: Right, right. That's what acting is all about, isn't it? After all, you become another person on the assumption that you get tainted by the sense of values of one particular time or another.

Satō: Yes, that's correct. But ultimately you really can't be certain of the past. I keep wondering about all kinds of things, like did those guys back then really think it was a good thing, or were they thinking that they really didn't want to go to war, you know? But such things are lost to us now; we can never know anymore.

Furuichi: By the way, the World Cup was held last year, right? Did you get all excited about that?

Satō: Oh yeah, I was thrilled. Until then, I wasn't in the habit of watching soccer matches, but the game I happened to be watching in a sports bar while I was drinking with my friends was the one where Honda clinched the victory for Japan with his free kick. I just went straight to Center Gai in Shibuya after that.

Furuichi: And did you live it up with everyone there, taking part in the celebrations?

Satō: Well, I didn't plan on it in the beginning, but the atmosphere was so wild and excited that even strangers were high-fiving each other. Since my friends and I were drunk ourselves, we cut across Shibuya, high-fiving along the way, too.

Furuichi: Ha, ha. Sounds like you had a lot of fun.

Satō: Yeah, it got really exciting. We had a good time.

Furuichi: This might be an odd question to ask, but I was wondering if the attitude of supporting Japan in the World Cup is all that different from the fanaticism you see during wartime? What do you think? As an act of supporting Japan, the two are the same, right?

Satō: Hmmm. When you watch the Olympics, you end up cheering for Japan. Certainly, as an act of supporting Japan, there's no difference, I suppose…But if it came to war, I couldn't support Japan, so I think it's different.

Furuich: I see.

Satō: Actually, I never thought about that.

Furuichi: That must be because in your mind the two forms of support must be so different that it never occurred to you. Oftentimes, the enthusiasm for the World Cup and the fanaticism for war are lumped together as signs of "patriotism."

Satō: Well, I haven't experienced war, so I don't know.

Furuichi: That's true. But was it fun to experience the sensation of being in the middle of that wild scene of excitement in Shibuya, high-fiving strangers?

Satō: It was a culture shock. Watching the game at the sports bar was really fun, but over at the Center Gai, where the crowd was going wild, I was more jolted by surprise than having fun, thinking to myself, "Oh, so this is what it all leads to in the end."

Furuichi: I went to Shibuya not because of the soccer match, but because I wanted to observe the people getting excited over the game. It was incredible! Even at the last game, which the Japan team lost, there were spirited exchanges of "*Otsukare!*" (Good job!) along with energetic high-fives before everyone went home. I thought then how peaceful Japan was.

Satō: Yes, that's true. Maybe everyone just wants to tag some kind of reason, some justification, to live it up, you know. But maybe I don't properly understand the true feelings of people who cheer in earnest.

Furuichi: So, in your case, you weren't cheering in earnest?

Satō: I suppose I was enthralled by how hard the players were trying, how much heart and soul they were putting into the game.

Furuichi: Still, the team you were rooting for was the Japan team, right?

Satō: Yeah, but I wonder why we cheer for Japan?

Furuichi: Yeah, frankly, it should be all right to root for Denmark, too.

Satō: It's all probably just an illusion.

Furuichi: The fact that we end up supporting Japan in soccer might be a sign that the illusion is still alive to some extent.

On Japan going forward

Furuichi: Are you interested in politics in general?

Satō: Umm, that's difficult to say. As far as I'm concerned, there's this sense that since I'm satisfied with my present life, slight developments in Japanese politics don't matter much. Regardless of whether the consumption tax rate rises, or who becomes the prime minister, I feel I can probably go on living happily. And that's why, truth be told, I can't bring myself to be that interested in politics.

Furuichi: Demographically speaking, the current population of Japan is made up of a small number of younger people and a large number of the elderly. And since the elderly tend to go to the polls and vote, more and more pro-elderly policies keep getting passed. Even for social security costs, according to a certain estimate, compared with the present-day generation of grandfathers and grandmothers, the generation of their grandchildren is apparently poised to be around a hundred million yen worse off.

Satō: Oh.

Furuichi: Exactly! That kind of talk can only make you say, "Oh," right? Do you think that kind of a reaction reflects an attitude of complacency, a feeling that everything's all right as long as you're having fun?

Satō: Rather than feeling that it's all okay as long as you're having fun now, there's this sense that you can't be certain about what lies ahead in life, you know. For example, even ten years from now, I think I'll be carrying on being an actor. But I can't say what that future will exactly be like, down to the detail of other things that happen in life, apart from my acting career.

Furuichi: I'm sure you couldn't have imagined five years ago the shape you find yourself in today, right?

Satō: Yes, that's right. And that's why, even with politics, I can't grasp the reality of it, at least for now. Maybe as we keep growing into adulthood, the day will come when politics will turn out to be a revelation to us, you know, like, "Oh, so that's what it's all about!"

Furuichi: Yes, though social security costs going forward will continue to rise because of the dwindling birthrate and aging population, the active, working generation will continue getting smaller in number. The generation of consumers will continue to steadily disappear. And that's why, when you think about twenty, thirty years into the future. . .

Satō: We're in trouble, aren't we?

Furuichi: Uh-huh, it's all quite chancy.

Satō: But the thing about people is that without failure, we never change, right? And that's why probably there will be no change until everybody becomes aware of the danger.

Furuichi: I'm of the same opinion. No matter how much TV and other media shout out about things happening in far-flung places of the world, unless change happens in the more immediate world of our own surroundings, we don't take action that readily.

Satō: Yes, we don't change. But still, even we young people, if we go on living thoughtlessly, anything can happen to us someday, right?

Furuichi: When something dire does happen, you'll be able to clearly tell those who have been prepared apart from those who haven't. But this kind of talk isn't something that will be immediately relevant starting tomorrow. And so there's no sense of impending crisis.

Satō: Yes, that's right. There's no guarantee that anything we might do now will turn out to be useful. And that's why it's difficult, right?

Furuichi: Yes, yes. There's no guarantee—in fact, doing something might prove to be a disadvantage to you personally. Instead of making an effort to change society, there are plenty of pleasant and fun things to do. Which is why I feel the situation is hopeless already. But frankly I shouldn't be saying things like that, since, as a researcher, I should be thinking about solutions [laughs].

Satō: But you can't help feeling hopeless.

Furuichi: That's why I think we're left with no option but to keep doing the obvious things we have been doing all this time, like valuing the friends around you. As you may recall, it was said in *Q10*, "As long as we can go on eating and avoid the worst-case scenarios, we'll be A-OK!" Now I think that this is what world peace is about.

Satō: That's certainly true.

Furuichi: Of course, the small slivers of happiness, the happiness you can get from being in the company of a tight-knit group of people, only becomes possible with various infrastructural support, so you never know what might happen going forward. However, the fact that people like you, Satō-san, are on the rise—that is, people who treasure the happiness you can get from the "small world" of everyday living, instead of from the "big world"—gives me hope. It's been such a pleasure to hear all kinds of stories today.

Satō: The pleasure is mine too. I usually don't get to talk about these things, so I had fun. Thank you. Please do take care of Japan [laughs].

Furuichi: Ha, ha. I can't do anything about Japan that easily, but I'd like to improve the comfortingly familiar world around me, even if only for just a little bit.

(Recorded on June 19, 2011)

Afterword

I'm not a terribly imaginative human being, though I have enough imagination to know the limits of my own imagination. For example, even though I have an informational grasp of lives lost in endless conflicts taking place in distant lands, of how they die while suffering; and child soldiers who, after receiving military training, go on to become disposable military forces at battlefronts, I am not taking any action to counter such realities.

Whenever I watch a documentary film depicting the poverty and violence in Africa, my heart aches like everyone else's. There are also times, when I look at the section of an official gazette running obituaries of people who died while traveling, I fall into an unspeakable despair imagining their lives from the clues their personal effects betray. But a little while later, I forget about it, and get back to my normal life as if nothing had happened.

Frankly, I couldn't care less about people I haven't met, objects I haven't seen, or places I've never been to.

The scope of the imagination of any person can only extend, at the most, to imaginings of "himself" and "the people and things around himself."

But the "himself" I'm referring to here is not just the "me" writing this afterword while listening to '90s J-pop in an air-conditioned room, or the me whose only concerns are getting rid of the reddish tinge of his face and losing the two kilograms he's gained.

In the world, unbeknownst to everybody, there must be innumerable switches, like the ones on railways, set up everywhere, causing the paths of our lives to fork in divergent ways; random, casual events serving to trigger these switches. And in this world, these switches, once they're switched, are contrived to be irreversible, making any attempt to simply start over again no easy task.

Whatever life decisions I have made, though no choice would ever have made me Takeru Satō (obviously), the possibility exists, more often than not, of me not being here.

My life to date is just twenty-six years long, but when I look back on it, I can see many crossroads: winning the prize, by chance, in a poetry contest when I was in high school; getting admitted into Keio SFC (Keio University Shonan Fujisawa Campus) via an entrance exam in which an interview played an important part (the AO *nyūshi* [Admissions office system] on the strength of that prize; meeting the friend at SFC who I continue to work with to this day; failing the preliminary exam to get into a CG modeling class and therefore taking the sociology class that happened to be available in the same time slot; traveling to Norway for a year on the university's overseas student-exchange program; drawing on my experience of studying in Norway to write my graduation thesis on the Northern European child care policy; the fact that there were people recommending I attend The University of Tokyo's graduate school; having, for some reason, made a trip around the world on the Peace Boat; having been lucky enough to have people interested in my research projects.

If any of these events had not occurred, I don't think "I" would be here.

Let me now ruminate on the "me" who wouldn't be here. Having run through a number of counterfactual assumptions, I have no way of knowing what the "me" who wouldn't be here would be doing, but I do have sympathy for the "me" who has changed my life by having acted slightly differently.

If he is in a happier place than I'm in now, I'm envious; but if he's not, I feel guilty.

This guilty conscience is something I feel for the "me" who exists in another world, and at the same time, for "somebody" in this world as well. In other words, this is because there probably is somebody (or more than one somebody) who has undertaken in this world the role I would have undertaken in a different world.

This can be paraphrased more directly as a responsibility I feel toward the people I have brought down—the people at whose expense I have advanced. Unlike first-rate entertainers or artists, I haven't fought successfully through a stringent selection process, but still, I can't deny that in universities there are those who pass and those who fail to get admitted, and perhaps there's a chair I have sat down on without realizing that it was meant for someone else.

For somebody unknown to me, I feel no responsibility, sympathy, or envy. It would even be arrogant of me if I did. However, for people whom the scope of my imagination allows me to identify as "myself" or "somebody" who could have been me, I will feel responsibility, sympathy, and envy: responsibility for somebody I have brought down, sympathy for the me who was unable to be here, and envy toward the me who might have been in a more wonderful place than here. My interest in young people probably lies in these considerations.

This book has meditated on my contemporaries, and on the country we find ourselves living in. This is not particularly out of any sense of enlightening society as a whole, nor is it out of any public desire to improve the nation, even for just a little bit. It was just out of merely wanting to gain some decent appreciation about "myself" and about "the people around me."

Of course, I couldn't be happier if this book, in the end, proves to be helpful to people other than "myself" and "the people around me." In fact, I would be extremely glad. However, at that point, it will no longer be "my" problem. But if there's anything I can say beyond that, it would be this: Use this book, people, as a launchpad to branch out and explore something new. I think you'll have a good time.

Within the materials and subject matter of this book, not a single thing in there is "special." For example, with regard to the conceited remark made by adults in chapter 2, namely that the youths nowadays are introverted, I have investigated and verified from a number of angles, but the statistical data I used at every turn was mostly drawn from the public opinion surveys carried out by the government, which are readily available on the Internet. The interviews, too, have all been stories I heard from people I simply ran into on the streets.

One of the great things about research in the field of humanities is that you don't necessarily have to make use of any "special" research apparatus or materials. If you read books, ask people to tell their stories, and search for statistics on the Internet, and then go on to arrange and put together all the collected data, you will end up with a body of "research."

Furthermore, "research" is fun. Drawing on data found anywhere, you can cast doubt on anything considered to be "common knowledge" or "common sense"; and just by reading several books, sometimes the world as you know it could be turned upside down.

The world we live in is so immense and complex that nobody can grasp the big picture. But if there is a silver lining, it's that we have the ability through "research" to keep clarifying, to keep shedding light on this picture, even if only incrementally. Shedding light on my world—the world of "myself" and "the people around me"—is a pleasure. And nothing would make me happier than to share this pleasure with more people.

Shouted cries fall short of reaching another world. But there are times when they resonate with each other, I believe.

Afterword to the English Edition

More than five years have passed since the publication of the first edition of this book. The prevailing mood in Japan at the time was a mixture of hope and despair, in the wake of the Great East Japan Earthquake and the accident at the Fukushima Daiichi Nuclear Power Station on March 11, 2011.

"This country may be finished now." —"No, Japan has experienced despair, and that's exactly why hope will arise." Adults were seriously having thoughts they'd ordinarily be ashamed of having. This book, too, ended up echoing the singular atmosphere of that time.

Enter 2017. Though the frequency has declined, aftershocks of the Great East Japan Earthquake still occur intermittently in Japan. We are told that the decommissioning of the Fukushima Daiichi Nuclear Power Station will not be completed for several decades at the earliest. It has not been decided how the decommissioning and compensation expenses, which are estimated to exceed 20 trillion yen, will be paid, and by whom. In other words, the issues arising from the Great East Japan Earthquake and nuclear plant accident have not been resolved at all.

However, I believe the mood in Japan has changed drastically in these five years. News coverage of the Great East Japan Earthquake and nuclear power has fallen off, as the mass media have been in a total frenzy about the Tokyo Olympics scheduled for 2020.

There are those who believe that the Tokyo Olympics are the last hope remaining in Japan. The country did see a successful Olympic precedent in the 1964 summer games, which took place during the period of high economic growth. It was a miraculous Olympic event that saw Japan, a nation once ruined by the defeat of war, return to the international limelight and become unified. People who have high expectations for the 2020 Olympics are praying for a revival of the 1964 Olympics and the times that accompanied them.

Back in 2013, when it was officially decided that the event would be held in Tokyo, there was much news welcoming this development. However, as it became clear that hosting the Olympics would entail a far greater cost than was originally assumed, cynicism began to spread. In addition, there was mounting mistrust due to the fact that important decisions concerning the Olympics would be made by a group of elders behind closed doors.

The Great East Japan Earthquake, a symbol of despair; and the Tokyo Olympics, a symbol of hope, share a common attribute: the fact that, in both cases, the voices of young people, who are supposed to be the persons concerned, have not been readily reflected. Young people and children are the ones who are going to live in Japan long after the earthquake disaster; and many of the athletes playing an active part in the Tokyo Olympics are likely people of the younger generation themselves. However, despite taking great interest in "young people," Japan has failed to positively listen to their voices.

The absence of young people from political and society-related decision-making isn't limited to the earthquake disaster and the Olympics. While the government finally lowered the age of voting eligibility from twenty to eighteen in 2016, candidates for office in the House of Representatives must be at least twenty-five; to run for office in the House of Councilors and prefectural governments, the minimum age remains thirty.

Of course, this reflects the fact that the "happy youth" themselves haven't felt the need to have their voices heard. The analysis made by this book in 2011 apparently remains valid to this day.

However, in the intervening years, there have been some outstanding exceptions, too. As I wrote in the postscript to chapter 4 of this book, in 2015 the SEALDs youth political movement was attracting significant attention.

In addition, in 2016, a blog post titled *Hoikuen ochita Nihon shine* (Couldn't get into daycare, go and die Japan) lit up the Internet. The post is the account of an anonymous woman who sought to work after pregnancy, but wasn't able to because her child hadn't won the daycare lottery. The author was enraged by the fact that an extreme shortage of daycare facilities and preschools continues to persist in urban areas, even when the government has been promising to realize a society where women shine, and to adopt measures to counter the problem of the declining birthrate. This blog post was also taken up in the Diet, and won the *Ryūkōgo taishō* (annual "buzzword" award) as well.

Will such instances continue to be such "exceptions" from now on, as well? Or will it turn out that Japanese youths will go on to carry out social movements so actively that they can no longer be called "exceptions"?

Those who have read this book will likely realize that this is a false dichotomy. In Japan, there are already many social entrepreneurs continuing a quiet social revolution. Instead of carrying out aggressive demonstrations in which Molotov cocktails are hurled at the Diet, they repeatedly engage in constructive talks with the national and local governments.

So it's not only people who find themselves in unfortunate, miserable circumstances who are raising their voices. Riots aren't the only means of instigating a social revolution. There's also the "Happy Youth" way of changing society.

However, no matter how active a role young people play, if you think Japan will turn into a "land of hope," think again. What can be said with certainty about the future of Japan is that hosting the Olympics again will not bring about another miraculous period of economic growth. Japan has been postponing implementation of full-scale countermeasures to combat the problem of the suddenly dwindling birthrate and an aging population. Even as social-security costs keep rising, social-security benefits for the active, working generation, such as the provision of daycare facilities, remain poor.

Despite this situation, in contrast to the groundswell of support for the Olympics, measures to counter the problem of the declining birthrate have not been recognized as a full-scale policy issue at all. Here's what a certain honest politician said in my interview with him:

> No matter how large the population of children becomes, they won't be eligible to vote for another twenty years or so. How many politicians do you think there are in this country who would seriously think about things that will happen twenty years from now? Ultimately, many politicians are people who can only think about the next election; and besides, young people don't always vote. And that's why politicians inevitably turn to the elderly who do show up at elections. In addition, while I believe the declining birthrate is a huge problem for the nation, its impact won't be felt immediately in any way.

Even as the number of children is declining, the number of elderly Japanese is rising. In particular, the number of patients suffering from dementia is estimated to reach 7 million by 2025. Lately, serious traffic accidents caused by elderly drivers have been occurring one after another, giving the people of Japan a look at what it will be like to be in the world's first "super-aged society."

However, the aging of society is not a problem that is unique to Japan; furthermore, it isn't the only problem the world has. Poverty, conflicts, infectious diseases, religious clashes, the threat of terrorism, gender discrimination, deterioration of the environment … I could go on and on, much to the dismay of the translator and publisher.

Fortunately for sociologists—and unfortunately for many people—there is a mountainous heap of reasons for despair in the world. For sociologists, there has been no interesting time more worthy of observing.

On the other hand, the world is filled with the seeds of hope, too. In particular, certain scientists and IT entrepreneurs are revealing a future we can be optimistic about, in which artificial intelligence takes the place of human labor; in which the causes of aging are discovered and pinpointed, dramatically extending healthy life expectancy; in which the aero-space industry blossoms, paving the way to humanity's successive waves of emigration to Mars. (It may just be my imagination, but it feels like these bright images of the future haven't been updated for half a century.)

Well, that should be enough of wondering about the future, a time rife with uncertainty. At any rate, one of these days the analysis in this book will lose its currency. From the day it is written, it is the fate of every book to begin aging. As an author, I can't help looking forward to what discoveries future readers of this book will make when it no longer has value as an analysis of its period. I wonder what the societies of these readers will be like; what "despairs," what "hopes" will they be colored with?

Acknowledgments

Though writing a book is solitary work, it is also the fruit of collaboration with numerous people. This book is jam-packed with new ideas gained from exchanging views with various people, as well as getting weary sighs from others.

Throughout the book, I believe I have made the most of my interview with Mr. Eiji Oguma (forty-nine years old, Tokyo), which took place at The University of Tokyo's Komaba festival in 2010. Most of my knowledge of sociology comes from what I learned in his classes in my undergraduate years. I am also grateful to Mr. Nobuo Kondō (twenty-four years old, Osaka) and everyone at The University of Tokyo Tachibana Takashi Seminars for organizing the interview. Without the great opportunity they offered me, I would have never mustered the courage to have a dialogue with Mr. Oguma. I am also very grateful to my advisor, Mr. Kaku Sechiyama (forty-eight years old, Nara) for his wide-ranging advice and unmitigated support. I would also like to acknowledge Ms. Yuki Honda (forty-six years old, Tokushima), who, despite not being my regular advisor, was gracious enough to always offer her guidance. She's truly a "mother bear" to me. Ms. Chizuko Ueno (sixty-three years old, Toyama) graciously took some time off from her extremely busy schedule to read the proofs and offer an immensely kind blurb. It was so enthusiastic, in fact, it made my heart pound.

Ms. Manami Oda (twenty-seven years old, Hyogo) tirelessly accompanied me on field expeditions. I was always encouraged and surprised by how boldly she approached interviewees to ask for their stories, no matter what kind of person they happened to be. Mr. Tōru Hasegawa (twenty-six years old, Aichi) also accompanied me on various field expeditions, even though he probably had absolutely no interest in doing so.

Mr. Takaaki Niji (twenty-three years old, Tokushima) has been kindly serving, for a long time now, as a sounding board for my unfocused ramblings. In fact, he may have been the first person I talked to about how surprisingly happy young people were. I am also indebted to Mr. Kazushi Matsumura (twenty-three years old, Tokyo), who's always teaching me bits and pieces of sociology. I don't know of anyone who is more in love with this subject than he is.

Furthermore, I am indebted to Ms. Akiko Nakazawa (forty-one years old, Tokyo) for taking the time to read the book from its rough-draft stage and to offer comments.

Thanks to her, I have the feeling that the draft has turned into something of a "good book." I also received thoughtful feedback on the rough draft from Mr. Sōichirō Maruo (twenty-one years old, Oita)—I can't believe he's five years younger than I am.

I am grateful to Mr. Takeru Satō (twenty-two years old, Saitama), who agreed to be interviewed at a time when he was extremely busy; he struck me as a very natural, open-minded, and clever person. I am also hugely indebted to Mr. Noriyoshi Murakami (thirty years old, Aichi) for magically making the interview happen.

Of course, my gratitude also extends to Mr. Ryūtarō Matsushima (twenty-eight years old, Chiba) and Mr. Ken'ichi Aoki (forty years old, Hyogo), who have allowed me, as always, to pursue my interests as freely as possible.

Above all, I owe a huge debt of gratitude to my editor, Mr. Takeo Inoue (forty years old, Hiroshima), without whom, I feel, this book would never have come to pass. Thanks to his unfailing counsel, I never felt alone while writing it.

Acknowledgments for the English Edition

Japan is a translation powerhouse, where books from all over the world are translated into Japanese every day. In particular, books that have become topical in the English-speaking world can be read in Japanese with hardly any time lag. The reverse, however, is extremely difficult. Opportunities for Japanese books to get translated into English are in short supply; though Chinese and Korean editions of this book had already been released, the English edition could not be realized readily.

The publication of this book has been made possible by the support of the following people. Firstly, the translator, Mr. Raj Mahtani (fifty-one years old, Yokohama), who turned this book, which contains many expressions unique to the Japanese language, into a witty work of English prose. I continued to be in the capable hands of Mr. Yū Aoyama (thirty-nine years old, Tokyo) and Mr. Katsunao Ishii (thirty-six years old, Tokyo), both of whom work at Kodansha, the publisher of the original work. I would also like to extend my thanks to Mr. Tuukka Toivonen (thirty-seven years old, Helsinki), who always directs my attention, which tends to remain domestic, toward the world.

I am glad to see this work—a critique of Japanese society—published as part of the JAPAN LIBRARY collection, a public project. (This demonstrates that ample tolerance and open-mindedness can still be found in Japan). Beginning with the Japan Publishing Industry Foundation for Culture and the JAPAN LIBRARY project division, I wish to thank everyone who played a part in the publication of the English version.

Having published this book, though, I have no idea how interested the readers of the English-speaking world will be in learning about an island nation in the Far East that's becoming steadily impoverished. But, you, dear reader, have at least looked through the tome all the way up to this address of gratitude. For that commendable act, I thank you, too.

About the Author

NORITOSHI FURUICHI was born in 1985 in Tokyo. He is a sociologist and a senior researcher at the Keio Research Institute at Shonan Fujisawa Campus. While still enrolled at The University of Tokyo, where he was studying in a Ph.D. program, he drew much attention with the publication of *Zetsubō no kuni no kōfuku na wakamono-tachi* (The Happy Youth of a Desperate Country; Kodansha, 2011). A recipient of the Japan Society for the Promotion of Science Ikushi Prize, he is also active in a wide variety of fields, including TV shows, in which he makes appearances as an emcee and commentator; in the field of publishing; and in politics as a member of a committee of experts at governmental conferences.

His other books include *Daremo sensō o oshierarenai* (Nobody can teach war; Kodansha, 2015), which makes comparisons between war museums around the world while analyzing the relationship between war and memory; *Dakara Nippon wa zureteiru* (That's why Japan is off; Shinchosha, 2014), which inquires into the issue of the generation gap; and *Hoikuen gimukyōikuka* (Making nursery schools compulsory; Shogakukan, 2015), which describes the absurd situation women find themselves in and points to a solution.

（英文版）絶望の国の幸福な若者たち
The Happy Youth of a Desperate Country:
The Disconnect between Japan's Malaise and Its Millennials

2017年3月27日　第1刷発行

著　者　古市憲寿
訳　者　ラージ・マタニ
発行所　一般財団法人 出版文化産業振興財団
　　　　〒101-0051 東京都千代田区神田神保町3-12-3
　　　　電話　03-5211-7282（代）
　　　　ホームページ　http://www.jpic.or.jp/

印刷・製本所　大日本印刷株式会社